The Changing Face of Home

The Changing Face of Home

The Transnational Lives of the Second Generation

Peggy Levitt and Mary C. Waters

Editors

Russell Sage Foundation • New York

Library of Congress Cataloging-in-Publication Data

The changing face of home : the transnational lives of the second generation / Peggy Levitt and Mary C. Waters, editors.
    p. cm.
  Includes bibliographical references and index.
  ISBN 10: 0-87154-517-9 (cloth)
  ISBN 13: 978-0-87154-517-6 (cloth)
  ISBN 10: 0-87154-516-0 (paper)
  ISBN 13: 978-0-87154-516-9 (paper)
    1. Immigrants—United States. 2. Transnationalism. I. Levitt, Peggy, 1957-
II. Waters, Mary C.

  JV 6455 .C434 2002
   305.9'0691—dc21

2002026990

RUSSELL SAGE FOUNDATION
112 East 64th Street, New York, New York 10021
10 9 8 7 6 5 4 3 2 1

For our own first and fourth generations:
Dylan, Harry, Katie, Maggie, and Wesley

Contents

Contributors

Peggy Levitt is associate professor of sociology at Wellesley College and a research fellow at the Weatherhead Center for International Affairs and the Hauser Center for Nonprofit Organizations at Harvard University.

Mary C. Waters is Harvard College Professor of Sociology at Harvard University.

Merih Anil is a doctoral candidate in political science at the City University of New York Graduate Center.

Susan Eckstein is professor of sociology at Boston University and former president of the Latin American Studies Association.

Yen Le Espiritu is professor of ethnic studies at the University of California at San Diego.

Nancy Foner is the Lillie and Nathan Ackerman Visiting Professor of Equality and Justice in America at Baruch College, School of Public Affairs, City University of New York.

Georges E. Fouron is associate professor of education and chair of the Social Sciences Interdisciplinary Program at the State University of New York at Stony Brook.

Nina Glick-Schiller is associate professor of anthropology at the University of New Hampshire.

Michael Jones-Correa is associate professor of government at Cornell University.

Philip Kasinitz is professor of sociology at Hunter College and the City University of New York Graduate Center and executive officer of the doctoral program in sociology at the Graduate Center.

Nazli Kibria is associate professor of sociology at Boston University.

Andrea Louie is assistant professor of anthropology at Michigan State University.

John H. Mollenkopf is professor of political science and sociology and director of the Center for Urban Research at the City University of New York Graduate Center.

Joel Perlmann is a senior scholar at the Levy Economics Institute of Bard College and a research professor at the college.

Rubén G. Rumbaut is professor of sociology and codirector of the Center for Research on Immigration, Population, and Public Policy at the University of California at Irvine.

Robert C. Smith is assistant professor of sociology at Barnard College, faculty fellow of the Institute for Social and Economic Research and Policy at Columbia University, and cofounder of the Mexican Educational Foundation of New York.

Thom Tran is an independent scholar who is especially interested in the lives of Vietnamese American youth.

Reed Ueda is professor of history at Tufts University.

Milton Vickerman is associate professor of sociology at the University of Virginia.

Diane L. Wolf is professor of sociology at the University of California at Davis.

Acknowledgments

T HIS BOOK WOULD not have seen the light of day without the support, encouragement, and patience of numerous friends and colleagues. We are especially grateful to Jorge Domínguez of the Weatherhead Center for International Affairs and John Coatsworth of the David Rockefeller Center for Latin American Studies at Harvard University for funding our conference and supporting our efforts. We also thank Parminder Bacchu, Levent Soysal, Marcelo Suárez-Orozco, and Karthya Um for their contributions to the conference upon which this volume is based. We are grateful to the two anonymous reviewers of the manuscript who helped us to improve it greatly. The Russell Sage Foundation and its president Eric Wanner have supported the field of immigration studies in myriad ways; we are fortunate indeed to have them as our publisher. Suzanne Nichols, Emily Chang, and Suzanne Washington shepherded us through the production phase of this project with expertise and good humor. And Ric Bayly and Robert Levers will always be our irreplaceable partners in crime.

Peggy Levitt
Mary C. Waters

EDITORS

Introduction

Peggy Levitt and Mary C. Waters

A T LUNCHTIME THE loud, cavernous cafeteria at Framingham High School fills with students talking and laughing with one another. They eat tortillas, rice noodles, and chapatis. They speak more than fifteen languages. Banners with flags from more than twenty-seven countries represented by the student body swing from one corner of the ceiling to the other.

Located twelve miles outside of Boston, Framingham is a microcosm of the United States. Once a predominantly white, working-class community, it is now home to numerous new immigrant communities. Many of the students at the high school are either immigrants themselves or members of the second generation: they were born to immigrant parents in the United States, or they came to this country when they were still very young. These trends mirror developments in the United States as a whole. In 2000 an estimated 27.5 million residents, or 10 percent of the nation's population, were children of immigrants, born primarily to the Latin American and Asian migrants who began arriving in the 1960s (Portes and Rumbaut 2001; Suárez-Orozco and Suárez-Orozco 2001). In 2000 approximately 56 million residents, or 20.5 percent of the population, were foreign stock (first- and second-generation individuals combined). In that same year immigrant children and the U.S.-born children of immigrants accounted for one out of every five children in the United States. They were the fastest-growing segment of the population under eighteen years of age.

There is much debate among researchers and policymakers about how the "new" second generation will fare. Will they follow the paths of the Irish, Italian, and Jewish immigrants who arrived in the early 1900s and gradually ascended the socioeconomic ladder? Or are there significant differences characterizing the contemporary migration experience that will shape mobility trajectories in fundamentally different ways?

Two partial answers to these questions come from different subfields of migration scholarship, although the researchers conducting this work have not always seen themselves as taking part in the same conversation. One body of scholarship focuses on the process of immigrant incorporation. Two broad views of assimilation characterize these debates. The theory of *segmented assimilation* proposes three patterns of adaptation for contemporary migrants and their children. One path involves increasing acculturation and subsequent integration into the white middle class. A second path predicts downward mobility and incorporation into the underclass. And a third pattern involves rapid economic advancement through the preservation of unique ethnic traits (Zhou 1999). An alternative view of the assimilation process revisits earlier ideas about straight-line assimilation, which viewed integration as linear, generationally driven, and a necessary prerequisite for successful incorporation into the United States. It emphasizes the agency of social actors in negotiating the incorporation process and stresses the influence of contextual factors. From this perspective, assimilation is an interactive, bumpy journey along multiple nonlinear pathways (Morawska 2002; Rumbaut 1997; Alba and Nee 1999; Gans 1992).

The second body of scholarship focuses on the kinds of attachments that contemporary migrants maintain to their homelands. Rather than severing their ties to their countries of origin and trading one membership for another, increasing numbers of migrants sustain economic, political, and religious ties to their homelands even as they work, vote, and pray in the countries that have received them. And although it is unlikely that the children of immigrants will be involved in their ancestral homes with the same frequency and intensity as their parents, the extent to which they will engage in transnational practices is still an open question.

This volume tries to wed these conversations. It grows out of a conference we organized at Harvard University in the spring of

1998 in which we brought together scholars of transnational migration and researchers working on the second generation. At this event we took stock of what we knew about how transnational the children of immigrants actually are and the kinds of activities they engage in. Given that more and more migrants participate in transnational activities, how widespread will these kinds of activities be among the second generation, and with what consequences? In many ways our efforts were premature. Most members of the second generation are still too young to know what kind of relationship they will have with their ancestral homelands. They may express strong attachments and formulate plans to act on them in the future, but it is impossible to predict what they will actually do. In addition, in many immigrant communities the size of the second generation is still quite small. Finally, survey data with which to assess these questions are only now becoming available.

Yet we still felt it imperative that migration scholars begin to lay the groundwork toward a better understanding of the transnational practices of the children of immigrants, for both intellectual and practical reasons. The concept of transnational migration, and its theoretical development, must grapple with the question of whether it extends beyond the immigrant generation. Researchers need to understand the relationship between transnational practices and assimilation among the first generation and examine how the character, intensity, and frequency of these activities might change among their children. The second generation is also expanding and maturing. Its members will play an increasingly important role in the economic and political life of this country and, perhaps, the countries from which their families came. The more information we have about the objective and subjective ties that the children of immigrants have to their ancestral homes, the better we will understand their experiences in this country and in their sending communities.

Thus, rather than propose definitive answers, this book presents the results of a first round of research on the transnational practices of the second generation. The chapters are organized into three parts. In part I, the authors address the content, meaning, and consequences of transnational practices among the second generation. They present findings from their own research on second-generation transnational engagements, descriptions of how these vary across groups and time periods, and some possible explanations for these variations. Although each of these contributors finds some evidence that the children of immigrants are transnational actors, they disagree over whether "the glass is half empty or half full," and over whether these activities will have any long-term, widespread impact. One perspective sees transnational activism among the second generation as confined primarily to certain groups of individuals who are, by and large, physically and emotionally rooted in the United States and lacking in the language and cultural skills or desire to live in their ancestral homes. Since these individuals are only occasionally transnational activists and their activities are confined to very specific arenas of social life, those activities are likely to have minimal long-term consequences. An alternative view sees the first view as overemphasizing the importance of physical movement and giving short shrift to the strong influences of the transnational social fields in which the second generation is embedded. This view stresses the importance of the sending-country individuals, resources, and ideas that are a constant presence in the lives of the second generation and holds that even selective, periodic transnational practices can add up.

The authors in part II comment on these analyses. They offer suggestions about how to bridge this analytical divide, introduce conceptual tools, and suggest directions for future research.

The chapters in part III are not, by and large, about actual transnational behaviors but instead use a transnational lens to analyze the second-generation experience. They examine the impact of home and host-country value systems on how the children of immigrants construct who they are, decide where to work, and choose civic and political communities. While the authors in part I actually conducted fieldwork in two settings or asked their respondents directly about their transnational affinities and behaviors, the authors in part III approach issues of transnational attachments more indirectly. While studying aspects of the lives of the second generation, many have come to realize that their respondents' lives cannot be adequately understood without reference to their ancestral homes.

We want to be clear from the outset, then, about what this book can and cannot do. It contributes to ongoing debates about transnational migration by expanding the range of groups previously covered. It includes Vietnamese, Filipino, and Chinese migrants in addition to those from Latin America and the Caribbean, who have been the focus of much of the prior research. It sheds light on the experiences of both upwardly mobile, middle-class migrants and their working-class counterparts. It includes work on groups with a high propensity toward transnational involvements, such as Dominicans, Mexicans, and Haitians, and on those whose networks and connections to their sending communities are not as well established, such as Koreans and Chinese. It advances a theoretical perspective stressing the synergy, rather than the antagonism, between assimilation and transnational practices. This volume cannot resolve questions, however, about how widespread or long-lasting transnational practices among the second generation are likely to be. Despite these limitations, we are confident that our contributors speak to concerns that are critical to ongoing immigration debates and are likely to become even more central in the future.

WHAT IS TRANSNATIONALISM?

Much early migration research predicted that migrants would sever their homeland attachments as they became integrated into the countries that received them. In the last decade, however, many scholars have come to acknowledge that international migration can no longer be seen as a one-way process. Events, communities, and lives, most observers now recognize, are increasingly linked across borders. The frequent and widespread movement back and forth between communities of origin and destination, and the resulting economic and cultural transformations, have prompted some researchers to speak of a set of activities grouped loosely together under the rubric of "transnationalism." Though the field is still in its infancy, those sympathetic to this perspective seek to recast our understanding of migration through their studies of the multilevel social, economic, and religious ties and practices that link migrants and nonmigrants to one another across borders.

Yet transnationalism remains a controversial topic. Some critics claim that transnationalism has become a catchall category that is used to describe everything under the sun. Others argue that transnational migration has a long history and that earlier waves of migrants also displayed strong connections to their homelands. Finally, while some scholars acknowledge the importance of transnational ties among the first generation, they predict that they will quickly weaken among their children.

Some of the confusion around these questions arises from the fact that those who ask them come from a variety of disciplines. Anthropologists, political scientists, cultural studies scholars, and sociologists have all thrown their hats into the ring. At present, vocabularies of "diaspora" and "transnationalism" are both used to describe the ways in which globalization challenges social organization and identity construction. Scholars using these terms are interested in how heightened social, economic, and political interconnectedness across national borders and cultures enables individuals to sustain multiple identities and loyalties, create new cultural products using elements from a variety of settings, and exercise multiple political and civic memberships. The different ways in which these terms are deployed stem more from their intellectual roots than from differences in their substantive concerns, and as the following discussion illustrates, it is sometimes difficult to differentiate between them.

The term "diaspora" is used in three principal ways in the literature (Vertovec 1997). First, there are those who use "diaspora" to describe a social form involving individuals living throughout the world but identifying collectively with one another, their host societies, and the lands from which they and their ancestors have come (Safran 1991). In addition to studies of classical diasporic groups, such as Jews, Armenians, and Greeks, these researchers now study voluntary and involuntary migrants from a variety of homelands, as well as their widespread connections to one another. Second, there are those who use "diaspora" to describe a type of social consciousness that locates individuals in multiple cultural and social spaces (Gupta and Ferguson 1997). Gilroy (1993) and Hall (1991), for example, reconceptualized the mid-Atlantic as a zone of movement, connections, and structures of domination and power that produce multiple black diasporic cultures. Nonini and Ong (1997) examined the multi-sited, multi-layered geography formed by networks of family ties, kinship, sentiments, and commerce that evolved from connections formed by earlier Chinese diasporas. Finally, there are those who use "diaspora" to describe a mode of cultural production involving the production and reproduction of transnational social and cultural phenomenon through creolization and hybridization (Hannerz 1992). Clifford (1988), for example, describes the formation of cultural subjectivities through the actual or imagined travel of intellectuals, business elites, or slum dwellers.

Many of these same social relations are of interest to those employing a transnational vocabulary. International relations scholars introduced the term "transnationalism" in the early 1970s to describe the proliferation of nonstate institutions and governance regimes acting across boundaries. They called these processes "transnational" rather than "international" to differentiate between activities that transcend national borders and relations between corporate actors whose boundaries are maintained (Keohane and Nye 1971).[1] Several years later anthropologists used "transnationalism" to describe the "process by which transmigrants, through their daily activities, forge and sustain multi-stranded social, economic, and political relations that link together their societies of origin and settlement, and through which they create transnational social fields that cross national borders" (Basch, Glick-Schiller, and Szanton-Blanc 1994, 6). These scholars explored the ways in which connections to collectivities constituted across space seem to override identities grounded in fixed, bounded locations (Hannerz 1992). They were also interested in the ways in which newly emerging transnational public spheres replace strictly bounded, geographically confined communities as sites where political claims are made (Gupta and Ferguson 1997).

Some scholars of transnationalism focus on the reorganization of the relationship between the global and the local through the logic of late capitalism, including the redistribution of corporate activities across the globe, the relocation of industrial production to global peripheries, and the reorganization of banking and investment relations. Instead of conceptualizing the global as macrolevel political and economic forces that stand in opposition to local cultural production, they explore where and how the global and the local meet and the ways in which relations of domination, as well as relations of reciprocity and solidarity, shape these encounters. Appadurai's (1996) work focuses on how media and travel influence identity, locality, and community creation. His notions of "ethnoscapes, ideoscapes, and mediascapes" bring to light how social actors use resources and construct identities that transcend traditional political and social boundaries. Ong (1999, 4) uses "transnationality" to describe the condition of "cultural interconnectedness and mobility across space." By doing so, she wants to call attention to the horizontal and vertical economic, social, and cultural practices that span space, the power hierarchies and citizenship regimes in which they are embedded, and the ways in which these practices are enabled and regulated by the changing relationship between states and capitalism. Kearney (1995, 548) also uses "transnationalism" to "call attention to the cultural and political projects of nation-states as they vie for hegemony in relations with other nation-states, with their citizens and aliens."

Another approach to transnationalism focuses on postnational politics. These scholars argue that national boundaries are no longer the principal axis around which social life is organized because the nation-state system is weakening, international governance bodies are proliferating, and global rights regimes protect individuals regardless of their national citizenship (Soysal 1994; Baubock 1994). Beck (2000) claims that the new dialectic emerging between the global and the local requires a transnational response because national political institutions can no longer resolve the kinds of challenges posed by globalism. An increasingly large body of work focuses on the international nongovernmental organizations (INGOs), intergovernmental organizations (IGOs), and transnational social movement organizations (TSMOs) that are changing the nature of politics (Keck and Sikkink 1998; Rivera-Salgado 1999; Brysk 2000).

This book focuses on one subset of activities included under the broad rubric of transnationalism—*transnational migration,* or how ordinary individuals live their everyday lives across borders and the consequences of their activities for sending- and receiving-country life. Portes, Guarnizo, and Landolt (1999) define transnational practices as the economic, political, and sociocultural occupations and activities that require regular long-term contacts across borders for their success. Clearly, not all migrants are engaged in transnational practices. Recent surveys find, however, that a small but significant group of migrants exhibits a distinct mode of transnational incorporation. Portes and his colleagues (2002) report that slightly more than 5 percent of the Salvadoran, Dominican, and Colombian migrants they studied were engaged in what they call "transnational entrepreneurship." The success of these business owners, who were more likely than their non-entrepreneurial counterparts to be male, to have higher incomes, and to be citizens, depended on frequent travel and constant contact with other countries. Guarnizo (2002) also has found that nearly 10 percent of the Colombians, Dominicans, and Salvadorans he surveyed were involved in some form of regular transnational political engagement. Their activities included membership in a home-country political party (9.9 percent), membership in a civic hometown association (13.7 percent), and participation in home-country electoral campaigns and rallies (7.7 percent). Nearly 20 percent reported occasional participation in these kinds of informal political activities.

We want to propose a somewhat more expansive view of the field. We are also interested in the connections that migrants sustain to their sending communities, the various kinds of social networks and social groups that result, and the ways in which these ties influence migrants' positions in their home and host countries. We also want to explore how these dynamics vary by race, class, and gender. But we are just as interested in the impact of transnational migration on those who stay behind as on those who move. We take cognitive and imagined elements of transnational livelihoods seriously. That is, our contributors are not only interested in migrants' actual behaviors and practices. They are also concerned about how social actors construct their identities and imagine themselves and the social groups they belong to when they live within transnational social fields and when they can use resources and discursive elements from multiple settings. Moreover, we analyze the ways in which non-economic transnational institutions create and are created by transnational migration. We explore religious, civic, and political institutions as sites of transnational belonging and how organizations respond to ensure that these loyalties endure (Levitt 2001a).

The size and impact of population movements increase through social networks. Sometimes these networks ultimately unravel as migrants are incorporated into host-country life. In other networks the effect of migration is so strong and widespread that a transnational social field or public sphere emerges between the sending and receiving countries. These social spaces extend beyond the networks of social relations and kin that actually connect each person located within them (Glick-Schiller 2000). Those who live within transnational social fields are exposed to a set of social expectations, cultural values, and patterns of human interaction that are shaped by more than one social, economic, and political system. Because their activities are influenced powerfully by the social fields in which they are carried out, the lives of individual actors cannot be viewed in isolation from the transnational social fields that they inhabit.

The transnational social fields that migration engenders encompass all aspects of social life. Though they may result at first from economic ties between migrants and nonmigrants, religious, political, and social connections soon emerge that also constitute and are constituted by these arenas. The thicker and more diverse a transnational social field is, the greater the number of ways it offers migrants to remain active in their homelands. The more institutionalized these relationships become, the more likely it is that transnational membership will persist.

Some researchers describe transnational social fields that encompass all migrants from a particular sending country residing in a key site of reception (Glick-Schiller and Fouron, this volume; Guarnizo 1998). These fields, however, often arise out of connections between multiple localities. Although there may be large overarching fields between the United States and Mexico, the Dominican Republic, or El Salvador, for example, the building blocks of these are the many smaller, bounded fields between particular sending villages and cities and specific urban or rural receiving points. Brazilian migration to the United States has created transnational social fields between residents of the city of Governador Valadares and migrants in New York City; Pompano Beach, Florida; Danbury, Connecticut; and the greater Boston metropolitan area (Margolis 1994). Transnational social fields also unite Dominicans in Venezuela and Spain to those who have stayed behind (Nyberg Sorensen 2000).

These arenas operate at multiple levels. Relations between local-level migrant and nonmigrant actors often produce ties between community-based sending- and receiving-country political party chapters. But these local, personalized ties also often form part of coordinated efforts between the party's national-level sending- and receiving-country operations. Similarly, relations between local parishes extend and deepen existing ties between national and regional sending- and receiving-country churches (Levitt 2001a).

The thick and expansive set of social relations that migration produces diminishes the importance of movement as a requirement for engaging in transnational practices. Those who travel regularly to carry out their routine affairs have been called "transmigrants" by some researchers (England 1999; Glick-Schiller 1995; Guarnizo 1997). Some individuals move infrequently and are rooted primarily in a single sending- or receiving-country setting, but their lives are integrally involved with resources, contacts, and people from far away. Finally, there are those who never move but who live their lives within a context that has become transnationalized because it is permeated by social remittances and cultural elements that migrants introduce.

Frequent travelers, periodic movers, and those who stay in one place engage in a wide variety of transnational practices. Guarnizo (2000) defines "core transnationalism" as those activities that form an integral part of an individual's habitual life, are undertaken on a regular basis, and are patterned and therefore somewhat predictable. "Expanded transnationalism," in contrast, includes migrants who occasionally engage in transnational activities, such as responses to political crises or natural disasters. Itzigsohn and his colleagues (1999) characterize "broad transnational practices" as those that are not well institutionalized, involve only occasional participation, and require only sporadic movement. These researchers contrast these practices with "narrow transnational practices," which are highly institutionalized and constant and involve regular travel.

These terms help to operationalize variations in the intensity and frequency of transnational practices, but cross-border engagements also vary by scope. Even those engaged in core transnational practices may confine their activities to one arena of social action. Or an individual may engage in core transnational activities with respect to one sphere of social activity and only expanded transnational activities with respect to another. There are those, for example, whose livelihoods depend on the frequent, patterned harnessing of resources across borders while their political and religious lives focus on host-country concerns. In contrast, there are those who engage in regular religious and political transnational practices but only occasionally send money back to family members or invest in homeland projects. Those individuals whose transnational practices involve many arenas of social life engage in "comprehensive transnational practices," while those involved in activities with a more limited purview engage in "selective transnational practices" (Levitt 2001b).

Highlighting variations in scope, intensity, and goals brings to light the multiple ways in which migrants and their children can combine transnational and assimilative strategies and the diverse outcomes these produce with respect to home- and host-country mobility. Doing so also reveals that transnational practices and assimilation are not diametrically opposed to one another (Levitt 2001a). Depending on their socioeconomic characteristics, immigrants and their children combine incorporation and transnational strategies in different ways at different stages of their lives. They use these to construct their identities, pursue economic mobility, and make political claims in their home or host country or in both. The resulting configurations produce different mixes of upward and downward mobility with respect to both contexts, depending on the kinds of activities in which migrants participate, the institutional arenas where these activities take place, and the class and life-cycle stage of individual migrants. Some migrants continue to play an active role in the economic, political, and religious lives of their homelands and achieve mobility in both home- and host-country contexts. Others engage in transnational practices but advance only in one setting. Still others engage in transnational practices that impede their mobility in both contexts (Levitt 2002; Morawska 2002).

A growing body of work uses a transnational lens to explore the experiences of the immigrant generation. But even those who now acknowledge that we must study migrants' and nonmigrants' experiences in their home and host communities to understand contemporary migration rightfully ask whether transnational practices will persist among the second generation. These questions are just beginning to attract serious attention from those who study these issues.

THE SECOND GENERATION

Studies of the second generation generally focus on the children of immigrants who were born in the United States (the classic second generation) and people who came to the United States as children, usually accompanied by their parents, but who grew up and attended school in this country (the "1.5 generation"). Almost

11 million are U.S.-born second-generation youth and 2.9 million are foreign-born. In 2000, 27.5 million U.S. residents, or 10 percent of the population, had one or two immigrant parents. Among these, over half are the new second generation—children of immigrants who have come to the United States since the 1960s. The remainder tend to be older individuals whose parents came to this country during the last great wave of immigration (1880–1920).

These two waves of immigration differ in terms of their racial origins. While the vast majority of immigrants who came between 1880 and 1920 were from Europe, 88 percent of immigrants who have entered the United States since the 1980s come from Latin America, the Caribbean, and Asia. Using Current Population Survey (CPS) data, Zhou (2001) calculates that 35 percent of the second generation are Latin American in origin and 7 percent are Asian. Most important for our purposes, these are precisely the regions whose migrants, researchers have found, engage in higher levels of transnational activism.

Members of the second generation, like their immigrant parents, are concentrated in gateway cities, especially Los Angeles, New York, Miami, and San Francisco. Immigrants and their children are a diverse lot. They are especially heterogeneous with respect to socioeconomic characteristics. Bipolar immigrant streams have brought large numbers of skilled professionals and entrepreneurs along with uneducated and unskilled laborers. Thus, immigrants are among the most educated and least educated Americans. Smith and Edmonston (1997) have found that overall about the same percentage of foreign-born and native-born are college graduates (20 percent), but that immigrants are overrepresented at the lowest educational levels: only 14.4 percent of native-born men had less than a high school diploma, but 37.1 percent of immigrant men had less than a high school diploma. Immigrant educational attainment also varies a great deal by national origin. Zhou (2001) reports that while 60 percent of foreign-born Indians report having a college degree, fewer than 5 percent of immigrants from El Salvador or Mexico have one. In gateway cities immigrant children have a particularly strong impact on the local school systems where they live because more than one-third of them speak a language other than English at home (Zhou 2001).

The difficulties of studying the second generation at the national level are well known (Zhou 1997; Portes and Rumbaut 2001;

Waters 1999).[2] The quantitative and qualitative work that has been done on this population to date generally compares the experiences of new immigrants and native minorities, analyzes their labor market status, examines patterns of naturalization and citizenship, measures language loss and retention, and examines strategies for economic mobility, including entrepreneurship and employment in ethnic enclaves. Immigration scholars have generally stressed the great variation in the social origins of the immigrants, who include highly educated professionals as well as unskilled laborers. They have also underscored the importance of legal conditions upon arrival, comparing legal immigrants, undocumented immigrants, and refugees. Attention has also been given to the regional distribution of the immigrants and their interaction with local labor markets and the geographic mobility patterns among the native-born. Finally, given the long history of castelike exclusion of America's nonwhite minorities, scholars have addressed the central question of how non-European immigrants are doing relative to native minority groups, not only to examine potential displacement effects but also to understand the long-run prospects for nonwhite immigrants.

The new scholarship on the second generation also stresses the changes in the American economy and the ways in which those changes shape the options available to the children of immigrants today. The decline in manufacturing and the growth of the service economy have combined with the impact of the civil rights movement and subsequent legal measures to open universities and the economy to all groups to make enormous opportunities available to well-educated immigrants and their children. Because of the growth of racial and ethnic tolerance and the acceptance of multiculturalism, this socioeconomic success does not come at the cost of cultural assimilation. At the same time the lack of well-paid jobs for those with less than a college education and the growth of low-level service jobs have combined to limit the opportunities and outlooks for those who did not do well in school.

This burgeoning literature has produced many intriguing findings and some speculation about the experiences of the new second generation. Taken as a whole, it suggests that the experience of twenty-first-century immigrant children will be quite different from that of late-nineteenth- and early-twentieth-century European immigrants and their children and grandchildren.

The "straight-line" model of assimilation was developed to explain the experiences of white ethnic groups of European origin. This model suggests that the second generation learns an immigrant culture at home but encounters the more highly valued American native culture in school, among their peer groups, and from the mass media. They internalize American culture and identity and reject their parents' culture and identity as foreign. These competing allegiances work themselves out through rebellion and profane behavior, total rejection of the immigrant culture, and ultimately the forging of an ethnic culture that combines the American and immigrant social systems. Whatever the psychic toll of this shedding of cultural identity for the immigrant's third- and fourth-generation descendants, assimilation was rewarded with substantial upward mobility. Generation has thus been a key term in assessing the assimilation of different ethnic groups in the United States (Gordon 1964; Lieberson 1980; Perlmann 1988; Hirschman 1983; Waters 1990; Lieberson and Waters 1988).

This description proved generally accurate for immigrant groups of European origin. Even as they have noted differences in the pace of change across ethnic groups, researchers have determined that the progress of once-stigmatized groups like the Greeks, Slavs, Irish, and Italians merits Greeley's (1976) description as an "ethnic miracle." They have found that time spent in the United States explains success because immigrants acquire the language skills, educational credentials, and general cultural knowledge needed to compete with native white Americans. Second-generation ethnic Americans may even *surpass* native Americans because of the selectivity of the immigrant generation and the drive and achievement orientation they instill in their children.

The new second generation, however, has elicited some disturbing hypotheses in recent years from thoughtful observers. Gans (1992) outlined several scenarios in which the children of the new immigrants could do worse than their parents or society as a whole. Gans speculated that second-generation immigrants who are restricted to poor inner-city schools, bad jobs, and shrinking economic niches will experience downward mobility. Using ethnographic case studies and a survey of second-generation schoolchildren in Miami and San Diego, Portes and Zhou (1993) have made a similar argument. The mode of incorporation of the first generation endows the second generation with differing amounts of cultural and social capital in the form of jobs, networks, and values and exposes them to differing opportunities, thus exerting differential pulls on their allegiances. Those who face discrimination and are close to American minorities adopt a "reactive ethnicity." Groups that arrive with strong ethnic networks, access to capital, and fewer ties to U.S. minorities, on the other hand, often develop a "linear ethnicity" by assimilating into existing ethnic communities. Still others practice a "segmented assimilation" in which they hold on to an immigrant identity to avoid being classified with American blacks or Puerto Ricans. Like Gans, they conclude that members of the second generation who cast their lot with America's minority groups, whose peer culture takes an adversarial view of upward mobility and school success, are likely to experience downward social mobility.

Recently some have criticized this "second-generation decline" hypothesis for concluding prematurely that today's second generation will not follow a pattern similar to that of earlier immigrants. Perlmann and Waldinger (1997) point out that earlier immigrants did not experience the effortless rise we sometimes attribute to them and that the heterogeneous nature of the second generation might just as well lead analysts to an optimistic assumption about their future prospects. They note that earlier waves of the European second generation also exhibited opposition toward school achievement, yet this attitude did not prevent them from doing well in the labor market.

Ethnographic studies support the notion that the children of voluntary migrants can resist mainstream American culture while not embracing an oppositional minority culture. Suárez-Orozco's (1987) study found that Central American immigrant schoolchildren contrasted their U.S. experiences with their experiences at home and developed an "immigrant attitude towards school that helped them to do well." Gibson's (1989) study of second-generation Punjabi Sikhs in California developed the concept of "accommodation without assimilation." The Sikh children, like the Central American children, saw success in school not as an avenue for individual mobility but rather as a way to bring honor and success to their families. Zhou and Bankston (1998) found that the social capital of a Vietnamese community protected its children against lowered educational performance in inner-city schools.

In the most comprehensive study of second-generation youth published to date, Portes and Rumbaut (2001) show very divergent paths for second-generation youth from different national origins and class backgrounds. They find three different trajectories of incorporation among the youth they studied in San Diego and Miami—dissonant, consonant, and selective acculturation. Dissonant acculturation occurs when young people quickly adopt American ways and the English language and their parents do not move as quickly. This is the trajectory that leads to role reversal: children must translate for their parents, and they become more worldly and sophisticated about American ways, leaving their immigrant parents relatively powerless and often dependent on them. Consonant acculturation occurs when parents and children learn the new culture and abandon the old one at the same pace. This occurs most commonly among middle-class immigrants and their children. Finally, with selective acculturation the second generation is embedded in a co-ethnic community that supports their parents, slows the loss of the parents' home language and norms, and cushions the move of both generations into American ways. This is characterized by a lack of intergenerational conflict, the presence of co-ethnics as friends, and full bilingualism in the second generation. Portes and Rumbaut conclude by extolling the benefits of selective acculturation and call for policy initiatives to promote it.

What might such policy initiatives mean for the second generation? Concepts such as second-generation decline, segmented assimilation, and selective acculturation all stress that, for the second generation, becoming American could lead to downward mobility and maintaining ties to their parents' culture and homeland could facilitate upward mobility. Portes and Rumbaut (2001) also show that first-generation immigrants with high levels of education and income are better able to provide a grounding in their own culture and language for their children. This has intriguing implications for the study of second-generation and transnational migration. Does the level of transnational involvement of the parental generation lead to more selective acculturation among the second generation? Does this hold even when we control for class background, or is all of the effect of transnational ties merely due to the fact that middle-class people are more likely to maintain transnational ties in the second generation? Or is the effect of transnational ties among the first generation not in the transmission of transnational ties or behaviors to the second generation, but rather in the beneficial effect of transnational ties among the first generation on the identities developed among the second generation? If indeed immigrants with higher levels of income and education are more likely to maintain transnational ties than immigrants from more modest class backgrounds, we might then expect to see more participation of the second generation in transnational practices now than in earlier periods, when fewer middle-class immigrants came to the United States (Foner 2000).

Race is the other crucial variable that at least in the theoretical literature plays an important part in both second-generation outcomes and in the maintenance of transnational ties. Many scholars have argued that contemporary immigrants may be more likely to maintain active involvement in their sending societies because of the racial discrimination they face in the United States (Foner 2000; Waters 1999; Kasinitz 1992). Glick-Schiller and Fouron (2001) suggest that the negative reception of people of color gives them more motivation to stay involved in a sending society in which they are members of the majority or in which their class status negates their racial status. This is another area ripe for empirical investigation in the second generation and for creative cross-fertilization between those who study transnational ties and those who study second-generation identity. What role does racial discrimination play in the second generation's maintenance of ties to their parents' sending countries? And what role does transnationalism play in how the second generation develops racial and ethnic identities and copes with racial discrimination when it does occur? Does multiculturalism in the United States create conditions that sustain transnational ties over generations? Does access to a global diasporic consciousness create opportunities for young people to acculturate selectively (to use Portes and Rumbaut's terms)? Or does the maintenance of ties to the parents' sending country cause second-generation young people to disengage from American society and become politically or socially isolated?

Again, we cannot resolve these questions in this volume. Instead, our aim is to present a range of initial responses to these questions and to pave the way for future research. The first part of this volume offers some initial insights into the kinds of transnational practices the second generation is engaged in and their variations across groups. The authors in this section agree that fairly small numbers of the second generation are actually engaged in transnational practices, but they disagree on the long-term impact of these engagements.

Part I opens with a chapter by Reed Ueda, who uses the case of Japanese American Nisei in Hawaii to place the contemporary second-generation experience in historical context. He argues that the second-generation consciousness that emerged in the 1920s func-tioned quite differently from the transnational identities expressed by the second generation today. It makes a difference, he con-cludes, that these identities were constructed within a cultural and policy context that favored the American national melting pot rather than the "globalizing multicultural mosaic" that currently prevails. Homeland connections during this earlier era were valued for their contribution to an emerging democratic, cosmopolitan amalgam and to the spirit of internationalism that also occupied center stage.

Rubén Rumbaut's chapter presents evidence from a decade-long longitudinal study highlighting the subjective and objective transnational attachments of a diverse sample of 1.5- and second-generation young adults from Mexico, the Philippines, Vietnam, China, and several other Latin and Asian countries. His findings reveal low levels of transnational activism (less than 10 percent) among his survey respondents, with significant differences between national-origin groups. Young people from Spanish-speaking coun-tries in the Americas, and especially Mexicans, are much more likely to be fluently bilingual into adulthood than the rest of the sample, and language plays a critical role in the maintenance of transnational ties. Religious involvement, legal and financial wherewithal, and, in the case of remittances, specific transformative events (such as natural disasters) also explain variations in transnational attachments.

In chapter 3, Philip Kasinitz, Mary Waters, John Mollenkopf, and Merih Anil present findings from the Second Generation in Metro-politan New York Study, which examines indicators of second-generation transnational activism, such as remittances by the second generation, remittances by their parents, interest in and involvement in home-country politics, use of home-country media, and visits to the home country. They found that the Dominicans in their sample displayed the highest levels of transnational activities, followed by the Colombians, Ecuadorans, and Peruvians (CEPs) and the West Indian samples. A significant minority ("but a minority nonetheless") seem highly embedded in transnational social structures and engage in frequent, comprehensive transnational practices. The majority, however, display much more selective, periodic transnational engagements and are therefore, according to these authors, clearly "here to stay."

These authors conclude that the scope and durability of transnational practices among the children of immigrants are confined to a small minority and are likely to become even less significant over time. In contrast, Peggy Levitt, Robert C. Smith, and Georges Fouron and Nina Glick-Schiller take issue with the time frame and social field implicit in these analyses. Although they too acknowledge that transnational activities are not central to the lives of most of the second generation, they say that to understand the impact of these behaviors we must look at the sending and receiving countries, and over time. From their perspective, the fact that most children do not want to return to live in their ancestral homes, are not completely fluent in their parents' ancestral tongue, or identify for the most part as New Yorkers on a survey questionnaire does not justify dismissing second-generation transnational practices out of hand. Such a gold standard overlooks the effect of the many periodic, selective transnational activities that some individuals engage in at different stages of their lives. It also underestimates the powerful influence of the transnational social fields in which these individuals are embedded. Such a perspective also privileges actual movement and mistakenly overlooks the resources, discourses, and social contacts in the homeland that strongly shape the lives of the children of immigrants. Over time, and taken together, these influences can have a cumulative effect, particularly at the local level.

Peggy Levitt describes three different types of transnational participatory patterns among the second-generation Irish, Dominicans, and Indians she studied and highlights several factors that explain variations in the emergence of these patterns among these groups. The first factor is the high level of institutional completeness and the persistence of strong, multigenerational social networks that afford migrants multiple arenas within which to participate and many choices about when and how to do so. The second factor is life-course effects. Levitt finds that her respondents displayed three intensities of transnational involvement across the life cycle: constant and frequent transnational practices; periodic but sustained transnational practices that have a cumulative effect over time; and intensive transnational activism at a particular life-cycle stage. The class and racial characteristics of immigrant groups constitute the final factor explaining the emergence of transnational practices.

Robert C. Smith's work on the children of Mexican immigrants also highlights the importance of life-course effects and the strong influence of the transnational social field occupied by the second generation. He argues that transnational activities among the second generation are a response to the racial, gender, and class hierarchies they experience in the United States. He highlights the ways in which transnational activities change as the children of immigrants move from adolescence to young adulthood and as they attempt to fulfill what Marcelo and Carola Suárez-Orozco (2001) call the immigrant bargain. Smith's work also stresses the importance of the dynamic interaction between the social worlds these individuals inhabit in the United States and in their parents' hometowns. The young adults he studied use transnational sites and practices to redefine second-generation social locations and the meaning of Mexican-ness in New York.

Georges Fouron and Nina Glick-Schiller also make a strong argument for the need to look at transnational practices to understand identity formation among the children of immigrants in the United States. They call for a redefinition of the term "second generation" to include the entire generation in both the homeland and the new land who grow up in transnational social fields. They claim that these individuals develop a sense of self that is indelibly shaped by personal, family, and organizational connections back home. At the same time identity formation is also the product of racial, ethnic, and national categories that are themselves produced transnationally.

The chapters in part II comment on the chapters in part I. In chapter 7, Susan Eckstein challenges the notion of generation as biologically based and urges us to reconceptualize generations as those who share a historically contextualized experience. Joel Perlmann also calls for greater conceptual and historical specificity. In chapter 8, he asks analysts to make a distinction between cultural and economic transnational practices; argues that discussions about events in the home country contribute little to our understanding of "what

if anything is special about the experiences of immigrants and ethnics in the United States today"; and differentiates between various
types of possible receptions in the host country. Although Michael
Jones-Correa concurs that we might be tempted to attribute little
significance to the transnational practices of the second generation
given that the relative numbers engaged in these practices are so
small, "there are good reasons to reflect before passing judgment."
Though these actors constitute only a small minority, their actual
numbers may be quite large. They will have a differential impact
depending on the region of the United States they live in, their own
wealth and influence, and the particular crises to which they may
be responding. Finally, Nancy Foner draws on her comparative
study of the two great waves of immigration to New York. She finds
that among the first wave, daily involvement in and connections to
sending-country community life declined sharply after the first generation. For their contemporary counterparts, however, "it seems
clear that connections to their parents' homelands will be more important, though those for whom this is central to their lives are
likely to be a minority."

In part III, contributors use a transnational perspective to make
sense of the second-generation experience. Several authors explore
the impact of parental transnational attachments and the transnational social spaces they engender on second-generation lives.
Although the majority of these youngsters do not actively engage
in transnational practices, their parents' involvements and the fact
that they are growing up in a context infused with homeland values and behaviors strongly affect their life trajectories. Other contributors emphasize that members of the second generation, in the
process of learning more about their family histories and ancestral
homes, incorporate elements of these narratives and experiences
into their own self-concepts. They may become more transnationally
active as a result, or they may come to new ways of thinking about
their place in the United States.

Diane Wolf claims in chapter 11 that the second-generation
Filipino youth she studied experience emotional transnationalism.
These individuals are situated between a variety of different, often
competing generational and locational points of reference, including those of their parents and their grandparents as well as their
own, both real and imagined perspectives. As a result, ethnic iden-

tity formation does not occur in one place. Instead, Filipino children are exposed to a range of "Home and home" discourses and cultural elements from which they construct their identities and life plans in ways that, Wolf claims, contradict conventional understandings of assimilation.

The second-generation Chinese and Korean American college students whom Nazli Kibria studied also reported that transnational practices did not play a major role in their everyday lives. However, their trips to the homeland affirmed the value and appeal of such engagements, the circumstances under which they developed, and the difficulties posed by creating them. They came to understand that Chinese and Korean membership could be strategically valuable, provide a means to take advantage of the rewards of a globalizing economy, and help them overcome the racial barriers to mobility that they may experience in their future professional lives. At the same time these homeland visits highlighted the barriers to their full acceptance in Chinese and Korean society.

Andrea Louie has also studied the genealogical projects and homeland trips of second-generation Chinese Americans. Her respondents used these experiences to locate themselves within the broader context of the Chinese–Asian American experience. But in contrast to Kibria's respondents, who courted transnational attachments in response to the social and occupational barriers they experienced in the United States, the Chinese Americans Louie studied were using such attachments to build strong ties to and achieve greater legitimacy within U.S. society. By piecing together their own account of Chinese culture, they bridged the divide between "China" and "Chinese American" that is central to U.S. multicultural politics.

Milton Vickerman discovered an interesting paradox from his research on second generation West Indians in New York City. These young people clearly live in a transnational social space that is increasingly vibrant. But, he predicts, the existence of such a space may diminish the incentive for the second generation to engage in actual transnational practices. Because the West Indian community in New York has recreated its culture so effectively and completely, the second generation can access their homeland without ever having to go home. West Indian ethnic enclaves represent reservoirs of West Indian culture that, to some extent, can substitute for actual contact with the West Indies.

Finally, Yen Le Espiritu and Thom Tran urge us to think about transnationalism not solely as actual transnational practices but as imagined returns to the homeland through memory, cultural rediscovery, and longing. For these authors, transnationalism is enacted both literally and symbolically. The homeland is thus not merely an actual physical place but also a place of desire that one returns to in one's imagination. Most of the second-generation Vietnamese these authors studied developed strong symbolic attachments to their ancestral home, although their factual knowledge about Vietnam was quite limited. Like the youth whom Diane Wolf and Nazli Kibria describe, these young people are caught between their inability to achieve full assimilation into the United States and their inability to achieve full membership in Vietnam, underscoring once again that identities are constituted from multiple places and from multiple components.

As Georges Fouron and Nina Glick-Schiller conclude in their chapter, our analyses of transnational migration and of the transnational practices of the second generation are not intended to celebrate unconditionally or lament these new forms of belonging across borders. Instead, our aim is to begin a conversation and to inspire a body of future research that will further advance our understanding of these relationships.

NOTES

1. In a recent article, Portes (2001) further delineates these arenas of social life. He defines "international" as those activities carried out by states and other nationally based institutions in other countries that take place across borders in pursuit of the goals of large organizations that possess clear national affiliations. "Multinational" refers to those institutions whose purpose and interests transcend the borders of the nation-state. He reserves "transnational" to describe those activities begun and sustained across national borders, many of which are informal and take place outside the boundaries of state regulation and control. These are goal-oriented initiatives that require coordination across borders by members of civil society.

2. Since 1980, when the U.S. Census Bureau replaced a question on parental birthplace with one on parental ancestry, adult children of immigrants who no longer live with their immigrant parents cannot be identified using census data. However, a growing body of research

tries to extrapolate future adult patterns of incorporation from the experiences of second-generation children and teenagers (Gibson 1989; Portes and Zhou 1993; Fernandez-Kelly and Schauffler 1996; Portes and Schauffler 1996; Zhou and Bankston 1998; Rumbaut 1995, 1996a, 1996b, 1997; Portes and Rumbaut 2001). Qualitative and ethnographic studies of second-generation young adults highlight generational transitions within immigrant communities (Waters 1996a, 1996b, 1999; Bacon 1994, 1996; Suárez-Orozco 1995; Smith 1994; Grasmuck and Pessar 1993). Quantitative analyses have also been carried out using 1990 census data (Hirschman 1996; Jensen and Chitose 1994; Landale and Oropesa 1995), and Kao and Tienda (1995) studied immigrant youth and the second generation using the National Education Longitudinal Study (NELS) longitudinal data set. (For an overview of these studies, see also Zhou 1997.) In addition, analyses from the Current Population Survey, which added a question on parental birthplace in 1994, have also begun to shed light on these issues, although, with the exception of Mexicans, the number of second-generation individuals in the sample is still very small (Zhou 2001).

REFERENCES

Alba, Richard, and Victor Nee. 1999. "Rethinking Assimilation Theory for a New Era of Immigration." In *The Handbook of International Migration,* edited by Charles Hirschman, Philip Kasinitz, and Josh Dewind. New York: Russell Sage Foundation.

Appadurai, Arjun. 1996. *Modernity at Large: Dimensions of Globalization.* Minneapolis: University of Minnesota Press.

Bacon, Jean. 1994. "Shared Rhetoric: Constructing a Second-Generation Identity in the Asian Indian Community." Paper presented at the American Sociological Association meetings, Los Angeles.

———. 1996. *Life Lines: Community, Family, and Assimilation Among Asian Indian Immigrants.* New York: Oxford University Press.

Basch, Linda, Nina Glick-Schiller, and Cristina Szanton-Blanc, eds. 1994. *Nations Unbound: Transnational Projects, Postcolonial Predicaments, and Deterritorialized Nation-states.* Switzerland: Gordeon and Breach.

Baubock, Rainer. 1994. *Transnational Citizenship: Membership and Rights in International Migration.* Brookfield, Vt.: Edward Elgar.

Beck, Ulrich. 2000. "The Cosmopolitan Perspective: Sociology of the Second Age of Modernity." *British Journal of Sociology* 51(1): 79–105.

Brysk, Alison. 2000. *From Tribal Village to Global Village.* Princeton, N.J.: Princeton University Press.

Clifford, James. 1988. *The Predicament of Culture: Twentieth-century Ethnography, Literature, and Art*. Cambridge, Mass.: Harvard University Press.

England, Sarah. 1999. "Negotiating Race and Place in the Garifuna Diaspora: Identity Formation and Transnational Grassroots Politics in New York City and Honduras." *Identities* 6(1): 5–53.

Fernandez-Kelly, Patricia, and Richard Schauffler. 1996. "Divided Fates: Immigrant Children in a Restructured U.S. Economy." In *The New Second Generation,* edited by Alejandro Portes. New York: Russell Sage Foundation.

Foner, Nancy. 2000. *From Ellis Island to JFK: New York's Two Great Waves of Immigration*. New Haven, Conn., and New York: Yale University Press and Russell Sage Foundation.

Gans, Herbert. 1992. "Comment: Ethnic Invention and Acculturation: A Bumpy-Line Approach." *Journal of American Ethnic History* 11(1): 42–52.

Gibson, Margaret A. 1989. *Accommodation Without Assimilation*. Ithaca, N.Y.: Cornell University Press.

Gilroy, Paul. 1993. *The Black Atlantic*. Cambridge, Mass.: Harvard University Press.

Glick-Schiller, Nina. 1995. "From Immigrant to Transmigrant: Theorizing Transnational Migration." *Anthropological Quarterly* 68: 48–63.

————. 2000. "Building a Transnational Perspective on Migration." Paper presented at the Conference on Transnational Migration: Comparative Theory and Research Perspectives, Oxford, England (June).

Glick-Schiller, Nina, and Georges Fouron. 2001. *Georges Woke Up Laughing: Long Distance Nationalism and the Search for Home*. Durham, N.C.: Duke University Press.

Gordon, Milton. 1964. *Assimilation in American Life: The Role of Race, Religion, and National Origins*. New York: Oxford University Press.

Grasmuck, Sherri, and Patricia Pessar. 1993. "First- and Second-Generation Settlement of Dominicans in the United States: 1960–1990." In *Origins and Destinies: Immigration, Race, and Ethnicity in America,* edited by Silvia Pedraza and Rubén Rumbaut. Belmont, Mass.: Wadsworth.

Greeley, Andrew. 1976. *Ethnicity, Denomination, and Inequality*. Beverly Hills, Calif.: Sage Publications.

Guarnizo, Luis. 1997. "The Emergence of a Transnational Social Formation and the Mirage of Return Among Dominican Transmigrants." *Identities* 4: 281–322.

————. 1998. "The Rise of Transnational Social Formations: Mexican and Dominican State Responses to Transnational Migration." *Political Power and Social Theory* 12: 45–94.

————. 2000. "Notes on Transnational." Paper presented at the Conference on Transnational Migration: Comparative Theory and Research Perspectives, Oxford, England (June).

————. 2002. "De la asimilación al transnacionalismo: Determinantes de la acción política transnacional entre los migrantes contemporáneos." Paper presented at the FLASCO Conference on Migración Transnacional: Sus Efectos y Tendencias en la Cuenca del Caribe, Santo Domingo (January 18–19).

Gupta, Akhil, and James Ferguson. 1997. *Anthropological Locations: Boundaries and Grounds of a Field Science.* Berkeley: University of California Press.

Hall, Stuart. 1991. "The Local and the Global: Globalization and Ethnicity." In *Culture, Globalization, and the World System,* edited by Anthony King. Binghamton: State University of New York Press.

Hannerz, Ulf. 1992. *Cultural Complexity.* New York: Columbia University Press.

Hirschman, Charles. 1983. "The Melting Pot Reconsidered." *Annual Review of Sociology* 9: 397–423.

————. 1996. "Problems and Prospects of Studying Immigrant Adaptation from the 1990 Population Census: From Generational Comparisons to the Process of 'Becoming American.' " In *The New Second Generation,* edited by Alejandro Portes. New York: Russell Sage Foundation.

Itzigsohn, José, Carlos Dore Cabral, Esther Hernández Medina, and Obed Vázquez. 1999. "Mapping Dominican Transnationalism: Narrow and Broad Transnational Practices." *Ethnic and Racial Studies* 22(2): 2316–40.

Jensen, Leif, and Yoshimi Chitose. 1994. "Today's Second Generation: Evidence from the 1990 U.S. Census." *International Migration Review* 28(4): 714–35.

Kao, Grace, and Marta Tienda. 1995. "Optimism and Achievement: The Educational Performance of Immigrant Youth." *Social Science Quarterly* 76(1): 1–19.

Kasinitz, Philip. 1992. *Caribbean New York: Black Immigrants and the Politics of Race.* Ithaca, N.Y.: Cornell University Press.

Kearney, Michael. 1995. "The Local and the Global: The Anthropology of Globalization and Transnationalism." *Annual Review of Anthropology* 24: 547–65.

Keck, Margaret E., and Kathryn Sikkink. 1998. *Activists Beyond Borders.* Ithaca, N.Y.: Cornell University Press.

Keohane, Robert, and Joseph Nye, eds. 1971. *Transnational Relations and World Politics.* Cambridge, Mass: Harvard University Press.

Landale, Nancy S., and R. S. Oropesa. 1995. "Immigrant Children and the Children of Immigrants: Inter- and Intra-group Differences in the United

States." Research Paper 95–02. East Lansing, Mich.: Population Research Group, Michigan State University.

Levitt, Peggy. 2001a. *The Transnational Villagers*. Berkeley and Los Angeles: University of California Press.

———. 2001b. "Transnational Migration: Taking Stock and Future Directions." *Global Networks* 1(3): 195–216.

———. 2002. "Keeping Feet in Both Worlds: Transnational Practices and Immigrant Incorporation." In *Integrating Immigrants in Liberal Nationstates: From Postnational to Transnational,* edited by Christian Joppke and Ewa Morawska. London: Macmillan-Palgrave.

Lieberson, Stanley. 1980. *A Piece of the Pie*. Berkeley: University of California Press.

Lieberson, Stanley, and Mary C. Waters. 1988. *From Many Strands: Ethnic and Racial Groups in Contemporary America*. New York: Russell Sage Foundation.

Margolis, Maxine. 1994. *Little Brazil: An Ethnography of Brazilian Immigrants in New York City*. Princeton, N.J.: Princeton University Press.

Morawska, Ewa. 2002. "The Sociology and History of Immigration: Reflections of a Practitioner." In *Reflections on Migration Research: Promises of Interdisciplinarity,* edited by Michael Bommes and Ewa Morawska. London: Macmillan-Palgrave.

Nonini, Donald, and Aihwa Ong. 1997. "Chinese Transnationalism as an Alternative Modernity." In *The Cultural Politics of Modern Chinese Transnationalism,* edited by Aihwa Ong and Donald Nonini. New York: Routledge Press.

Nyberg Sorensen, Ninna. 2000. "Notes on Transnationalism to the Panel of Devil's Advocates: Transnational Migration—Useful Approach or Trendy Rubbish?" Paper presented at the Conference on Transnational Migration: Comparative Theory and Research Perspectives, Oxford, England (June).

Ong, Aihwa. 1999. *Flexible Citizenship: The Cultural Logics of Transnationality*. Durham, N.C.: Duke University Press.

Perlmann, Joel. 1988. *Ethnic Differences: Schooling and Social Structure Among the Irish, Italians, Jews, and Blacks in an American City, 1880–1935*. New York: Cambridge University Press.

Perlmann, Joel, and Roger Waldinger. 1997. "Second-Generation Decline?: Children of Immigrants, Past and Present—A Reconsideration." *International Migration Review* 31(winter): 893–922.

Portes, Alejandro. 2001. "The Debates and Significance of Immigrant Transnationalism." *Global Networks* 1(3): 195–217.

Portes, Alejandro, Luis Guarnizo, and Patricia Landolt. 1999. "Introduction: Pitfalls and Promise of an Emergent Research Field." *Ethnic and Racial Studies* 22: 463–78.

Portes, Alejandro, William Haller, and Luis Guarnizo. 2002. "Transnational Entrepreneurs: An Alternative Form of Immigrant Economic Adaptation." *American Sociological Review* 67: 278–98.

Portes, Alejandro, and Rubén Rumbaut. 2001. *Legacies: The Story of the New Second Generation.* Berkeley: University of California Press.

Portes, Alejandro, and Richard Schauffler. 1996. "Language and the Second Generation: Bilingualism Yesterday and Today." In *The New Second Generation,* edited by Alejandro Portes. New York: Russell Sage Foundation.

Portes, Alejandro, and Min Zhou. 1993. "The New Second Generation: Segmented Assimilation and Its Variants." *Annals of the American Academy of Political and Social Science* 530: 74–97.

Rivera-Salgado, Gaspar. 1999. "Political Organizing Across the U.S.-Mexican Border: The Experience of Mexican Indigenous Migrant Workers." Paper presented to the University of California Comparative Immigration and Integration Program Research Workshop, San Diego (February).

Rumbaut, Rubén G. 1995. "The New Californians: Comparative Research Findings on the Educational Progress of Immigrant Children." In *California's Immigrant Children: Theory, Research, and Implications for Educational Policy,* edited by Rubén G. Rumbaut and Wayne A. Cornelius. La Jolla, Calif.: Center for U.S.-Mexican Studies, University of California.

————. 1996a. "The Crucible Within: Ethnic Identity, Self-esteem, and Segmented Assimilation Among Children of Immigrants." In *The New Second Generation,* edited by Alejandro Portes. New York: Russell Sage Foundation.

————. 1996b. "Origins and Destinies: Immigration, Race, and Ethnicity in Contemporary America." In *Origins and Destinies: Immigration, Race, and Ethnicity in America,* edited by Rubén Rumbaut and Silvia Pedraza. Belmont, Mass.: Wadsworth.

————. 1997. "Ties That Bind: Immigration and Immigrant Families in the United States." In *Immigration and the Family,* edited by Alan Booth, Ann C. Crouter, and Nancy Landale. Mahwah, N.J.: Erlbaum.

Safran, William. 1991. "Diasporas in Modern Societies: Myths of Homeland and Return." *Diaspora* 1(1): 83–99.

Smith, James, and Barry Edmonston. 1997. *The New Americans: Economic, Demographic, and Fiscal Effects of Immigration.* Washington: National Academy Press.

Smith, Robert C. 1994. "Upward Mobility or Social Marginalization: The Contingent Futures of Second-Generation Mexican Immigrants in New York City." Proposal submitted to the Russell Sage Foundation (September 30).

Soysal, Yasemin. 1994. *Limits of Citizenship: Migrants and Postnational Membership in Europe.* Chicago: University of Chicago Press.

Suárez-Orozco, Carola, and Marcelo Suárez-Orozco. 2001. *Children of Immigration*. Cambridge, Mass.: Harvard University Press.

Suárez-Orozco, Marcelo M. 1987. "Becoming Somebody: Central American Immigrants in U.S. Inner City Schools." *Anthropology and Education Quarterly* 18(4): 287–99.

———. 1995. "The Cultural Patterning of Achievement Motivation: A Comparative Study of Mexican, Mexican Immigrant, and Non-Latino White American Youths in Schools." In *California's Immigrant Children: Theory, Research, and Implications for Educational Policy,* edited by Rubén G. Rumbaut and W. A. Cornelius. San Diego: Center for U.S.-Mexican Studies, University of California.

Vertovec, Steven. 1997. "Three Meanings of Diaspora Exemplified Among South Asian Religions." *Diaspora* 6(3): 277–99.

Waters, Mary C. 1990. *Ethnic Options: Choosing Identities in America.* Berkeley: University of California Press.

———. 1996a. "Ethnic and Racial Identities of Second-Generation Black Immigrants in New York City." In *The New Second Generation,* edited by Alejandro Portes. New York: Russell Sage Foundation.

———. 1996b. "The Intersection of Gender, Race, and Ethnicity in Identity Development of Caribbean American Teens." In *Urban Adolescent Girls: Resisting Stereotypes,* edited by Bonnie Leadbeater and Niobe Way. New York: New York University Press.

———. 1999. *Black Identities: West Indian Dreams and American Realities.* New York: Russell Sage Foundation.

Zhou, Min. 1997. "Growing up American: The Challenge Confronting Immigrant Children and Children of Immigrants." *Annual Review of Sociology* 23: 69–95.

———. 1999. "Segmented Assimilation." In *The Handbook of International Migration,* edited by Charles Hirschman, Philip Kasinitz, and Josh Dewind. New York: Russell Sage Foundation.

———. 2001. "Contemporary Immigration and the Dynamics of Race and Ethnicity." In *America Becoming: Racial Trends and Their Consequences,* edited by Neil Smelser, William Julius Wilson, and Faith Mitchell. Washington: National Academy Press.

Zhou, Min, and Carl L. Bankston. 1998. *Growing up American: How Vietnamese Children Adapt to Life in the United States.* New York: Russell Sage Foundation.

— Part I —

Historical, Empirical, and Theoretical Perspectives

An Early Transnationalism? The Japanese American Second Generation of Hawaii in the Interwar Years

Reed Ueda

Hawaii, being the Cross-Roads of the Pacific, we have notables of the world passing through here nearly every week. How many of us realize this fact? By conducting ourselves as we should, the American-born Japanese citizens are in a position to bring about closer and more amicable relations between the United States and Japan. They are in a position to correct any misunderstandings, they are able to nail lies that are published by yellow journals and peanut politicians on both sides of the ocean.

—A. K. Ozawa, "The Japanese Boy in Hawaii" (1918)

SCHOLARS HAVE EXPLORED the presence of transnational identity among the children of immigrants by examining the dynamics for forming perceptions of the homeland. For example, in this volume, Nazli Kibria and Andrea Louie study the domains for cultural contact that produce knowledge and awareness of the homeland in today's Asian American second generation. For a segment of this cohort, study and travel in the homeland in managed settings arranged by the home state provide a means for learning transnational identifications. For them and for most second-generation Asians, direct firsthand experiences in the homeland are still quite limited, discontinuous, and subject to management or supervision by outside authorities. In daily life in the United States various domains for indirect contact with the homeland play a prominent role in shaping transnational consciousness. Consuming those commodities of mass culture and commercial markets that reflect images of the homeland is central to the formation of transnational identifications. These "reconnections" are ultimately related by second-generation members to their position in the host society, to their experience of local cultural and racial boundaries, and to their construction of an ethnic American identity.

Scholars can obtain a deeper perspective on the intercultural dynamics shaping transnational identity among the new Asian American second generation by examining the parallel historical situation of the Japanese American Nisei. They were the most sizable and culturally cohesive Asian American second-generation cohort to emerge in early-twentieth-century Hawaii, a U.S. territory influenced by extensive international contact. The case of the Hawaiian Nisei offers evidence for understanding a historical transnational consciousness that functioned very differently from the transnational awareness forming today. This was a transnationalism that shaped American ethnic identity, articulated group relations, responded to racial marginality, and promoted assimilation.

Nisei students at Honolulu's McKinley High School in 1926 wrote revealing autobiographies showing how they, as educated members of the second generation, were building a Japanese American ethnic identity. William Carlson Smith, a sociologist who had been trained at the University of Chicago and who held a position at the University of Southern California, collected these brief autobiographies, with the approval of the Hawaii Territorial Department of Instruction.[1] Examined here are seventy-six of these "life histories" (denoted hereafter as *MK*), written by thirty-five male and thirty-one female students who were themselves born in the U.S. territory of Hawaii and whose parents were both Japanese-born. These students' descriptions of their "life-worlds" reveal a multidimensional acculturation process underlying their emerging second-generation identity. For the young Nisei in prewar Hawaii, American national consciousness and identity coexisted with an ethnic life shaped by the family and community (Yamamoto 1949).

Nisei youngsters learned informally about homeland customs and life in their families, but they also learned in the sphere of public life about linkages to the home culture. Occasions for direct contact and direct cultural learning, such as trips to the homeland for study and tourism of the kind described by Kibria and Louie, were indeed quite rare in the interwar years, when the Nisei hardly traveled outside of the Hawaiian Islands. Instead, the Nisei gained an idea of Japan and its traditions through indirect experiences of cultural learning. The content of the resulting perceptions of the home country could not be mediated by face-to-face, on-site, empirical cross-checks, and thus much of it tended to be imagined, idealized, or even romanticized (Anderson 1991, 6–7).

The Japanese were the most populous immigrant group in Hawaii during the interwar years and created the largest commercial market for ethnically oriented goods and services in the Islands (Nordyke 1989, tables 3.3a–3.3k; Kimura 1988, 176–77; Fuchs 1961, 123). Japanese-owned and Japanese American–owned retail establishments merchandised a plethora of items from Japan, including food, medicine, clothing, utensils, dishware, tools, sporting goods, newspapers, magazines, and phonograph records. The Nisei sense of their culture was shaped in early life by perceptions of "things Japanese" derived from their Issei parents' patronage of these ethnic stores and their patterns of consumerism. The Nisei gained additional impressions of Japanese life by viewing feature films from Japan in local theaters, hearing Japanese-language radio programs, and listening to recorded Japanese popular music on the phonograph, frequently while in the company of their parents.[2] Japanese movies were especially effective in conveying vivid and idealized images of Japan and Japanese people. Feature films set in the preindustrial era of Japanese history (jidai-geki) and samurai adventure movies (chambara) were very popular in the community. They acquainted the Nisei with mythical national heroes and sagas of the bravery and loyalty of samurais, and they celebrated the moral strength of the Japanese people.

Another key public domain for indirect cultural learning about the home society was the Japanese language school. This institution primarily served the Nisei as a place where they learned how to read and write Japanese, but it also functioned as a cultural vehicle for supplying an appreciation of the history and traditions of their ancestral country. From their teachers and textbooks students obtained a glimpse of the land and the people of Japan that stimulated their wonder and innate curiosity. The education at the language school cultivated the Nisei's ability to identify with the home country and to take pride in the ancestral culture, which their parents had taught them to admire (Daniels 1988, 176; Miyamoto 1984 [1939], 57).

Concurrent with these experiences of indirect cultural learning about the home country, the Nisei encountered American national identity in their history and civics courses in the public schools. Hawaii's public educators organized the curriculum to promote Americanization, much as their counterparts did in the immigrant districts of the mainland in the 1920s (Tamura 1993, 56–57). The progressive educators of Hawaii endeavored to "Americanize" the Japanese second generation to ensure that they would have exclusive political ties to the United States. The goal of inculcating American citizenship among Hawaii's Nisei could not be extricated from the geopolitical context. These residents of Japanese ancestry in an island territory midway between Japan and the American mainland represented to U.S. officials a potential security factor in an era of escalating Japanese-American tensions.

The public high school exerted a powerful cultural influence on the Nisei generation. A comparatively large proportion of Nisei in their late teen years attended high school because of the willingness of their parents to invest in schooling up to the secondary level; at the time most children in the United States ended their formal education at the eighth grade. Thus, a large number of Nisei were exposed to Hawaii's progressive education programs in citizenship and Americanism. A curriculum centered on teaching citizenship complemented extracurricular efforts at cultivating institutional civic participation through essay contests, oratorical contests, student government programs, and public lectures promoting patriotism (see the McKinley High School newspaper *The Pinion,* November 6, 1925, 1; February 19, 1926, 1; February 21, 1927, 1; March 8, 1927, 1; April 26, 1927, 2; January 23, 1929, 3; February 26, 1929, 1; May 1, 1930, 2; May 12, 1932, 1).

The Nisei were pulled culturally in two directions defined by different national public spheres. The extent to which young Nisei developed a transnational identity in this situation can be gauged by looking at the autobiographies written by McKinley High School students in 1926. These personal testimonies reveal aspects of conscious self-identity that parallel the subjective parameters of transnational identity touched on by the studies of Kibria and Louie, including: contextualizing and personalizing one's perspective on self-identity; using a language of globalism; experiencing transnationalism "as a vision, a possibility for the future," in Kibria's phrase; conceptualizing transnationalism as a cultural advantage; locating transnational identity in relationship to the host-society ethnic identities made official by state institutions and politics; and relating transnational identity to second-generation identity in the private realm of the ethnic community.

In their autobiographies, these Nisei students expressed a profoundly felt need to exhibit publicly their American citizenship. One student remarked, for example, "We are true Americans and we must prove that we are true Americans" (*MK*-101). Another student explained that it was necessary to do so because "white people do not consider American-born Japanese as Americans. . . . They confuse largely . . . their native tongue [and] nationality" (*MK*-204).

As they strove to make their American national identity highly visible, these students also publicly avowed their sense of connection to their Japanese heritage. While believing that their cultural background endowed them with attitudes and beliefs that predisposed them to becoming "good" American citizens, Nisei students also felt that their Japanese cultural inheritance was a practical advantage in their lives. One student cited economic globalist incentives for knowing the "mother tongue." He predicted that "in the future trade will be carried on with Orientals exclusively and in order to be friendly we must know this [Japanese] language." More generally, Nisei students felt that being bilingual would open up greater opportunities in life for them. As one student argued:

> I believe we Japanese should go to the Japanese schools because . . . [if a] person understands and speaks Japanese well, as well as English, this would help him because the "haole" [Caucasian] wouldn't be able to understand the Japanese customers while the Japanese can understand both the English and Japanese customers and any employer would rather have a man who can do more work for him. (*MK*-19)

The most ambitious students described creative plans for future careers in which they would help to build better relations between the United States and Japan. A Nisei who had spent three years in Japan described his career goal as the promotion of international cultural understanding.

> I wished to become a translator of modern literature of English into Japanese and Japanese into English. . . . To my judgement, [the] majority of the Japanese people do not know the real nature of English literature. On the other hand most of the Americans do not know the real appreciation of the Japanese literature. I have studied the Japanese language for only these years, yet I discovered many pieces of literature that is worth reading by all people of all nations. . . . And my ambition of becoming a medium between the two literatures still exists. (*MK*-97)

Another student unveiled an even more ambitious career plan:

> [My] desire [is] to do something for America by so educating myself in Japanese and English, and so distinguish[ing] myself in the eyes of America that there would be the possibility of her wanting my service as an ambassador to Japan. . . . I had dreams of an ambassadorship that I may serve Americans and the American-Japanese at the same time. . . . I wanted to do something for America for the opportunity she had given my parents. Also, to serve her that the Japanese may not be thought of as a menace and burden to her. As my parents are Japanese natives of Japan, I would like to see the best of friendship between the two nations. (*MK*-125)

One student announced her intention to go to Japan to work as a teacher and thereby become a kind of cultural ambassador. In the homeland of her parents she would tell the Japanese people about American ideals, which she felt would help to improve their lives.

Nisei high school students fervently expressed a desire to promote the public good that united their adopted country and their ancestral country. Seeing themselves as equipped with knowledge about both the United States and Japan, these students aspired to become cultural interpreters to help better relationships between the two nations. The most ambitious believed if they pursued careers that promoted the progress of U.S.-Japanese relations, they would enhance their social standing as Nisei. Ultimately, by promoting international concord they would render the highest possible service as both Americans and world citizens. One student pledged:

We are the younger generation, upon whose shoulders are placed the responsibility and duty to distinguish ourselves as ideal American citizens, and at the same time, to pay obedience and respect due our Japanese parents, to create understanding and good fellowship between the East and the West, thus establishing the foundation of the realization of World Wide Brotherhood. (*MK*-45)

Nisei students saw that working to harmonize relations between Japan and the United States was an international mission that Hawaii was uniquely positioned to facilitate. In their view, Hawaii was a laboratory in which an experiment in multiracial democracy was taking place, and its outcome could make Hawaii a social and ethical touchstone for the entire world.

Nisei students wove a common thread through their autobiographies: the sense of a self in which the "best" qualities of American culture had been internalized and were reinforced by their cultivation of cherished features of their ancestral culture. Moreover, they felt that many Japanese values were American values, such as respect for education, devotion to family, loyalty to country, honesty, and moral rectitude. From Issei parents, from Japanese schoolteachers, and from the daily patterns and institutions of the ethnic neighborhood they learned to identify with their heritage in terms that allowed them to feel that the best of Japanese culture was congruent with the best of American culture. As a Nisei girl explained, "I have both the American and Japanese ideas so I shall . . . use the best of both and endeavor to be useful to my country, America" (*MK*-116). Nisei students tried to explain how their positive identification with Japanese culture prepared them to participate fully in the project of building American democracy in Hawaii. They were expressing a cosmopolitan American national identity consistent with international citizenship. Primordialist racial and cultural factors were devalued in this second-generation ideological vision. Their response to racial marginality was to strive to overcome it through new civic relations and an American civic identity.

On the Japanese side of the international relationship in the interwar years, Tokyo was receptive to a view of the national identity of immigrants as elective. In fact, the Japanese government acceded to Issei parents who petitioned to sever their children from Japanese nationality. Representatives of Japanese prefectural associations (kenjin-kai), who were first-generation Issei, asked the government of Japan to change its citizenship policy for their children, the second-generation Nisei. The existing policy was based on jus sanguinis and automatically made the children of Japanese immigrants citizens of Japan. The Issei wanted instead to facilitate the acculturation of their children by expatriating them so that they would no longer have Japanese citizenship. Tokyo gave its approval to their petitions. In 1916 Japanese nationality law was revised to permit Nisei (except for males between the ages of seventeen and twenty-eight who were eligible for military service) to renounce their Japanese citizenship. In 1924 another law was passed that automatically expatriated American Nisei within fourteen days of their birth unless their parents took out special papers with the Japanese consulate to preserve their children's Japanese nationality (Petersen 1971, 48–50).

The consul general of Japan stationed in Honolulu at that time, Keiichi Yamasaki, was a vocal proponent of the expatriation of the Nisei from Japan. "No consul general stationed in Hawaii urged Japanese born in Hawaii to expatriate themselves from the Japanese government more openly than Consul General Yamasaki," summarized a column in the English section of the Japanese-language newspaper *Nippu Jiji* on November 13, 1922. The column reported at length on Yamasaki's speech to the Nisei at Makiki Church on Armistice Day, in which he openly avowed that the Nisei were "American citizens, not Japanese": "Japan is not your country. Japan does not claim your allegiance. She hopes you will be loyal citizens of America. I hope you will cultivate your personal character, be faithful and loyal to the American flag." Yamasaki added: "I envy you because you were born in America, country of liberty and freedom, which is prosperous in industry and commerce." The attitude of this official forms a sharp contrast with the late-twentieth-century "home nation without boundaries" outreach policies in China, South Korea, and Cambodia directed to the overseas second generation.

The Nisei experience of subjective transnationalism suggests that, in assessing the influence of the structures of national life in host and home societies on transnational identity, it must be kept in mind that national systems are in motion and historical shifts in their political direction periodically affect how immigrant ethnic minorities absorb transnational influences.

In the current era of globalization and multiculturalism, transnational cultural connections reinforce the construction of second-generation identities in the public realm that center on ethnic differences and strong group boundaries. Transnational identities play out in host-society official multiculturalism, particularistic international linkages, and public arenas where primordial racial identities can be used for symbolic power. Thus, we might ponder Kibria's suggestion that transnational identity challenges the concept of assimilation by bypassing "two-worlds" oppositionalism and providing an alternative to Americanization. In an era of accelerating globalization, multiculturalism, and racialization, are second-generation identities increasingly being worked out in a social and cultural domain that overarches national boundaries, in a transnational space that is beyond the assimilationist dilemmas of the past?

As this chapter indicates, it makes a difference when we turn to the role of transnational cultural connections in historical eras when U.S. and immigrant homeland policies promoted the American national melting pot rather than the globalizing multicultural mosaic now in favor. During the 1920s, when the Nisei identities examined here were evolving, transnational connections shaped second-generation public identities so that they expressed immigrant homeland heritages in terms of their contributions to an ever-improving and democratic national amalgam, to a cosmopolitan host-society pluralism, and to an idealistic Wilsonian internationalism.

NOTES

1. William Carlson Smith Collection, "Life Histories of Students," Hamilton Library, University of Hawaii, Manoa.
2. An extensive historical collection of popular-culture artifacts from pre–World War II Hawaii, initiated by Kiyoshi Okubo, is housed at the Japanese Museum of Hilo, Hawaii.

REFERENCES

Anderson, Benedict. 1991. *Imagined Communities: Reflections on the Origin and Spread of Nationalism,* rev. ed. London: Verso.

Daniels, Roger. 1988. *Asian America: Chinese and Japanese in the United States Since 1850*. Seattle: University of Washington Press.

Fuchs, Lawrence H. 1961. *Hawaii Pono: A Social History*. New York: Harcourt, Brace.

Kimura, Yukiko. 1988. *Issei: Japanese Immigrants in Hawaii*. Honolulu: University of Hawaii Press.

Miyamoto, S. Frank. 1984 [1939]. *Social Solidarity Among the Japanese in Seattle*. Seattle: University of Washington Press.

Nordyke, Eleanor. 1989. *The Peopling of Hawai'i*. Honolulu: University of Hawaii Press.

Ozawa, A. K. 1918. "The Japanese Boy in Hawaii (To the American-born Japanese of Hawaii)." *Mid-Pacific Magazine* (March): 226–31.

Petersen, William. 1971. *Japanese Americans: Oppression and Success*. New York: Random House.

Tamura, Eileen H. 1993. *Americanization, Acculturation, and Ethnic Identity: The Nisei Generation in Hawaii*. Urbana: University of Illinois Press.

Yamamoto, Misako. 1949. "Cultural Conflicts and Accommodations of the First and Second Generation Japanese." *Sociology and Social Research* (May–June): 40–48.

Chapter 2

Severed or Sustained Attachments? Language, Identity, and Imagined Communities in the Post-Immigrant Generation

Rubén G. Rumbaut

America is coming to be, not a nationality but a trans-nationality, a weaving back and forth, with the other lands, of many threads of all sizes and colors.

—Randolph S. Bourne, "Trans-National America" (1916)

Migration as a social phenomenon must be studied not merely in its grosser effects . . . but envisaged in its subjective aspects.

—Robert E. Park, "Human Migration and the Marginal Man" (1926)

It is language, more than land and history, that provides the essential form of belonging.

—Michael Ignatieff, *Blood and Belonging: Journeys into the New Nationalism* (1993)

A WOMAN IN a camp in Croatia captured in a vivid metaphor the war-torn refugees' sense of loss of homeland: "They are like people who have lost a limb. Amputees. They can still feel their homeland, even though it's gone. It tingles. . . . They can dream it's still there" (Merrill 1995). Less metaphorically, Benedict Anderson asked in his *Imagined Communities: Reflections on the Origin and Spread of Nationalism* what explains "the *attachment* that peoples feel for the inventions of their imaginations," even to the point of being ready to die for these inventions:

> In an age when it is so common for progressive, cosmopolitan intellectuals to insist on the near-pathological character of nationalism, its roots in fear and hatred of the Other, and its affinities with racism, it is useful to remind ourselves that nations inspire love, and often profoundly self-sacrificing love . . . *amor patriae* does not differ in this respect from the other affections, in which there is often an element of fond imagining. (Anderson 1991, 141, 154)

Indeed, a language of kinship and of home—"homeland," patria, "fatherland," "mother tongue," "blood ties," a "birth connection"— is often invoked to describe these attachments to an imagined common origin or ancestry, so that while ethnic and national identities may be socially and politically constructed, they are experienced and expressed as "natural" (Cornell and Hartmann 1998; Horowitz 1985).[1] Such bounded attachments may be taken for granted by natives under conditions of normal order, but they are made salient by jolting change, rivalry, conflict, war . . . and international migration. Of the approximately 6 billion people on the planet, more than 120 million—slightly more than 2 percent of the world's population—are immigrants or refugees residing outside their countries of birth (Stalker 2000). Whatever the motives and circumstances that led them to move across national borders, the overwhelming majority remain linked, in one way or another, real or imagined, objectively or subjectively, to their native land. That is neither new nor news; despite the hackneyed one-way imagery of "uprooting" and "assimilation," adult migrants have seldom detached themselves radically from the ties and memories that bind and orient them to their origins (Foner 1997). As has been amply noted in a burgeoning literature, a revolution in transportation and communication technologies and a renewed globalization of the international economy has facilitated migrants' ability to sustain those ties, to the point of creating "transnational communities" in the process (Levitt 2001). Such transnational communities, as Portes (1996, 76) and others have argued, "include an increasing number of people who lead dual lives. Members are at least bilingual, move easily between different cultures, frequently maintain homes in two countries, and pursue economic, political, and cultural interests that require a simultaneous presence in both."

To be sure, transnational communities do not emerge ex nihilo; their formation and the movements of people crossing national borders that occasion them need to be placed and understood in concrete historical contexts. International migrations are rooted in historical relationships established between the sending and receiving countries—including colonialism, war and military occupation, labor recruitment and economic interaction, and sociocultural exchanges. Through these connections, migration footholds are formed, kinship networks expand, and remittances (in the tens of billions of dollars annually, second only to oil sales worldwide) sent by immigrants to their families abroad link communities across national borders. All of this turns migration into a social process of vast transformative significance, for both countries of origin and countries of destination. Moreover, migration pressures as a result of global inequality can be expected to mount in a world that is more and more a place with a declining proportion of rich people and a growing proportion of poor people. For those on the move, by hook or by crook, the United States remains the premier destination—and putatively a premier node for transnational networking. But while today's immigrants to the United States come from virtually every country in the world, some regions and nations send many more than others, despite the equitable numerical quotas provided to each country by U.S. law. In fact, only about a dozen countries have accounted for the majority of all immigration to the United States for the past few decades. The major sources of (legal and illegal) immigration are located either in the Caribbean Basin—in the immediate periphery of the United States, with Mexico being by far the predominant source—or in a handful of Asian nations also characterized by significant historical ties to the United States—notably the Philippines, China, Korea, and Vietnam.

Nonetheless, the numbers involved are sizable: millions of first-generation adult immigrants in the United States today are embedded in often intricate webs of family ties, both here and abroad.

Such ties form extraordinary transnational linkages and networks that can, by reducing the costs and risks of migration, expand and serve as a conduit to additional and thus potentially self-perpetuating migration (see Massey et al. 1998; Massey and Espinoza 1997). Thus, for example, by the end of the 1980s national surveys in Mexico found that about *half* of adult Mexicans were related to someone living in the United States, and that one-third of all Mexicans had been to the United States at some point in their lives. In the mid-1990s a poll in the Dominican Republic found that *half* of the 7.5 million Dominicans had relatives in the United States, and that *two-thirds* would move to the United States if they could. Despite four decades of hostile relations, at least one-third of Cuba's population of 11 million (and maybe half of Havana's) now have relatives in the United States and Puerto Rico, while over 75 percent of first- and second-generation Cubans in Miami have relatives in Cuba, according to the 1997 Cuba Poll conducted by Florida International University. Ironically, this is a greater degree of structural linkage than ever before in the history of U.S.-Cuba relations (Rumbaut 1997a, 1998). Not surprisingly, when in July 1999 the U.S. diplomatic mission in Havana held a lottery for 20,000 immigration visas to the United States, it received 541,000 applications in thirty days—meaning that about 10 percent of the total eligible population of Cuba applied to leave. Immigrants in the United States in 1990 who hailed from the English-speaking Caribbean, notably from Jamaica, Trinidad and Tobago, Barbados, Belize, and Guyana, already constituted between 10 and 20 percent of the 1990 populations of their respective countries—as did also those from El Salvador. (In the case of some Lesser Antillean countries, almost one-quarter of their entire populations can now be found residing in New York City alone!) Potentially vast social networks of family and friends are implied by these figures. These microsocial structures can shape both future migration and adaptation processes, as well as patterns of settlement in areas of destination and the ties they may maintain over time to their homelands.

The question that this book raises is whether and to what extent such attachments, in creed and deed, are sustained *in the generation of their children,* particularly those born here who lack the memories and the metaphorical birth connection of their emigrant parents. Where is home—or perhaps homes—for the *second* generation? Do they imagine themselves in multiple sites of belonging?

Are they able to lead dual lives or to maintain dual frames of reference? Are they even interested? Or will they become merely curious visitors to their ancestral lands, incidental genealogists or accidental ethnics (Liu 1999), largely indifferent to the transnational possibilities of the present age? After all, no matter how cheap and fast the travel or how advanced the communications technologies, motivated and resourceful actors are still required to avail themselves of those means of attachment and to pursue a meaningful transnational project of "dual lives." As is the case with the maintenance of a second language in the United States, so too may be the fate of transnationality in the "post-immigrant" new second generation: if you don't use it, you lose it. That is an open empirical question, and it is that question that I address here.

This chapter is intended principally as an empirical contribution to this volume. It aims to do so in two ways. First, it seeks to specify in detail the size and composition—and definition—of what is loosely called the "second generation" in the United States, nationally and in metropolitan areas of principal settlement. And second, it seeks to assess whether attachments (both subjective and objective) to the parental homeland are severed or sustained into early adulthood among children of immigrant parents. In addition, the analysis focuses on factors that either promote or undermine the maintenance of transnational ties over time in that post-immigrant generation. Thus, for a volume on what is transnational about the second generation, my aim is to advance our research and understanding of both based on specific operational definitions of these concepts and on new survey data from representative national and regional samples.

THE NEW FIRST AND SECOND
GENERATIONS IN THE UNITED STATES

The measurement of the size and composition of the first and second generations—which together comprise the country's "immigrant-stock" population—depends on what is meant by these terms, which have not been uniformly defined in the literature. Differences in nativity and age at arrival, which are criteria used to distinguish between generations, are known to affect significantly the modes of acculturation of adults and children in immigrant families, especially with regard to language and identity, and thus may also affect their propensity to sustain transnational attachments over time. When referring to the first generation, immigration scholars in the United States commonly have in mind persons born and socialized in another country who immigrate as adults, although (with certain technical exceptions) all foreign-born persons, regardless of age at arrival, are considered and aggregated as immigrants in official statistics. Similarly, the second generation technically refers to the U.S.-born and U.S.-socialized children of foreign-born parents, although under this rubric immigration scholars also often and imprecisely lump together foreign-born persons who immigrated as children, as well as U.S.-born persons with one U.S.-born parent and one foreign-born parent. None of these definitions accurately captures the experience of youths who fall in the interstices between these groupings. Nor do they account for the different developmental contexts at the time of immigration among those born abroad.

Thomas and Znaniecki (1958 [1918–1920], 1776), writing over eighty years ago in *The Polish Peasant in Europe and America,* referred in passing to the "half-second" generation to describe foreign-born youths coming of age in the United States. Warner and Srole (1945), in *The Social Systems of American Ethnic Groups,* distinguished the foreign-born—which they called the "parental" or "P" generation—from the U.S.-born generations, the first of which (the offspring of the immigrants) they dubbed the "filial first" or "F1" generation, the second (the grandchildren of the immigrants) "F2," and so on. They divided the immigrant generation, in turn, into those who entered the United States after the age of eighteen (labeled the "P1" generation) and those who entered at age eighteen or younger (the "P2" generation). Both the P2 and the half-second concepts are akin to the terms "one-and-a-half" or "1.5 generation," which I coined in studies of Cuban and then Southeast Asian youths and applied especially to those who had come to the United States after reaching school age but before reaching puberty (Rumbaut and Ima 1988; Rumbaut 1991). Adolescents and preschool immigrant children are at different developmental stages at arrival and closer to the experience of the "first" and "second" generations, respectively, and can be classified accordingly.[2]

However, while more precise distinctions based on age and developmental stage at arrival are not only possible but important for the analysis of modes of acculturation (and hence, theoretically, of the level of transnational attachment), the aim here is simpler and more limited. For purposes of depicting the size and composition of the immigrant-stock population of the United States, I rely on a fourfold classification. First, I distinguish by nativity between the first and second (or P and F1) generations; and then within each of those I distinguish between the 1.0 and 1.5 (or P1 and P2) and between the 2.0 and 2.5 groupings. By "1.0" I refer to all foreign-born persons who arrived in the United States as adults age eighteen and over, while the "1.5" grouping here absorbs all foreign-born persons who arrived in the United States as children under the age of eighteen. By "2.0" I refer to persons born in the United States of two foreign-born parents, while the "2.5" designation refers to persons born in the United States of one foreign-born parent and one U.S.-born parent (who are in that sense closer to the third generation, or F2 in Warner and Srole's terminology). The data are drawn from an analysis of special merged annual demographic files of the U.S. Census Bureau's Current Population Survey (CPS), which since 1994 has reinstated the question of paternal and maternal country of birth (unlike the past three decennial censuses). The CPS is the only national-level annual survey that permits a systematic assessment of the immigrant-stock population (the first and second generations of persons of foreign parentage) versus the third and higher generations of natives of native parentage.[3]

THE SIZE, COMPOSITION, AND CONCENTRATION OF THE IMMIGRANT-STOCK POPULATION

Based on the CPS merged data files, tables 2.1 and 2.2 provide a generational breakdown of the relevant populations in the United States today about whom the debate over transnationality centers. As table 2.1 shows, by 1997 there were an estimated 55 million people of foreign birth or parentage in the country—that is, the first generation of the foreign-born (26.8 million) and the second generation of U.S.-born persons with at least one foreign-born parent (27.8 million). That figure—already one-fifth of the national total—did not include 2.8 million others residing in the fifty states

(*Text continues on p. 52.*)

TABLE 2.1 Immigrant-Stock Population (First and Second Generations) of the United States, 1997, by Regional and National Origin

| National Origin | Immigrant Generation | | | | | Total Persons | |
| | First Generation | | Second Generation | | | (First and Second Generations) | |
	Foreign-Born N	Age (Mean)	U.S.-Born N	Age (Mean)		Total N	Foreign-Born (Percentage)
Latin America and Caribbean	13,260,671	35.7	10,209,048	18.0		23,469,719	57
Mexico	7,218,506	33.2	6,381,103	18.9		13,599,609	53
Cuba	869,722	50.8	507,711	18.2		1,377,433	63
Dominican Republic	584,954	36.9	390,337	12.5		975,291	60
El Salvador[a]	608,421	33.9	404,134	12.8		1,012,555	60
Guatemala	430,597	33.5	251,602	9.1		682,199	63
Nicaragua	277,035	34.0	122,763	15.8		399,798	69
Other Central America	465,299	37.2	277,799	14.8		743,098	63
Colombia	374,770	37.9	218,052	14.7		592,822	63
Other South America	991,097	37.4	519,945	16.6		1,511,042	66
Haiti	401,694	37.6	201,738	14.1		603,432	67
Jamaica	453,090	38.9	281,551	15.3		734,641	62
Other West Indies	585,486	39.6	362,863	18.6		948,349	62
Asia and Middle East	7,184,825	38.1	3,515,830	18.3		10,700,655	67
Philippines	1,257,729	41.4	733,932	17.1		1,991,661	63
China	903,690	44.9	355,783	22.9		1,259,473	72
Hong Kong, Taiwan	480,631	34.5	179,791	11.7		660,422	73
Vietnam	801,132	36.3	281,862	8.7		1,082,994	74
Laos, Cambodia	354,498	36.6	249,156	10.3		603,654	59

India	734,120	37.9	283,109	13.2	1,017,229	72
Korea	645,283	36.2	215,937	11.0	861,220	75
Japan	323,279	38.4	419,490	38.1	742,769	44
Other Southeast Asia	781,206	31.6	221,227	11.2	1,002,433	78
Iran	284,631	41.2	124,603	12.9	409,234	70
Israel	136,079	31.7	56,994	15.8	193,073	70
Arab Middle East	482,547	37.5	393,946	23.5	876,493	55
Europe and Canada	5,392,604	48.5	13,368,683	52.8	18,761,287	29
Canada	746,047	48.0	1,745,543	45.3	2,491,590	30
Great Britain	659,075	45.7	1,174,667	46.5	1,833,742	36
Ireland	191,959	53.9	689,073	55.5	881,032	22
Germany	725,794	48.7	1,740,100	43.8	2,465,894	29
Northwest Europe	500,473	51.6	1,681,164	56.4	2,181,637	23
Italy	495,098	58.0	2,328,525	58.2	2,823,623	18
Poland	477,484	47.9	1,203,265	61.7	1,680,749	28
Russia, former USSR	743,923	43.2	1,053,911	61.6	1,797,834	41
Southeast Europe	852,751	47.5	1,752,435	50.6	2,605,186	33
All other regions	1,007,280	37.0	703,453	27.3	1,710,733	59
Africa	499,017	34.6	248,619	13.0	747,636	67
Australia, other	508,263	39.4	454,834	35.1	963,097	53
Total population	26,845,381	39.0	27,797,013	35.0	54,642,395	49

Source: Merged 1997 and 1996 Current Population Survey demographic files (March CPS). Totals do not include an estimated 2.8 million persons residing in the fifty states who were born (or whose parents were born) in Puerto Rico or other U.S. territories.

[a] The 1997 CPS estimate for the Salvadoran second generation has been adjusted downwards based on more recent data (CPS 2000).

who were born (as were their parents) in Puerto Rico or other U.S. territories, nor the even larger number who resided in Puerto Rico and the other territories (Rumbaut 2001).[4] Further, net immigration to the United States (legal and illegal) has been adding an estimated one million more per year to the foreign-born population. Between 1990 and 1997 the foreign-born population of the United States increased from 19.8 million to 26.8 million; by the year 2000, as the U.S. Census Bureau recently reported, the foreign-born population exceeded 30.5 million people.[5] Meantime, the number of their children has grown commensurately; indeed, immigrant children and U.S.-born children of immigrants constitute the fastest-growing segment of the U.S. child population (under eighteen years of age). The 1990 census showed that they already comprised over 60 percent of all children classified as "Hispanic" and almost 90 percent of all "Asian American" children in the country; by 1995 foreign-born mothers, whose fertility rates are higher than those of native-born women, already accounted for nearly one-fifth (18 percent) of all U.S. births (Landale et al. 1999; Oropesa and Landale 1997; Zhou 1997).

The data presented in table 2.1 allow for an approximate rank ordering by size and mean age of the largest national-origin groups within the first and second generations. As the data show, the Mexican-origin population clearly dwarfs all others in both the first and second generations. By 1997 Mexican immigrants totaled about 7.2 million persons—about 6.0 million more than the next sizable immigrant groups (from the Philippines, China, Cuba, and Vietnam), and with a mean age of thirty-three, they were one of the youngest immigrant populations in the United States as well. The Mexican American second generation added another 6.4 million persons; this group was three times larger than the next largest second-generation group (Italian Americans, estimated at 2.3 million), but with a mean age of under nineteen years, the Mexican American second generation was much younger than Italian Americans of foreign parentage (whose mean age was fifty-eight, mostly the children of Italian immigrants who had come to the United States in the early twentieth century). Both through immigration and natural increase, the Mexican-origin population of the United States is growing more rapidly than virtually any other group and, as such, is of central interest for the study of transnational ties.

More than three out of every four immigrants in the United States today come from Latin America, the Caribbean, and Asia, with Mexico alone accounting for more than one-fourth of the total. While less than one-fifth of the 26.8 million in the immigrant first generation hailed from Europe or Canada, nearly half of the 27.8 million in the second generation did so. Indeed, not only the Italian but also the Canadian, German, British, Polish, and Russian second generations are larger than any other except for the Mexican. Their mean ages, however, are generally in their fifties, reflecting the fact that they consist largely of the surviving offspring of immigrants who came to the United States before World War II. As table 2.1 shows, the mean age of the combined European and Canadian second generations was fifty-three, compared to a much younger average of eighteen years for the U.S.-born offspring of Latin American, Caribbean, and Asian immigrants. For the latter groups, the mean age of the generation of their children is still very young—in fact, they mostly consist *of* children with mean ages ranging from nine to eighteen years for almost all the groups, the sole exception being the Japanese Nisei, whose mean age was thirty-eight years. This telling marker not only reflects how recently the first-generation groups immigrated but also suggests that a full assessment of the level of sustained transnationality in the second generation is only now beginning to be made possible. (Indeed, this book is a pioneer in this respect.)

A more precise rendering of the generational composition of the immigrant-stock population is presented in table 2.2. The data are here broken down by the four main cohorts described earlier: the "1.0" generation of persons who arrived in the United States as adults (age eighteen or older); the "1.5" generation of persons who arrived in the United States as children (age seventeen or younger); the "2.0" generation of persons who were born in the United States of two foreign-born parents; and the "2.5" generation of persons who were born in the United States of one foreign-born parent and one U.S.-born parent (approximating a more acculturated and intermarried population situated between the second and third generations). As table 2.2 shows, each of these groupings numbered between 11 and 16 million persons in 1997. Theoretically, each is likely to differ significantly with regard to its transnational attachments and orientations. As noted earlier, that is an open empirical

(*Text continues on p. 57.*)

TABLE 2.2 Immigration Era, Region of Origin, Age Groups, and Ten Top Areas of Metropolitan Settlement of the Immigrant-Stock Population of the United States, 1997, by 1.0, 1.5, 2.0, and 2.5 Generations

	First Generation (N/Percentage)		Second Generation (N/Percentage)		Total
	1.0	1.5	2.0	2.5	
Total U.S. Population of Immigrant Stock	15,801,623 100.0	11,043,757 100.0	15,083,922 100.0	12,713,090 100.0	54,642,392 100.0
Immigration era[a]					
New immigration (post-1960)	14,021,699 88.7	10,242,424 92.7	9,096,284 60.3	6,924,676 54.5	40,285,083 73.7
Old immigration (pre-1960)	1,779,924 11.3	801,333 7.3	5,987,638 39.7	5,788,414 45.5	14,357,309 26.3
Region of origin by immigration era					
New immigration (post-1960)					
Latin America, Caribbean	6,651,487 47.4	6,051,355 59.1	5,724,272 62.9	3,016,537 43.6	21,443,651 53.2
Asia and Middle East	4,555,108 32.5	2,410,108 23.5	2,055,923 22.6	984,668 14.2	10,005,807 24.8
Europe and Canada	2,215,046 15.8	1,432,667 14.0	1,106,860 12.2	2,633,101 38.0	7,387,674 18.3
All other regions	600,058 4.3	348,294 3.4	209,228 2.3	290,370 4.2	1,447,950 3.6
Old immigration (pre-1960)					
Latin America, Caribbean	344,481 19.4	213,349 26.6	670,854 11.2	797,384 13.8	2,026,068 14.1
Asia and Middle East	113,131 6.4	106,479 13.3	291,844 4.9	183,395 3.2	694,849 4.8

Europe and Canada	1,279,619	465,270	4,949,623	4,679,097	11,373,609
	71.9	58.1	82.7	80.8	79.2
All other regions	42,693	16,235	75,318	128,537	262,783
	2.4	2.0	1.3	2.2	1.8
Age groups					
Children (under eighteen)	—	2,962,090	6,586,248	4,213,507	13,761,845
	—	26.8	43.7	33.1	25.2
Young adults (eighteen to thirty-four)	3,620,028	5,534,612	2,268,659	2,344,967	13,768,266
	22.9	50.1	15.0	18.4	25.2
Middle age (thirty-five to sixty-four)	9,292,543	2,484,866	2,059,314	3,845,318	17,682,041
	58.8	22.5	13.7	30.2	32.4
Elders (sixty-five and older)	2,889,052	62,190	4,169,701	2,309,298	9,430,241
	18.3	0.6	27.6	18.2	17.3
Metropolitan areas[b]					
Los Angeles	2,012,434	1,513,961	1,784,264	604,760	5,915,419
	12.7	13.7	11.8	4.8	10.8
New York	1,844,886	1,056,087	1,307,218	573,771	4,781,962
	11.7	9.6	8.7	4.5	8.8
San Diego–Orange–Riverside	1,125,735	866,031	889,507	606,423	3,487,696
	7.1	7.8	5.9	4.8	6.4
New Jersey MSAs	935,094	536,798	992,262	629,838	3,093,992
	5.9	4.9	6.6	5.0	5.7
San Francisco–Oakland–San Jose	818,161	450,476	648,312	430,747	2,347,696
	5.2	4.1	4.3	3.4	4.3
Chicago	644,238	437,332	727,983	465,289	2,274,842
	4.1	4.0	4.8	3.7	4.2

(*Table continues on p. 56.*)

TABLE 2.2 *Continued*

	First Generation (N/Percentage)		Second Generation (N/Percentage)		Total
	1.0	1.5	2.0	2.5	
Total U.S. Population of Immigrant Stock	15,801,623	11,043,757	15,083,922	12,713,090	54,642,392
	100.0	100.0	100.0	100.0	100.0
Miami	704,489	404,130	380,374	141,046	1,630,039
	4.5	3.7	2.5	1.1	3.0
Ft. Lauderdale–West Palm Beach–Tampa	453,209	265,924	471,195	380,253	1,570,581
	2.9	2.4	3.1	3.0	2.9
Houston	396,561	266,094	299,398	184,888	1,146,941
	2.5	2.4	2.0	1.5	2.1
Washington, D.C.	401,633	223,823	181,580	193,276	1,000,312
	2.5	2.0	1.2	1.5	1.8
All other MSAs	5,570,829	4,264,565	6,146,849	6,624,811	22,607,054
	35.3	38.6	40.8	52.1	41.4
Not MSA	894,355	758,536	1,254,979	1,877,989	4,785,859
	5.7	6.9	8.3	14.8	8.8

Source: Merged (March) 1997 and 1996 Current Population Survey (CPS) demographic files. Totals do not include an estimated 2.8 million persons residing in the fifty states who were born (or whose parents were born) in Puerto Rico or other U.S. territories. Generations are here defined as follows: 1.0 = foreign-born persons, arrived in the United States as adults (eighteen years old or older); 1.5 = foreign-born persons, arrived in the United States as children (under 18 years); 2.0 = born in the United States of two foreign-born parents; and 2.5 = born in the United States of one foreign-born parent and one U.S.-born parent.

[a] Immigration eras are here defined as follows: "Old immigration" = arrived in the U.S. before 1960, or born in U.S. before 1960; "New Immigration" = arrived in the U.S. in or after 1960, or born in the U.S. in or after 1960.

[b] Primary metropolitan statistical areas (PMSAs), or contiguous MSAs (the San Francisco Bay Area; the New Jersey areas across the Hudson River from New York City; the counties of San Diego, Orange, and Riverside adjacent to Los Angeles; and the corridor north of Miami-Dade stretching from Fort Lauderdale to West Palm Beach and Tampa, Florida). These ten metropolitan regions accounted for half of the 55 million people of immigrant stock in the United States in 1997.

question, although it may prove fruitful for future research to break down the "second generation" with regard to parental birthplace and age at arrival, rather than lumping together the 1.5, 2.0, and 2.5 generational segments and treating them all as "second-generation."

Table 2.2 divides the immigrant-stock cohorts into two main immigration eras: those who either arrived or were born in the United States before 1960 (the *old* immigration era); and those who either arrived or were born in the United States on or after 1960 (the *new* immigration era).[6] By this definition, the new post-1960 first and second generations totaled over 40 million persons in 1997, and the old pre-1960 first and second generations totaled about 14 million persons (12 million of whom were born in the United States before 1960)—one-quarter of the total immigrant-stock population and its oldest components, but still significant overall. Note that the data in table 2.2 are broken down by both regional origin and immigration era for each of the four generational types, as well as by age group. This makes clearer the differential location generationally of Europeans and Canadians (who make up a substantial segment only among the 2.5 cohort) vis-à-vis the Latin Americans (who dominate the 1.5 and 2.0 cohorts) and the Asian-origin populations (who are most sizable among the 1.0 cohorts of immigrants who arrived as adults). Children under eighteen make up by far the largest share of the 2.0 generation (as well as one-third of the 2.5 cohort); young adults eighteen to thirty-four account for half of the 1.5 generation (immigrants who arrived in the United States as children); and middle-age adults thirty-five to sixty-four make up the lion's share (almost 60 percent) of the 1.0 cohort.

Lastly, table 2.2 breaks down these data by the ten largest metropolitan concentrations in the United States, where half of the 55 million people of foreign birth or parentage resided in 1997. The results vividly document the huge significance of southern California and the New York region; those two regions alone absorbed fully one-third of the national immigrant-stock total population. In that year 62 percent of Los Angeles County's 9.5 million people were of immigrant stock, as were 54 percent of the residents of adjacent Orange County and 43 percent of San Diego's, so that the corridor stretching from San Diego to Los Angeles alone contained 17.2 percent of the country's foreign-stock population. New York City and the New Jersey metropolitan areas on the other side of the

Hudson River combined for another 16.5 percent of the country's first and second generations. The Bay Area in California—encompassing San Francisco, Oakland, and San Jose—absorbed 4.3 percent of the national immigrant-stock total; the corridor stretching from Miami to Fort Lauderdale and Palm Beach contained another 4.8 percent. Nearly three-fourths (72 percent) of metropolitan Miami's population was either foreign-born or of foreign parentage, the highest proportion in the United States (Portes and Rumbaut 2001, ch. 2). Theoretically, in contrast to more dispersed populations, such dense ethnic concentrations could enable the development of a bilingual-bicultural second generation and hence enhance the prospects for their maintenance of transnational attachments.

THE TRANSNATIONAL ATTACHMENTS OF ADULT CHILDREN OF IMMIGRANTS

For the second objective of this chapter—to assess whether attachments (both subjective and objective) to the parental homeland are severed or sustained into early adulthood among children of immigrant parents—I have turned to a decade-long panel study, the Children of Immigrants Longitudinal Study (CILS). CILS has followed representative samples of 1.5- and second-generation youth from several dozen different national origins on both coasts of the United States (the San Diego and Miami metropolitan areas) from late 1991 (when the sample was drawn) to the present. The initial survey, conducted in the spring of 1992 (T1), interviewed more than five thousand students enrolled in the eighth and ninth grades in public and private schools, when most were fourteen or fifteen years old. Follow-up surveys were done in 1995–1996 (T2) with 82 percent of the original respondents, and again in 2001–2002 (T3) when most were about twenty-five years old. The baseline sample was drawn in the junior high grades, a level at which dropout rates are still relatively low, to avoid the potential bias of differential dropout rates between ethnic groups at the senior high school level. For purposes of the study, students were eligible to enter the sample if they were U.S.-born but had at least one foreign-born parent, or if they themselves were foreign-born and had come to the United States at an early age (most before age ten). Among the seventy-seven nationalities represented in the CILS sample are found the principal types of immigrants in contemporary American society—immigrant laborers, professionals, entrepreneurs, and refugees with sharply contrasting socioeconomic origins, migration histories, and contexts of exit and of reception (see Portes and Rumbaut 1996). Although the 26.8 million foreign-born persons in the United States in 1997 came from over 150 different countries, over 40 percent came from only five: Mexico, the Philippines, China, Cuba, and Vietnam. Children of immigrants from those five countries make up about 60 percent of the overall CILS sample, and about 80 percent of the San Diego CILS sample (where all of these groups except the Cubans are represented in sizable numbers).

Specifically, the principal nationalities represented in the San Diego baseline sample—on which I focus here—were Mexicans, Filipinos, Vietnamese, Laotians, Cambodians, Chinese, and smaller groups of other children of immigrants from Asia (mostly Japanese, Korean, Indian, and Thai) and Latin America and the Caribbean (including some from virtually all of the Central and South American countries, as well as a few Haitians, Jamaicans, Dominicans, and Cubans). Table 2.3 presents a profile of the demographic and socioeconomic characteristics of these respondents and their families, which differ significantly by national origin. Note that the baseline sample in San Diego was divided exactly evenly by gender. By nativity, 56 percent were foreign-born (the 1.5 generation) and 44 percent were U.S.-born (the second generation); 15 percent of the respondents had one U.S.-born parent (the 2.5 generation). For the foreign-born, their year of arrival in the United States is indicated. Table 2.3 also presents data for all of the main national-origin groups in San Diego on the structure and cohesion of their families, their parents' level of education and home ownership, the socioeconomic characteristics of their neighborhood, and objective measures of the respondents' educational attainment (math and reading achievement test scores in 1991–1992, final high school grade point average, and dropout rates by 1995–1996).

CILS results have been reported in a variety of publications and two recent books (Portes and Rumbaut 2001; Rumbaut and Portes 2001). However, that literature reports on results only through the end of high school, when these youths were about eighteen years of age and still resided at home with their parents. We returned to the field in 2001 to locate (wherever they may be now residing) and reinterview for a third time the entire baseline sample, who by now were

(Text continues on p. 63.)

TABLE 2.3 Characteristics of Children of Immigrants in San Diego, 1992, by National Origin

Characteristics	Mexico	Philippines	Vietnam	Cambodia, Laos	China, Taiwan	Asia Other	Latin America Other	Total
$N=$	727	808	361	301	52	82	89	2,420
Sex								
Female	49.2	50.1	47.6	52.8	50.0	50.0	56.2	50.0
Male	50.8	49.9	52.4	47.2	50.0	50.0	43.8	50.0
Year of birth[a]								
1975	2.1	1.4	3.6	4.0	0	1.2	3.4	2.3
1976	17.5	16.8	22.7	23.6	7.7	15.9	25.8	18.8
1977	43.9	51.0	42.4	44.2	48.1	47.6	42.7	46.2
1978	36.5	30.8	31.3	28.2	44.2	35.3	28.1	32.7
Nativity and (if foreign-born) year of U.S. arrival								
U.S.-born	59.8	54.2	15.2	3.3	50.0	54.9	49.4	43.5
Foreign-born	40.2	45.8	84.8	96.7	50.0	45.1	50.6	56.5
1975 to 1979	9.2	9.5	17.5	16.3	1.9	13.4	6.7	11.3
1980 to 1984	10.9	16.3	35.5	51.8	21.2	13.4	20.2	22.1
1985 to 1990	20.1	19.9	31.9	28.6	26.9	18.3	23.6	23.1
One parent born in the U.S.?								
No	82.4	80.7	97.5	99.7	84.6	53.7	73.0	85.0
Yes	17.6	19.3	2.5	0.3	15.4	46.3	27.0	15.0
Family structure, 1992								
Intact family	59.0	79.3	73.1	72.1	76.9	69.5	46.1	69.8
Stepfamily	14.3	9.3	3.9	7.0	3.8	8.5	21.3	10.0
Single parent, other	26.7	11.4	23.0	20.9	19.2	22.0	32.6	20.2

Family cohesion, 1995								
Low	28.6	33.8	41.7	32.7	47.1	25.4	34.4	33.4
Medium	32.6	37.3	30.7	37.4	31.4	28.2	29.7	34.4
High	38.7	28.8	27.7	29.9	21.6	46.5	35.9	32.2
Father's education								
Under twelve years	67.3	15.2	62.0	73.4	38.5	8.5	24.7	45.7
High school graduate	26.4	55.7	23.5	19.6	26.9	47.6	44.9	36.3
College degree	6.3	29.1	14.4	7.0	34.6	43.9	30.3	18.0
Mother's education								
Under twelve years	73.9	21.0	69.8	83.4	32.7	18.3	33.7	52.6
High school graduate	22.4	40.7	21.9	13.3	36.5	58.5	41.6	29.5
College degree	3.7	38.2	8.3	3.3	30.8	23.2	24.7	17.9
Homeownership, 1992								
Rent	68.8	26.4	66.2	84.1	23.1	40.2	59.6	53.8
Own	31.2	73.6	33.8	15.9	76.9	59.8	40.4	46.2
Poverty rate of neighborhood, 1990								
Under 15 percent	8.0	58.6	34.8	6.0	46.4	64.5	27.8	35.3
15 to 50 percent	43.7	39.5	37.0	31.9	50.0	29.0	52.8	39.8
Over 50 percent	48.3	1.9	28.1	62.1	3.6	6.5	19.4	24.9

(*Table continues on p. 62.*)

TABLE 2.3 *Continued*

Characteristics	Mexico	Philippines	Vietnam	Cambodia, Laos	China, Taiwan	Asia Other	Latin America Other	Total
N=	727	808	361	301	52	82	89	2,420
Rate of foreign-born residents in neighborhood, 1990								
Under 20 percent	27.7	24.5	35.7	17.4	67.3	62.2	56.2	29.6
21 to 39 percent	32.3	56.7	39.9	33.8	30.8	31.7	31.5	41.7
Over 40 percent	40.0	18.8	24.4	48.8	1.9	6.1	12.4	28.7
National percentile in Stanford Achievement Test (eighth or ninth grade), 1991 to 1992								
Math	30.7	58.9	60.1	37.5	81.0	62.7	46.4	48.2
Reading	25.7	51.1	37.2	18.0	63.7	61.2	50.4	38.3
Achievement outcomes (by end of high school), 1995 to 1996								
Dropped out (percentage)	8.8	4.0	5.5	4.0	0.0	7.3	5.6	5.7
Mean GPA	2.24	2.86	3.02	2.72	3.69	3.16	2.74	2.71

Source: Children of Immigrants Longitudinal Study (CILS), 1992. Data on achievement test scores were collected by the San Diego school system in 1991 to 1992, when the students were in eighth or ninth grades; data on achievement outcomes by the end of high school in 1995 to 1996 (dropout status, academic grade point averages) were collected from the school system for the full baseline sample (See Rumbaut 2001).
[a] A small number of respondents born in 1979 are included under 1978.

in their midtwenties. For comparative purposes we included in our T3 survey instruments a variety of items about transnational activities identical to those that had been asked in the recent New York City Second Generation Study directed by Mary Waters, John Mollenkopf, and Phil Kasinitz. (Some of the results of that study are reported in this volume.) The NYC study focused on the immigrant and refugee groups that have concentrated in that city—Dominicans, Chinese, West Indians, Soviet Jews, and certain South American nationalities—thus significantly broadening the comparability and scope of the CILS research reported here. This chapter is limited to preliminary results from 1,100 completed T3 surveys collected in 2001 from the original San Diego sample.[7]

We turn now to an analysis of those results, organized as follows: tables 2.4, 2.5, and 2.6 present detailed information, by national-origin groups, on respondents' educational, occupational, marital, and residential status by 2001–2002; their patterns of language use and proficiency across the decade from 1992 to 2002; and change over time in their self-reported ethnic-national identities, the parents' degree of prior ethnic-national socialization of their children (drawn from separate interviews with their parents in 1995–1996), and the children's knowledge and perceptions of the parents' homeland. Table 2.7 then summarizes our findings on key indicators of subjective and objective transnational attachments (perceptions of "home" and frequency of visits and remittances to the country of origin) for all of the main ethno-national groups. Finally, tables 2.8 and 2.9 present bivariate and multivariate analyses of predictors (the independent variables detailed in tables 2.3 through 2.6) of transnational attitudes and behaviors (the dependent variables in table 2.7) in this sample of 1.5, 2.0, and 2.5 cohorts of adult children of immigrants. Note that all of the data in tables 2.4 through 2.9 are for the 1991–2001 longitudinal sample; that is, the same 1,100 respondents are reflected in each of these tables.

CHARACTERISTICS AND TRAJECTORIES OF ADULT CHILDREN OF IMMIGRANTS, 1992 TO 2001

Table 2.4 presents a set of current social characteristics, measured in 2001–2002, for each of the major ethnic groups in the longitudinal

(Text continues on p. 66.)

TABLE 2.4 Socioeconomic Characteristics of Adult Children of Immigrants in San Diego, 2001, by National Origin (Percentage)

Characteristics	Mexico	Philippines	Vietnam	Cambodia, Laos	China, Taiwan	Asia Other	Latin America Other	Total
Highest level of education attained, 2001								
Not high school graduate	7.1	1.7	4.3	5.8	0	3.0	5.6	3.9
High school graduate, GED	25.4	12.6	7.2	38.0	3.6	9.5	19.4	18.1
College, one to two years	39.9	26.9	8.7	23.9	10.7	12.5	25.0	26.6
College, three to four years	18.7	29.8	34.1	17.4	39.3	31.3	19.4	26.0
College graduate	7.1	24.3	42.0	14.9	35.7	34.4	27.8	21.9
Graduate school	1.9	4.8	3.6	0	10.7	9.4	2.8	3.6
Marital status, 2001								
Single	51.9	74.9	87.0	68.6	89.3	75.8	77.8	70.4
Married	31.0	12.3	3.6	21.5	3.6	9.1	5.6	16.4
Engaged	6.3	6.4	3.6	2.5	3.6	3.0	5.6	5.3
Cohabiting	7.1	5.0	3.6	5.0	0	9.1	8.3	5.4
Divorced, separated, other	3.7	1.4	2.2	2.5	3.6	3.0	2.8	2.5

Do you have any children?								
No	60.4	84.2	94.9	77.7	100.0	84.8	86.1	79.3
Yes	39.6	15.8	5.1	22.3	0	15.2	13.9	20.7
Where do you live now?								
Parents' home	50.6	62.9	55.8	52.1	46.4	48.5	41.7	55.9
Own place	41.6	28.1	31.2	25.6	35.7	45.5	47.2	33.1
Other	7.9	9.0	13.0	22.3	17.9	6.1	11.1	11.0
Religion, 2001								
Catholic	71.3	79.0	19.6	3.3	10.7	6.1	36.1	54.8
Protestant	3.4	4.5	1.4	1.7	14.3	12.1	2.8	3.9
Buddhist	0	0.5	45.7	67.8	3.6	9.1	0	14.6
Other	15.6	7.1	6.5	10.7	10.7	27.3	27.8	10.9
None	9.7	9.0	26.8	16.5	60.7	45.5	33.3	15.8
Current work situation, 2001								
Employed, full-time	63.2	49.1	47.1	65.3	40.7	51.5	52.8	54.3
Employed, part-time	21.4	31.8	23.5	14.9	18.5	27.3	41.7	25.9
Unemployed, looking for work	6.0	7.1	12.5	9.1	14.8	0	2.8	7.6
Unemployed, not looking for work	2.3	1.9	1.4	3.3	3.7	3.0	0	2.1
Full-time student, not working	3.8	7.3	14.7	5.8	22.2	18.2	2.8	7.8
Full-time homemaker	3.4	2.9	0.7	1.6	0	0	0	2.3

Source: Children of Immigrants Longitudinal Study (CILS), 2001.

sample. In effect, it sketches a portrait of the transition to early adulthood among respondents in their midtwenties with respect to their educational attainment and labor force status, living arrangements, marriage and family formation, and religion. The data provided here include variables that were analyzed for their hypothesized association with transnational attachments and activities, as elaborated later in the chapter. One of these factors, religion, has until recently been largely ignored in the research literature on the new immigration, yet as research by some of the contributors to this volume, among others, has suggested, it is an important factor to consider in the analysis of transnational ties (Levitt 2001; Ebaugh and Chafetz 2000). Note in particular the large proportion of Chinese (over 60 percent) who adhere to no religion at all, compared to fewer than 10 percent of the Mexicans and Filipinos (who are mostly Catholics).

As table 2.4 shows, only about 4 percent of the sample were high school dropouts (the Mexicans, Cambodians, and Laotians had somewhat higher rates); about the same percentage were in graduate school or had completed advanced degrees (with the Chinese and "other Asians" disproportionately represented among them). About one-fourth were college graduates (including nearly half of the Vietnamese and Chinese); one-fourth had completed three to four years of college but had not graduated; and another one-fourth reported having attended college for only one to two years (disproportionately among them the Mexicans and Filipinos). Nearly one in five (18 percent) had finished their formal education after obtaining a high school diploma or a GED (including 38 percent of the Cambodians and Laotians and 25 percent of the Mexicans). About two-thirds of those three groups were employed full-time in 2001, in contrast to only about half of all the others, many of whom were still enrolled in colleges or universities (especially the Chinese, Vietnamese, and "other Asians"). The Mexicans, Cambodians, and Laotians were also much more likely to be married and to have children. Indeed, none of the Chinese had had any children to date, compared with 40 percent of the Mexicans. All of these intergroup differences underscore the sharp ethnic segmentation in their socioeconomic trajectories to date.

Table 2.5 focuses detailed attention on one of the central factors examined in this study: language use, proficiency, and preferences (in both English and the non-English mother tongue), as measured in 1992, 1995 to 1996, and 2001, and their patterns of change across the span of a decade. Although a language other than English was spoken in the homes of over 95 percent of these individuals during their teen years, as table 2.5 documents, already by 2001, 17 percent reported knowing no language other than English—including one-third of the Filipinos and "other Asians" and over one-fourth of the "other Latin Americans." Language extinction, however, was rare among the Mexicans, Vietnamese, Laotians, and Cambodians, fewer than 4 percent of whom reported speaking English only by 2001. Among all respondents, the percentage of those who could *speak* English "very well" increased from 74 percent in 1992 to 84 percent in 2001, and those who could *read* English "very well" increased from 69 to 84 percent over the same period. By contrast, the percentage of those who could speak a foreign language "very well" increased slightly overall from about 27 percent in both 1992 and 1995 to 31 percent in 2001; those who could read a foreign language "very well" also increased slightly from 17 to 23 percent over time. However, those figures are distorted by the fact that the improvement in foreign language proficiency, and especially in reading literacy, was observed largely among the Spanish users, as table 2.5 shows. This was particularly the case among the Mexican-origin respondents, whose ability to speak and read in Spanish did not atrophy but rather improved appreciably from their teens to their twenties. Thus, although English proficiency trumps their competency in the mother tongue, certain groups actually improved in their non-English language abilities by early adulthood, above all the Spanish speakers.

Table 2.5 presents longitudinal data on the maintenance (or not) of fluent bilingualism among the various ethnic groups over the 1992 to 2001 decade, as well as a typology of language dominance and detailed patterns of current language use with parents, spouse or partner, children, close friends, and coworkers. A much higher proportion of Mexicans (52 percent) and "other Latin Americans" (44 percent) could be classified as fluent bilinguals by 2001

(*Text continues on p. 71.*)

TABLE 2.5 Language Patterns Among Children of Immigrants in San Diego, 1992 to 2001, by National Origin (Percentage)

Characteristics	Mexico	Philippines	Vietnam	Cambodia, Laos	China, Taiwan	Asia Other	Latin America Other	Total
What is the main language spoken in your home? (asked in 1992 and 1995)								
Non-English	96.2	95.6	100.0	100.0	92.9	87.1	84.8	96.2
English	3.8	4.4	0	0	7.1	12.9	15.2	3.8
Do you know a language other than English? (asked in 2001)								
No	3.7	31.8	2.2	1.7	17.9	33.3	27.8	16.8
Yes	96.3	68.2	97.8	98.3	82.1	66.7	72.2	83.2
Percentage who could speak a foreign language "very well" in								
1992	53.7	7.3	30.4	38.0	28.6	12.1	41.7	27.7
1995	56.5	6.6	23.0	41.5	14.3	18.8	36.4	27.2
2001	62.7	8.7	26.8	51.2	10.7	18.2	44.4	31.4
Percentage who could speak English "very well" in								
1992	66.0	88.9	64.5	44.6	75.0	84.8	80.6	73.9
1995	66.9	91.4	60.7	47.5	67.9	93.8	81.8	75.1
2001	84.3	90.4	70.3	76.9	78.6	100.0	94.4	84.0
Percentage who could read a foreign language "very well" in								
1992	39.6	7.8	8.7	7.4	7.1	6.1	33.3	16.8
1995	48.8	5.9	10.4	8.5	10.7	6.3	33.3	18.8
2001	57.5	9.2	11.6	8.3	3.6	12.1	41.7	22.8
Percentage who could read English "very well" in								
1992	57.3	88.9	57.8	37.3	64.3	83.9	72.2	69.4
1995	67.3	91.8	60.6	47.0	67.9	93.5	81.8	75.3
2001	82.4	90.1	69.6	75.4	78.6	96.8	94.4	83.8

Percentage classified as fluent bilinguals in[a]								
1992	25.4	4.0	7.2	2.5	0	3.0	25.0	10.3
1995	38.1	5.4	3.7	3.4	3.6	12.5	30.3	14.3
2001	52.2	9.5	5.8	9.1	3.6	15.2	44.4	21.1
Level of language dominance (English, bilingual, or foreign language), 1992[a]								
English dominant	23.5	74.2	46.4	24.8	60.7	78.8	47.2	50.7
Fluent bilingual	25.4	4.0	7.2	2.5	0	3.0	25.0	10.3
Non-English dominant	32.5	5.4	10.1	7.4	10.7	6.1	19.4	13.8
Limited bilingual	18.7	16.3	36.2	65.3	28.6	12.1	8.3	25.1
Percentage who preferred to speak English, as reported in								
1992	41.8	90.8	57.2	55.4	82.1	87.9	72.2	68.8
1995	71.9	97.3	77.0	78.0	85.7	96.9	84.8	85.1
Language uses with parents, 2001								
Non-English	53.5	4.3	68.4	67.2	39.3	18.2	25.7	34.7
Both the same	33.0	13.1	19.8	27.7	10.7	24.2	14.3	21.1
English	13.5	82.6	11.8	5.1	50.0	57.6	60.0	44.2
Language uses with spouse or partner, 2001								
Non-English	16.0	1.9	7.7	5.3	6.7	0	6.9	7.0
Both the same	36.2	5.3	17.9	33.3	0	0	20.7	18.6
English	47.8	92.8	74.4	61.4	93.3	100.0	72.4	74.4

(*Table continues on p. 70.*)

TABLE 2.5 *Continued*

Characteristics	Mexico	Philippines	Vietnam	Cambodia, Laos	China, Taiwan	Asia Other	Latin America Other	Total
Language uses with close friends, 2001								
Non-English	9.1	1.0	2.3	4.2	3.6	0	2.9	3.7
Both the same	43.4	3.3	23.3	27.1	14.3	0	11.4	19.4
English	47.5	95.7	74.4	68.7	82.1	100.0	85.7	76.9
Language uses with co-workers, 2001								
Non-English	5.9	0.5	2.3	2.7	4.2	0	0	2.4
Both the same	26.1	1.2	1.6	4.4	4.2	3.2	8.6	8.4
English	68.0	98.3	96.1	92.9	91.7	96.8	91.4	89.2
Prefers to speak English, Non-English native tongue, or both the same, 2001								
Non-English	6.3	0.5	0.7	3.3	0	3.0	0	2.4
Both the same	56.3	9.5	40.4	52.1	25.0	12.1	38.9	32.0
English	37.3	90.0	58.8	44.6	75.0	84.8	61.1	65.6
Wishes to raise own children in English, Non-English native tongue, or both the same, 2001								
Non-English	4.9	0.5	3.7	0.8	0	0	0	2.0
Both the same	86.8	43.7	83.0	86.4	55.6	54.5	75.0	66.5
English	8.3	55.8	13.3	12.8	44.4	45.5	25.0	31.5

Source: Children of Immigrants Longitudinal Study (CILS), 2001.

[a] The level of bilingualism is determined from mean scores in two 4-item indices of language proficiency, measuring the respondent's ability to speak, understand, read and write in English and in a non-English language, each scored 1 to 4 (where 1 = poor or not at all, 2 = not well, 3 = well, and 4 = very well). Fluent bilinguals are defined as respondents who speak-understand-read-write English "very well" (English Language Proficiency Index score of 4) and a foreign language "well" (Foreign Language Proficiency Index score of 3.25 or above). For a detailed discussion of these measures, see Portes and Rumbaut (2001), chapter 6.

(albeit using a relaxed measure of fluent bilingualism, as explained in table 2.5) than any of the Asian-origin groups (less than 10 percent on average). Still, the data on language *preferences* are particularly relevant (and will be shown later to have significant effects on transnational outcomes). In 1992 over two-thirds of the sample (69 percent) preferred English over their parents' native language; in 1995 to 1996 their preference for English had swelled to 85 percent; and by 2001 fewer than 3 percent indicated a preference for the non-English language. Note in this context the disconnection in their patterns of actual language preference and use versus the ideal language in which they say they would like to raise their own children. That is, two-thirds report that they wish to raise their children as bilinguals, speaking both languages the same, while fewer than one-third say they wish to raise their children speaking English only. However, 44 percent of them speak with their own parents in English only, as do about 75 percent of them with their spouses and close friends and 89 percent with their coworkers.

Table 2.6 shifts the focus of attention from language to questions of ethno-national socialization, attitudes, and identities. The top panel of table 2.6 presents data from the separate interviews we carried out with the respondents' parents in 1995 to 1996; as in the previous tables, these are broken down by national origin. The parents were asked how proud they were of their homeland, how important it was for the children to know about the homeland and to keep in touch with others living there, and how often they talked to their children about the homeland and celebrated patriotic and festival days connected to the homeland. In short, these items measured the parents' beliefs and practices in the ethnic socialization of their children, which were later tested in multivariate analyses of transnational outcomes. In all of these indicators, the Vietnamese parents were far and away the group that was most concerned with inculcating in their children a sense of pride in and attachment to their country of origin, although most parents scored high on most of the measures shown in table 2.6.

Table 2.6 then reports the results of an index we used in the 1992 survey to measure the youths' knowledge about their (or their parents') country of origin. Three questions were asked to ascertain their level of basic knowledge: the capital of the country, the

(*Text continues on p. 74.*)

TABLE 2.6 Perceptions, Practices, and Identities among Children of Immigrants and their Parents in San Diego, 1992 to 1995, by National Origin (Percentage)

Characteristics	Mexico	Philippines	Vietnam	Cambodia, Laos	China, Taiwan	Asia Other	Latin America Other	Total
Parents (interviewed in 1995)[a]								
How proud is parent of homeland?								
A lot	81.3	76.7	88.5	66.5	52.9	60.0	70.0	76.8
How important is it for child to know of homeland?								
A lot	80.7	72.5	82.3	71.8	64.7	46.7	50.0	74.6
How often parent talks to child of homeland?								
A lot	44.0	41.5	73.5	59.1	35.3	33.3	40.0	49.9
How often celebrates days connected to homeland?								
A lot	21.7	28.8	84.1	56.4	35.3	20.0	10.0	40.2
How important is it to keep in touch with others from the homeland?								
A lot	46.1	51.3	69.0	56.9	25.0	23.1	31.6	52.2
Children (surveyed in 1992 and 1995)								
Knowledge of parents' homeland (out of three questions asked), 1992[b]								
Knew zero of three	35.8	16.1	53.6	53.7	35.7	27.3	27.8	31.7
Knew one of three	35.8	25.3	44.2	41.3	39.3	48.5	52.8	34.4
Knew two of three	25.4	55.1	2.2	5.0	21.4	15.2	13.9	31.1
Knew three of three	3.0	3.5	0	0	3.6	9.0	5.6	2.8

Is the United States the best country in the world to live in?

Agree, 1992	54.1	66.4	68.1	68.6	75.0	75.8	47.2	63.6
Agree, 1995	60.4	78.0	85.2	63.6	71.4	65.6	72.7	72.0

Ethnonational self-identity, reported in 1992[c]

American	1.5	4.0	1.5	1.7	10.7	18.2	8.3	3.5
Hyphenated-American	32.5	61.7	53.6	38.0	39.3	45.5	0	47.2
National origin	21.3	27.9	40.6	54.5	39.3	18.2	8.3	30.3
Racial-panethnic	43.3	2.1	0.7	0.8	0	3.0	58.3	14.2
Mixed-other	1.5	4.3	3.6	5.0	10.7	15.2	25.0	4.8

Ethnonational self-identity, reported in 1995[c]

American	1.9	1.5	0.7	0	3.6	9.4	9.1	1.9
Hyphenated-American	30.0	38.4	35.6	19.4	21.4	31.3	0	31.7
National origin	38.5	54.3	46.7	63.6	32.1	28.1	0	47.1
Racial-panethnic	25.4	1.0	16.3	15.3	32.1	12.5	75.8	14.6
Mixed-other	4.2	4.9	0.7	1.7	10.7	18.7	15.2	4.7

Source: Children of Immigrants Longitudinal Study (CILS), 1992 to 1995.

[a] Listed only are the percentage of parents who responded "a lot" to each question, out of four possible choices: "not at all," "a little," "somewhat," or "a lot."

[b] The three questions asked to ascertain level of basic knowledge about their or their parents' country of origin were: the capital of the country, the size of its population (just a rough approximation), and the name of a political leader (for example, a president or prime minister).

[c] Responses to an open-ended survey question, "How do you identify, that is, what do you call yourself?" "Filipino-American" and "Vietnamese-American" are examples of hyphenated-American self-identities; "Mexican" or "Cambodian" are national-origin identities; "Hispanic," "Latino," "Black," and "Asian" are classified as racial or panethnic identities; "Cuban-Mexican" or "Chinese-Thai" are examples of "mixed" identities.

approximate size of its population, and the name of one of its political leaders (for example, a president or prime minister). Virtually no one (fewer than 3 percent) answered all three questions correctly. But nearly one-third got two right (with the Filipinos being the most knowledgeable by far), another one-third answered one question correctly, and one-third could answer none of them correctly (including more than half of the Vietnamese, Laotians, and Cambodians). With regard to their attitudes about the United States over time, in both the 1992 and 1995 to 1996 surveys the respondents were asked to agree or disagree with the statement: "The United States is the best country in the world to live in." The proportion agreeing with that statement increased from 64 percent in 1992 to 72 percent three years later. (The Vietnamese were the strongest endorsers of this statement, with 85 percent indicating their agreement by 1995 to 1996.)

Finally, table 2.6 presents CILS data on the reported ethno-national self-identities of respondents over time. These have been analyzed in a number of publications for the full CILS sample (see, for example, Rumbaut 1994, 1997b, 2001; Aleinikoff and Rumbaut 1998; Portes and Rumbaut 2001). For our purposes here it suffices to point out that the direction of change over time was exactly in the opposite direction of the change observed for linguistic outcomes. While in 1992 just over half of the sample identified as an American or as a hyphenated American and fewer than one-third identified themselves by their national origin, by 1995 (in the aftermath of the passage of Proposition 187 in California) these figures were reversed, with only about one-third identifying as an American or hyphenated American and about half by their parents' national origin, even among the U.S.-born. This "reactive ethnicity" phenomenon was especially noted among the Mexicans (a plurality of whom had chosen racial or pan-ethnic identities such as "Hispanic" or "Latino" in 1992) and the Filipinos. All the other Asian-origin groups, who had evidenced scarcely any sign of Asian pan-ethnicity in 1992, showed substantial increases in this type of self-identification by 1995. However, in multivariate analyses of transnational outcomes in 2001, it turns out that not a single ethnic identity type chosen by the respondents proved to have a determinant effect on any of the transnational indicators examined. It was language—and several other factors to be noted presently—rather than made-in-the-USA ethnic identities that accounted for the most significant effects.

TRANSNATIONALITY AMONG ADULT CHILDREN OF IMMIGRANTS, 2001

Table 2.7 reports the first results to date from the CILS study on several subjective and objective (attitudinal and behavioral) transnational indicators found among our sample in early adulthood. Again, these results are portrayed for each of the major ethno-national groups. The first (subjective) indicator shown in table 2.7 is a question asking respondents which place feels most like "home": the United States; their homeland or their parents' homeland; both the United States and the homeland; or neither. The overwhelming majority—88 percent—said that the United States was home, while minuscule proportions (just over 1 percent) indicated that either their country of origin or neither country most felt like home. However, the nearly one in ten (9.5 percent) who indicated that both countries felt like home are the ones who can be said to best reflect a transnational attachment, at least symbolically. Fifteen percent of the Mexicans so responded, as did 14 percent of the other Latin Americans, and 10 percent of the Chinese and Vietnamese.

A second (objective) indicator was a question asking how many times respondents had been back to visit their homeland or their parents' country of origin. Three out of four respondents reported that they had either *never* done so or had done so only once or twice in their lives. As would be expected, the Mexicans living on the U.S.-Mexico border in San Diego were far and away the most likely to have made repeated visits: 18 percent of the sample reported having visited Mexico more than ten times. The children of the Southeast Asian refugees from Vietnam, Laos, and Cambodia were the least likely to have ever returned. As table 2.7 shows, a follow-up question asked whether any of these visits had ever lasted for six months or more. Only 4 percent reported visits of that duration; once again, the Southeast Asians were the least likely to have ever returned for a prolonged stint.

A third (objective) indicator—of particular interest to current debates—measured the frequency with which respondents sent remittances to anyone in their country of origin. Again, about three out of four had *never* done so. It should be noted, however, that

(*Text continues on p. 78.*)

TABLE 2.7 Transnational Indicators Among Adult Children of Immigrants in San Diego, 2001, by National Origin (Percentage)

Characteristics	Mexico	Philippines	Vietnam	Cambodia, Laos	China, Taiwan	Asia Other	Latin America Other	Total
Which feels most like "home" to you: the United States, or your or your parents' country of origin?								
United States	82.5	90.8	87.1	91.7	82.1	90.9	77.8	87.6
Both	15.3	6.6	10.1	5.8	10.7	3.0	13.9	9.5
Neither	0.3	1.4	1.4	2.5	3.6	6.1	2.8	1.5
Country of origin	1.9	1.2	1.4	0	3.6	0	5.6	1.4
How many times have you ever been back to visit your or your parents' country of origin?								
None	22.8	34.8	73.9	85.1	21.4	36.4	33.3	42.3
One or two times	17.9	49.4	23.2	12.4	57.1	24.2	38.9	32.7
Three to five times	26.5	13.2	2.2	1.7	14.3	21.2	11.1	14.0
Six to ten times	14.6	1.9	0.7	0.8	7.1	9.1	13.9	5.6
More than ten	18.3	0.7	0	0	0	9.1	2.8	5.3
Has any visit to your or your parents' country of origin lasted six months or more?								
No	94.4	95.3	99.3	97.5	92.9	93.9	91.7	95.6
Yes	5.6	4.7	0.7	2.5	7.1	6.1	8.3	4.4
How often do you send money (remittances) to anyone there?								
Never	79.5	67.2	73.2	65.3	89.3	90.9	69.4	72.3
Less than once a year	4.5	10.6	5.8	16.5	7.1	3.0	2.8	8.5

Once or twice a year	7.1	13.2	11.6	9.9	0	6.1	5.6	10.2
Several times a year	8.9	9.0	9.4	8.3	3.6	0	22.2	9.0
Type of transnational attachment (attitudinal and behavioral)[a]								
Both countries are "home"								
Visits and remits	6.3	1.2	0	0	0	0	8.3	2.4
Visits or remits	7.5	3.3	3.6	5.0	7.1	0	5.6	4.7
Neither	3.4	3.3	8.0	0.8	7.1	3.0	5.6	3.8
The United States is "home"								
Visits and remits	6.7	4.3	0.7	0	0	0	2.8	3.6
Visits or remits	41.8	23.8	18.8	15.7	17.9	45.5	27.8	27.5
Neither	34.3	64.1	68.8	78.5	67.9	51.5	50.0	58.0
Citizenship, 2001								
U.S. citizen	80.6	93.9	89.1	49.6	96.4	87.9	80.6	84.1
Not U.S. citizen	17.9	5.2	10.9	50.4	3.6	9.1	13.9	14.8
Dual citizenship	1.5	0.9	0	0	0	3.0	5.5	1.1

Source: Children of Immigrants Longitudinal Study, 2001.

[a] The typology of transnational attachment classifies respondents on the basis of two objective-behavioral indicators (frequency of visits and remittances to the country of origin) and one subjective-attitudinal indicator (their perception of "home"). A minimum threshold of transnational activity is defined as having made more than "one or two" lifetime visits to the country of origin, or sent remittances at least once a year to the country of origin. The *highest* level of transnational attachment is seen among those who consider *both* countries (*or* only the country of origin) as "home" *and* who have visited and sent remittances beyond the minimum threshold noted (only 2.4 percent of the sample). The majority (58 percent) exhibit no transnational attachment at all; they consider the U.S. as "home" and neither visit nor send remittances to the country of origin. The rest are classified in four categories between those poles.

about half the sample overall still resided with their parents, and some of the affirmative responses among those respondents may have referred to the *family*, not the individual, sending money back to the country of origin. Still, 10 percent reported sending remittances about once or twice a year, and another 9 percent said that they did so several times a year. The Filipinos were somewhat more likely to do so than any other group, while the Chinese and other Asians were the least likely to do so in this sample.

On the basis of these three indicators—a subjective one (where is home?) and two objective ones (frequency of visits and remittances to the country of origin)—I constructed a *typology of transnational attachment* (as shown and explained in table 2.7 and illustrated graphically in figure 2.1). The lowest level of transnationality in this typology—characterized by *detachment* rather than *attachment*—was found among those who neither visited nor remitted and who felt that the United States was home. That category, indicative of no transnational attachment at all, encompassed three out of five of our respondents overall (58 percent). Another 28 percent felt that the United States was home but occasionally either visited *or* sent remittances to the country of origin (but not both). At the other end, and accounting for only 2.4 percent of the overall sample, were those who exhibited the highest level of transnational attachment: they felt that *both* the United States and the country of origin were home, and they occasionally visited *and* sent remittances. (Note that this category of highest transnational attachment is operationally defined in terms of a minimum threshold; that is, it does not necessarily reflect a strong transnational attachment, nor does it establish that respondents so classified are actively engaged in a project of leading "dual lives.") The rest of the sample fell in between these poles, as shown in the table, although there is clearly a great deal of difference between the various ethno-national groups in their propensity to sustain these types of transnational attachments.

Finally, table 2.7 presents data on current citizenship status for these respondents: by 2001, 84 percent were U.S. citizens (either by birth or naturalization, including about 95 percent of the Chinese and Filipinos), 15 percent were not U.S. citizens (including 18 percent of the Mexicans), and 1 percent indicated that they had dual citizenship or nationality (mostly among the "other Latin Americans"). The Laotians and Cambodians (only 3 percent of whom are U.S.-born,

FIGURE 2.1 **Typology of Transnational Attitudes and Behaviors**

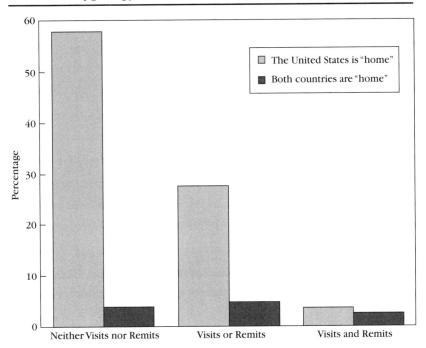

Source: Children of Immigrants Longitudinal Study (CILS), 2002.
"Visits" is defined as having made more than one lifetime visit to the country of origin; "remits" is defined as sending money at least once a year to the country of origin.

as seen earlier in table 2.3) were by far the most likely to report that they were not U.S. citizens: over half remained noncitizens and had no passports from any country. Ironically, however, the Laotians and Cambodians were the groups most likely to consider the United States to be home.

PREDICTORS OF TRANSNATIONAL OUTCOMES AMONG ADULT CHILDREN OF IMMIGRANTS

Table 2.8 offers a bivariate analysis of selected correlates of these three main types of transnational outcomes. Levels of statistical significance (chi-square or ANOVA) are shown to test the probability

(*Text continues on p. 84.*)

TABLE 2.8 Correlates of Attitudinal and Behavioral Transnational Outcomes Among Adult Children of Immigrants, 2001

Correlates	Which Feels Most Like "Home" to You?					Frequency of Visits and Remittances[a] to Country of Origin			
	U.S. (Percentage)	Both Countries (Percentage)	Country of Origin (Percentage)	Neither Country (Percentage)	p	Number of Visits (Ever) (Mean)	p	Remittances (Frequency) (Mean)	p
Gender, generation, family, socioeconomic status									
Sex									
Female	87.4	9.9	1.4	1.4		3.15		0.56	
Male	87.8	9.0	1.5	1.7	NS	3.60	NS	0.62	NS
Nativity									
U.S.-born (second generation)	90.9	7.4	1.0	0.8		2.24		0.69	
Foreign-born (1.5)	84.5	11.4	1.9	2.2	*	4.52	**	0.47	**
One parent born in U.S.?									
No	86.2	10.3	1.7	1.8		3.17		0.60	
Yes	95.0	5.0	0	0	*	4.35	NS	0.53	NS
Family structure, 1992									
Intact family	88.3	8.6	1.5	1.6		3.42		0.58	
Stepfamily	87.1	10.0	0	2.9		3.03		0.64	
Single parent, other	84.0	13.6	1.9	0.6	NS	3.15	NS	0.60	NS

Family cohesion, 1995					**		NS		NS
Lower	90.5	6.4	1.4	1.7		3.20		0.57	
High	82.1	15.3	1.3	1.3		3.89		0.66	
Homeownership, 1992					**		NS		NS
Rent	83.4	12.4	2.2	2.0		3.65		0.65	
Own	90.7	7.3	0.8	1.2		3.13		0.54	
Poverty rate of neighborhood, 1990					*		**		NS
Under 15%	91.1	6.2	0.8	1.9		1.84		0.53	
15 to 50%	86.4	9.7	2.4	1.5		3.11		0.58	
Over 50%	84.6	13.5	0.8	1.2		5.71		0.68	
Language proficiency, preference, and use									
Foreign language proficiency (verbal and written), 1992					**		**		**
Not well	92.6	5.1	0.6	1.8		1.97		0.50	
Well	82.9	14.2	2.1	0.8		6.45		0.75	
Very well	70.3	23.4	4.7	1.6		4.88		0.74	
Level of language dominance (English, bilingual, or foreign language), 1992[b]					**		**		**
English dominant	91.5	5.8	0.8	1.9		2.50		0.48	
Fluent bilingual	80.6	15.7	2.8	0.9		8.55		0.69	
Non-English dominant	71.7	22.8	4.1	1.4		3.97		0.86	
Limited bilingual	91.3	6.8	0.8	1.1		2.60		0.62	

(Table continues on p. 82.)

TABLE 2.8 *Continued*

Correlates	Which Feels Most Like "Home" to You?					Frequency of Visits and Remittances[a] to Country of Origin			
	U.S. (Percentage)	Both Countries (Percentage)	Country of Origin (Percentage)	Neither Country (Percentage)	p	Number of Visits (Ever) (Mean)	p	Remittances (Frequency) (Mean)	p
Preferred to speak English, 1992									
No	79.5	16.5	2.1	1.8		5.10		0.64	
Yes	91.2	6.3	1.1	1.4	**	2.56	**	0.56	NS
Language uses with parents, 2001									
Non-English	82.2	13.6	2.5	1.7		4.38		0.63	
Both the same	85.4	12.8	0.9	0.9		4.35		0.64	
English	92.6	4.8	0.9	1.8	**	2.13	**	0.54	NS
Language uses with spouse or partner, 2001									
Non-English	73.6	22.6	3.8	0		6.25		0.62	
Both the same	81.4	15.0	2.1	1.4		4.99		0.69	
English	90.9	6.8	1.3	1.1	**	2.74	**	0.60	NS
Language uses with close friends, 2001									
Non-English	78.9	15.8	5.3	0		6.58		0.53	
Both the same	75.5	21.5	1.5	1.5		5.55		0.78	
English	90.9	6.2	1.3	1.6	**	2.69	**	0.55	*
Language uses with co-workers, 2001									
Non-English	83.3	12.5	4.2	0		7.63		0.71	
Both the same	75.9	19.3	3.6	1.2		8.55		0.58	
English	88.5	8.7	1.2	1.5	**	2.84	**	0.61	NS

Identity, perceptions of U.S., citizenship

Ethnonational self-identity, 1992									
American	91.9	5.4	2.7	0		3.78		0.41	
Hyphenated-American	89.7	7.3	1.4	1.6		3.26		0.56	
National origin	87.1	10.1	0.9	1.9		2.57		0.61	
Racial-panethnic	79.9	17.4	1.3	1.3		5.46		0.70	
Mixed-other	90.0	6.0	4.0	0	*	2.62	*	0.46	NS
Believes that the United States is the best country in the world to live in, 1995									
No	82.0	13.4	2.1	2.5		4.12		0.65	
Yes	90.3	7.4	1.1	1.2	**	3.14	NS	0.57	NS
U.S. citizenship, 2001									
Not a U.S. citizen	84.0	12.8	1.9	1.3		1.81		0.64	
Naturalized	84.4	11.0	1.9	2.7		2.52		0.71	
Citizen by birth	90.9	7.4	1.0	0.8	*	4.41	**	0.48	**

Source: Children of Immigrants Longitudinal Study (CILS), San Diego Longitudinal Sample, 1991 to 2001.

[a] Frequency of visits to the country of origin is scored as the mean of total visits ever made from the U.S., as reported by respondents in 2001. Frequency of remittances are mean scores, measured on a 0 to 4 scale, where 0 = never, 1 = less than once a year, 2 = once or twice a year, 3 = several times a year, and 4 = once or twice a month.

[b] The language dominance typology is derived from mean scores in two four-item indices of language proficiency, measuring the respondent's ability to speak, understand, read and write in English and in a non-English language, each scored 1 to 4 (where 1 = poor or not at all, 2 = not well, 3 = well, and 4 = very well). *Fluent bilinguals* are defined as respondents who speak-understand-read-write English "very well" (English Language Proficiency Index score of 4) and a foreign language "well" (Foreign Language Proficiency Index score of 3.25 or above). Probabilities that results are due to chance (chi-square, ANOVA): ** p < .01. * p < .05. NS = Not significant.

that the differences in means for the predictor variables selected are due to chance. The association of the following variables with the main forms of transnational attachment are examined in the table: gender and nativity (of self and parents); family structure and cohesion; homeownership and poverty rate of neighborhood; language proficiency, preference, and use; and identity and citizenship. Many other variables were examined for their potential relationship with the three attitudinal and behavioral transnational indicators but are not included in table 2.8 since none showed any statistically significant associations in bivariate or multivariate analyses. Among them were the parents' degree of ethno-national pride and socialization of their children, and the children's ethno-national self-identity choices.

The results shown in table 2.8 are straightforward and need not be belabored here; only a few main points will be highlighted. Gender has no significant association with any of the indicators of transnational attitudes or behaviors; that is true at the bivariate level of analysis, and as will be seen, it remains the case in multivariate models as well. There are moderate associations in table 2.8 between generation and transnationality: the 1.5ers (foreign-born) are more likely to report that *both* countries feel like home and to visit the homeland (but are less likely to send remittances); and the 2.5ers (those with one U.S.-born parent) are more likely to feel that the United States is home than either the 1.5 and 2.0 cohorts (with two foreign-born parents). Note that the selected predictor variables listed in table 2.8 were measured six or nine years *prior* to the transnational outcomes in question in order to establish unambiguously the temporal order of effects. Thus, for instance, there is a significant correlation between the level of *family cohesion* (measured in 1995 to 1996) with the likelihood that the respondent would feel (in 2001) that *both* countries are home; the higher the level of early family cohesion and solidarity, the greater the level of subjective attachment to the homeland of the parents. There are also clearly very strong and significant associations between the language variables measured in 1992 and almost all of the transnational outcomes measured in 2001. The next step, then, is to sort out which of these correlations prove spurious when controlled simultaneously in a multivariate analysis, and to identity those variables that retain independent net effects on the transnational outcomes in question.

Table 2.9 presents the results of three multivariate analyses that seek to identify the strongest and most significant determinants of each of the three dependent variables (objective and subjective): the frequency of visits and remittances to the country of origin, and an identification of both the United States and the country of origin as home. Basically the same set of predictor variables is regressed on each of the three outcomes, except that in the last regression I also examine the effect on attitudinal transnationality ("both countries are home") of behavioral transnationality (visits and remittances). The first two are continuous dependent variables (the frequency of visits and remittances), and thus I employ least squares multiple linear regression as the analytical technique of choice. The third is a dichotomous variable (both countries are home or not), and logistic regression is the method employed. For the sake of simplicity, table 2.9 shows only the final results, with all predictors entered in each model.

For our limited purposes here—to identify the most significant determinants of these transnational outcomes net of all other factors examined—the statistics of greatest interest are two measures of strength of effects: the t-ratios in the first two models (the ratio of the regression coefficient to its standard error, so that the higher the number the stronger and more significant the effect) and the Wald statistic in the logistic regression (the square of the ratio of the regression coefficient to its standard error, so that again the higher the number the stronger and more significant the effect). The logistic coefficient is also shown, especially to note from its sign whether an effect is positive or negative (since the Wald statistic, as the square of a number, can only be positive).

A remarkable result is that to a certain extent it is possible to predict ten years in advance the probability of transnational engagement and orientation. Table 2.9 shows that several variables measured in early 1992 retain strong and significant effects in 2001, despite the fact that many other contemporary predictors were entered into different models, including socioeconomic status. Those tend to wash out, however, underscoring the resilience of the midadolescence predictors measured in 1992. Of those, as the results reveal, none are more important than language.

(*Text continues on p. 88.*)

TABLE 2.9 Predictors of Transnationality Among Adult Children of Immigrants, 2001

| | Objective Indicators | | | | | | Subjective Indicator | | |
| | Visits to Country of Origin[a] | | | Frequency of Remittances[a] | | | Both Countries are "Home"[b] | | |
Predictor Variables	Beta	T-Ratio	p[c]	Beta	T-Ratio	p[c]	B	Wald	p[c]
Gender, age, nativity, citizenship									
Gender (1 = female, 0 = male)	-.03	[-1.20]	NS	-.03	[-1.05]	NS	.06	[0.06]	NS
Age	.01	[0.30]	NS	.06	[1.96]	**	.19	[1.39]	NS
Born in the U.S.	.02	[0.63]	NS	-.05	[-1.16]	NS	-.01	[0.01]	NS
Not a U.S. citizen	-.12	[-3.89]	***	-.02	[-0.67]	NS	.09	[0.07]	NS
Economic situation, life events									
Family owned home, 1992	.07	[2.25]	**	-.05	[-1.46]	NS	.11	[0.14]	NS
Family annual income, 2001	.08	[2.61]	**	.07	[2.33]	**	-.06	[1.01]	NS
Death of a parent	.03	[1.14]	NS	.09	[2.83]	***			
Cared for ill family member	-.00	[-0.08]	NS	.08	[2.58]	***			
Language, acculturation, religion[a]									
Knowledge of country, 1992	.15	[5.19]	***	-.03	[-0.86]	NS	.08	[0.28]	NS
Fluency in mother tongue	.13	[3.38]	***	.15	[3.42]	***	1.94	[9.50]	***
Prefers English language, 2001	-.07	[-2.19]	**	-.06	[-1.80]	*	-.96	[10.83]	***
Frequency of religious activity	-.01	[-0.44]	NS	.07	[2.18]	**	.14	[2.02]	NS

Ethnonational origin								
Mexican	.24	[5.10]	***	-.10	[-1.83]	*	-.31	[0.39]	NS
Filipino	-.16	[-3.37]	***	.12	[2.04]	**	.20	[0.16]	NS
Vietnamese	-.21	[-5.49]	***	-.00	[-0.09]	NS	.51	[0.84]	NS
Lao-Hmong-Cambodian	-.19	[-4.73]	***	-.01	[-0.16]	NS	-.28	[0.20]	NS
Transnational activity								
Visits to home country							.33	[7.97]	**
Remittances to home country							.49	[31.77]	***
Constant	—	[1.05]	NS	—	[2.43]	**	10.51	[0.73]	NS
R^2	.338			.078					
Model chi square (degrees of freedom)							133.4	(16)	***

Source: Children of Immigrants Longitudinal Study, San Diego Longitudinal Sample, 1991 to 2001.

[a] Results of least-squares multiple linear regressions predicting, respectively, the frequency of visits and remittances to the country of origin (measured in 2001). Standardized regression coefficients (betas) are shown; the t-statistic, in brackets, is the ratio of the unstandardized regression coefficient to its standard error. Higher numbers indicate stronger and more significant effects.

[b] Results of a logistic regression predicting the probability of reporting that both the United States and the country of origin feel like "home." Logistic regression coefficients [B] are shown; the Wald statistic, in brackets, is a measure of strength of effects (the square of the ratio of the logistic coefficient to its standard error). Higher numbers indicate stronger and more significant effects.

[c] ***Strong effect (coefficient exceeds three times its standard error, p < .001).
**Moderate effect (coefficient exceeds two times its standard error, p < .05).
*Weak effect (coefficient approximates two times its standard error, p < .10).
NS: Statistically insignificant effect.

[d] Predictors include the three-item index of knowledge about the country of origin (measured in 2001), composite mean scores in the four-item index of foreign language proficiency (measured in 1992, 1995, and 2001), and a measure of frequency of attendance at religious services, scored on a five-point scale from "never" to "once a week or more" (measured in 2001).

Interestingly, focusing first on the analysis of visits to the country of origin (the left column of table 2.9), the strongest and most significant effect (the largest t-ratio) was found for the three-item index of knowledge of the country of origin, measured in 1992 (t = 5.19, meaning that the regression coefficient exceeded its standard error by more than five times). Fluency in the non-English language (a composite measure of speaking, understanding, reading, and writing proficiency measured across the three survey periods) was strongly predictive of more visits (t = 3.38), while preference for English was negatively associated with transnational visiting behavior (t = −2.19). Significantly, *not* being a U.S. citizen was strongly associated with *fewer* visits (t = −3.89), underscoring the importance of legal status and passports for international travel. And in addition, the frequency of visits was clearly facilitated by the financial wherewithal of the respondents and their families, as indicated by the significant positive effect of current family income and of parental homeownership in 1992 (an indicator of early economic stability). Even with these factors controlled for, all of the ethno-national groups entered in the equation (as dummy variables) showed very strong effects: not surprisingly, the Mexicans in San Diego were very strongly associated with more visits, as had been seen earlier at the bivariate level (t = 5.1), while compared to all other groups not entered into the equation (who serve as reference groups for this analysis), the Filipinos and especially the Vietnamese, Laotians, and Cambodians were significantly much less likely to visit their countries of origin.

The strongest and most significant effect found in the analysis of remittances sent to the country of origin (the middle column of table 2.9) is seen for the level of fluency in the mother tongue (t = 3.42), while preference for English was negatively if weakly associated with transnational remittance behavior. Not surprisingly, the level of current family income (t = 2.33) is also significant. More notably, a measure of frequency of religious attendance was significantly associated with greater frequency of sending remittances to the country of origin (t = 2.18). This finding lends support to ethnographic and qualitative studies that have linked religious participation with sustained transnational ties and attachments. In addition, Filipinos emerge as moderately more likely to send remittances even after controlling for all other factors, while Mexicans (who visit the most by far) are slightly less likely to send remittances frequently compared to the reference groups in this analysis.

Unexpectedly, two stressful life events turned up as having among the strongest effects in this analysis: whether a parent had died (t = 2.83), and whether the respondent had had to care for an ill or disabled family member over the past six years (t = 2.58). These findings suggest that young adults may assume moral responsibility for the remittance assistance that had been provided by the parent to family members back home, and that family health plays an important role in sustaining such attachments. In any event, these significant effects are suggestive for future in-depth qualitative research on the nature of transnational attachments.

Finally, the last equation in table 2.9 seeks to identify the predictor variables that exert the strongest independent effects on the likelihood of respondents seeing *both* countries as their home. Here, among the set of predictors we have been considering, the overriding determinants of this subjective outcome involve the respondents' level of acculturation, as indicated (positively) by their level of fluency in the mother tongue and (negatively) by a preference for English. Note that in this equation the two objective behavioral measures of frequency of visits and remittances to the country of origin were then entered as predictors. As may be expected, both have significant and positive effects, but it is the frequency of remittance behavior that emerges as by far the strongest predictor of a subjective attachment, and commitment, to the country of origin (the Wald statistic is 31.8). Once those factors are controlled for, all other variables wash out of the equation, including all of the ethnicities.

CONCLUSION

In sum, the evidence of this decade-long longitudinal study shows that the level of transnational attachments, both subjective and objective, among a diverse sample of 1.5- and second-generation young adults from Mexico, the Philippines, Vietnam, China, and a host of other Latin American and Asian countries is quite small—always under 10 percent. However, there are significant differences in transnational propensities among different national-origin groups, with those from Spanish-speaking countries in the Americas, and especially from Mexico, being much more likely to maintain a level of fluent bilingualism into adulthood than the rest. The Mexican-origin population in the United States is so large that even a relatively small proportion of sustained transnationality in the second generation can nonetheless translate into large-scale social consequences. Of course, the fact that the Mexicans in this sample reside in a city that is situated right on the Mexican border (and was once *part* of Mexico) greatly facilitates their transnationality, especially the frequency of visits across the border. Perhaps the surprise is that despite that advantage of nearness and familiarity, the level of binational and bicultural engagement is as low as it is. There *are* small pockets of transnational possibility among various groups of young adults in our sample, notably those located next to the border and those who are able to maintain a fluent bilingualism into adulthood and thus the potential for transnational attachments. Time will tell whether, as these young adults mature and struggle to forge lives that are meaningfully linked to their pasts, their degree and modes of transnational attachment evolve and expand. But for the great majority of the new second generation (1.5ers and 2.5ers now included), let alone a third generation still in gestation, what the empirical tea leaves seem to suggest (in English) is that theirs is an American future, not a bilingual or a binational one.

The role of language emerges here as central to the maintenance of transnational ties, both attitudinally and behaviorally. The findings echo Michael Ignatieff's observation, cited in the epigraph, that "it is language, more than land and history, that provides the essential form of belonging." Also playing a part is religious involvement, which may foster the transmission of ethnicity and ethnic socialization from the parent generation to that of their children, although the evidence by the second generation is of decreased levels of religiosity and increased secularism. "Thick" ethnographies more than "thin" survey data, however, will be needed to explain convincingly how and why. Additional factors in transnational involvement among young adult children of immigrants are their legal status, their financial wherewithal, and, in the case of remittances, certain types of jolting life events and defining moments. National origin, which is itself a proxy for different types of migration histories and contexts of reception in the United States (such as that accorded the refugees from the Indochina War, for many of whom the bridges of return have been burned politically), also adds to the explanation of particular forms of transnational propensities.

Still, the most compelling conclusion to be drawn thus far from the findings yielded by this study—and a preliminary answer to the "open empirical question" posed at the outset—is that there is very little evidence that the kinds of attachments that are fundamental to pursuing a meaningful transnational project of "dual lives" are effectively sustained in the post-immigrant new second generation. For most of them, unlike their parents—to return to our opening metaphor—there appears to be no "tingling" sensation, no phantom pain, over a homeland that was never lost to them in the first place.

I gratefully acknowledge the support provided by research grants from the Russell Sage Foundation and the Andrew W. Mellon, Spencer, and National Science Foundations to Alejandro Portes and Rubén G. Rumbaut, principal investigators for the Children of Immigrants Longitudinal Study, 1991–2001; and by the William and Flora Hewlett Foundation for a fellowship year (2000 to 2001) in residence at the Center for Advanced Study in the Behavioral Sciences, Stanford University.

NOTES

1. The words *natural, native,* and *national* share a common etymology: the Latin root means "birth" (see Rumbaut 1994).
2. I found Thomas and Znaniecki's (1958 [1918–1920]) half-second concept awkward and reversed the term to "one-and-a-half" for clarity's sake. Similarly, what Warner and Srole (1945) call the "P2" generation can be further refined into three developmentally distinct groups of immigrant children, depending on their age at immigration. I have distinguished between preschool children (ages five and younger), who retain virtually no memory of their birthplace, who are largely socialized here, and whose experience and adaptive outcomes are most similar to

the U.S.-born second generation, whom I labeled the "1.75" generation; preadolescent, school-age children (ages six to twelve), which I labeled the "1.5" generation; and adolescents (ages thirteen to seventeen), the "1.25" generation whose experience and adaptive outcomes are closer to those of the first generation of immigrant adults. For an empirical test of this classification, see Oropesa and Landale (1997).

3. To obtain more reliable estimates of the immigrant-stock population of the United States, the March 1997 Current Population Survey data file was augmented by unduplicated cases from the March 1996 CPS (U.S. Bureau of the Census, annual demographic files). Still, the accuracy of the estimates decreases as the sample size decreases, and thus care should be taken when interpreting the results, especially for the smaller national-origin groups. For a discussion of sampling and nonsampling error in the March 1997 CPS, see U.S. Census Bureau (1999, 54–61).

4. My estimate of 26.8 million *includes* approximately 1.0 million persons who were born in a foreign country but had one parent who was a U.S. citizen. The U.S. Census Bureau classifies such persons as part of the "native-born population" and *excludes* them from the "foreign-born population," even though many are in fact recent U.S. arrivals. On this basis, the Census Bureau (1999) officially reported a 1997 foreign-born population of 25.8 million.

5. The data come from the Census 2000 Supplementary Survey, or American Community Survey (ACS), based on a national sample of 700,000 households. ACS results can be accessed online at: *www.census.gov/acs/www*. With the U.S.-born second generation estimated at about 30 million as well, immigrants and their children now add up to some 60 million persons and account for approximately 22 percent of the total U.S. population.

6. Conventionally, 1965 has been seen as the "great divide" in U.S. immigration history because of the amendments to U.S. immigration law passed that year (not fully implemented until 1968). However, the revised law principally affected immigration from the Eastern Hemisphere (especially benefiting Asian countries, which had been largely barred for decades), not from Western Hemisphere countries (although the latter account for more than half of all immigration to the United States). During the decade from 1960 to 1969 more Mexicans legally immigrated to the United States than from any other country, followed by Canadians and Cubans; the much-vaunted transformation in the national-origin composition of the "new" immigration was already well under way prior to 1965.

7. Data collection for this third-wave CILS survey will extend past the summer of 2002. The sample of 1,100 respondents on which this analy-

sis is based represents more than 50 percent of the 2,063 who completed the second survey in San Diego in 1995–1996 and is largely representative of the sociodemographic characteristics of the baseline sample. Nearly three-fourths of the respondents were still living in San Diego; another one-fifth lived elsewhere in California; and the remainder (fewer than 10 percent) have been located in thirty-two different states and one foreign country. T3 data from the original Miami sample have not yet been processed at this writing and are not included here.

REFERENCES

Aleinikoff, T. Alexander, and Rubén G. Rumbaut. 1998. "Terms of Belonging: Are Models of Membership Self-fulfilling Prophecies?" *Georgetown Immigration Law Journal* 13(1): 1–24.

Anderson, Benedict. 1991. *Imagined Communities: Reflections on the Origin and Spread of Nationalism*. New York: Verso.

Bourne, Randolph S. 1916. "Trans-National America." *Atlantic Monthly* 118: 86–97.

Cornell, Stephen, and Douglas Hartmann. 1998. *Ethnicity and Race: Making Identities in a Changing World*. Thousand Oaks, Calif.: Pine Forge.

Ebaugh, Helen Rose, and Janet Saltzman Chafetz. 2000. *Religion and the New Immigrants: Continuities and Adaptations in Immigrant Congregations*. Walnut Creek, Calif.: AltaMira Press.

Foner, Nancy. 1997. "What's New About Transnationalism?: New York Immigrants Today and at the Turn of the Century." *Diaspora* 6(3): 355–75.

Horowitz, Donald L. 1985. *Ethnic Groups in Conflict*. Berkeley: University of California Press.

Ignatieff, Michael. 1993. *Blood and Belonging: Journeys into the New Nationalism*. New York: Farrar, Straus & Giroux.

Landale, Nancy S., R. S. Oropesa, and Bridget K. Gorman. 1999. "Immigration and Infant Health: Birth Outcomes of Immigrant and Native Women." In *Children of Immigrants: Health, Adjustment, and Public Assistance,* edited by Donald J. Hernández. Washington, D.C.: National Academy of Science Press.

Levitt, Peggy. 2001. *The Transnational Villagers*. Berkeley: University of California Press.

Liu, Eric. 1999. *The Accidental Asian: Notes of a Native Speaker*. New York: Vintage Books.

Massey, Douglas S., Joaquín Arango, Graeme Hugo, Ali Kouaouci, Adela Pellegrino, and J. Edward Taylor. 1998. *Worlds in Motion: Understanding International Migration at the End of the Millennium.* Oxford: Clarendon Press.

Massey, Douglas S., and Kristin E. Espinoza. 1997. "What's Driving Mexico-U.S. Migration?: A Theoretical, Empirical, and Policy Analysis." *American Journal of Sociology* 102(4): 939–99.

Merrill, Christopher. 1995. *The Old Bridge: The Third Balkan War and the Age of the Refugee.* Minneapolis: Milkweed Editions.

Oropesa, R. S., and Nancy S. Landale. 1997. "In Search of the New Second Generation: Alternative Strategies for Identifying Second-Generation Children and Understanding Their Acquisition of English." *Sociological Perspectives* 40(3): 427–55.

Park, Robert E. 1926. "Human Migration and the Marginal Man." *American Journal of Sociology* 33(6): 881–93.

Portes, Alejandro. 1996. "Global Villagers: The Rise of Transnational Communities." *The American Prospect* (March–April): 74–77.

Portes, Alejandro, and Rubén G. Rumbaut. 1996. *Immigrant America: A Portrait.* 2nd ed. Berkeley: University of California Press.

———. 2001. *Legacies: The Story of the Immigrant Second Generation.* Berkeley and New York: University of California Press and Russell Sage Foundation.

Rumbaut, Rubén G. 1991. "The Agony of Exile: A Study of the Migration and Adaptation of Indochinese Refugee Adults and Children." In *Refugee Children: Theory, Research, and Practice,* edited by Frederick L. Ahearn Jr. and Jean Athey. Baltimore: Johns Hopkins University Press.

———. 1994. "The Crucible Within: Ethnic Identity, Self-esteem, and Segmented Assimilation Among Children of Immigrants." *International Migration Review* 28(4): 748–94.

———. 1997a. "Ties That Bind: Immigration and Immigrant Families in the United States." In *Immigration and the Family: Research and Policy on U.S. Immigrants,* edited by Alan Booth, Ann C. Crouter, and Nancy S. Landale. Mahwah, N.J.: Erlbaum.

———. 1997b. "Assimilation and Its Discontents: Between Rhetoric and Reality." *International Migration Review* 31(4): 923–60.

———. 1998. "Growing up American in Cuban Miami: Ambition, Language, and Identity in the '1.5' and Second Generations." Paper presented at the Twenty-first International Congress of the Latin American Studies Association, Chicago.

———. 2001. "Transformations: The Post-Immigrant Generation in an Age of Diversity." In *In Defense of the Alien,* vol. 23, edited by Lydio F. Tomasi. New York: Center for Migration Studies.

Rumbaut, Rubén G., and Kenji Ima. 1988. *The Adaptation of Southeast Asian Refugee Youth: A Comparative Study.* Washington: U.S. Office of Refugee Resettlement.

Rumbaut, Rubén G., and Alejandro Portes. 2001. *Ethnicities: Children of Immigrants in America.* Berkeley and New York: University of California Press and Russell Sage Foundation.

Stalker, Peter. 2000. *Workers Without Frontiers: The Impact of Globalization on International Migration.* Geneva and Boulder, Colo.: International Labor Organization and Lynne Rienner Publishers.

Thomas, William I., and Florian Znaniecki. 1958 [1918–1920]. *The Polish Peasant in Europe and America.* New York: Dover.

U.S. Census Bureau. 1999. *Profile of the Foreign-born Population of the United States: 1997.* Current Population Reports, Series P23–195. Washington: U.S. Government Printing Office.

Warner, W. Lloyd, and Leo Srole. 1945. *The Social Systems of American Ethnic Groups.* New Haven, Conn.: Yale University Press.

Zhou, Min. 1997. "Growing up American: The Challenge Confronting Immigrant Children and Children of Immigrants." *Annual Review of Sociology* 23: 63–95.

Chapter 3

Transnationalism and the Children of Immigrants in Contemporary New York

Philip Kasinitz, Mary C. Waters,
John H. Mollenkopf, and Merih Anil

T HE UNITED STATES is once again a nation of immigrants. About 850,000 documented and at least 225,000 undocumented immigrants arrive in the country every year, and about one-third of the nation's population growth is now the result of migration from abroad. The political debate over immigration has generally been dominated by "hard-headed" issues of economics and demographics: Do immigrants "take" jobs from natives? Do they contribute more than they take from the public coffers? Is the population growth to which immigration contributes a good or bad thing? Yet the passion with which these issues are debated reveals, we suspect, a deeper concern, one that might be termed "assimilation anxiety." In many quarters there is fear that today's "huddled masses" are not becoming "American" with anything like the speed or enthusiasm that earlier immigrants are at least imagined to have shown. Today's communication and transportation technologies make it easier for immigrants (or, as some would describe them, "transmigrants") to remain embedded in the social lives of their nations of origin.

What this means for U.S. national identity and for the long-term incorporation of migrant groups is still unclear. One reason these outcomes are uncertain is that while the issues raised by transnationalism are generally framed as part of the immigration debate, their long-term consequences actually have as much to do with the experiences of the U.S.-born children of the immigrants as with the experiences of the immigrants themselves. The experience of the second generation (along with what Rubén Rumbaut has termed the "1.5 generation"—children born abroad but substantially raised in the United States) will determine whether the patterns of incorporation into U.S. society echo or diverge from those of the past. As these young people, who are only now emerging from their parental households, become independent actors in the labor force and the political and cultural life of their communities, we will see whether the desire to maintain strong ties to nations of origin and to live social lives across borders is a passing phenomenon or the signal of a permanent change in the way a significant part of the American population constructs its notions of place, identity, and citizenship.

International migration can no longer be seen as a one-way process. Events, communities, and lives are increasingly linked across borders. Those who advocate a transnational perspective on migration have set forth a research agenda that seeks to: "(1) explore how transnational migration is shaped by and contributes to the global capitalist system; (2) rethink the analytical concepts used in migration studies; and (3) analyze how 'transmigrants' construct racial, ethnic, class, national and gender identities as they move between countries of origin and countries of settlement" (Friedman-Kasaba 1996, 198; see also Glick-Schiller, Basch, and Szanton-Blanc 1992). This transnationalism has a variety of sources: the increased flow of goods and capital across international borders has consistently led to increased labor flows as well. With telephone connections, fax machines, the Internet, high-speed air travel, and the ability to send audio- and videotapes around the globe, even working-class populations, if not the poorest migrants, may be able to participate in the social and political life of their communities of origin and retain membership in local networks even when their bodies are thousands of miles away.

Yet the great appeal of the term "transnationalism" may also betray a potential weakness in its use as a social scientific concept. The term "transnationalism" (along with the parallel concept "globalization") has come to be used so broadly as to make us question whether all of those who use it are addressing the same, or even related, phenomena. For some, transnationalism is nothing less than a new phase of capitalism in which global flows of capital, labor, and culture threaten to leave the nation-state, if not quite "withered away," at least increasingly irrelevant (Glick-Schiller et al. 1992; Appadurai 1996). Others make more modest claims, pointing to the increased importance of remittances—economic and cultural—and circular migration in the lives of many communities. Some see transnationalism as a highly local phenomenon, since "transmigrants" continue to participate in and sometimes even come to dominate the local affairs of small communities, sometimes bypassing the national state in the process (Smith 1997; Levitt 1997, 1998, 2001a). Others concentrate on state-sponsored or at least state-supported efforts to extend various forms of citizenship and political participation to migrants outside the nation's geographic boundaries.[1] For these analysts, far from becoming less important, nation-states have sought a continuing role in the lives of their nationals abroad, who in turn may become advocates for the state or even of certain political parties. Still others have found transnationalism at the supra-state level, pointing to the importance of nongovernmental organizations, trade groups, refugee advocates, and so on, in transnationalizing the political sphere (Soysal 1994). World-traveling business men and women, carrying a variety of passports, are said to be transnational, but so are impoverished workers struggling to support faraway villages while surviving on extremely low-wage jobs in the United States. Even some people who never leave home but are part of a community and cultural system reshaped by global flows of capital and labor (Fouron and Glick-Schiller, this volume) are also said to be transnationals.

Some have described emigrant involvement in national and international political movement of a highly ideological nature as transnational: emigrant support for contemporary Hindu nationalism (see Lessinger 2001), for example, or support for Irish independence in times past. Such support is particularly volatile precisely because in the emigrant world it is cut loose from the practical give-and-take of local politics. Yet this use of the term is very different from using it to describe the commonly felt sense of allegiance to and pride in one's sending society, which does not differ strongly from what we traditionally call "ethnicity."

Out of this plethora of uses of the term "transnationalism," an inevitable question arises: as Foner (2001) has asked, what, if anything, is really new in all of this? Surely the speed of travel and the importance of communication technologies are new and important developments. Yet recently historians have been jumping on the transnationalism bandwagon by pointing out that in times past bi- and tridirectional flows of money, ideas, and people have been more common than we generally remember.[2] Once it was common for migration history to be written as the first chapter of "ethnic history"—in the case of several of the classics of American ethnic history, literally the first chapter (see Handlin 1951; Howe 1976). However, as the transnational perspective has made us increasingly aware, writing about the immigrant experience as the "World of Our Fathers" underestimates the amount of back-and-forth migration in the past, presumably because the most transnational of the migrants of the past were disproportionately represented among those who "went back" to become someone else's father and thus drop out of the story. However, while rediscovering the long history of transnational connections, most historians would concede that among earlier migrations, at least to the United States, continuing day-to-day involvement in the communal life of sending societies fell off sharply after the first generation. Even though some of the connections we now call transnational were present in earlier times, the ability of today's migrants to sustain transnational connections is unprecedented. Further, as Portes (2001) reminds us, just because a phenomenon is not wholly new does not mean it is not important. Sometimes it is the conceptual framework that is new, shedding a fresh light on old history.

It is also important to note a confusion that the comparison of past and present sometimes raises in popular discussion. Both those who decry the supposed "balkanization" of U.S. society (of which transnationalism is often cited as an extreme example) and those who celebrate the maintenance of transnational ties often assert that today's immigrants do not *want* to assimilate. This probably overstates the importance of conscious volition in this process, both now and in the past. Certainly there were some nineteenth- and early-twentieth-century immigrants who deliberately chose to break ties with their former societies and who rejoiced in their children becoming "real Americans." Others, however, were only reluctantly resigned to the inevitability of their children's assimilation, while still others actively resisted it, making sometimes heroic efforts to maintain ties to their former lands and keep the forces of Americanization at bay. In the end it hardly mattered. Second-generation assimilation and the attenuation of transnational ties that accompanied it were not the result of a single conscious decision, but the cumulative effect of a thousand small decisions. Immigrants learned English, not to "assimilate" but to improve their job options. They moved out of immigrant ghettos, not to reject old ties or because they preferred mainstream American neighbors, but because the housing, schools, and services were better elsewhere. Ties to the "old country" were rarely given up all at once but gradually replaced by new ties and more pressing obligations in the new country. As Alba and Nee (forthcoming) have argued, assimilation is what happened while people were trying to do other things, often despite their best efforts to forestall it. Obviously, transnational ties are easier to maintain today, and it may well be that assimilation and transnationalism are less incompatible. But we should not assume that homeland ties were ever given up willingly or cheerfully by the vast majority of earlier immigrants.

In the last few years the concept of transnationalism has undergone a considerable strengthening and improvement in precision; several efforts have been made to narrow and delineate the concept as well as to point out different types of transnational relationships (Portes, Guarnizo, and Landolt 1999; Guarnizo, Sanchez, and Roach 1999; Vertovec 1999; Levitt 2001a, 2001b). A broad, if by no means universal, consensus seems to be emerging that the term "transnationalism" should be reserved for "economic, political and cultural fields that involve individuals and institutions located in more than one nation state," and that the activities in these fields must be engaged in regularly by a substantial number of people and form an "integral" part of the "habitual life" of at least substantial segments of the migrant community (Guarnizo and Portes 2001, 3). Beyond this, we now distinguish between "strong" and "weak" transnational ties, between transnational politics from "below" and from "above," and between different levels of institutionalization (see Portes et al. 1999). We have particularly highly developed typologies of transnational economic activities (see Landolt, Autler, and Baires 1999; Faist 2000).

To these efforts at definition building we would add a few thoughts on what transnationalism is *not*. Transnationalism, as it is now being used in the literature, is more than just the cosmopolitanism of world cities, although, of course, the two concepts are related. The culture produced and consumed in cosmopolitan cities clearly draws on their diverse populations, and the fact that diverse cities tend to foster a cosmopolitan cultural outlook has been well known since at least the days of Babylon. (For an excellent look at the connection between certain cities and cosmopolitanism, see Kahn 1987.) Thus, using the word "transnationalism" in connection with cosmopolitan cities is confusing; the notion of urban cosmopolitanism long predates the modern idea of the nation. But there is a more serious problem. While cities with large transnational communities sometimes develop the tolerance and appreciation for diversity at the core of the cosmopolitan outlook, such an outlook does not necessarily sustain embeddedness into transnational social spheres. Indeed, it probably erodes it. When the New York City Second Generation Study asked young people what they liked about New York and what they missed about it when visiting their parents' homelands, cultural variety was one of the things most often mentioned. What is distinct about the cultural life of cosmopolitan cities is the role of pastiche and innovation, the mixing of a variety of influences (see Taylor 1988; Kasinitz 1999). As the current emphasis on "post-ethnic" (Hollinger 1995) culture illustrates, cosmopolitanism draws on the vibrance of transnational communities, but at the same time it erodes and remakes their boundaries.

Nor is transnationalism merely diasporic nationalism, although they are related. Clearly many, if not most, of the new nations of the nineteenth and twentieth centuries were conceived in exile. To paraphrase Anderson (1981), communities can be "imagined" differently from a distance. One need only think of the Irish Republican Brotherhood or the Fenians seeking solace in New York while out of favor in Ireland, or the Zionists imagining a Jewish Palestine from Eastern Europe and the Lower East Side. But if this is transnationalism, then what is nationalism? Although exiled nationalists often find support and shelter in transnational communities, this is largely a matter of convenience. Far from superseding the nation-state, their project is to build one. The action remains back home.

Perhaps most important, transnationalism is not ethnicity, although again, the two are related. Some ethnic groups do maintain strong transnational connections, but others do not. In the United States, however, ethnicity is usually an American creation. Or as Rumbaut and Portes (2001, 302) put it:

> The rediscovered national identities and the cultural origins among today's children of immigrants do not represent linear continuations of what their parents brought along. They are rather a "made in USA" product born of the children's experience of growing up American. . . . Second-generation youth who loudly proclaim their Mexican-ness or Haitian-ness often do so in English, and with body language far closer to their American peers than anything resembling their parents' culture.

Those who contrast transnationalism to assimilation sometimes forget this pluralist alternative. Yet in New York at least, ethnic pluralism is probably the dominant model of ethnic relations in the popular mind, reflecting how a good many of the natives *expect* newcomers to behave. The Jews, Irish, and Italians whom Glazer and Moynihan (1963) wrote about were quite "assimilated" in some ways. They all spoke English, other languages surviving mainly in a handful of colorful terms of endearment, curses, and food words. They lived in similar houses and watched the same movies and television, and their children danced to the same African American music. They even ate the same except on special occasions. They had very few real transnational connections. Yet they had not "melted." Even three and four generations past Ellis Island, they remained real and distinct groups largely voting for different candidates, living in different neighborhoods, and working in different jobs (see also Waldinger 1996). Their corporate existence as "ethnic groups" had come to have a widely recognized, almost official, status. And at least as long as they stayed in New York (the speed with which they could become regular "white Americans" upon crossing the Hudson was remarkable), they had not assimilated in the structural sense.

Will this be true for today's immigrants and their children, arriving as they do in a more transnational economic context? It is probably too early to say. In some cases ethnic identities are also transnational ones. Ethnic business may embed economic actors in transnational networks, and ethnic media and cultural activities may connect migrants to folks back home or in other parts of a diaspora. But ethnicity also represents shifts in the nature and content of social identity and even in group boundaries, shifts that make sense only in the U.S. context. Many of the South American young people in the New York City Second Generation Study describe themselves as "Hispanic" or "Spanish." They are quick to point out that they are *not* Puerto Rican, but what they *are* seems to be a work in progress. As they come to share neighborhoods, jobs, and love lives, they are developing a non–Puerto Rican, non-white, Hispanic identity that makes sense to them and probably makes no sense to their Ecuadoran, Colombian, or Peruvian parents. There are also a number of transnational businesses in New York today that advertise "Ecuadoran and Mexican Products." There is even one called EcuaMex, which does international money transfers as well as retailing. Perhaps there are a host of cultural affinities between Ecuador and Mexico. But we suspect that EcuaMex is more a product of the fact that *in New York* Ecuadorans and Mexicans often live in the same neighborhoods, work at the same jobs, arrived about the same time, and are seen as similar by the native population.

Sometimes transnational connections "bounce" these shifts in ethnic identity back to the home country. In recent years, for example, traditional Dominican ideas about race have undergone a strong challenge from young people putting forward more positive notions of "blackness" and African heritage. This is almost certainly a spillover from the racial politics of Washington Heights, with a dash of influence from black studies pursued on U.S. college campuses. The evolution of Anglophone West Indians into a single ethnic group in New York (Kasinitz 1992) has had a huge impact on Caribbean culture, often at the expense of local particularity. Trinidadian calypsonians, for example, complain that the social and political satire that was once the mainstay of carnival music has been increasingly replaced by dance tunes with generic lyrics that can be marketed throughout the region and the diaspora. Yet there is little sign that this transnational culture supports any transnational politics. The governments of the thirteen independent states and two colonies that once made up the British West Indies are now more structurally separate than ever. We do not know whether, in time, the children of Ecuadoran and Mexican New Yorkers will come to see themselves as more or less part of the same group. (It would take a fair amount of intermarriage.) But we are fairly sure that Ecuadorans and Mexicans in their homelands will not.

TRANSNATIONALISM AND THE SECOND GENERATION

Does the new research on transnational communities reveal a new way of conceptualizing identity on the part of migrants? Or are today's transnational communities merely a new (or not so new) one-generation variant on the familiar immigrant incorporation stories? To answer this question, it seems vital to look not just at migrants but at their U.S.-born and U.S.-raised children.

To examine this question we review some data from our study of the second generation in metropolitan New York. The New York City Second Generation Study included a telephone survey of 4,081 respondents; in-depth, open-ended, in-person follow-up interviews with a subsample of 10 percent of the survey respondents; and six strategically positioned ethnographies in the city. We selected for study young adults ages eighteen to thirty-two who were either born to post-1965 immigrant parents in the United States or born abroad but arrived in the United States by age twelve. We focused on five migrant groups—Anglophone West Indians, Dominicans, South Americans (Colombians, Ecuadorans, and Peruvians–hereafter CEPs), Chinese, and Russian Jews—as well as native-born whites, blacks, and mainland-born Puerto Ricans. As we compared these groups with one another, and as we implicitly compared them with the historical record on previous waves of immigrants, a number of concrete questions about transnationalism arose. Does the second generation have the language skills to participate in their parents' home society? How much contact does the second generation have with their parents' national-origin country? How much circular migration is there? Does the second generation pay attention to parental home-country politics? Are members of the second generation sending social or economic remittances back to their parents' country of origin?

Not surprisingly, the groups show different patterns of transnational activity. Distance and politics seem to play important roles.

On every activity we looked at (remittances by the second generation, remittances by their parents, interest and involvement in home-country politics, use of home-country media, and visits to their parents' homelands), Dominicans showed the highest levels of transnational activity, followed by the CEPs and the West Indians. Chinese and Russian Jewish levels were far lower.

One of the reasons often cited in the literature to explain the persistence of transnational ties is the modern ease of travel back and forth between the United States and home countries. Indeed, Latin American and Caribbean immigrants are often described as partaking in a "circular migration"—that is, spending some time in both countries. We asked our respondents about visits to their parents' home country to ascertain the degree to which this held true for the second generation.

In every group except one, the Russian Jews, the majority of respondents had visited their parents' home country at least once (see table 3.1). Among the Russians, 82 percent had never been to the former Soviet Union since emigration (or since birth in the case of the "true" second-generation respondents). However, even this group showed considerable transnational activity directed toward Israel, which one-third had visited. As members of what their political organizations are now calling "the Russian-*speaking* Jewish diaspora," many of our in-depth interviewees reported extensive connections with Russian communities in Israel (where some would consider living, although others describe it as not diverse enough) and Western Europe, but not in Russia, where almost none could ever envision living. The shape of the Russian Jewish transnational community also reflects an important aspect of the

TABLE 3.1 **Respondents Who Never Visited Parents' Country**

	Chinese	CEP	Dominican	Russian Jews[a]	West Indian	Puerto Rican	Total
Never visited	232	60	46	200	73	186	853
Percentage	38	15	11	64	18	43	33
N	609	410	428	311	407	429	2,594

Source: The Second Generation Project.
[a] Never visited Israel or Russia.

New York context. This group is related, if distantly, to a large and powerful ethnic group already in New York. The Jewish social service organizations of New York provided a variety of services to virtually all new Russian Jewish arrivals during the 1970s and 1980s and in many ways smoothed their transition to American life. (At the same time what some immigrants saw as a sometimes patronizing attitude on the part of established American Jews led to some resentment; see Kasinitz, Zeltzer-Zubida, and Simakhodskaya 2001.) These Jewish organizations had a strong interest in fostering connections to Israel. They even paid for many to take "heritage tours" there. They had no such interest in sustaining connections to the former Soviet Union.

Among the Chinese, 62 percent had visited China (including Taiwan and Hong Kong)—a surprisingly high number given the distance and difficulty of travel. However, few had visited more than three times (see table 3.2). By contrast, 47 percent of Dominicans, 39 percent of CEPs, and 34 percent of West Indians had visited more than three times, and an astounding 22 percent of Dominicans reported having been to their parents' homeland

TABLE 3.2 **Number of Visits by Respondents to Parents' Home Country**

	Chinese	CEP	Dominican	Russian Jews[a]	West Indian	Puerto Rican	Total
Never visited	232	60	46	200	73	186	852
	38%	15%	11%	64%	18%	44%	33%
One to three visits	309	186	169	48	189	126	1,027
	51%	46%	41%	15%	47%	30%	40%
Three to nine visits	57	110	112	7	78	56	420
	9%	27%	27%	2%	19%	13%	16%
Ten or more visits	10	48	90	1	61	53	263
	2%	12%	22%	0%	15%	13%	10%
N	608	404	417	311	401	421	2,562

Source: The Second Generation Project.
[a] Number of respondents never visited Russia = 255
Number of respondents never visited Israel = 200.

TABLE 3.3 Respondents Who Lived More Than Six Months in Parents' Country

	Chinese	CEP	Dominican	Russian Jews	West Indian	Puerto Rican
	8%	19%	27%	8%	24%	15%
N	609	410	428	311	407	429

Source: The Second Generation Project.

more than ten times. This contrasts with 2 percent of the Chinese and .03 percent of the Russians. The numbers who had spent more than six months in their parents' home country showed the same pattern. Only 8 percent of Chinese and Russians had done so, contrasting with 27 percent of Dominicans, 24 percent of West Indians, and 19 percent of CEPs (see table 3.3).

The majority of every group except the Russians reported that their parents sent remittances home, although most of the Chinese reported that their parents did so only about once a year. By contrast, 44 percent of Dominicans and CEPs and 34 percent of West Indians reported that their parents regularly sent money home several times a year (see table 3.4). Remittance activity among the second generation was much lower than it was among their par-

TABLE 3.4 Frequency of Remittances by Parents to Family in Home Country

	Chinese	CEP	Dominican	Russian Jews	West Indian	Puerto Rican	Total
Never visited	195	102	118	169	101	152	837
	32%	25%	28%	54%	25%	35%	32%
Visited once	210	77	60	69	78	45	539
	34%	19%	14%	22%	19%	10%	21%
Visited several times to frequently	100	182	188	48	138	75	731
	16%	44%	44%	15%	34%	17%	28%
N	609	410	428	311	407	429	2,594

Source: The Second Generation Project.

TABLE 3.5 **Frequency of Remittances by Respondents to Family in Home Country**

	Chinese	CEP	Dominican	Russian Jews	West Indian	Puerto Rican	Total
Never visited	522 86%	277 68%	282 66%	240 77%	271 67%	251 59%	1,843 71%
Visited once	58 10%	51 12%	58 14%	39 13%	70 17%	27 6%	303 12%
Visited several times to frequently	17 3%	77 19%	87 20%	31 10%	60 15%	32 7%	304 12%
N	609	410	428	310	407	429	2,593

Source: The Second Generation Project.

ents. Of course, given their age, it is not surprising that most respondents did not send remittances themselves, although in some groups a significant minority—20 percent of Dominicans and 19 percent of CEPs—sent remittances several times a year (see table 3.5). Once the parents retire or die, the second generation may begin to take up the responsibility of caring for relatives back home. Or they may not, leading to an overall decline in the level of remittances sent abroad.

Constructing a scale of transnational practices (frequency of remittances by respondent, frequency of remittances by parents, and frequency of visits to parents' home country) shows that Dominicans have the strongest transnational ties, followed by CEPs and then West Indians, with Russians and Chinese showing much lower levels of transnational practices (see table 3.6). Although very few of the respondents were married, those with co-ethnic spouses were more likely to report high levels of transnational practices than those who were outmarried. Women were more likely than men to exhibit high levels of transnational practices. While this finding contrasts with some studies that show that men have a greater interest in returning home (Grasmuck and Pessar 1990), it probably indicates that the burdens of maintaining family ties disproportionately fall on young women. Not surprisingly, those who prefer to speak English over their parents' native language are slightly less likely to show strong transnational practices, while

TABLE 3.6 **Transnational Practices Scale by Sociodemographic Variables—Horizontal Percentages**

	Transnational Practices	
	Weak	Strong
Group (*N* = 1,810)		
Chinese (500)	14.8%	3.2%
CEP (356)	6.8	31.8
Dominican (359)	4.5	35.1
Russian Jews (285)	50.9	6.7
West Indians (310)	8	25.1
Sex		
Male (853)	16.6	17.8
Female (958)	14.8	20.9
Country of birth		
U.S.-born (860)	12.7	20.6
Foreign-born (951)	18.4	18.4
Interested in NYC politics		
Not interested (801)	15	18.2
Interested (996)	16	20.7
Watching or listening to ethnic media		
Rarely (467)	29.4	5.8
Occasionally (309)	15.9	16.5
Frequently (1,013)	9.6	26.6
Language		
Prefer English (1,007)	17.5	16.8
Other (804)	13.3	22.9
Mother's citizenship status		
Citizen (1,170)	16.2	18.3
Not citizen (540)	13.3	23.1
Father's citizenship status		
Citizen (1,021)	17.3	18.5
Not citizen (492)	12.4	21.8
Ethnic organization		
Member (260)	13.8	24.9
Not a member (1,523)	16.2	18.5
Political organization		
Member (113)	9.8	21.4
Not a member (1,696)	16	19.4

(*Table continues on p. 110.*)

TABLE 3.6 *Continued*

	Transnational Practices	
	Weak	Strong
Registered to vote		
Registered (983)	14.1	19.6
Not registered (447)	15.4	18.1
Church attendance		
Now attending (634)	15.3	27.9
Not attending (705)	17.9	18.6
Age at arrival		
Under six (299)	15.4	17.4
Over six (649)	19.7	19.1
Parents' education		
Neither parent has college education (822)	11.5	21.6
At least one has college education (556)	24.6	17.1
Parents' citizenship status		
Neither parent is citizen (283)	11.5	21.6
At least one is citizen (1527)	24.6	17.1
Spouse or partner of same ethnicity		
Partner of different race (187)	11.2	28.9
Partner of same race (294)	16.3	23.8
Spouse or partner of same ethnicity when controlled for proximity		
Latino and West Indian respondents with spouse or partner of same ethnicity (189)	6.9	34.4
Latino and West Indian respondents with spouse or partner of different ethnicity (145)	6.2	33.1
Chinese and Jewish respondents with spouse or partner of same ethnicity (106)	33	4.7
Chinese and Jewish respondents with spouse or partner of different ethnicity (42)	28.6	14.3
Proximity to home country		
Western Hemisphere (1,026)	6.3	31
Eastern Hemisphere (785)	27.9	4.5

Source: The Second Generation Project.
Note: The Transnational Practices Scale is an additive scale, ranging from 0 to 9, composed of three items: parent sending cash to home country, respondent sending cash to home country, and respondent's visit to parents' home country (average inter-item correlation = .35, alpha = .53, $N = 1,810$). Respondents with weak transnational practices are those scoring 0. Respondents with strong transnational practices are those scoring above 5.

those who prefer a language other than English are more likely to have strong transnational ties, although, as the regression analysis (table 3.7) shows, this relationship is weaker than might be expected once other factors are controlled for. Those who belong to ethnic organizations are more likely to exhibit strong transnational practices, and this not very surprising result turns out to be highly significant once other factors are controlled for. Church attendance is correlated with high levels of transnational practices, but this relationship disappears in the regression model once other forms of organizational membership are introduced.

Working in a place where most of one's coworkers and one's supervisor were co-ethnics—that is to say, in an "ethnic niche"—had surprisingly little impact on the strength of transitional practices. Indeed, those who worked with members of other ethnic groups were actually more likely to show high levels of transnational activity. On the other hand, frequent use of the ethnic broadcast media—that is, listening to ethnic radio or watching ethnic TV—was closely associated with high levels of transnational activity. This is significant in the first regression model and is even stronger when the three groups with high levels of transnational activity (the Dominicans, CEPs, and West Indians) are examined separately.

Finally, we constructed regression models looking at each of the three groups which showed high levels of transnational activity (see table 3.8). For the CEPs, younger people were significantly more likely to be highly transnational than older respondents, and members of ethnic organizations showed the most such activity. Ethnic media were not a significant predictor of transnationalism for this group, although it was a very strong predictor among both Dominicans and West Indians. For West Indians, interestingly, interest in *New York* politics was a strong predictor of transnationalism–showing that for this group at least there is no contradiction between involvement in U.S. affairs and ties to the home country. (The relationship is also positive for the other two groups, although not significant.)

Our in-depth interview data fill out the picture of very low levels of second-generation transnationalism among the Russians and Chinese and higher levels among the Caribbean and South American groups, for whom a significant minority–but a minority

(*Text continues on p. 115.*)

TABLE 3.7 Determinants of Transnational Ties of Second- and 1.5-Generation Immigrants: OLS Regression

	For Five Groups		For Three Groups	
	Standardized Coefficient	T-values	Standardized Coefficient	T-values
Demographic measures				
Male gender	−.071	−1.246	−.185	−1.631
Age	.026	.451	−.172	−1.469
Group (dummy variable, Chinese omitted)				
CEP	−.316***	4.448	(omitted)	
Dominicans	.316***	4.718	.030	.239
Russian Jews	−.105	−1.288	(omitted)	
West Indian	.286***	4.585	.159	1.069
Came to the United States before age six	.019	−.325	.015	−.132
Naturalized citizen	−.073	−1.077	−.300**	−2.194
Prefers to speak English	−.106*	−1.780	.038	.286
Parental measures				
Mother is a citizen	−.035	−.481	−.115	−.840
Father is a citizen	−.071	−.956	−.063	−.474
At least one parent has a college-level education (dummy variable)	−.002	−.024	.015	.134

Sociopolitical measures

Coworkers and supervisors are of same race	−.090	−1.615	−.098	−.859
Watches ethnic programming frequently (dummy variable)	.142**	2.266	.344**	2.884
Registered to vote	.046	.734	−.229*	1.697
Regularly attends church	−.010	−.180	.067	.584
Member of an ethnic organization	.200***	3.434	.316**	2.694
Member of a political organization	.097*	1.728	.039	.323
Interested in NYC politics	.027	.468	−.041	−.317
Interested in home country's politics	.093	1.526	.264**	2.097
Constant (unstandardized coefficient)	1.708*	1.771	6.098**	2.499
R-squared		.536		.458
Adjusted R-squared		.482		.258
N		1,810		1,026

Source: The Second Generation Project.
*** T-value significant at the .001 level.
** T-value significant at the .05 level.
* T-value significant at the .1 level.

TABLE 3.8 **Determinants of Transnational Ties of Second- and 1.5-Generation Immigrants: OLS Regression**

	Standard Coefficient		
	CEP	Dominican	West Indian
Demographic measures			
Male gender	−.206	.130	.039
Age	−.326*	−.333	.587**
Came to the United States before age six	.221	.130	−.467*
Naturalized citizen	.048	−.736**	—
Prefers to speak English	−.179	−.078	—
Parental measures			
Mother is a citizen	−.357*	−.289	−.677
Father is a citizen	.050	.077	.535
Socioeconomic measures			
Coworkers and supervisors are of same race	.178	−.211	.152
Watches ethnic programming frequently (dummy variable)	.110	.361**	.735**
Registered to vote	.089	.302	.044
Regularly attends church	.275	.147	−.005
Member of an ethnic organization	.370*	.164	.399*
Member of a political organization	−.022	.152	−.051
Interested in NYC politics	.135	.179	.452*
Constant (unstandardized coefficient)	7.063**	1.667**	−4.708
R-squared	.407	.742	.836
Adjusted R-squared	.112	.479	.582
N	356	359	310

Source: The Second Generation Project.
*** T-value significant at the .001 level.
** T-value significant at the .05 level.
* T-value significant at the .1 level.

nonetheless–seemed highly embedded in transnational social structures. This transnational subgroup visited annually or semiannually, sent money home, and sometimes even contemplated settling there. A surprising number of West Indians and Latinos were sent back home to live with relatives at some point during their teen years by parents terrified by the dangers of the New York streets. Ironically, these teenagers often found that the education back home stood them in better stead when it came to getting into U.S. colleges and being hired for U.S. jobs than the education acquired by their cousins in the New York City public schools. Thus, Third World taxpayers now subsidize the production of First World workers, and just as immigration provided many of their parents with a second chance after setbacks at home, some young people now use a hiatus in their parents' homeland as a second chance to "make it" in the United States. One Taiwanese respondent recalled a nightmare New York adolescence. Shunted off to relatives after her parents' divorce, she had dropped out of high school, learned Cantonese (an ironic twist on the idea of assimilation that horrified her Mandarin-speaking family), and spent several years running with a Chinatown gang. Finally sent back to Taiwan by her father, she managed to acquire fake Taiwanese high school transcripts and return to New York. When we interviewed her a few years ago, she was doing well in a four-year college.

Yet for most of the people we spoke to, these sorts of strong ties to their parents' country are the exception, not the rule. For them, the United States was indisputably home. Even those who fondly recalled trips "back home" returned to the United States realizing how profoundly they had been shaped by this country (and by New York). Chinese respondents often complained of the strange "lifestyle" of China as well as the lack of amenities. (Squat toilets and the lack of air conditioning were particularly noted.) One Queens resident dismissed Guangzhou as dirty and crowded—"like Chinatown, only on a bigger scale." Few of the people we spoke to envisioned living in their parents' homeland for any sustained length of time. As one Dominican woman put it, "You go, you visit all these relatives that are there. You kind of see how they live their life. It was fun. It is kind of like country mouse and city mouse, and you get to go to the country and do all sorts of crazy things, like take a bath in a lake. Things that you can't do here. But you are kind of glad that you are going back home to civilization."

There were other reasons for the reluctance to consider a permanent return to their parents' homeland. Many Latino second-generation respondents did not read Spanish well, although most claimed to speak and understand it. Women also noted that they would face a lack of opportunities in Latin America. "In Ecuador," said one, "I'd already be married and be a housewife." On the other hand, among many groups the home country was thought of as a better place to raise children. Dominicans and West Indians were particularly convinced that the traditional values and more relaxed lifestyle of the Caribbean made for better child-rearing than the dangerous streets of New York. One woman, who claimed she would never live permanently in the Dominican Republic, was nonetheless considering sending her son there to live with her husband's parents: "Well, my husband wants him to go to school in the Dominican Republic. . . . He plans to send him to his grandparents so he can study there . . . because the educational system here doesn't work. And the kids over here are still undisciplined."

Still, few second- and 1.5-generation Dominican and West Indian respondents could imagine relocating to the Caribbean. The lack of economic opportunities and amenities were often mentioned. As one Dominican man noted:

> I'm used to living here, and I don't want to say that their technology is bad, you know, but when you are used to living in a place, it's hard to, like, for example, when I went back, I remember I couldn't drink the milk, it gave me a stomachache, and also when I went to the bodega my mom gave me money and told me to buy what I want, and I started looking around and I did not see anything I liked, nothing.

Low levels of transnationalism among New York's Chinese young people, while not surprising given the distance, are particularly interesting in light of the fact that both Taiwan and the People's Republic of China make considerable efforts to court overseas Chinese (and even such marginally connected "overseas relations" as the American parents of adopted Chinese children) as a source of economic and political support. In a classic example of transnationalism "from the top down," Taiwan and the People's Republic both have programs of cultural awareness tourism aimed at second-generation youth, and Taiwan subsidizes tours specifically for single young adults to get in touch with at least Taiwan's version of their Chinese heritage. Yet the ubiquitous nickname for this tour among young Chinese Americans, "the Love Boat," points to its deeper function, one more ethnic than transnational. Most parents who send their young adult children off on the Love Boat are probably less concerned with fostering ties with Taiwan than with providing them with the opportunity to meet eligible, middle-class Chinese Americans. Although it no doubt helps foster ethnic ties, we strongly suspect the Love Boat will ultimately prove no greater threat to assimilation than singles weekends at Grossinger's were for an earlier generation of immigrants.

Overwhelmingly, the young people we spoke to see themselves as here to stay. Although they do not always consider themselves "Americans"—indeed, they often use the term "American" to mean the white, native-born, not obviously ethnic Americans whom many know primarily through television—they generally do see themselves as New Yorkers, at home in the increasingly diverse city. Even moments of seeming separatism may actually attest to the assimilation process. In recent years churches catering specifically to the second generation have sprung up in both the Chinese and Korean communities: Chinese and Korean second-generation young people sometimes now worship together, live near each other, and join the same political groups. In fact, becoming an "Asian" (as opposed to Chinese, Filipino, or Korean) may be the most profound form of assimilation. It means, in effect, internalizing the racial definitions of the dominant society. Many Asian (and some Latino) respondents report first taking up a pan-ethnic identity in college. In groups like the New York Committee on Anti-Asian violence, recent college graduates who are highly politicized and largely Korean American take up the cause of downtrodden Chinese factory workers and South Asian taxi drivers. The "Asian" solidarity that underlies this stance mystifies many immigrant parents, for whom Asian is often a meaningless category.

The feelings of these respondents about questions of identity and home may change when they get older. But in only a minority of cases did we find the kind of sustained commitment to maintaining meaningful ties to the parental home societies that would seem to be necessary for transnationalism to flourish in the second generation.

This conclusion, however, does merit some caveats. First, it is important to remember that in a context of sustained replenishment, it is possible to see widespread transnationalism and assimilation at the same time, among people of the same age. In mid-twentieth-century New York the drop in immigration after the restrictions of the 1920s created a confluence of immigrant generation and chronological age. By midcentury, in many ethnic communities, many of the old people were immigrants and almost all of the young people were U.S.-born. Today, however, even if most second-generation people in an immigrant community are not maintaining transnational ties, the presence in these communities of recent immigrants of the same age who are maintaining such ties may serve to blur the lines considerably.

The second caveat is to recognize that significant minorities in at least the Caribbean and South American communities are maintaining transnational social structures into the second generation. This is most visible in the Dominican community, but it can also be seen among the West Indians and South Americans. These people are more likely to belong to ethnic organizations and to use ethnic media than others in their communities, although they are not the only ones who belong to such organizations or who use these media. And counter to the notion that having one foot still embedded in social fields "back home" discourages full incorporation into U.S. society, they turn out to be no less likely to take an active interest in New York politics and affairs than their less transnational co-ethnics. Indeed, in the case of West Indians, they are actually significantly more likely to do so.

Further, the New York context of reception will also play a role in shaping the sort of transnational ties our respondents maintain. (Paradoxically, all transnationalism is local!) The New York political structure and culture not only foster the existence of transnational organizations and transnational politics but encourage those active in such groups to also be engaged with New York politics. At the cultural level, New York's celebration of diversity, while initially friendly to the maintenance of transnational ties, also encourages transformations in identity that make more sense in the New York context than in the home country. In some cases something more ethnic than transnational is created. For those who favor a cosmopolitan culture, this is an exciting prospect. But it does not bode well for continued embeddedness in transnational social structures.

However, in each group we studied there is a minority—and among the three Western Hemisphere groups we examined a significant minority—for whom transnational ties continue to play a regular, sustained, integral role in their lives. The activities of these minorities are important, because it is these truly transnational minorities that will maintain the structures and networks that can occasionally be employed by the ethnic majority, for whom such ties are less integral and less habitual, but for whom such ties nonetheless will continue to play a role in their sense of who they are. The presence of a transnational minority among the second generation probably ensures that structural ties between the home countries and their diaspora communities in New York will endure as the second generation comes of age. Such structural ties will thus be available to be revitalized when and if historical circumstances dictate. Because a small minority of New York's Irish community continued to be directly involved in Irish nationalism into the fourth and fifth generations, vague ethnic sentiment could be effectively mobilized into real transnational politics in the form of material support for Sinn Fein and the IRA when interest in Ireland among Irish Americans rose during "the troubles" of the late 1960s and early 1970s. This support relied on the ability of someone in the ethnic community with ongoing transnational connections to get resources to these groups over the objections of the Irish government. Similarly, the relatively small number of New York Jews with sustained transnational connections to Israel played a vital role in mobilizing support for Israel during the 1967 war and in Middle East crises since among a majority whose connections are more symbolic and sentimental—that is to say, more "ethnic." We suspect that in those communities in which a significant minority exhibits strong transnational ties into the second generation (in our study, the Dominicans are the strongest case), such ties will also be multifaceted as people who continue to be embedded in transnational networks maintain ties to a variety of people, places, and organizations in the home country. In those communities in which the number of second-generation transnationals is small, such as the Chinese and probably the Russian Jewish communities, a strong interest in the home country may also continue, and it will probably be connected with close ties to the ethnic community in the United States. However, in the absence of significant ongoing transnational networks, ties between that ethnic community and the home country, if they survive at all, are likely to be mediated through formal organizations and national governments.

NOTES

1. At times this type of transnationalism is a conservatizing force. Emigrant communities, long feared by many governments as potential hothouses of oppositional émigré politics, are now sometimes seen as potential lobbying forces on behalf of sending-society governments.
2. In this respect, our understanding of migration to the United States has perhaps been overly shaped by the example of the Eastern European Jews, who, for a variety of reasons, loom large in the popular and scholarly image of early-twentieth-century immigration. Jews were actually quite exceptional in their extremely low levels of return migration and remittance activity.

REFERENCES

Alba, Richard, and Victor Nee. Forthcoming. *Remaking the American Mainstream Assimilation and the New Immigration.* Cambridge, Mass.: Harvard University Press.

Anderson, Benedict. 1981. *Imagined Communities: Reflections on the Origins and Spread of Nationalism,* rev. ed. London: Verso.

Appadurai, Arjun. 1996. *Modernity at Large: Dimensions of Globalization.* Minneapolis: University of Minnesota Press.

Faist, Thomas. 2000. "Economic Activities of Migrants in Transnational Social Spaces." In *Minorities in European Cities: The Dynamics of Social Integration and Social Exclusion at the Neighborhood Level,* edited by Sophie Body-Gendrot and Marco Martiniello. Houndmills, Eng.: Macmillan.

Foner, Nancy. 2001."Transnationalism Then and Now: New York's Immigrants Today and at the Turn of the Twentieth Century." In *Migration, Transnationalization, and Race in a Changing New York,* edited by Hector R. Cordero-Guzman, Robert C. Smith, and Ramon Grosfoguel. Philadelphia: Temple University Press.

Friedman-Kasaba, Kathie. 1996. *Memories of Migration: Gender, Ethnicity, and Work in the Lives of Jewish and Italian Women in New York 1870–1924.* Albany: State University of New York Press.

Glazer, Nathan, and Daniel P. Moynihan. 1963. *Beyond the Melting Pot: The Negroes, Puerto Ricans, Jews, Italians, and Irish of New York City.* Cambridge, Mass.: MIT Press.

Glick-Schiller, Nina, Linda Basch, and Cristina Szanton-Blanc. 1992. "Transnationalism: A New Framework for Understanding Migration." *Annals of the New York Academy of Sciences* 645.

Grasmuck, Sherrie, and Patricia Pessar. 1990. *Between Two Islands.* Berkeley: University of California Press.

Guarnizo, Luis E., and Alejandro Portes. 2001. "From Assimilation to Transnationalism: Determinants of Transnational Political Action Among Contemporary Immigrants." Working Paper Series. Princeton, N.J.: Center for Migration and Development, Princeton University.

Guarnizo, Luis E., A. Ignacio Sanchez, and E. M. Roach. 1999. "Mistrust, Fragmented Solidarity, and Transnational Migration: Colombians in New York City and Los Angeles." *Ethnic and Racial Studies* 22: 367–95.

Handlin, Oscar. 1951. *The Uprooted.* Boston: Little, Brown and Company.

Hollinger, David A. 1995. *Postethnic America: Beyond Multiculturalism.* New York: Basic Books.

Howe, Irving. 1976. *World of Our Fathers.* New York: Harcourt Brace Jovanovich.

Kahn, Bonnie Menes. 1987. *Cosmopolitan Culture: The Gilt-Edged Dream of a Tolerant City.* New York: Atheneum.

Kasinitz, Philip. 1992. *Caribbean New York: Black Immigrants and the Politics of Race.* Ithaca, N.Y.: Cornell University Press.

———. 1999. "A Third Way to America." *Culturefront* (summer): 23–31.

Kasinitz, Philip, Aviva Zeltzer-Zubida, and Zoya Simakhodskaya. 2001. "The Next Generation: Russian Jewish Young Adults in Contemporary New York." Working Paper 178. New York: Russell Sage Foundation.

Landolt, Patricia, L. Autler, and S. Baires. 1999. "From Hermano Lejando to Hermano Mayor: The Dialectics of Salvadoran Transnationalism." *Ethnic and Racial Studies* 22: 290–315.

Lessinger, Johanna. 2001. "Class, Racc and Success: Two Generations of Indian Immigrants Face the American Dream." In *Migration, Transnationalization, and Race in a Changing New York,* edited by Hector R. Cordero-Guzman, Robert C. Smith, and Ramon Grosfoguel. Philadelphia: Temple University Press.

Levitt, Peggy. 1997. "Transnationalizing Community Development: The Case of Boston and the Dominican Republic." *Nonprofit and Voluntary Sector Quarterly* 26: 509–26.

———. 1998. "Local-level Global Religion: The Case of U.S.-Dominican Migration." *Journal for the Scientific Study of Religion* 3: 74–89.

———. 2001a. *The Transnational Villagers.* Berkeley: University of California Press.

————. 2001b. "Transnational Migration: Taking Stock and Future Directions." *Global Networks* 1(3): 195–216.

Portes, Alejandro. 2001. "Introduction: The Debates and Significance of Immigrant Transnationalism." *Global Networks* 1(3): 181–94.

Portes, Alejandro, Luis E. Guarnizo, and Patricia Landolt. 1999. "Introduction: Pitfalls and Promise of an Emergent Research Field." *Ethnic and Racial Studies* 22: 463–78.

Rumbaut, Rubén G., and Alejandro Portes, eds. *Ethnicities: Children of Immigrants in America.* Berkeley: University of California Press.

Smith, Robert. 1997. "Transnational Migration, Assimilation, and Political Community." In *The City and the World: New York in Global Context,* edited by Margaret Crahan and A. Vourvuoulias-Bush. New York: Council on Foreign Relations.

Soysal, Yasemin. 1994. *The Limits of Citizenship: Migrants and Postnational Membership in Europe.* Chicago: University of Chicago Press.

Taylor, William. 1988. "The Launching of a Commercial Culture." In *Power, Culture, and Place: Essays on New York City,* edited by John Hull Mollenkopf. New York: Russell Sage Foundation.

Vertovec, Steven. 1999. "Conceiving and Researching Transnationalism." *Ethnic and Racial Studies* 22: 447–62.

Waldinger, Roger. 1996. *Still the Promised City?: African Americans and New Immigrants in Postindustrial New York.* Cambridge, Mass.: Harvard University Press.

Chapter 4

The Ties That Change:
Relations to the Ancestral
Home over the Life Cycle

Peggy Levitt

J UST WHEN SHE was about to begin her freshman year at Yonkers High School in New York, Lizzie Santos's parents decided to send her to live with her Dominican grandparents so that she could attend school in Santo Domingo. They wanted to protect her from the gangs, drugs, and violence that they felt plagued their urban neighborhood. Although Lizzie worried that she would not fit in after having spent so many years in the United States, she soon realized that her fears were unfounded. At least 20 percent of her 425 private-school classmates were also U.S.-born—reverse migrants like herself.

In 1998 Dominican educators and government officials estimated that as many as 10,000 students formerly enrolled in U.S. schools had made similar journeys. The number has risen especially dramatically in recent years in response to changes in the Dominican constitution, which now counts those born to Dominican parents in the United States as Dominican citizens. The transition homeward that these youngsters undertake is not always smooth. Some do not speak fluent Spanish. Others find themselves excluded from social events and clubs by Dominican parents who associate those milieus with the problems in the United States from which they want to protect their children. The admissions catalog at the Colegio

Padre Fortin, for example, openly states that candidates who have lived in the United States during the last three years need not apply (Rohter 1998).

Lizzie Santos's story is a striking example of the ways in which migrants' and nonmigrants' enduring social and economic ties to one another influence the second-generation experience. Though she spent most of her formative years in New York, the people, opportunities, and values that shape Lizzie's life still continue, to a large degree, to be found in Santo Domingo. She is exposed to cultural elements from both contexts not only in her current life but most likely in her future as well.

Lizzie Santos is not alone. Increasing numbers of contemporary migrants continue to be active in the life of their homeland even as they are integrated into the United States. They do not exchange one membership for another but instead enact various aspects of their lives across borders. For many groups these ties will weaken with each generation. But for others the second generation will sustain ties to their ancestral homes from a firm base in the United States.

As the chapters in this volume reveal, there is little agreement about the nature of transnational practices among the second generation. Skeptics predict that individuals either born in the United States or socialized primarily in this country will be only minimally involved in their ancestral homelands. They point to recent survey results indicating that many children of immigrants are not completely fluent in their parents' mother tongue, and that these youth have no desire to return to live in their parents' country of origin. Though these children may be "ethnic," these observers say, they are not likely to be "transnational."

This is probably true for a large proportion of the second generation. In this chapter, however, I argue that it is far too early to sound the death knell for transnational practices among the children of immigrants. Much of this research sets the bar too high, causing us to miss many of the smaller, less frequent transnational practices that the children of immigrants engage in. Although these are not comparable to the regular, comprehensive transnational practices of their parents, they nevertheless reflect a transnational approach to social and economic advancement that combines sending- and receiving-country elements at distinct stages of the life course.

SECOND-GENERATION TRANSNATIONALS:
THREE CASE STUDIES

In this section, I profile three second-generation individuals who enact selective transnational strategies. They do not visit their ancestral homes on a regular basis. Their commitments and activities have varied at different stages of their lives. Yet they all display some kind of strong attachment to their parents' country of origin that they combine, with varying degrees of success, with economic and social activities in the United States. In the next section, I highlight three factors which explain the emergence of these practices: high levels of institutional completeness and the persistence of strong, multigenerational social networks that give migrants extensive opportunities for transnational participation and choices about where and how they want to do so; life-course effects that produce different levels of intensity of transnational practices at different stages of the life cycle (including constant, frequent transnational involvements, periodic but sustained transnational practices, and fervent transnational activism at particular life-cycle stages); and the class and racial characteristics of immigrant group members.

My comments are based on an ongoing, comparative, historical study of the transnational religious, political, and social activities of six immigrant communities in the greater Boston metropolitan area. Each group in this study was selected because large numbers of migrants left a particular sending-country village, city, or state and settled near one another in Massachusetts. The project team includes myself, my colleagues in each sending country, and a group of graduate and undergraduate researchers. In the United States we collect data by interviewing first- and second-generation individuals and organizational leaders, by observing meetings and special events, and by reviewing pertinent documents. After each interview in Boston we ask for the names of nonmigrant family members to contact. We then travel to the sending country and conduct a parallel set of interviews with individuals and organizational leaders at the local, regional, and national levels. Presented in this chapter are findings from our work on three of the six groups: Dominicans from the village of Miraflores and the neighboring city of Baní who live in the Jamaica Plain neighborhood of Boston; Irish from the Inishowen Peninsula who live in the Dorchester section of the city; and Indians from Gujarat State who have settled around the city of Lowell.[1]

Eduardo: Keeping His Feet in Both Worlds and Not Knowing Which Way Is Up

Shortly after they married, Marcela and her husband, Diómedes, decided to try their hand at life in the United States. Though Diómedes' family had land in the Dominican Republic, it was getting harder and harder to make a good living by farming. Diómedes left for Boston first, and Marcela began the long wait for her visa. She was finally granted one when baby Eduardo was six months old. Since she could not get a visa for her infant, and she had already been waiting two years, Marcela decided to leave Eduardo with her mother and sister and go to work in the United States. She tried to come back regularly, but Marcela would miss Eduardo's baptism, his first steps, and his first tooth.

By the time Eduardo joined his mother and father in Boston five years later, they were divorced. Marcela soon remarried and started a new family. Though he knew that his mother and stepfather cared for him, and he was pleased to be with his mother again, Eduardo also felt forcibly uprooted from the place he loved. He did not like the cold or the fact that children had to stay inside, away from the dangers of the neighborhood. Though he tried to fit in, he always seemed to get into trouble at school and was unable to get along with other students or the teachers. When he fell behind in his schoolwork and began having difficulty expressing himself in both Spanish and English, his parents decided he would be better off living on the island. They put in place what would become a recurrent strategy—sending Eduardo back to live with his grandmother, in the hopes that things would improve, and then bringing him back to Boston when he became too much for her to handle. Though Eduardo's behavior usually got better at first and it looked like he might be turning around, problems always resurfaced. After each move Eduardo felt more and more that he was not entirely comfortable anywhere.

Eduardo is now eighteen. He has been back and forth between Boston and Miraflores five times. Saying that she is too old to take care of him, his grandmother throws her hands in the air to express how overwhelmed she feels. Because Eduardo disobeys her when she tells him to be home by midnight, she waits up half the night to make sure he comes back in one piece. His aunt, who was responsible for his day-to-day care when he was an infant, now has a son of her own. It pains her that she cannot reach him anymore, since she was the one who changed his diapers and shared his bed when he was little. She tries to talk to him about staying in school and about staying away from the delincuentes (delinquents) in the village. Though he promises to change, the next day he is back at it again, doing the same things. This hurts her, she says, but she is just not the person responsible anymore.

Back in Boston, Marcela is also at her wit's end. Eduardo no longer fits easily into the new family she has created. She grew tired of the constant phone calls she received from teachers at school. She has a job and three other children to take care of. Eduardo recently returned to live in Boston after a year and a half on the island. It is now time for him to look for a job and to start earning his own money. Every weekend she and her husband cajole, scream at, and implore him to "get his life together," but Eduardo spends his days lying on the couch and watching television. Even when she found a position for him at a hospital cafeteria just a bus ride away, he complained about the hours and the commute and quit after only two days on the job. Marcela feels that, like so many youth in Miraflores, he has become accustomed to the dole of the migration check that arrives each month from Boston. He has never had to work to put food on the table, and now he expects that it will magically appear.

Eduardo is an example of a second-generation transnational actor who physically moves frequently between two settings. Each time he does his ability to negotiate the social and cultural demands of either place diminishes further. He neither reads nor writes English or Spanish particularly well. He is not well trained for the factory or the farm. And his ability to decode cues in social and work settings in the Dominican Republic or the United States is limited. His particular mix of transnational practices and host-country involvement has resulted in social and economic marginality in both settings.

Thomas: Discovering His "Home" at Middle Age

Many of the Irish who came to the United States in the 1920s wanted desperately to forget the communities they left behind. They had been raised on farms that produced so little that there was barely enough to feed the family. Extra children were sometimes loaned out to other farmers, sometimes kin and sometimes not, because they were too much of a burden at home. Before someone migrated, the community often held what they called an American wake, reflecting their expectation that the migrant would never come back.

When these migrants had children of their own, they told them little about Ireland except that their lives had been full of hardship. They wanted to forget the bleak, cold, unproductive landscape and wanted their offspring to be firmly established in the United States. There was little talk of the old country in the household in which Thomas Byrne, a fifty-four-year-old second-generation Irish American, grew up. Though they lived in a neighborhood surrounded by other Irish, Thomas's parents and his friends' parents spoke little about their former lives. "You knew they remembered it and that their memories ran deep," he said, "but it was like they could not bring themselves to talk about the poverty and misery they escaped from."

As a result, during his childhood and young adult years Thomas learned little about his family's history. He knew that letters came regularly from his unmarried aunt who still lived in the family home on the Inishowen Peninsula in County Donegal. He knew that his mother always sent packages filled with the old clothes that he and his brothers had outgrown. But that was as far as it went. His images of Ireland, he said, were the same stereotypical ones held by most Americans—potatoes, thatched-roof cottages, green, fog-filled rocky meadows, and Irish brogues. Nothing challenged these ideas as he completed his college degree at a predominantly Catholic college, trained as a lawyer, and moved his wife and first-born child to an Irish lower-middle-class suburb just outside of Boston. Work, baseball practice, and parish activities consumed his life. But the letters that Thomas's parents, and others like them, wrote and received on a regular basis kept their emotional ties to Ireland strong. Normally, one sibling among the many who journeyed to the United

States continued to write letters, wire money, or send packages of clothing, often containing dollars tucked away in a pocket, as John Doherty, a middle-aged second-generation lawyer, described:

> Well, see there was a lot of transmittal of information back and forth. Someone had left the village thirty-five years before, but they were not forgotten, at least among their contemporaries. They would always get drips and drabs of information from people who were visiting, either coming over here, or coming over there, to live. They were always very interested in people and what they were doing. The good thing about village life is that it was very personal in terms of people keeping track of people and knowing what people were doing and people talking about other people. The bad thing is if you're living there everyone knows your life, what you're doing, what you're not doing, your sins. There's no anonymity in these Irish villages.

Inishoweners also exchanged news and gossip about what went on at home when they saw each other at church, in the pub, at kitchen rackets, or at wakes. Though few returned or participated from afar in the economic or political life of their villages in Ireland, among families and within these informal settings the social and emotional connections between Inishowen and Boston were not allowed to die.

That Inishoweners, like many of the other groups in this study, sustained these connections, albeit weakly and sporadically, enabled the second generation to rekindle them when they reached the stage in their lives when they were willing and able to do so. At middle age, with enough time and money to travel, many members of the second generation became curious and eager to understand the mystery that was their parents' lives. They were taken completely by surprise to discover a community of people who, despite never having laid eyes on them, were quick to know who they were and welcome them "home." The second generation, in a sense, reaped the fruits of the transnational seeds their parents had planted, without ever having known they had been sown.

For example, when Maureen and her brother Bob, both in their sixties and raised in the Charlestown neighborhood of Boston, made their first trip over, they stopped in a pub before heading back to the bed-and-breakfast where they were staying. After talking with them, the pub owner realized that a cousin of theirs lived just up the road. He told them this, but they thought little of it, thinking that they did not want to bother a stranger. Later that evening their cousin came to find them and demanded to know why they had not come to visit before.

Thomas Byrne was also baffled the first time he traveled to Ireland. He began thinking about his Irish roots when he reached the age of forty-five. He had a successful law practice and lived in a comfortable home in a middle-class community. One of his children had finished college, and the other would soon graduate. When he found a box in his attic filled with the letters his mother and her sister had written to each other, he realized how much and how often his mother thought about her relatives back home. Though she had never returned, and her sister had never visited Boston, they wrote frequently, revealing a rich narrative of small-town life in Ireland that his mother somehow remained part of.

Thomas decided to visit Ireland. He finally had enough money, time, and stability to be able to do so. He was completely unprepared for what he found and how it transformed his life. "It's amazing," he said:

> When I go up to Malinhead, it's "Welcome home, Tom." Down in Mayo, where there are lots of family, an old-timer—late seventies, early eighties, all bent over on the cane and problems with his back—I see him running out the door to see me! He was running out the door. It's humbling. But that's what it's like to go there. That's why I can't wait to go back. [*crying*] Sorry, I get carried away with it. It doesn't at all feel like I'm an American, you know, there's a family party someplace, and I go just like anybody else. "He's one of us." In fact, one of my cousins over there and we happened to be talking about the first time I went over there, in '83, and there was a party at their father's house. "But, Tom, do you remember the first night we were at that party?" Oh God, remember, I'll never forget it, it was one of the greatest times I ever had in my life! "And I'll never forget," he says, "remember, we were pouring the booze on you pretty good that night." I said, "I don't remember it was just me, I thought it was everybody." "Oh yeah, we were," he said. Somebody comes out with the accordion, the guitar, two sons all play the guitar, and people start singing, and so I started singing. And he told me how his father told him, "Give him plenty to drink, give him plenty to drink." So once the night was over and I had got up and sang a few songs, his father said to him, "By God, he's one of us." Pretty powerful stuff. I can almost *sense* it walking there, something just comes over me. Like I've been . . . I was there sometime before. Before this life. Just have a sense of it. Good. Wonderful.

Many of Thomas's contemporaries have also made similar "roots journeys." They begin to go back to Ireland on vacation every year.

Each time they meet new members of their extended family and systematically fill in the gaps of the puzzle that is their past. For others, like Thomas, their return transforms them in much more fundamental ways. Their relatives' "Welcome home" greeting resonates somewhere deeply within them. They feel they have discovered a missing piece of who they are but had never really known was lacking. "When I went back to Ireland for the first time," Clare Murphy recalled,

> I understood why I am a Democrat, why I have spent so much of my life fighting for liberal values. I realized that these had somehow been transmitted to me from Ireland—caring for your family, a concern for others, responsibility to the community. I felt like I finally understood myself. That for all these years I had somehow been out of sync with everyone around me and that all of a sudden I felt like I completely fit.

Though Thomas has no plans to move back to Ireland, like Clare, he became a transnational activist once he began traveling there. He felt such a strong connection to the family and friends he became "reacquainted" with in his mother's hometown that he began working on community development. He and several other "sons of Inishowen" raised money to build a soccer field. He has also joined forces with a local group in Malinhead to promote tourism to the area. His activities include lobbying the Irish American community and Irish elected officials to approve plans he helped to develop for a visitors' center at Ireland's most northern point.

Second-generation individuals like Thomas are paradigmatic examples of straight-line assimilation. Though his parents arrived with little, Thomas exhibits many of the traditional markers of social, economic, and cultural assimilation. This assimilation in fact is precisely what gave Thomas the resources and time he needed to become a transnational actor. In Thomas's case, assimilation enabled transnational participation, and at least so far, these two allegiances peacefully coexist.

Priti: A Part of Her Always Faces East

Ever since Priti's family arrived in Massachusetts when she was just seven years old, she has lived in communities with few Indian children. In the garden apartment complex where her family first lived, and later in the new subdivision located twenty miles west of

Boston where her parents bought their first home, one hardly saw another South Asian face.

Priti, who is now twenty-seven, says that she led a schizophrenic childhood. At school she tried her best to fit in with her American friends and play down her Indian-ness. She never wore Indian clothing, and she pleaded with her mother to send sandwiches instead of japatis for lunch. There were obvious differences, however. Unlike her peers, she was not allowed to sleep over at a friend's house. She could not attend school dances. For six months out of the year, when her grandmother visited, Priti had to come directly home from school to be with her grandmother so that she would not feel lonely while her parents were away at work.

When friends came to visit, a few inquired about the different foods and smells that permeated her house, but most expressed little interest. It did not matter, her parents told her. Her real friends and the people who were important, they said, consisted of the ever-widening circle of Indian relatives and family friends and their children whom Priti's family visited and were visited by every weekend. During these gatherings, held at a different home each week, she was expected to abide by Indian values. Her many adopted aunties and uncles took it upon themselves to ensure that all the children in this extended group studied hard, respected their elders, did not date, and learned to chant the bhajans or sacred verses they sang together.

Priti deeply resented the double life that she led during most of her childhood. She felt angry about not being able to participate in the same kinds of activities as her classmates. This began to change, however, when her father started attending meetings of the Devotional Associates of Yogeshwar, or the Swadhyay movement. The group met every Sunday in rooms they rented from a yoga school located in a strip mall near the New Hampshire border. While the adults gathered to watch videotapes of lectures by Dadaji, the group's leader (the same videotapes watched by Swadhyay members around the world), younger members participated in the Divine Brain Trust (DBT). During these meetings the group's motobhais, or elder brothers, taught the children about Dadaji's teachings.

I must have been about fourteen or fifteen when my father decided that we should start going regularly to Swadhyay. Every Sunday Deepti [her sister] and I would attend the DBT while our parents sat with the other parents and listened to Dadaji. Since Dadaji's lectures were in Gujarati and some of us could not understand Gujarati fluently, Ganesh and Ranjit uncle would tell us about Dadaji's message. They would teach us some of the stories from the Gita. The lessons were always about how one should live one's life according to Indian values, that to be good and kind one had to live according to these teachings.

At first I hated going. I felt like this was just another way my family was different and that my father was trying to keep me away from my American friends. But gradually I came to really value the lessons I was learning. I saw how some of the kids I knew in high school were starting to drink and smoke and get away from their studies and that going to Swadhyay helped me never to be tempted by that stuff. My Swadhyay friends became my best friends because we all understand and are interested in living the same way. When I went to college, this made me strong. I didn't care about "being brown" because I am a Swadhyayee, so when people were ignorant about India or about Hinduism, I had a support system and confidence in myself. I had a set of principles, a philosophy, that could guide my life and help me live in a good and healthy way.

When Priti's family visits India, they also attend Swadhyay meetings. Whether they are staying in her father's homeplace, a small, rural village near Baroda, or in town with her aunt and uncle, it is easy to find a gathering to attend. It is also easy to follow what goes on because Swadhyay meetings are similar all over the world. These experiences, Priti said, made her gradually become more interested in her Indian background.

I wanted to learn a lot more about my religion, the holidays, the festivals. When we would travel back to India, I wasn't resentful anymore. Instead, I felt proud. I felt connected to my cousins who were also Swadhyayees. And there was a feeling about watching Dadaji when we were in India, about feeling close to him. It made me feel that an important part of me was there and to want to continue to go back. As long as I belong to Swadhyay, I will always feel linked to India. I imagine myself as part of a community with deep roots there.

It is through Priti's membership in Swadhyay that she establishes a connection to India. Not only do her religious activities transform her Indian ethnicity into something that she values, but they orient her toward and connect her to India as well. As long as she is a Swadhyayee, she will look to India for spiritual guidance and sustenance. Her ties are reinforced because they are partially expressed within a transnational religious institutional context that is inextricably linked to the motherland and that continuously looks to India for guidance, direction, and support.

EXPLAINING VARIATIONS
IN THE TRANSNATIONAL PRACTICES
OF THE SECOND GENERATION

Priti, Eduardo, and Thomas all participate in some kinds of activities that connect them to their parents' ancestral homes. Eduardo spent most of his school years circulating back and forth between Boston and Santo Domingo. If his uncle's experience is any indication—and it may be, since they both have limited education and few job skills—Eduardo is likely to spend much of his adult life moving between the United States and the island as he attempts to piece together a secure livelihood. Thomas lives, works, and has raised his family in the United States but has become actively involved in community development projects in Inishowen. His discovery of Ireland at middle age has given new meaning to his life. Finally, while Priti lives, studies, and works in the United States, her religious identity binds her inexorably to India. She engages in selective transnational involvements that evoke strong loyalty and commitment because of their deep spiritual roots.

In these examples, at least three factors explain the emergence of transnational practices among the second generation. I will discuss each in turn.

Institutional Completeness

Breton (1964) used the term "institutional completeness" to refer to ethnic communities that create such a diverse array of institutions that it is possible for members to satisfy most of their needs within the community itself. I extend this concept to describe communities that are institutionally complete across borders. When large numbers migrate, the political, religious, and civic groups that serve them often organize themselves transnationally to accommodate their new constituencies. They fund-raise, lead, strategize, and act across borders, thereby enabling migrants to meet most of their needs within this transnational institutional field and reinforcing their membership in multiple settings.

The Dominican case provides a good example of this. A multi-layered, multi-sited transnational institutional field emerged between Boston and the Dominican Republic that affords migrants a variety of arenas within which to express their transnational allegiances. The Partido de la Liberacíon Dominicana (PLD) and the Partido Revolucionario Dominicano (PRD), two of the principal Dominican political parties, each created structures, raise funds, campaign, and implement their activities across borders. The PRD even authorized the formation of local-level support committees among children born to Dominican parents in the United States. In 1996 the Dominican government formally institutionalized these memberships by approving Dominican citizenship for the children of Dominican immigrants who are born in the United States.

Religious arenas are also sites of dual belonging. Strong ties between churches in Baní and Boston grew out of personal connections between priests, parishioners, religious movement members, and seminary students who circulated back and forth between both settings. At first the religious lives of many migrants consisted primarily of popular folk practices conducted largely outside the formal church. Climate, lifestyles, and Catholic Church requirements, however, pushed many toward more church-based practices. When these migrants visited Miraflores, or when their family members visited them in Boston, they modeled this more formal religious style, which gradually prompted nonmigrants to adopt more church-based rituals. Subsequent migrants arrived already partially socialized into the pan-Latino religious program the church in Boston had to offer. This convergence in religious practices allowed migrants and nonmigrants to participate almost seamlessly in the religious life of both settings, making the church a powerful institutional arena for asserting dual membership.

Finally, sister chapters of the Miraflores Development Committee (MDC) in Boston and Miraflores also provide opportunities for migrants and nonmigrants to work jointly on community development. Members in Boston and on the island identify problems, raise money to address them, and implement solutions together. When migrant members return to Miraflores to visit, or when nonmigrants come to Boston, they are expected to attend MDC meetings. These connections also reinforce migrants' transnational commitments, not only among the first generation but among the second as well.

When the children of immigrants attend fund-raising events or accompany their parents or visiting relatives to MDC meetings, they are encouraged to feel a sense of loyalty and continuing responsibility to their ancestral home. They are also exposed to a broad range of elements from which to construct livelihood strategies and sources of social and cultural capital. The greater the number of institutional opportunities, and the more fully children are socialized into them, the more likely it is that the second generation will engage in transnational activism (Levitt 2001).

The Inishowen case also attests to the role of institutional completeness. Thomas got help reactivating the ties that lay dormant between Inishowen and Boston because a set of institutions and cultural assumptions were in place that reinforced these connections. Numerous clan associations have been created throughout Ireland to reunite extended family members and help them trace their Irish roots. For example, members of the Doherty clan, which comes from the Inishowen region, can visit the clan headquarters in Buncrana and request that paid staff members conduct customized genealogical searches to trace their family histories. Staff also organize worldwide clan reunions every five years. The Irish government actively promotes this "heritage industry." In many counties heritage centers detailing the history of a particular region have become important stops on the tourist trail traversed by the thousands of Irish descendants who visit the country each year. These institutional arrangements allow and encourage individuals like Thomas to reclaim and celebrate their Irish heritage and, by so doing, also enable transnational involvements for those who choose to pursue them.

These institutional arrangements helped preserve the multigenerational social networks that are so important in Thomas's story. But even without them, the fact that social ties persisted over generations, however weakly, helped Thomas become a transnational actor. It is too early to predict how strong the actual personalized connections between migrant and nonmigrant Gujaratis and Dominicans in this study will remain. But Thomas's experience suggests that very little is needed to rekindle the transnational connection, especially when the institutional climate is supportive of cross-border connections.

Institutional completeness is also key to understanding Priti and the lives of other second-generation Gujaratis like her. The majority of the first-generation Gujaratis in this study enjoy high levels of economic and residential assimilation. Many are fluent in English. They generally work with people from diverse racial and ethnic backgrounds. By and large, their children attend Anglo-dominated public schools and universities. Yet many consider Western culture inferior to their own. They intentionally segregate themselves and their families socially and culturally. They can do this, in part, because of the range of Indian cultural and religious organizations they have established, many of which also connect them back to India.

Children whose parents did not participate actively in these groups generally engaged in fewer transnational practices. Though many said they agreed with Indian values and planned to raise their children as they had been raised, the identities they constructed did not depend on ongoing relations with—and thus replenishment through—some form of contact with India. Nor did they construct livelihood strategies involving resources and contacts abroad. Rather, although many expressed a strong sense of being Indian in America, they felt this would have less to do with India with each generation. Shefali, a first-generation parent of two children born in the United States, explained:

> My husband and I never participated in those kinds of groups. So our children never grew up going to events, socializing with other Indians. We lived in a town where there were few other Indian families. Our kids are Americans. They like Indian food. They respect their elders. But they are no more interested in voting or starting a business in India than they are in voting in South Africa. This is their home.

Children, like Priti, whose families participate actively in Indian cultural and religious groups tend to feel more strongly connected to their ancestral home. Because their families spend so much time attending meetings, weddings, prayer sessions, cultural presentations, and holiday dinners with other Gujaratis, these second-generation children experience their connection to India as a constant in their everyday lives. They are often reminded of the value and meaning of these connections.

Furthermore, unlike migrants who join social and religious groups that are part of U.S. organizations, many Gujaratis participate in groups that are franchises or chapters of groups in India and are still run, to varying degrees, by parent organizations in the homeland. As a result, these chapters are regularly exposed to new infusions of Indian values and norms, which are then communicated to their first- and second-generation members. Participation underscores the superiority of connections to other Indians and strengthens the barriers between Indian immigrant and Anglo life. Members look to India as the source of their faith, and because, for some, religion plays such a significant role in their everyday lives, the homeland is a strong magnet.

The Swadhyay movement has modified its activities to encourage long-term, long-distance membership, and it has tailored its social justice work requirements to make them easier to complete in the United States. The principles and values guiding Swadhyay activities are the same, leaders say, but they take different forms in each country. For example, all followers are to "devote time to God" by participating in Yogeshwar Krishi. In India these are cooperative farms or fishing enterprises established by the movement. Members donate their labor, and their earnings are then distributed to the poor. To do Yogeshwar Krishi in Chicago, Swadhyayees formed a small company that makes ink refills for pens, and in Massachusetts groups of families get together and assemble circuit boards on contract from computer companies. These activities are more compatible with the demands of the U.S. lifestyle but still allow members to fulfill their responsibilities to the group.

The Uda Bhakta Society, another religious group based in Puniyad, about thirty-five kilometers outside of Baroda, provides another example of a homeland religious organization that is modifying its activities to encourage loyalty among the children of immigrants. When I asked its leader, Punjya Shri Jagdishchandra Maharaj, how his message has changed since so many of his followers have migrated, he said that it has not, because his disciples are "still very much Indian in the United States." They continue to engage in the same rituals and do the same good works they have always done. The group, however, recently began printing a small magazine for its expatriate members. On the last page is a letter written in English by the leader's son and successor, Shri Premjivan Swami, because, as his father explained, "We want to help them keep in touch with us." The letter states: "My young friends, the expectations of the Indian Bhagat Society are very high for you. Please don't ignore their feelings." He ends his message assuring them that he will stay in touch, saying, "We will continue to [shed] light on the preachings of Kabiriji and Jivanji in further issues regularly."

In sum, institutional opportunities strongly influence the degree to which the second generation enacts transnational practices. When powerful, expansive organizations involve the second generation in activities that bring them into contact with their ancestral homes on a regular basis, they are more likely to become transnational actors. The persistence of multigenerational transnational networks, be they institutionalized or not, enables these allegiances as well.

Life-Course Factors

A second factor influencing the extent to which the second generation engages in transnational practices is life-course effects. Transnational activities do not remain constant across the life cycle. Instead, they ebb and flow at different stages, varying with the demands of work, school, and family.

Several different patterns are suggested so far by our findings. First, there is Eduardo, and others like him, whose transnational activities remain fairly stable over time and who move regularly in order to conduct them. Eduardo was raised and educated transnationally. His social and emotional life has always been, and is likely to continue to be, conducted across borders.

Such lifestyles create opportunities and obstacles. For Eduardo, these experiences add up to not belonging anywhere. Moreover, he is likely to continue as a long-term transnational actor because he cannot gain a secure foothold in either the United States or the Dominican Republic. But this is not always the case. As I will argue, given different educational, language, or class status, other children involved in equally intensive transnational activities can function effectively and successfully in both worlds.

A second pattern involves children who participate only periodically, although repeatedly, in transnational activities over an extended period of time, when specific events or family circumstances arise. Though their parents do not send them to formal language and cultural schools, these youngsters grow up in environments that are sufficiently infused with immigrant and sending-community influences that they can participate in sending-country activities when and where they are called on to do so. Most of the Gujarati youth in our study, for example, have attended enough Indian dance performances (garba), religious celebrations, and parties for weddings and births that they join these events easily when in India. Likewise, most of the Miorafloreño youth brought up in Boston have spent enough time dancing the merengue and celebrating fiestas patrias (patron saint day celebrations) that they can also participate fully when they visit Santo Domingo.

In general, these kinds of experiences do not seem to produce frequent, comprehensive transnational practices. Instead, homeland involvements occur in response to special events such as births or deaths, national holidays, fund-raising efforts, political campaigns, and homeland visits. The children of immigrants have usually learned enough about homeland practices to handle themselves in these settings. They can act transnationally when called on to do so. Their periodic engagement with or exposure to homeland practices can have a cumulative effect. It renews youngsters' sense of sending-country attachment and endows them with the skills they need to participate again, or more fully, at some later date.

The third level of engagement among the second generation is one of intense transnational activity at a particular life-cycle stage. Thomas is a clear example of this, but some of the second-generation Gujaratis in our study told of similar experiences as well. Several reported that they had not been interested in their cultural heritage as young children. Though their parents performed certain religious rituals each morning and they sometimes visited the Hindu temple near their home, they understood little of what went on. It was when they left home to attend college and their fellow students assumed that they would know things about their culture and traditions that they did not that they began to think more about where they came from. According to Lakshmi, a nineteen-year-old second-generation Indian American:

> When I got to Whitehead College, everyone sort of assumed I would know everything about Hinduism. They expected me to belong to the South Asian Students Association. I literally knew next to nothing when I got here. But I felt pressured by these assumptions to learn more. Not to be a spokesperson for my group, but at least to be able to answer some basic questions. In retrospect, I'm glad. I've learned a lot, and it's very rich. I've become very proud of my cultural heritage.

This was also clearly the case for Priti, who became a transnational actor because of her membership in Swadhyay. Other respondents developed more individualistic, informal attachments to their parents' place of origin that were not based on organizational membership, such as choosing careers that involve work in India, studying Indian topics that require extended in-country stays, or managing family property or business interests. This has been the experience of Vaishali, a twenty-three-year-old M.B.A. graduate student. Her periodic contacts with India seem to be evolving into a more intensive commitment as she enters her working years. Asked how she identifies herself, she replied: "I don't like to be called just American. . . . My dad bugs me, because he always calls me American, and I always say, 'No, I'm Indian American.' " Her sense of Indian identity has intensified recently,

> because, I think, I'm living at home now, and I'm experiencing it more. It started when I was at college. I was never interested in all the things my parents did. But then when I got to school, I thought maybe this is something to be proud of. All the Indian kids would get together, and we knew exactly what we were talking about when we talked about our families. We had all grown up with the same pressures and expectations. During my junior year our family went back to India. We were always going back, but somehow that time it was different. I realized that India was part of me and that I wanted to make some decisions that would let me make India part of my life. That's why I chose finance. I thought I could get a job working in a multinational company and I could do something for the country.

Vaishali now works in the South Asian division of a large financial services firm. Her job requires that she travel to India at least three or four times a year. She has also become active in a group of South Asian coworkers who are trying to pressure her company to divert some portion of its philanthropic contributions to India since so many of its employees are from the region and it conducts so much business there. Vaishali's discovery of her South Asian roots is both affective and instrumental. She has found part of herself, and it is deeply satisfying. The skills that are both creating and reinforced by these reactive transnational ties also stand her in good stead professionally.

Socioeconomic Characteristics

The third factor that explains variations in transnational practices among the second generation involves socioeconomic characteristics. Some children of immigrants are compelled to engage in transnational practices because they do not have the education, language, or job skills to succeed in their country of origin or in their parents' ancestral homes. Like Eduardo, they are not culturally and linguistically fluent in either setting. Their skills and the kinds of job opportunities they face as a result prevent them from achieving minimal economic gains in either context. Their marginalization worsens with each circular journey, making a transnational livelihood a necessity rather than a choice.

Others, like Vaishali, choose a transnational lifestyle. They have the education, language, and job skills to function effectively in multiple settings. They have the cultural capital and manners to handle themselves in boardrooms, alumnae meetings, and cocktail parties. They see themselves as choosing from a wide range of potential opportunities they can strategically combine in multiple settings to get ahead. Some respondents, like those described by Kibria and Louie in this volume, see their transnational capabilities as a safety net that they can put into place when they encounter racial barriers to their mobility in the United States.

Pravin, a second-generation Indian American whose family is from Baroda, for example, describes himself as hedging his bets. While his primary professional life takes place in the United States, he carries out a second set of activities in India that contribute to his economic portfolio. His investments in India provide him with a small cushion and enable him to help his family there.

> When I graduated from engineering school, I went to work for Brown and Marshall. I was doing well and moving up. Then, I thought, now I have the money, I have the know-how, I can start a small company in Baroda. My uncle's career was sort of floundering, so I asked him if he wanted to go into business with me. We could never live on what we make by doing business there, but it is a nice cushion for us, and it helps my uncle and his family. It helps me help my family even though I am so far away.

Shefali, a twenty-seven-year-old who was born in the United States to Gujarati parents, sees her ties to India as a means to circumvent the roadblocks to her mobility that she anticipates encountering in the work world:

> I have been out in the work world for several years now, and I am doing well. But I see who gets promoted and who does not. I think companies

are happy to have South Asians. We are smart, we work hard, we are educated—the whole model minority thing. But we are still a minority. I know that someday I will achieve a position and then I will not be able to get any further. They will look at my skin, at my gender, and say, that's it, no more. That's why I figure if I learn as much as I can about working in India I have more options. I can get over the bar here by working over there, or by working for a company that needs people like me. I see my background as a plus. It can help me fight back.

While Pravin, who uses his connections to India to diversify risk and produce additional income streams, Shefali uses her transnational capabilities to overcome obstacles placed in her path by race. She also diversifies risk in her own way by deploying multiple skill sets and expecting her transnational one to prove particularly valuable.

CONCLUSION

Lizzie Santos is one among many members of the second generation who will live some aspect of their adult lives across borders. Her experiences suggest that it is premature to summarily dismiss the importance of transnational practices among this group. Although the vast majority of the children of immigrants are likely to be firmly rooted in the United States, and are unlikely to engage in the same kinds of long-term transnational practices as their parents, there may still be a small but important number who continue to contribute to the political economic, and social life of their ancestral homes.

In this chapter, I suggested three patterns of transnational participation among the second-generation Irish, Dominicans, and Indians in my study, and I proposed several factors explaining their emergence. The first is the high levels of institutional completeness and the strong multigenerational networks that persist among certain groups. These characteristics provide the second generation with a wide range of arenas to participate in and many choices about when and where to do so. The second factor is life-course effects. My research revealed at least three levels of transnational involvement that varied over the life course: regular and frequent transnational participation, periodic but enduring transnational practices that may have a cumulative impact over time, and intensive transnational activism at a particular lifecycle stage or in response to a specific event. Finally, the class and racial characteristics of the second generation are the third factor that explains transnational participation among the second generation.

These patterns underscore the importance of a long-term longitudinal approach to the study of transnational activism. If we only examine the activities of the second generation at a single point, we will miss significant ebbs and flows in involvement. Because the second generation's interest in, need for, and ability to participate in their ancestral homes varies considerably over time, such a strategy will be necessarily incomplete.

NOTE

1. The larger study also includes Israelis, Pakistanis, and Brazilians. We have conducted 240 interviews among first- and second-generation Irish, Indian, Dominican, and Brazilian migrants. In addition, 90 leaders of religious, political, and social organizations were interviewed. Fieldwork was carried out in Ireland, Brazil, and India between 1997 and 2001. Fieldwork in the Dominican Republic was conducted between 1992 and 1994 and in 1997. The name "Miraflores" and the names of individuals and workplaces are pseudonyms. I wish to thank Erin Collins, Rafael de la Dehesa, Breda Gray, and N. Rajaram for their work on this study.

REFERENCES

Breton, Raymond. 1964. "Institutional Completeness of Ethnic Communities and the Personal Relations of Immigrants." *American Journal of Sociology* 70: 193–205.

Levitt, Peggy. 2001. *The Transnational Villagers*. Berkeley: University of California Press.

Rohter, Larry. 1998. "Island Life Not Idyllic for Youths in U.S." *New York Times*, February 20.

Chapter 5

Life Course, Generation, and Social Location as Factors Shaping Second-Generation Transnational Life

Robert C. Smith

WHY AND HOW would second-generation Mexicans in New York participate in transnational life? And what factors would affect the nature of that participation in the short and long terms? I pursue answers to these questions in this chapter by analyzing second-generation transnational life among the children of migrants from a town in rural Puebla, Mexico, that I have called Ticuani. The analytical work is twofold: to demonstrate that transnational life exists among the second generation, and to theorize about its etiology—how it emerges, what its nature and limits are, and how it matters. My intent is to offer a corrective to both those who dismiss the study of things transnational out of hand and those who see transnationalism everywhere, as well as to point out ways of getting empirical and conceptual purchase on this important social reality.

My argument is that transnational life among second-generation Mexicans in New York is a result of the dual processes of assimilation and settlement and related processes such as social locationing in New York City, migration from and return to Mexico, and the transnationalization of adolescence. (For a fuller development of this argument, see Smith 2001a.[1]) I argue that transnational life in the second generation: results from the second generation's engagement with racial, gender, and class and status hierarchies in the United States (and sometimes in Mexico); evolves as the second generation moves from adolescence into early adulthood, an important step in the life course; and reflects their attempt to keep the immigrant bargain with their parents (see Suárez-Orozco and Suárez-Orozco 2001). My answer underlines the importance of the dynamic interaction between the American context and the parents' hometown, focusing on the ways in which transnational sites and practices are used to redefine second-generation social locations and the meaning of Mexican-ness in New York. Mexican-ness is redefined internally, for example, as the second generation returns to their parents' hometown as college students, enjoying that status and keeping the immigrant bargain as they mature. Mexican-ness is also redefined when they reject its negative images in New York—as powerless undocumented workers or dangerous gang members—by learning about religious or cultural practices in Ticuani. But fighting these images within the American context pushes the second generation into a tight engagement with New York's racial hierarchies and the need to negotiate their ambiguous social location with respect to what Du Bois (1969 [1901], 1992 [1935]) called America's "color line." Many in the second generation demonstrate their positive social location in New York by showing themselves to be "not black" and "not Puerto Rican," as did the Irish and other white immigrants before them. Being "not black" is part of being "good immigrants" like their parents, and hence fit for full membership and upward mobility in what some call the "immigrant analogy" (see Omi and Winant 1986; Roediger 1991; Ignatiev 1997; Smith 1995, 1996, 2001a, 2002; Basch et al. 1994; Portes and Rumbaut 2001).[2] This dynamic engages both assimilation and transnationalization: they return to Mexico to help escape negative assimilative pressures and end up transnationalizing their own lives.

Concretely, in this chapter I analyze the Ticuani Youth Group, a conscious attempt to create a transnational second-generation institution. I analyze the reasons for the failure to fully realize this ambition, as well as the proximate and longer-term latent effects that the group nevertheless has had on the social lives of its members in New York and Ticuani. Although transnational life is different for the second generation, it does exist. Theoretically, this chapter engages one of the most frequent criticisms of transnational research—that transnationalism, to the extent that it exists at all, is a first-generation phenomenon, and that it is squashed under the foot of second- and third-generation American monolingualism and acculturation. I document the second generation's conscious participation in transnational life, and with what effects, and the impact of the life course on this process for the second generation (see Levitt 2001; Smith 1997, 1999). I argue that rather than squashing transnationalization, assimilative pressures actually foster it by giving the second generation a reason to want to redefine their Mexican-ness in a new context.

Ticuani is a good case for looking at transnational life in the second generation for several reasons. It has a high degree of first-generation participation in strongly institutionalized transnational life (see Smith 1995, 1998, 2001a). For example, since the early 1970s Ticuani has funded major public works projects through its New York Committee for the Progress of Ticuani, and its politics is practiced in both New York and Mexico. About 60 percent of Ticuani's population now lives in the United States, mainly in New York, and about 40 percent in Mexico. Moreover, large numbers of first- and second-generation youth return to the town every two or three years for the Feast of the Patron Saint, Padre Jesus, giving these second- and 1.5-generation youth significant lived experience there. Although some would point to cases like Ticuani as outliers (without actually having a universe from which to make such an assessment), massive exits like that experienced by Ticuani are becoming more and more widespread in parts of rural Mexico (Thompson 2001), making the kinds of dynamics described in this chapter increasingly likely. In one political region I studied in Puebla, one-third of the municipios (counties) have had electoral processes and outcomes changed by migrant participation. Many believe that migrants in the United States contributed to President Vicente Fox's electoral victory in 2000 (Smith 2001a, 2001b). Finally, Ticuani is a good case because the period of research—the fourteen years from 1988 to the present—is an ethnographically long time and hence it has been possible to watch carefully as the processes of second-generation transnational life unfold.[3]

Before proceeding, a word about terminology is in order. I use the term "transnational life," and in some places "transnationalization," to emphasize processes and lived experience, and I avoid using the popular "transnationalism," which is sometimes understood to indicate a kind of "third space" divorced from both the home and host societies.[4] The implication of this usage of "transnationalism" is that there is an entirely new way of being as a migrant—a transnational—whose entire life is lived simultaneously in two places. My understanding of transnational life is somewhat more modest and circumscribed but still yields important effects. I understand transnational life as that sphere of life that flows out of the regular contact between sending and receiving societies, a social field of relations that, in the second generation especially, has a character akin to associational life and is particularly strong in particular phases of life. For many in the second generation transnational life has a significance similar to that of the Jewish summer camps in the Catskills during the middle decades of the last century: one's friends came from there, one's social life revolved around the camp experience, and it was most intense during adolescence but persisted into adulthood (see also Smith 2001a, 2001b). I return to these issues in the conclusion.

THE TICUANI YOUTH GROUP: ITS GOALS AND EARLY HISTORY

Among the forms of second-generation participation in transnational life—returning with parents, returning to escape gang violence in New York, returning for major ceremonies such as marriage and baptism, participating in a set of rituals of adolescence (Smith 2001a)—the Ticuani Youth Group is one of the most institutionalized. The group represents an attempt to form a second-generation transnational institution modeled on the New York Committee for the Progress of Ticuani, run by first-generation men and dedicated to improving life in Ticuani (Smith 1995, 1998). Although the latter organization ultimately failed to fully realize this objective, it did have a number of other important effects on transnational life, including support for a long-term practice of return and the cementing of a primary friendship group among its members. Its failures and successes are important for what they suggest about the possibilities and limits of long-term, local-level transnational life, as well as for what they reveal about the ways in which the processes of settlement and assimilation are involved in creating the desire to participate in transnational life. Racialization and social location in New York are two key processes of the push toward transnationalization, and life course is a key dimension in setting its limits and possibilities.

The Ticuani Youth Group held sports tournaments and other events to raise funds with the goal of refurbishing a small chapel to Padre Jesus and the kindergarten in Ticuani. The group raised about $20,000 toward these goals over the course of the two years from 1991 to 1993. About half of the members of the group were teen migrants, one-third were 1.5-generation migrants, and one-fifth were second-generation, U.S.-born children of migrants. The 1.5 and second generations seemed to have more in common and to remain more active than the teen migrants. The group's manifest goals were understood by its leaders to achieve latent goals that were tightly linked to the contexts in which the second and 1.5 generations and the teen migrants found themselves. One important latent goal of the group was to differentiate its Mexican members from the Puerto Ricans and blacks whom they said victimized Mexican youth, especially teen migrants. One of the group's presidents was Walker, a teen migrant who had also been involved in founding one of the earliest Mexican gangs in New York, a group that had the same racialized understanding of where Mexicans fit into the social hierarchy. The primary purpose of both that gang and the Ticuani Youth Group was to protect Mexicans from Puerto Ricans and blacks. He said in 1997:

> So I remember that at the time I made the Youth Group I was thinking about so much abuse, too much abuse of the Mexicans. And because of this I wanted to be like a guardian and all this, but it was impossible. It was very difficult to watch over all of New York City, you would need an enormous movement to be able to defend your race, to defend the human rights so they were not violated, that they respect the conscience of each person. It was very difficult.[5]

One of Walker's gang's names was ODR, or Organization for the Defense of the Race, where the race included Mexicans, Central and South Americans, and Puerto Ricans born on the island. The gang's goal was to defend this "Hispanic race" against the blacks and the Puerto Ricans born in New York whom they said were preying on them. This is a very clear elaboration of racialization through the immigrant analogy that also asserts that Mexicans have more honor and occupy a socially and morally superior place in the status hierarchy in New York (see Sanchez Jankowski 1995; Smith 1995, 2001a).

The group also served the linked purposes of distinguishing its members from other Mexican teen migrants and members of the 1.5 and second generations who were not upwardly mobile or who were "going on the wrong path," and proving to their elders that they themselves had kept the immigrant bargain. They wanted to show their parents that their sacrifices had not been in vain; they were not wasting their time but using the opportunities given to them in the United States to prosper. All the members of the Ticuani Youth Group either continued with their education—many earned an associate's degree, some a bachelor's degree, and one even obtained a master's degree—or did well in their work; some even opened their own businesses. Walker described the group's purpose to me this way in a 1997 interview in New York:

> More than anything, the group was to try to support the pueblo (Ticuani). From contributing a little bit, so that the older people would notice that we young people had our eyes open. That we wanted to do something for our pueblo. That we had desire. Because we are all Ticuani citizens, it does not matter if you were born here [New York].

Other group members described another function as fighting against the negative image of Mexicans in New York, while simultaneously keeping the immigrant bargain. My question in this 2001 interview refers to various conversations in the early and mid-1990s.

> JUANA: Yeah, because it was like an image. "Oh, Mexicans are little, short, and ugly—and Indians." And I didn't want to be part of that. But . . .
>
> RS: So I remember another thing you said, in an interview that we did then [1994]. You said that you were watching a TV show—"Cristina" or something—and there was this thing about the flower vendors. And . . . part of the reason of the group was to show people that Mexicans weren't just flower vendors. . . .
>
> JUANA: Yeah, we talked about that a lot. It's like, we need to get more educated Mexicans. First of all, we're a very rich culture. We have a lot of culture here. The thing is that people that go over there, the poor people that come from the town, you know . . . so that's their image of what Mexico is or Mexicans are. But it's not like that. You know, we always talk, we need to give our children education. . . .
>
> ELIANA: [In our meetings] we used to share, our personal things. . . . We used to talk about it—what do you think, give me your opinion on this—we used

to talk about, you know, our problems. And sometimes we even used to cry, yeah. . . . We wouldn't only talk about the pueblo, but our personal lives as well. Yeah. And then we would try to help each other. Like, you know, like, let's lead her to the right path, or, you know, it's like helping, because we went through it. . . . Like, to encourage each other, you know, education-wise, if you need help with school or anything, we used to help each other with that, you know?

JUANA: Or, you know, like, you're young, you can do it; you should take advantage of this, or, you know, your parents worked so hard, why should you go on in the wrong path? And, you know, a lot of things. Like I said, a lot of people, even our generation, instead of taking the route, take education, get educated and stuff, [they] get married, have kids, and stop going to school. And it just becomes the same circle over and over, and we're never gonna get out of that. . . . But, you know, we haven't probably gotten to where we wish we were, but we've gone a lot further, you know, and I think we should be proud of that, you know. We all have decent jobs. . . . We're not, you know, having to work in factories like our parents had to, you know, and stuff like that. . . .

ELIANA: We have a different lifestyle [than] our parents did.

JUANA: Right, but I think that's good because that's what they wanted, that's what they worked so hard for, so we wouldn't do the same thing.

The group did several related things at the same time for its members. It fought against the image of Mexicans as poor and un-educated, while also creating a context for its members in which they could talk explicitly about upward mobility and link it with their parents' sacrifice. In other words, they simultaneously fought against the image of Mexicans as powerless immigrants and against the "wrong path" that they saw many of their peers taking, as they worked to realize some of the promise that their parents had held out for them. They wanted to be upwardly mobile, keep the immigrant bargain, and have a "different lifestyle" and work more "comfortably," as their parents wanted for them. By doing this, they also differentiated themselves from the blacks and Puerto Ricans with whom they felt they wanted to have nothing in common, despite attending the same schools and living in the same neighborhoods.

At this point in the interview, I told them that it sounded like they were describing the immigrant bargain, whereby the parents' sacrifice in leaving home is redeemed by the success of their children in the United States, and I asked them whether they thought they had kept their part of the bargain.

JUANA: Not fully. . . . I think we could have done a lot more . . . but I think we've done pretty well, we haven't fallen into the routine that was set for us [not finishing school, getting pregnant, marrying young, and so on]. . . . I should've been farther. . . . I left school for one or two years . . . wasted time.

Honestly, but like I said, you know, we have decent jobs, we can travel, and you know . . . I feel like I've kept my . . . you know, so far . . . I did okay . . . [but] we still have to put out that money and cumplir nuestra promesa [keep our promise] to build the chapel.

RS: What's the bargain? How would you describe it?

JUANA: I guess they've never asked anything from us. . . . But just to go to school, you know, and that was it.

ELIANA: To get an education for us. To be able to survive. . . .

JUANA: Like my mother used to tell me, "Finish school, get yourself something that, whatever happens to you, you'll be able to take care of yourself, to get a job. Then after that, you could marry."

In his 1997 interview, Walker also had a generally positive assessment of the mobility of members of the Ticuani Youth Group and noted that each member had either opened a business or gone to college and acquired a profession.[6]

The group also helped to change life trajectories as its members moved through adolescence. Juana, for instance, felt that the group and her visits to Ticuani had a significant impact on her own life. From not wanting to be Mexican as a young girl, she embraced her Mexican-ness in both positive and negative ways in her midteens. First, she became a female gang member. She did not participate in any hard-core gang activities but was the girlfriend of a gang member and cut school a lot to go to hooky parties. She was nervous about some of the violence she saw among the men. She said that she came to understand her Mexican-ness in a positive way at the age of fifteen "when I came here"—to Ticuani. She suddenly realized that being Mexican was not about being a "short, ugly Indian" but about the respect that people demonstrated for each other in the town and about the connection she felt to her roots in Ticuani.

Despite not getting along with some of its members, she joined the Ticuani Youth Group when they invited her. She would later credit her involvement with the group as an important factor in her transformation: "The group took me away from a lot of bad stuff. . . . I was hanging out in gangs. . . . I came [to Ticuani] for a week . . . I found people like me." When she started attending meetings, she not only discovered people like herself, but she "saw people doing something." She noted that another group member who had a job and was attending college was someone who "had her money, and I wanted that for me and for my kids," because, she remarked, "life would be easier."

After coming back from her first trip to Ticuani, she started spending less time with her gang friends and more time with the group, stopped cutting school so much, and graduated from high school. The group gave her different models to follow. Instead of seeking a closer link with her Mexican-ness through the "lost little kids" in the gang—who were mainly teen migrants—she was able to find people she could also identify with but who showed her a different way to be Mexican. Since that time Juana has gone to college and works now in a responsible office job.

The linkage between the immigrant bargain and doing well in school and work was a recurrent theme in the conversation of these youth and others in discussing the group and the situation of their peers. Both doing well in their own lives and showing their elders that they loved the pueblo and had a desire to help back in Ticuani were strategies for vindicating their parents' sacrifice. These strategies said to their parents: Look, we have not forgotten or rejected where we come from, and we are doing well, as you wanted, to realize the promise of your sacrifice.

GENERATIONAL CONFLICT, LIFE COURSE INERTIA, AND THE DISSIPATION OF THE TICUANI YOUTH GROUP: THE VIEW FROM 2001

In the eight to ten years since the Ticuani Youth Group's heyday, it is clear that it has not become an enduring transnational institution in the way that some had hoped it would. Although its members will not say it is moribund, they are also too busy to revive it and have not organized any activities in several years. The funds they gathered were never actually donated to Ticuani. At one point the money was used to bail out a member of the group on charges that were ultimately dismissed; the remaining funds raised now sit in an account, awaiting the reassembly of the group so that it can act. In addition, the Ticuani Youth Group members and others in their generational cohort return less frequently to Ticuani—they now make one trip every year or two or three, and usually for special occasions, instead of making one or more trips annually, as they did before.

That this institution has not persisted in its original form, as has the New York Ticuani Committee, is not to say that these particular members of the second generation do not participate in transnational life. They do so in different forms, and the cohort of teens coming up behind them are also beginning to enter into this kind of transnational adolescence, for some of the same reasons as their young adult siblings.

There are several reasons why the Ticuani Youth Group lost its steam and failed to institutionalize itself in the same way as the committee. One involved the relations between the first-generation institution of the committee and the second- and 1.5-generation and teen-migrant institution of the youth group. As its members tell the story, they started the group independently but also attempted to work cooperatively with the committee. But the committee wanted the group to become a sort of auxiliary to itself and to submit to its authority. For example, the committee had asked the youth group to do a census of all Ticuanenses in New York for them. The youth group balked; they had been considering some other kind of collaboration or coordination of independent action, not simply becoming youthful labor for their older counterparts. Youth group members felt as if the committee did not understand the myriad pressures they faced as students or aspiring young entrepreneurs. Walker explained the problem in the relationship:

> Well, almost all of the group had their own business or were in the university or had a profession. . . . It was a more or less well educated group. . . . With the committee we were not in accord always, they were very different than us. Then this was very difficult. In the committee, you are talking of a man of fifty years or so, and his ideas are very different than yours. . . . So they put us to do the census of the Ticuanenses in New York for the simple reason that we were young, and that we had more time to go up and down stairs in buildings. But that was work! So you can imagine that we thought, Why do the census that has nothing to do with anything? It is hard, visiting every house. You don't know how people are going to receive you.

Walker and his peers felt that the committee not only failed to understand that, despite their youth, the members of the youth group were all working, but that their group was independent of the committee: "If we work on a committee for the town, we would be very independent. We would not work with contributions or cooperations . . . or with any committee that had to do with the president of Ticuani. We were definitely apart . . . neutral. With no one."

The problem was based in several of the dimensions of first-generation transnationalization and captures some of the limits of locally based transnationalization among the second generation. Here, the aspirations and lack of time of the second generation—due to their educational and occupation pursuits, signs of assimilation—conflicted with the requirements of participating in the work of this particular transnational institution, the New York Committee. Ticuani also occupied a less central space in the social world of the second generation, who saw the town increasingly as a place for vacation and status demonstration but did not see their futures bound up with the political future of the town. The problem is also one of regenerating transnational institutions. The New York Committee could not work out a relationship with this younger generation's self-created institution, just as it had not been successful in drawing other younger teen migrants or members of the 1.5 or second generations into its work. A lesson is that assimilation and transnationalization can work in complementary ways when they engage the interest and ability of upwardly mobile second-generationers to participate in transnational life, but also at cross-purposes when the pressures of this same upward mobility allow less time for transnational life as these young people pass into early adulthood.

A related problem was that the group members saw the committee as "very machista." They felt that the committee did not want to listen to them because their group was largely women and because they were young. Group members contrasted the progressive structure of their organization—they elected two presidents, one woman and one man—with the "macho" way the committee was organized—all men, with the same president for its whole history. They also saw the departure of the one woman who had worked in a responsible position on the committee, Marla Lanita, as a macho expulsion of a woman who had tried to be independent (though she herself refuses to characterize her departure this way). In a 2001 interview, they summarized their view of relations between the committee and the youth group:

> They're older men, and they think different. . . . It [the committee] was mostly men, and we [the group] were mostly women. They didn't think we were capable. They were always opposing our ideas. Marla Lanita [who served briefly as the committee's treasurer], they pushed her out because she was a woman. Ellos son muy poco liberal [they are not very liberal]. Don Miguel didn't even let [the female president of the youth group] finish her sentences! . . . We had too much respect. But my father would have smacked me for disrespecting an older man. The committee is very machista.

In the opinion of these youth group members, relations with the committee were also strained because "we had a woman and a man president, so it was never, like, the man thing. . . . we all had very strong attitudes. We did discuss things. But no dejamos dominar por el hombre [we did not let things be dominated by the men]."

In their telling, the egalitarian structure of the group and the youth of its members conflicted with the macho style of the committee. The younger generation felt that the women in their number were not accorded any respect by the older generation, and that the committee would never give them the authority to do real work with them.

A third problem was that the youth group members—particularly the 1.5ers, the teen migrants, and those who had lived in the village as teens after being raised in the United States—did not wish to get too involved in what they considered to be Ticuani's corrupt politics. They talked about how undemocratic and violent it was in the Mexican village and said that talking to the wrong person had gotten people killed in the past. With their futures looking bright in the United States, why enter into that? One important member of the youth group described the relationship between the committee and municipal authorities:

> According to them, they [the committee and municipal authorities] work together, and according to them, what they let you know is that they work together, but in this we are defensively not informed, or maybe you hear rumors and nothing else. But to me it looks like they work together because they collect the cooperations [donations] here and send the money there, it's logical that they are together. For this, what they do, only they know. They speak apart, and they never tell anything of what they have said, never include anyone, including the people in Ticuani, to tell them how they work. . . . But we want democracy on a world level, and in Ticuani there is none. There, there is no vote when they choose the president. There, only five or six people decide who will be president. We need democracy because always who decides should be the people but in Ticuani it never is.

Although they saw the town's political future as relevant to their own lives in important ways, they did not see any way to change things in Ticuani. According to these youth, its corrupt politics was an absolute impediment to deepening their involvement in Ticuani public life.

In addition to the problems working with the committee, the group fell victim to the life course as its members moved from adolescence into early adulthood and began to be weighed down with such adult responsibilities as jobs and children. The youth group had been formed when its members were mainly in college or just out—in their late teens to midtwenties. In the intervening eight or ten years, most had married and had children or taken on responsible jobs with inflexible hours and greater time commitments. These changes had recentered their lives in the challenging business of raising children with, often, both parents working. Hence, they had less time for travel to Ticuani and less time to engage in Ticuani-related activities. Moreover, some group members married people not from Ticuani; for women especially this usually led them away from participation in Ticuani activities. In 2001 they described the dissipation of the organization:

> At first, every Saturday or Sunday we had meetings, and we'd plan events for the summer. For two years. Then the group started to disintegrate. Two people married outside Ticuani. . . . It was harder to get together than when we were all single. . . . Gradually, less people came to the meetings. Slowly, then only four or five members were coming. We all said, "Even when we get married and have children we won't stop coming." . . . But people started leaving the group. AC married someone from another pueblo, and since you usually follow your husband's group, they were gone.

The group's egalitarian gender structure and the changing division of labor between the first and second generations were also important factors that constrained any emulation by the Ticuani Youth Group of the model of the New York Committee. Most first-generation women worked to some extent outside the home but also assumed almost complete responsibility for domestic work. This freed up the first-generation men to go collecting "cooperations" on nights and weekends while their wives and children waited at home. Many second-generation women renegotiated this gendered division of labor, or at least were attempting to do so (Hondagneu-Sotelo 1994; Gonzalez de la Rocha and Escobar Latapi 1991). Many men were also doing more voluntarily, such as spending more time with their children and less time with their male friends, as their fathers had done (Gutmann 1995). Hence, the men did not have the freedom to conduct public affairs that their fathers had while their wives took care of the home. The women did not feel that they too served by staying home and waiting. And neither the man nor the woman in most of these couples saw the sacrifice of lost family time as being compensated by the prestige and honor they might get as leaders in the community, as both men and women among the first generation did. Similar changes are happening with young migrant families in Mexico, where women have become less willing to wait at home while their husbands migrate.

ENDURING EFFECTS OF THE TICUANI YOUTH GROUP AND OTHER SECOND-GENERATION RETURN

That the demands of young adulthood have crowded out much of the time that the second and 1.5 generations would have used for youth group activities in the past does not mean that they do not still participate in transnational life, nor that transnational life does not persist in other forms or continue to have important effects. Many second-generationers who have entered fully into young adulthood—marrying, having children, taking on jobs—continue to return to Ticuani, not only for special events but because they feel close to their relatives there—and to God. The dedication to Padre Jesus that emerges in adolescence among many in the second generation (analyzed in Smith 2001a) persists into young adulthood.

When Eliana was enduring a difficult pregnancy, she promised Padre Jesus that if her child was born healthy, she would bring him back to Ticuani for baptism.

> I used to get a lot of urinary tract infections and inflammation of the kidney. So it was hard. I was taking antibiotics during my pregnancy, and I made a promise to Padre Jesus that if everything would be fine, I would do Xavier's christening again [in Ticuani] . . . I guess also when we come back here we feel a lot closer to God. [*Others in interview voice agreement.*] Like, more religious, like, we come here and the first thing you do when you come, you like, thank God. [*Others agree.*] That you're here. It's just—like going to church in New York is a lot different from coming to church here. . . .
>
> I took a lot of medication, and I was concerned that maybe Xavier would be disabled, you know, because that was one of the risks. The doctor said,

you know, you're gonna be on antibiotics for some time. He even suggested that . . . maybe I shouldn't have the baby, maybe I should have an abortion. And I wasn't willing to do that. I was like, I'm gonna have the baby, and I'm just gonna pray to Padrecito, and hopefully everything will be fine. And that's when I promised that I would bring Xavier.

When she was blessed with a healthy child, the entire family returned from Brooklyn for the baptism of the child in Ticuani's beautiful old church and the reception that followed.

For many, the friends they made in the group remained their central friendship group some eight to ten years later, partly because they met as teenagers, and partly because of the intensity of the experiences they had together in their weeks or months in Ticuani. Juana described her Ticuani Youth Group friends as "still my main friends. Carolina's mother called me her mugre. . . . I see [Carolina] almost every day." Calling Juana Carolina's "mugre" was a gentle way of teasing her; "mugre" is the Mexican word for the dirt under one's fingernails. Juana's descriptions of the group's gatherings suggest the closeness of an extended family: "I mean, we see them, like if we're ready to go out, we'll see them, or like I said, when they cook [a meal for everyone] in their house, we'll see them, or when there's a birthday, we all get together. We still pass Christmas together. Yeah, over Christmas, we all get together and stuff like that." The emergence of such primary, enduring friendship groups has been linked in studies of the effects of Jewish and Protestant religious camps and programs to the enduring importance of religion and ethnicity (Friedman and Davis 1998), and anecdotally to the effects of the experience of Jewish summer camps in the Catskills.

Ticuani had other emotional and social offerings for young adults. For example, just as the teens in New York saw many of their friends mainly in Ticuani Youth Group meetings because their parents restricted their ability to go out, the young adults' social lives were restricted by their jobs, children, and limited free time. So young adults could also return to Ticuani each year knowing that they would find some of their old friends, or that, with a little planning, a small reunion could be organized. Juana related her experience to the group in a 2001 interview. Now twenty-six years old, employed full-time, and living with her boyfriend, she described her intense desire to return to Ticuani after a three-year absence:

> It means a lot to me to come back. You know, for three years. . . . I used to
> see all my people come back, and I would stay [in New York], you know,
> and that felt horrible. But now, I'm like, I'm ecstatic. Like, that night that I
> flew here, I wanted to come straight here, I didn't want to stop anywhere
> else [not] Puebla . . . Mexico [City]. I wanted to come here. And I came
> straight from the airport.

For Juana, as for many others, this intense emotional attachment did not exist when she was a child, but rather formed through her participation in Ticuani's emerging adolescent rituals. The passion in her words testifies to the continued importance of Ticuani in her social and emotional world.

Young adult returnees also have important roles to play in the younger adolescent rituals, both formal and informal. Carolina, who still returned most years, helped out the local organizers with the beauty pageant for the young women. She helped them learn how to walk in the desired way, to put on their makeup, and to speak in public. The presence of these older women in their twenties or early thirties was important. Also, the annual return provided a context in which these single men and women could meet other single people with whom they were certain to have at least Ticuani in common. And many of these young adults still derived great satisfaction from participating in the religious and civic rituals and ceremonies related to the Feast of Padre Jesus. Moreover, the returns provided opportunities for multigenerational socialization that resembled the extended family that Ticuani really was. For example, young adults in their twenties danced at the Baile with their younger cousins in their teens, while the former's children ran about the dance floor. The same group would walk together in a religious procession the next day, and then go to los toros (a rodeo) together that afternoon.

CONCLUSION

This chapter has attempted to analyze how second-generation transnational life is embedded within processes of migration, on the one hand, and processes of settlement and assimilation, on the other hand. It has focused on one conscious attempt to create a second-generation transnational institution, the Ticuani Youth Group. The chapter reviewed both continuities and obstacles and limits in the reproduction of transnational life between the first and second generations. It located the second generation's primary motivations for wanting to participate in transnational life in the assimilative pressures it was facing in the United States. The second generation used its return to Mexico to reject negative images of Mexican-ness—as either powerless undocumented workers or dangerous gangsters—and to embrace a different version of Mexican-ness. In doing so, many in the second generation returned to New York with better images of what it meant to be Mexican, but they also often engaged the immigrant analogy. By defining their Mexican-ness in part in contradistinction to the social location of blacks and U.S.-born Puerto Ricans, Mexicans sought to negotiate their ambiguous social location within the white-black dichotomy that has run like a fault line through American life. In recent years, applying the immigrant analogy in the Mexican case has become more complex as Mexican youth have become more involved in gangs, and as some in the second generation have sought to put social distance between themselves and their compatriots and co-ethnics.

Another impetus for participation in transnational life has been the desire of the second generation to keep the immigrant bargain with their parents (Suárez-Orozco and Suárez-Orozco 1995, 2001; Smith 2000, 2001a; Guerrero-Rippberger 1999) and to show them and the pueblo that they have not forgotten their roots. That it matters so much to these second-generation youth what people living several thousand miles away think of them is an important indication that some socially significant processes are at work here. Their lived experiences going to the town, especially during their adolescence, made Ticuani an important reference point for them. Keeping the immigrant bargain—by going to school and retaining links to Ticuani and its culture—is an important part of settlement and assimilation and sets the stage for transnationalization.

Yet this analysis has shown that a desire to keep the immigrant bargain does not lead to an automatic replication of the same forms of transnational life between generations. Indeed, the problems plaguing the reproduction of a second-generation transnational institution on the model of the New York Committee of the first-generation Ticuani migrants were myriad. These included the uneven power relations between the first and second generations, the second generation's desire to be autonomous, and the first generation's failure to establish a mechanism for "passing the torch" to the third generation. Moreover, the more "Americanized" second generation perceived the "machismo" of the committee as an obstacle to their collaboration. While the youth group adopted an explicitly gender-neutral governing structure, all of the committee's main players have always been men, with only one brief exception. These strong differences in gender roles and strategies contributed to the disjuncture between the two organizations.

Also contributing to the differences between the first- and second-generation forms of transnational life are their different relations to the processes of settlement and transnationalization and life course (Levitt 2001; Smith 1997, 2001a; Portes 2001). As the second generation moves into adolescence, participation in transnational life becomes incredibly important for many of them, but the demands of young adult life, beginning in their midtwenties, lessen their ability to participate. In particular, they lose their freedom to travel as they get responsible jobs, have children, and move into their own apartments with their own rents to pay. The urgency of transnational life seems to peak during mid- to late adolescence, particularly in the high school and college-age years, when the saliency of peer groups and ethnic identity increases. Part of the failure of the Ticuani Youth Group to endure as a second-generation transnational institution can be traced to this problem of aging members being more encumbered and preoccupied with the settlement process and their own upward mobility, and by their resolution of many adolescent identity issues.

But to say that transnational life changes does not mean that it does not persist in some form, or that it does not merit study. Indeed, many members of the second generation bring their children back to Ticuani for baptism, return with their families for vacation, and maintain important friendship groups formed in their Ticuani or youth group experiences long after their peak involvement in these transnational activities. These practices are especially intense among former Ticuani Youth Group members. Moreover, Ticuani itself is now set up to accommodate such types of return and involvement. The water runs all day long, there are several video stores in town, and new restaurants are opening up that sell New York–style food, including pizza made by an ex-migrant who learned the trade in New York. Moreover, second-generation people build new houses, maintain old houses, or inherit or use their parents' houses in Ticuani, adding to the sharply inverse relationship between the number of people in the town and the number of houses.

This chapter thus engages both the assimilationist critique of a transnational perspective—that assimilation is overtaking it—and the strident transnationalist position—that it offers some third way of being for immigrants. In my analysis, it becomes clear that assimilative pressures are clearly an important factor in producing transnational life in the second generation: not only do those pressures supply a main impetus for going to Ticuani, but migrants use them to differentiate themselves from the negative images of Mexicans in New York. Hence, assimilation helps create transnationalism. But assimilation clearly combines with other factors to limit its identical reproduction in the second generation. Treating everyone involved in transnational life as equally "transnational" does not capture the processes described in this chapter.

In closing, I would like to make two more observations about the durability of transnational life among the second generation. First, suppose for the sake of argument that transnational life will sunset after this second generation, let's say even in another ten years. As I have described it here and elsewhere in greater depth (Smith 1995, 1998, 2001a), Ticuani transnational life, by persisting since the late 1960s, has lasted for at least fifty years and through two generations. It has also had significant effects on the experiences of migration, assimilation, ethnicity, and racialization of first- and second-generation Ticuanenses. It is not a "third way" that produces a completely new transnational or global world, but it certainly seems like something that is worth keeping an eye on to see what effects it will actually have in our lifetimes. And while there has been extensive documentation of transnational life in history in the first generation (see Foner 1999; Glick-Schiller 1999; Guarnizo and Smith 1998; Portes 2001; Fouron and Glick-Schiller, this volume), there has been almost no documentation of it among the second generation in the earlier wave of migration. Ostergren's (1988) thorough study of Swedish immigration over the course of nearly one hundred years discusses extensive transnational political and social flows between Minnesota and Rattvik, Sweden, among the first generation, but not among the second generation, even though their lives in Minnesota were quite "Swedish." Ostergren describes this as a "community transplanted": they spoke Swedish, sought spouses in

Swedish marriage pools, read Swedish-language newspapers, and had their social life organized in almost identical ways in Minnesota and Sweden. Yet there was no mention of significant return among the second generation. Similarly, studies of Italian migration document return rates for migrants of between one-third and two-thirds and extensive transnational activity, yet they do not mention any significant second-generation transnational activity. This includes contemporary accounts like Foerster's (1919) massive volume, Child's (1943) *Italian or American: The Second Generation in Conflict,* and more recent work (Gabaccia 2000).

A second observation is that even in the Ticuani case there are developments not analyzed here that point to a continuation of other forms of transnationalization and transnational life. I will sketch two of these examples, which are analyzed at greater length elsewhere (Smith 2001a) but are worth mentioning here because they open up the cramped horizons that the assimilationist objection attempts to put on the study of transnational life. The first observation is that the assimilation of teen migrants in New York has changed the pattern and content of transnational life significantly. In a nutshell: the extensive family reunification stemming from IRCA (Immigration Reform and Control Act of 1986) in the later 1980s and early 1990s contributed to a huge surge in the Mexican population in New York, a hostile reaction by native minorities, especially Puerto Ricans, and rapid growth in the Mexican gangs in New York. One result has been an increase in the number of migrants who are coming to the United States as young boys or teens instead of as older teens or young adults. They experience a harsh secondary socialization and end up pressured to join gangs, then drop out of school and encounter either legal or gang violence problems. To escape they end up returning to Mexico, where they resume their gang activities, profoundly changing youth culture there, transnationalizing it in new ways. New York gangs now organize much of youth life in Ticuani. Analytically, this is a case of migration producing pressurized assimilation and causing remigration back to Mexico and a transnationalization of youth gangs. This constellation of relations and structures will not disappear quickly, and it merits further analysis.

A second example of how transnational life may persist in the Ticuani case comes in the form of the extended return visits of older, retired first-generation "pioneer" women migrants. These pioneer women migrated many years before and have retired in the United States and are receiving small pensions or Social Security. Most of them also perform child-care duties for their second-generation adult children. A significant minority of them take their third-generation charges back to Mexico to live with them for one or two months or more during the winter and summer vacations from school. These visits enable them and their grandchildren to enjoy nature and the outdoor world in ways not possible in New York and provide cultural, linguistic, and religious immersion that seems to be contributing to the development of a Ticuani identity and practices among the young third generation. In this case, we have a first-generation woman taking care of her third-generation children in Ticuani while their second-generation parents work in New York. This kind of significant life experience among the third generation is something that is not documented in the literature for the last great wave of migration and is likely to make the processes of assimilation, settlement, and transnationalization play out very differently.

NOTES

1. My argument benefits from Basch et al. 1994; Guarnizo and Smith 1998; and Portes et al. 1999.
2. Many embrace the immigrant analogy, whereby the greater socioeconomic success of the descendants of white immigrants compared to that of African Americans is used as evidence of the latter's inferiority rather than of the effects of systematic discrimination in the way the two groups were incorporated into the United States.
3. The most intensive research periods were 1990 to 1993 and 1997 to 2000. My thanks to Ph.D. student Sandra Lara, and undergraduates Sara Guerrero-Rippberger, Carolina Perez, Griscelda Perez, and Agustin Vecino for their excellent research assistance in different parts of this project.
4. Other useful discussions can be found in Guarnizo and Smith 1998; Portes et al. 1999; Portes 2001; Smith 2001a, 1998; Basch et al. 1994; and Glick-Schiller 1999.
5. All translations of excerpts from interviews are by the author.
6. The youth group's upward mobility also made it a subject of ridicule, as in one youth who called them a "bunch of fucking conceiteds" (pinches presumidos), and others who made clear in our conversations that they were not part of that crowd.

REFERENCES

Basch, L., N. Glick-Schiller, and C. Blanc-Szanton. 1994. *Nations Unbound*. Langhorne, Penn.: Gordon and Breach.

Child, Irving. 1943. *Italian or American: The Second Generation in Conflict*. New Haven, Conn.: Yale University Press.

Du Bois, W. E. B. 1969 [1901]. *The Souls of Black Folk*. In *Three Negro Classics: Up From Slavery*. New York: Avon Books.

————. 1992 [1935]. *Black Reconstruction in America, 1860–1880*. New York: Atheneum.

Foerster, Robert. 1919. *The Italian Emigration of Our Times*. Cambridge, Mass.: Harvard University Press.

Foner, Nancy. 1999. "What's So New About Transnationalism? New York Immigrants Today and at the Turn of the Century." *Diaspora* 6(3): 355–75.

Friedman, Nathalie, and Perry Davis. 1998. *Faithful Youth: A Study of the National Conference of Synagogue Youth*. New York: National Council of Synagogue Youth.

Gabaccia, Donna. 2000. *Italy's Many Diasporas*. Seattle: University of Washington Press.

Glick-Schiller, Nina. 1999. "Transmigrants and Nation-States: Something Old and Something New in the Immigrant Experience." In *Handbook of International Migration: The American Experience*, edited by C. Hirschman, J. DeWind, and P. Kasinitz. New York: Russell Sage Foundation.

Gonzalez de la Rocha, Mercedes, and Agustin Escobar Latapi. 1991. *Social Responses to Mexico's Economic Crisis of the 1980s*. La Jolla: Center for U.S. Mexico Studies.

Guarnizo, Luis, and M. P. Smith. 1998. *Transnationalism from Below*. New Brunswick, N.J.: Transaction.

Guerrero-Rippberger, Sara. 1999. " 'But for the Day of Tomorrow': Negotiating Femininity in a New York-Mex Identity." Senior Thesis, Sociology Department, Barnard College.

Gutmann, Matthew. 1995. *The Meanings of Macho: Being a Man in Mexico City*. Berkeley: University of California Press.

Hondagneu-Sotelo, Pierette. 1994. *Gendered Transitions: Mexican Experiences of Migration*. Berkeley: University of California Press.

Ignatiev, Joel. 1995. *How the Irish Became White*. New York: Routledge.

Levitt, Peggy. 2001. *The Transnational Villagers*. Berkeley: University of California Press.

Omi, Michael, and M. Winant. 1986. *Racial formation in the United States: From the 1960s to the 1980s*. New York: Routledge & Kegan Paul.

Ostergren, Robert. 1988. *A Community Transplanted: The Trans-Atlantic Experience of a Swedish Immigrant Settlement in the Upper Midwest, 1835–1915*. Madison: University of Wisconsin Press.

Portes, Alejandro. 2001. "Introduction: The Debates and Significance of Immigrant Transnationalism." *Global Networks* 1(3): 181–94.

Portes, A., L. Guarnizo, and P. Landholdt. 1999. "Introduction: Pitfalls and Promise of an Emergent Research Field." *Ethnic and Racial Studies* 22: 217–38.

Portes, A., and R. Rumbaut. 2001. *Legacies*. Berkeley: University of California Press.

Roediger, David. 1991. *The Wages of Whiteness*. New York: Routledge.

Sanchez Jankowski, Martin. 1995. "The Significance of Status in Race Relations." In *The Bubbling Cauldron: Race, Ethnicity, and the Urban Crisis*, edited by Michael Peter Smith and Joe R. Feagin. Minneapolis: University of Minnesota Press.

Smith, Robert C. 1995. "Los Ausentes Siempre Presentes: The Imagining, Making and Politics of a Transnational Migrant Community Between Ticuani, Puebla, Mexico, and New York City." Ph.D. diss., Department of Political Science, Columbia University.

———. 1996. "Mexicans in New York City: Membership and Incorporation of New Immigrant Group." In *Latinos in New York*, edited by S. Baver and G. Haslip Viera. Notre Dame, Ind.: University of Notre Dame Press.

———. 1997. "Transnational Migration, Assimilation and Political Community." In *The City and the World*, edited by Margaret Crahan and Alberto Vourvoulias-Bush. New York: Council on Foreign Relations.

———. 1998. "Transnational Localities: Technology, Community, the Politics of Membership within the Context of Mexico-U.S. Migration." In *Transnationalism From Below: Journal of Urban and Comparative Research*, edited by Michael Peter Smith and Luis Eduardo Guarnizo. New Brunswick: Transaction.

———. 1999. "Social Location, Generation and Life Course as Social Processes Shaping Second Generation Transnational Life." Draft paper (June).

———. 2000. "How Durable and New is Transnational Life? Historical Retrieval through Local Comparison." *Diaspora* 9(3).

———. 2001a. *Migration, Settlement and Transnational Life*. Book manuscript.

———. 2001b. "Mexicans: Social, Educational, Economic and Political Problems and Prospects in New York." In *New Immigrants in New York*, edited by Nancy Foner. New York: Columbia University Press.

———. 2002. "Gender, Ethnicity and Race in School and Work Outcomes of Second Generation Mexican Americans." In *Latinos in the Twenty-First Century*, edited by Marcelo Suárez-Orozco and Mariela Paez. Berkeley: University of California Press.

Suárez-Orozco, Carola, and Marcelo Suárez-Orozco. 1995. *Transformations: Immigration, Family Life, and Achievement Motivation among Latino Adolescents*. Stanford, Calif.: Stanford University Press.

Suárez-Orozco, Marcelo, and Carola Suárez-Orozco. 2001. *Children of Immigration*. Cambridge, Mass.: Harvard University Press.

Thompson, Ginger. 2001. "An Exodus of Migrant Families Is Bleeding Mexico's Heartland" *New York Times,* June 17, section 1: 1.

Chapter 6

The Generation of Identity: Redefining the Second Generation Within a Transnational Social Field

Georges E. Fouron and Nina Glick-Schiller

GEORGES WOKE UP laughing. He had been dreaming of Haiti, not the Haiti he had visited last summer, but the Haiti of his youth. But it wasn't actually the Haiti of his youth either, as he realized when he tried to explain to his wife, Rolande, the feeling of happiness with which he had awakened. He was walking down Grand-Ruc, the main street of his hometown of Aux Cayes. The sun was shining, the streets were clean, and the port was bustling with ships. He and his friends were laughing, joking, and having a wonderful time. Once he was awake, Georges laughed again, but this time not from joy. Georges had been dreaming of a Haiti that never was.

The Haiti of Georges's youth had actually been more nightmare than joy. The Duvalier dictatorship was clamping down on all dissent. Wearing an Afro, speaking out at school, or joining any form of organization could lead to disappearance, beatings, imprisonment, torture, and murder. Besides being afraid, Georges was constantly anxious about how he would get an education and find some sort of a job. He couldn't even take his next meal for granted, although his father was the director of a technical school and his mother did sewing and fancy embroidery to supplement the family income.

Georges's joyful dream of his dear, sweet homeland would have been familiar to immigrants from around the world whose days as well as nights are filled with memories of things past. In the pain of resettling in a new country, reminiscence is often replaced by nostalgia. The deprivations or repression that prompted migration often are put aside. This nostalgia persists even though for Georges and for millions of contemporary immigrants from all over the world, the longed-for homeland is a location of ongoing experience. These immigrants are transmigrants living simultaneously in two countries. They participate in personal and political events in both their homeland and their new land. They live their lives across borders in a social world that includes the often harsh realities of their homeland. Nonetheless, many immigrants continue, as does Georges, to dream of a homeland in which "the sun is shining and the streets are clean."

What of the next generation, who were born or grew up in the United States rather than in Haiti? How have they been affected by the fact that the pattern of their lives is shaped not only by their parents' nostalgia but also by their families' enduring transnational connections? And if, as we and a growing number of scholars have been documenting, immigrants' transnational social relations connect homeland and new land into a single social field, how do we delimit the boundaries of the generation born to immigrants, the second generation? After all, many young people living in Haiti are also children of immigrant families, living in Haiti while their parents or other relatives who maintain their households live incorporated into the United States.

In this chapter, we employ a transnational perspective to examine the second generation. We look at the effects of transnational migration on young people born in the United States of Haitian parentage and on young people living in Haiti within transnational social fields. We also examine the similarities and differences in identification with Haiti between children of Haitian parentage living in the United States and Haitian youth born in Haiti. Our conclusions are based on research we conducted on Haitian transnational migration and Haitian ethnic, racial, and national identities in New York and in Haiti. This research extended from 1969 to 1999. When we describe the experience of one of the authors, we use the third person, referring to "Georges" or "Nina." To describe our joint analysis we speak in the first person plural. Between 1985 and 1997, in addition to participant observation, we conducted surveys, two in the United States and three in Haiti. In total we interviewed 229 poor and middle-class people and asked about the relationship between those who have left Haiti and those left behind.

To discuss the experience of a generation living within the daily realities of transnational migration, we will use quotations from interviews conducted in 1996 and 1997 with two samples of young people, one in New York and one in Haiti, and observations of a conference called in New York in 1996 to build what became the Haitian American Community Action Network. While we draw on data from all the interviews and discuss the identities of the second generation and how they vary over time and in location, degree of education, class position, and political involvement, we highlight the voices of youth who served as the unpaid staff of a radio program in Aux Cayes, Haiti, young people who participated in the 1996 conference in New York, and Haitian students at the State University of New York at Stony Brook. We present these particular voices because they contribute to the public debate within Haitian transnational social fields about the identity of the second generation and the relationship between those in Haiti and the Haitian diaspora. However, we wish to stress that there is not a single voice of Haitian youth, either in Haiti or in the diaspora. There are many experiences and imaginings of Haiti, of the United States, and of their relationship.[1] We use our findings to argue for a new and expanded concept of the second generation and to examine long distance nationalism as an ideology of belonging that extends across the territorial boundaries of states, as well as across generational divides (Anderson 1993, 1994; Glick-Schiller and Fouron 2001).

DEFINITION OF TERMS

A growing number of scholars are constructing a "transnational perspective for the study of migration" and documenting the connections that first-generation immigrants to the United States who are part of the "post-1965" immigration maintain with their native land (Glick-Schiller, Basch, and Szanton-Blanc 1992; Glick-Schiller and Fouron 1990; Goldring 1996; Guarnizo 1997; Kearney 1991; Mahler 1998; Margolis 1998; Portes, Guarnizo, and Landolt 1999;

Rouse 1991, 1992; Smith 1995; Smith and Guarnizo 1998). Although there is now an emerging scholarship of transnationalism, there is no common understanding about what is meant by transnational migration. The effort to create a common set of definitions for the study of transnational migration is complicated by the fact that political leaders in many emigrant-sending countries are now working to engage their emigrant populations in economic or political projects. These leaders have developed a set of policies and laws that redefine membership in these emigrant-sending states, in some cases by constitutional changes that provide dual nationality to transnational migrants and their children (Basch, Glick-Schiller, and Szanton-Blanc 1994; Guarnizo 1998; Graham 1996; Sanchez 1997; Smith 1997, 1998b). Even those states that have not changed their legal definitions have formulated tax regulations or created public agencies that strive to incorporate emigrants and their descendants into the sending society.

To facilitate the study of the effects of transnational migration on the political identities of immigrants and their descendants, we propose the following definitions. Transnational migration is a process of movement and settlement across international borders in which individuals maintain or build multiple networks of connection to their country of origin while at the same time settling in a new country. Persons who live their lives across borders so that they are simultaneously incorporated in two or more states can be defined as "transmigrants" (Glick-Schiller, Basch, and Szanton-Blanc 1992, 1). That is to say, such migrants do more than stay in touch with family members left behind. They organize their daily economic, familial, religious, and social relations within networks that extend across the borders of two nation-states. Transnational connection takes many forms, all of which go beyond immigrant nostalgia in which a person who is removed from his or her ancestral land tries to re-create in the new land a sense of the old, through foods, music, and storytelling.

While transmigrants may emigrate and settle without returning home, they consistently engage in various social interactions that cross borders. Georges, for example, does much more than dream of Haiti. His transnational relations range from sending money and gifts to sporadic attendance at meetings, demonstrations, and forums called by various organizations that conduct activities in both the United States and Haiti.

Even in the periods when he did not visit Haiti, first because he was undocumented, and then because his burden of supporting family in the United States and Haiti left him no money to visit, he was embedded within transnational networks that intimately connected him to the place he continued to call home. We must point out that to speak about the transnational connections of persons who have emigrated from their homeland to settle abroad is to describe only one set of relationships that such persons establish. For example, many persons from Haiti have become well incorporated in their new country, developing relationships at work and in their neighborhood. Economic, religious, and social activities link them to persons of varying nationalities with whom they may identify in various ways: coworker, union member, neighbor, Catholic, Protestant, Mason, black, Caribbean, or woman. In this chapter, we focus on the transnational domain of social relationships established by migrating populations not because it is their exclusive sphere of action but because the effects of this domain on the second generation have yet to be addressed.

The most useful way to conceptualize the domain created by the social relationships of persons who visit back and forth in their country of origin and persons who remain connected even if they themselves do not move is to speak of a "transnational social field" (Basch, Glick-Schiller, and Szanton-Blanc 1994; Glick-Schiller 1999a; Glick-Schiller, Basch, and Szanton-Blanc 1992, 1995; Glick-Schiller and Fouron 1999). We build our understanding of social field on the network studies developed by the Manchester School of Social Anthropology (Barnes 1954, 1969; Mitchell 1969; Noble 1973; Turner 1967). A network is best understood as a chain of social relationships specific to each person. A social field can be defined as an unbounded terrain of interlocking ego-centric networks.[2]

The concept "transnational social field" provides a conceptual and methodological entry point into the investigation of broader social, economic, and political processes through which migrating populations are embedded in more than one society and to which they react. It facilitates an analysis of the processes by which immigrants as well as their descendants can continue to be part of the fabric of daily life in their home state, including its political processes, while they simultaneously engage in activities in their new country, at their jobs, in their neighborhoods, and as citizens participating in

the political process. The study of transnational social fields focuses on human interaction and situations of personal social relationship.[3] Underlying the use of this concept is the hypothesis that
ongoing transnational social relations foster different forms of social
and political identification than connections made simply through
transborder forms of communication.

To facilitate the analysis we differentiate between the maintenance of transnational networks and an ideology of belonging and
call the ideology of belonging built within a transnational social field
"long distance nationalism." Georges is not only a transmigrant but
also a long distance nationalist. We define long distance nationalism
as ideas about belonging that link people living in various geographic locations and motivate or justify their taking action in relationship to an ancestral territory and its government. Through such
ideological linkages, a territory, its people, and its government become a transnational nation-state. Long distance nationalism binds
immigrants, their descendants, and people who have remained in
their homeland into a single transborder citizenry. It provides the
transborder nationalist narratives that constitute and are constituted by everyday forms of state formation. As in other versions of
nationalism, the concept of a territorial homeland governed by a
state that represents the nation remains salient, but national borders are not thought to delimit membership in the nation. Citizens
residing within the territorial homeland view emigrants and their
descendants as part of the nation, whatever legal citizenship the
émigrés may have.[4]

Long distance nationalism does not exist only in the domain of
the imagination and sentiment. It leads to action. These actions link
a dispersed population to a specific homeland and its political system. Long distance nationalists may vote, demonstrate, contribute
money, create works of art, give birth, fight, kill, and die for a
"homeland" in which they may never have lived. Meanwhile, those
who live in this land will recognize these actions as patriotic contributions to the well-being of their common homeland.[5] Georges is
a long distance nationalist not only because he dreams about Haiti
but also because he takes action on behalf of Haiti while continuing
to live in New York. He believes that when he assists family members in Haiti, speaks out about problems in Haiti, or counsels young
people of Haitian descent born in the United States, he is working

to reconstruct Haiti. People living in Haiti are also long distance nationalists if they continue to claim Georges as their own and maintain that he continues to be responsible for Haiti and that his actions abroad reflect on the reputation and future of Haiti.

Transnational migration and long distance nationalism are not new. In previous publications, Nina has explored the late-nineteenth- and early-twentieth-century nation-state building projects of U.S. immigrants in order to better understand the role of contemporary globalization in shaping long distance nationalism (Glick-Schiller 1999a, 1999b, 1999c). As in the past, long distance nationalists today build their homelands and emigrant-sending states continue to claim the loyalty of their emigrants. However, current-day states no longer expect their emigrants to return home to rebuild the motherland; they are urged to do this work from afar. Recently, emigrant-sending states such as Mexico, Colombia, the Dominican Republic, Ecuador, Brazil, and Haiti have adopted policies that turned them into transnational nation-states. Many have changed their laws and created government agencies to ensure that transmigrants remain incorporated in their native land. Some governments have granted dual nationality so that emigrants can carry two passports; others have extended voting in the homeland to emigrants who have become U.S. citizens. Through these changes, as well as the establishment of special ministries responsible for the diasporic population, the political leaders of these countries signal that transmigrants, as well as their children, remain members of the nation of their birth. These countries urge their dual nationals to vote, lobby, and demonstrate on behalf of the land of their ancestors.[6] This alteration in the relationship between emigrant-sending countries and their populations abroad has important consequences for a transnational second generation.

The emergence of a scholarship on transnational migration constitutes a challenge to the dominant model of the immigrant experience that has portrayed immigrants as "uprooted" and examines their incorporation into their new country without regard to their continuing relationship to their native land. Generated from the experience of European immigrants who arrived at the end of the nineteenth century and the beginning of the early twentieth century, the dominant model of immigrant incorporation projects a unilineal process of acculturation and assimilation that takes several generations

(Gleason 1982; Gordon 1964; Simpson and Yinger 1958; Warner and Srole 1945). In this model, U.S. society is defined as the sole domain of structural and cultural pressures that shape the identities and cultural repertoire of the second generation. Even the naming of immigrants' children as a "second generation" reflected and contributed to the notion of the incorporation of immigrants as a steplike irreversible process and one in which immigrants' children were socialized solely by forces within the land of their birth.

More recently, scholars concerned with a new second generation that is growing up in the wake of the recent immigration from Latin America, the Caribbean, and Asia have developed a more nuanced reading of immigrant incorporation. The emerging paradigm of immigrant incorporation foresees a range of trajectories for the second generation rather than a straightforward pattern of assimilation (Portes 1995; Portes and Zhou 1993; Rumbaut 1996; Stepick 1998; Waters 1996, 1999). Factors of race, class, region, and city of residence are seen as contributing to variations in the identities of the second generation whose parents were part of the post-1965 immigration.

For example, Alejandro Portes and Min Zhou (1993), working with data sets that included Haitian youth in Miami, theorized that race enters into the experience of second-generation youth in two contradictory processes, neither of which resembles the classic model of immigrant incorporation. Some second-generation youth who are racialized as black do assimilate rapidly but take on a black American identity. The adoption of this identity by a sector of second-generation young people constitutes a rejection of white mainstream culture and values that, through processes linked to race and class, marginalize black youth. In contrast, other sectors of the second-generation youth respond to racialization by joining with their parents in embracing the national identity of their country of origin. Mary Waters's (1996, 178) research reveals a range of responses among Caribbean second-generation youth in New York to the experience of racialization. These responses included "identifying as [black] Americans, identifying as ethnic Americans with some distance from black Americans, or identifying as immigrant in a way that does not reckon with American racial or ethnic categories." (Alex Stepick [1998] has reported similar findings among Haitian youth in Miami.) This significant rethinking of the

Americanization process has not addressed, however, the transnational social and political processes that shape the lives and identities of a significant sector of both immigrants and their children.

In investigating the forces that contribute to these variations of identity, Portes and Zhou (1993), Stepick (1998), and Waters (1996) examine only the structure and processes within U.S. society. Furthermore, they tend to see racial and ethnic identifications as fixed in time and singular. That is to say, the model they develop suggests that a person develops only one racial, ethnic, or national identity and tends to keep it as he or she matures. But as young people mature they develop multiple, overlapping, and simultaneous identities and deploy them in relation to events they experience at home, at school, at work, in the country of their birth, and in the country of their ancestry.

At various conferences at which we have presented evidence of transnational migration, scholars who remain within the older assimilationist perspective have dismissed our work as only a "first-generation phenomenon" that will vanish with the coming of age of a second generation. Even if this were true, home ties would clearly be a phenomenon of note, since these ties affect the incorporative strategies of immigrants and the political rhetoric and practices of political leaders. Moreover, there has been little research about the degree to which children born in the United States embrace or reject transnational processes and relations.[7]

To establish the parameters in which members of the second generation develop their identities we need to employ both a concept of transnational social fields and an understanding that immigration is currently an ongoing process. Often discussions of the second generation implicitly assume that migration stops after the first generation. In this approach, whether in its classic or recent formulations, the old country is represented in the United States only by an aging population of immigrants; a second generation grows up as a cohort surrounded by people their age who were also U.S.-born and -bred. But this view of immigration was inspired by a migration stream that was abruptly cut by immigration restriction, depression, and world war. If attacks on immigration do not succeed in halting the flow of newcomers, and if the current pace of family reunions continues, young people born in the United States will continue to find in their households, and all around them, compatriots their age who recently have arrived from the home country.[8] These young people influence and socialize one another. In addition, immigrant households host a constant flow of relatives of various generations who engage in a circuit of visiting.

Once a migration is firmly established, child-rearing is a transnational process. This means that in research on the second generation, we cannot assume that adults who have immigrated and settled in the United States will have children born and reared in the United States only. This is a question for empirical investigation. For example, many Haitian parents have children born in Haiti who are brought to the United States only when they are teens, children born in the United States after their parents have migrated but sent home to be raised in Haiti, and children born and reared in the United States. Consequently, households contain children with many different degrees of knowledge about Haiti.

YOUTHFUL VOICES IN NEW YORK

Her presence was not imposing. Her rhetoric was not fiery. She stood before the large lecture hall filled with people, mostly young, mostly Haitian, and spoke very quietly. But the audience hung on her words because she was Edwidge Dandicat, a successful author at the age of twenty-seven. "I am not a politician," she told the audience. "I am just a Haitian and our community is in crisis." Her message was as much in her presence at this occasion as in her specific words. She seemed the perfect symbol to open this conference that had been called to initiate the Haitian American Community Action Network (HACAN).

The Haitian American Community Action Network envisioned by the conference conveners as a means of "initiating a national network of community groups and individuals dedicated to promoting the well-being and the civil and political rights of Haitians in the United States" (HACAN 1996). But to many of the participants in the conference, the location of this Haitian community and the domain of community action were not stable. Dandicat stood as a symbol of "Haitian American" success, but on what ground did she stand? Dandicat ended her speech by quoting the slogan on the Haitian flag, "L'Union Fait la Force" (Through Union Comes Strength). That flag along with the U.S. flag decorated the speaker's podium. Much of Dandicat's critically acclaimed fiction is set in both the United States and Haiti, carrying readers into the world of Haitian transmigrants who travel back and forth between Haiti and the United States (Dandicat 1996, 1998a, 1998b).[9] Her life story, which was known to this audience, includes a childhood in Haiti, migration to the United States at the age of twelve, degrees from Barnard College and Brown University, and continuing ties to Haiti. Her English is flawless, but she addressed the conference in Kreyòl.

The conference addressed political concerns in Haiti as well as in the United States. The first session, entitled "Building Haitian American Political Leadership," offered, "in an increasingly hostile environment, . . . a broad overview of the socio-political environment in which Haitian-Americans live." But the final session on the agenda, "Politics and Democratic Trials in Haiti," focused on Haiti and the responsibility of Haitian Americans to Haiti. "How can Haitian-American communities honestly contribute to Haiti's democratic well-being?"

Not all the organizers and participants at the conference were equally comfortable with the transnational scope of the agenda. There was a noticeable difference between the older generation and the youth, a second generation who had come of age within families structured by transnational migration and in the context of efforts of Haitian leaders to portray Haiti as a transnational nation-state. Those who spoke for an older generation of leadership saw the goal of the community action network in the terms of the traditional U.S. paradigm of immigrant settlement: the development of immigrants as an ethnic "community" that celebrates its roots but gets on with the business of carving a place for itself within the U.S. political and economic structure. For example, Jocelyn McCalla (Americanized as "Johnnie"), in his forties and a spokesperson for the National Coalition for Haitian Rights (NCHR), the organization that attempted to launch HACAN, urged the audience to speak in "American" rather than "Haitian terms" "because we are here and we are here to stay." He made no mention of Haiti. He called on Haitian professionals to help improve life for Haitian immigrants. "We have more power than we think we have at the local, state, and federal levels. We should build strong lobbies. We should build alliances and we need to link up to other groups."

It should be noted that many in this older generation of leadership were engaged in politics in Haiti. However, they had learned in the United States to separate political organizations linked to Haiti from efforts to create ethnic constituencies. They had found that foundations and churches that helped fund Haitian community organizing efforts, such as the proposed network, expected to see ethnic activities focused on incorporating immigrants into the United States.

The majority of the participants in this conference and a significant section of its leadership came from a second generation that was born or has lived since childhood in the United States. This generation has a different vision of the meaning of community. Young, confident, well educated, they felt comfortable building an organization that connected them to Haiti as well as the United States. They simply did not acknowledge the boundaries. Their experience growing up in the United States convinced them that they needed to have a public identity. Public identity meant they had a label and a culture they could claim as their own. This identity became Haitian, but for them Haitian was not confined to a concern for building a Haitian "community" in the United States. At one point, the assembled body was called on to chant, "A strong Haitian community equals a strong Haiti; a strong Haiti equals a strong Haitian community." Their ability to use the word *community,* sometimes for Haitians in Brooklyn, sometimes for Haitians in the New York metropolitan area, sometimes for Haitians in the United States, sometimes for the Haitian diaspora, and sometimes for all Haitians abroad and in Haiti, gave the slogan layers of meaning.

In three decades of research on Haitian incorporation in the United States, we have found an identification with Haiti to be common among persons of Haitian descent born in the United States. In certain ways our findings resemble those of Portes and Zhou (1993) and Waters (1996), who describe a sector of study of second-generation Caribbean youth who maintain an identification with the homeland of their parents. These findings take on new meaning, however, when placed within the transnational perspective on the second generation that we are proposing. To make this point we draw on quotations from eleven lengthy interviews Georges conducted in 1996 with seniors at the State University of New York at Stony Brook who were born in the United States but whose parents had emigrated from Haiti. All the students we interviewed spoke some Kreyòl, but not all were fluent in Kreyòl, and the interviews were conducted in English. Although education is highly valued by the Haitian immigrant population and a significant segment of Haitian young people in the United States have some form of postsecondary education, these young people are more educated than many second-generation Haitian immigrants.[10] The students we interviewed did not come from elite backgrounds, either in Haiti or in the United States; in the United States their parents worked as nurse's aides, office cleaners, and mechanics.

Although these students were U.S. citizens, none of them identified himself or herself as American.[11]

> GEORGES: Do you classify yourself as Haitian American, African American, or Haitian?
> TOUFI: Haitian.
> GEORGES: Haitian, no hyphen?
> TOUFI: No, no hyphen. I am a Haitian.

Sandra, age twenty-two, discounted the influence of birthplace on her identity:

> I know I say I'm Haitian because I have a Haitian background. My family is from Haiti and the only thing I have from here is that I was born here. I picked up the American culture, but at the same time, I think that about 60 percent of me, if not more, is Haitian. . . . I automatically say I'm Haitian.

Sandra maintains she has always thought of herself as Haitian, but several of these young people speak of their identification with Haiti as something that they consciously adopted as they grew up. Carline sees herself as growing up "more as an African American . . . but as of late incorporating more of the Haitian culture into my daily life." Toufi explains:

> When I went into high school, I started to realize a little bit more of who I was and started getting more in touch with my Haitian side, and that is the only side I have ever seen since then. And that is the side I want to help.

We have observed this maturing of a sense of Haitian identity among many young adults of Haitian parentage in the New York metropolitan area. It seems to be a direction taken more frequently by those who obtain higher education, but the acquisition of a sense of being Haitian also seems linked to participation in the workforce in the New York metropolitan area. Whether they saw themselves as mostly or completely Haitian, all of the Stony Brook students expressed pride in being Haitian. As these young people matured they learned to turn to their Haitian origins as a wellspring of strength that allowed them to live their lives in the United States. Several directly said in almost the same words, "Haiti is me, Haiti is my pride." To be Haitian is defined as being proud. When Claudia was asked, "What does it mean to you to be Haitian?" she responded, "A lot of pride, a lot of history, strength."

This pride in Haiti is linked to a catalog of Haiti's historical accomplishments that were recited or referred to in each of the interviews. Among those accomplishments mentioned were that Haiti was "the first country to defeat slavery"; it is a country that maintains "an African religion," a country with its own language, a country that fought for its independence, and "the first black republic to defeat a white army." The statement that Haiti "defeated a white army" is highly significant. One of the forces that impel youngsters of Haitian descent toward an identification as Haitian is their racialization in the United States as blacks.

All of these young people held jobs while attending school, and all had their most direct experiences of discrimination in the workforce. There, being viewed as black meant being defined as somehow not American. They said that they had learned that despite their citizenship and their fluency in English, the United States "is not your country."

These students were treated by the larger society as if they were African American, and they experienced discrimination because of this identification. Yet, by the time they were teenagers they were not able to easily identify as African American. African Americans often treated them as different and sometimes inferior. Meanwhile, their parents continued to teach them to differentiate themselves from African Americans. As college seniors they chose to be Haitian, at least some of the time. However, we want to stress that they were not antagonistic to African Americans or to an overarching identity politics that united them with other blacks and placed them within an African diaspora. For them, being Haitian does not exclude them from other forms of identification.

Without a transnational perspective, these students' specification that they were Haitian can be interpreted as evidence of the persisting importance of ethnicity within American life. Pride in Haiti can be construed as a politics of cultural roots within a discourse about membership in a multicultural United States. Or continuing identification by a second generation with their ancestral homeland can be interpreted as solely a response to the racialization that the second generation experiences. And certainly several of the students told us that the discrimination they faced convinced them that they should "go back to some place where they expect something of you, where they appreciate you, where they don't discriminate against you." That place becomes your true home, no matter where you were born. For example, Toufi told us, "When I go home, there is no discrimination. I don't feel it."

An adequate interpretation of the experience of the second generation, however, must assess their transnational ties and experiences. All eleven of the students we interviewed were raised within transnational social fields. All but one had visited Haiti, and that one young woman's plans were abruptly disrupted in 1991 when the military coup against Jean-Bertrand Aristide made the prospective journey dangerous. However, direct experience in Haiti was only one aspect of their ongoing relationships to Haiti. Their childhoods were structured by the sending of remittances, packages, and news to and from Haiti and the visiting back and forth of various relatives. Sandra provided a description of the taken-for-granted interchange of visits: "My grandmother has come here . . . I think only twice, but that's because she was sick. My cousins have come from time to time, and I think all of them have come once or twice, but I think there are one or two . . . different cousins and aunts who haven't been here yet." All of these young people also grew up with and continued to confront their parents' relationships to Haiti. Of the eleven students, two had parents planning to return to Haiti to live, one to establish a business and the other to retire.

The transnational context of these students' lives makes it logical for them to see themselves not just identifying with Haiti but assuming some responsibility for Haiti. For example, Carline linked her ability to confront racism in the United States with her responsibilities to Haiti: "My strength derives from my Haitian nationality.

I feel I have an obligation to Haiti." Sabrina had returned the previous year from her first trip to Haiti with a commitment to assume some of the burden of supporting kin in Haiti that had previously been carried by her mother: "What I do once a month is send money to my family, 'cause they are so much in need."

Haitian youth born in the United States and living within transnational social fields come to believe that identification with a homeland is a matter of action as well as words. Therefore, when they speak about their Haitian identity, they speak about future plans as well as their sense of self. All the students we interviewed had such plans that ranged from the personal to the political. But of course in this context the personal was political. To identify with another nation as part of a personal sense of self and to plan to take some action in relation to that nation provides a base for political leaders seeking to rally persons living in the United States on behalf of Haiti.

Some students planned to work in Haiti, others just to visit. Sabrina mentioned becoming a doctor and possibly opening a private practice in Haiti: "It would be good if I go back, and as far as helping my country and my people, that's something I would always do." In their discussions of education the students made a link between their Haitian identity and their education. They also told us that their obtaining an education reflected well on Haiti and provided them ways to help the country. We have found this elision between self and the Haitian nation among young people who grew up in Haiti, as well as among members of the second generation in the United States.

Two students envisioned for themselves a directly political role in relation to Haiti. Toufi told us: "I want to be involved in politics in Haiti. My father always tells me no because I may never be able to go back to Haiti, which would be a problem. True, but I just think I can go back and volunteer and do things."

In the 1960s young men who were born in Haiti but had emigrated to the United States often declared their intentions to become president of Haiti. Nina encountered this aspiration repeatedly when she worked with Haitian young people in Haitian summer youth programs in New York in 1969–70. By the 1990s the situation had changed. The dream of leading Haiti had not disappeared, but now Georges heard the same aspiration from a young woman born in the United States. Carline told Georges: "Well, one of my biggest ambitions is to get involved in politics in Haiti. And even one day run for president. . . . Even though I was born in America, . . . with or without a [Haitian] citizenship I still have patriotism for the country, so!"

It is important to note that Carline differed from the other students Georges interviewed. She had lived for significant periods of her life in both Haiti and the United States. Although born in the United States, she had been sent back to Haiti for part of her education. While Carline was the only young person in our sample to have had this experience, living for several years in Haiti is an important part of the socialization of many children born in the United States. In our assessment of the identities and loyalties of the second generation, we must consider the experiences of young people who grow up across borders. Youth brought up this way, as well as young people born and reared in Haiti and then brought to the United States, often form a cohort within school populations in regions of the country with large numbers of Haitian immigrants, such as New York, New Jersey, and Miami. This cohort pressures other Haitian second-generation youngsters who know less about Haiti to identify themselves as Haitian and to become involved in activities linked to Haiti. All the students we spoke with described such pressures within the Haitian Student Organization at Stony Brook, in which all but one of them participated.

Many Haitian student clubs in New York, including the one at Stony Brook, have been active in articulating long distance nationalism and in building transnational activities that link them to Haiti. Students contributed to the movement against the Duvalier regime and participated in Aristide's Lavalas movement.[12] By 1996 the political disarray in Haiti was accompanied by a lull in Haitian student activism in the United States. Those students who had not recently visited Haiti seemed removed from the country's political discourse. Nonetheless, we were told, "I have to defend Haiti. . . . I feel at times I am the voice of the country." It is also important to note that a core of the young people engaged in building HACAN who seemed more immersed in current transnational political discussion had come out of Haitian student clubs.

Claudia was among those of this second generation who envisioned themselves as a force to "rebuild Haiti." She told us:

> I have a lot of people who are just like me who are getting their education
> here who want to go back. . . . It can be, you know, a very fulfilling future
> as far as Haiti is concerned because a lot of us who are getting our educa-
> tion here we gonna plan to go back and to build the country. So I see, in a
> few years, Haiti will be a good country again to live in.

And Carline concluded: "I can see my future in Haiti. It could be here and helping over there or totally there. Definitely my eyes will be focused on Haiti."

These students take into their vision of the future not only their own experiences in the United States but also their parents' imagery of a beautiful Haiti that once was. Sabrina, for example, used the word *rebuild* in discussing her own plans for the future: "I hope for the best for my future, and as far as Haiti, it's my country and I will definitely be going back. . . . It can be rebuilt." Georges asked, "What do you mean rebuilt? Was there a time when it was beautiful?" And she replied: "That's all I heard, when I went to Haiti. All I heard was, 'You came at the wrong time. Haiti's at its worst. This was once a beautiful place.' "

Most of the students we interviewed were familiar with this projection of Haiti's past, the same imagery of Haiti that haunts Georges's dreams. Past becomes linked to the future. Politics and nostalgia meet in the concrete organizations, practices, and plans of the second generation to reconstruct and reclaim Haiti for their generation and for the future.

YOUTHFUL VOICES IN HAITI

In 1996 we visited Aux Cayes, Georges's hometown, as part of our research on long distance nationalism. On our first day in Aux Cayes, we turned on the radio and found ourselves in an air space that the young people in Aux Cayes were claiming as their own. A team of young women and men, most of them in their early twenties, were broadcasting a daily radio program, designed to speak to young people. The radio program was broadcast on Men Kontre (Hands Together), a noncommercial station sponsored by the Catholic Diocese of Aux Cayes. Men Kontre originated under the Duvalier dictatorship as part of a broad-based social movement that led in 1986 to the toppling of the twenty-nine-year-old Duvalier regime. While many of the radio stations that had contributed to the struggle had been silenced by 1996, Men Kontre continued to provide political information and serve as a political forum. The young people who participated in the station as either broadcasters or audience were linking themselves to a particular history of struggle against political repression, using a particular discourse about the Haitian nation and state that had been shaped by a grassroots movement for social justice, more than a decade old, and demanding that the state take responsibility for the welfare of the nation.

At the time of our research the station's youthful broadcasters had successfully initiated a dialogue among the youth of Aux Cayes. The broadcasters called on their listeners to participate in the live broadcast by calling the station or, since most of their audience did not have access to a telephone, by writing to the station and receiving personalized answers. Hundreds of young people responded to this invitation to become "pen pals" and wrote to the station.

We spoke with six members of the radio staff, one man and five women, ranging in age from eighteen to twenty-nine; their average age was twenty-three.[13] All six were born in the countryside. Four of the six had fathers who worked the land as "cultivators," selling crops to support the family; only one had a father with any formal training and profession.[14] Four had mothers who were commerçante, small-scale retailers selling agricultural products, cooked food, and a broad array of new or second-hand manufactured goods. Two of those interviewed had the same mother but because they had different fathers they had different family members living abroad.

These youth grew up in the crucible of political struggles that popularized a transnational project of rebuilding the Haitian nation-state. Before Aristide became president in 1991, Haitian political discourse sharply delineated between those living in Haiti and the Haitian diaspora. The diaspora were defined as outside of the nation or even traitors to it. In a sharp reversal, Aristide in 1991 began to define the Haitian diaspora as one of the territorial departments of Haiti (the Dixième, or Tenth). The young people of the radio program staff responded enthusiastically to this redefinition as part of their embracing Haiti as a transnational nation-state. Though they were isolated from the rest of Haiti by poor roads and a grossly inefficient telephone service, they were connected to Haitians who lived in other nation-states. They understood that they inhabited a global terrain of settlement that included the United States (Miami, New York, Chicago, and Boston), Guadeloupe, and France. This knowledge shaped their definition of the term *Haitian*. Marjorie, for example, who had an aunt and cousin abroad, said:

> A Haitian is a person who is fighting for Haiti, who loves his brothers and sisters who live in Haiti, who loves the flag, who loves the culture. A person who is living abroad for a long time is a Haitian. Even if you are naturalized [as a U.S. citizen], you keep Haitian blood. The only way to keep them from being Haitian is if they cut their meat and took all your blood.

Her definition of Haitian extended into the second generation. She stated, "I believe if the parents are Haitian and always speak with him and say who he is and what nationality he is, that person is not totally [American]. He has Haitian blood in his veins."

Carmelle took up this theme, differentiating between legal definitions of citizenship and questions of political loyalty by using the language of blood. She informed us, "According to the constitution of the foreign country, once you naturalize, you adhere to their nationality and reject your native one, but for me, regardless of what the other country says, you have Haitian blood in your veins."

By using the concept of blood, Haitians in Haiti find a way to reclaim persons of Haitian descent as Haitians—even if those persons have changed their language, culture, and nationality. For this reason, all six members of the radio staff expressed opposition to the concept of dual nationality because they felt one could never stop being Haitian. They agreed that the ties of blood were not an abstract claim of identity—they came with an agenda. Those abroad were a key to changing Haiti, and the diaspora had obligations toward Haiti. They differed, however, about whether the diaspora has fulfilled these obligations. Anna explained:

> It is an obligation because they know the conditions the country is in and the sufferings that exist in Haiti. If the country was good, they would never have left. They know what they left behind. They know that they left these people in the same conditions that existed prior to their departure. How can they ignore them and not lend a helping hand?

The young people we interviewed in Haiti did not all have connections with family abroad, and those who did have transnational family connections differed in whether these ties provided resources.

The absence and degree of intensity of transnational family connections shape their life prospects, affecting both their daily standard of living and their sense of the future for themselves and for Haiti. While not all young people have transnational family connections, the fact that many do have such ties affects the outlook of the entire generation. Young people all over Haiti live within networks of people who do have family abroad and are aware of acquaintances who do receive money and benefits from such connections. Those who receive money and gifts from family abroad appeared more positive and self-confident. They expected either assistance in obtaining education in Haiti or sponsorship to go abroad and study. They prefer to study abroad.[15] Anna, whose parents are both in the United States, informed us: "Haiti doesn't offer any real university education. I have been calling my mother regularly, asking for my mother to send for me so that I can attend college in the United States."

In contrast, those without such prospects, although still in their twenties, were already bitter. Their sense of frustration was deepened by the widespread belief in Haiti that kin have an obligation to help their family. The transnational flow of money from families in the United States and Haiti, while providing material evidence of interconnection, at the same time contributes to class divisions within Haiti and tremendous tensions within family networks that extend from Haiti to persons settled abroad. The transnational ties of Haiti's youth have been a basis for them to judge conditions in Haiti and envision themselves studying and working abroad. As Carmelle, age twenty-three, stated:

> When I was young, I wanted to study medicine, but I never asked myself was it possible to get admitted to medical school. I thought that once I finished my studies, I could just go and register at the medical school, and get accepted. But I used to hear people say that it is a comedy to be in philo [the terminal year of high school], but the tragedy begins when you pass the exam. I am now realizing that it is true. I want to study, but the tragedy of the reality is that I can't.[16]

Carmelle abandoned her dream of becoming a doctor, and even though she obtained technical clerical training, she found herself without a job or a future. Her hopes lie in migration from Haiti. She told us, "If right now I could leave Haiti, it would be good for me." Emilia, looking at her older sister's fate, was even more despondent.

Look at the others already living abroad. They are already working and making money. Even when I finish my studies I won't have anything to do in a country that doesn't offer you anything. Three of my mother's children are grown and none of them is working and doing anything. What a sad story. Alas. Sometimes I sit and cry and cry because there is no future for me.

Given the worsening living conditions and the tenuous political situation, the staff of the radio program saw their personal futures and the future of the country very much connected to the Haitian diaspora, and especially to the United States. These youth were aware of the racial discrimination in the United States but nonetheless saw it as a land of possibility rather than of restriction. Marjorie reported, "My aunt and boyfriend told me that they are mistreated a great deal because they are black. They reserve the harder, dirtier work for them." But she and the others wanted to go anyway. Without employment or educational opportunities in Haiti, these young people saw no choice but to leave. They saw as a more insurmountable barrier to their aspirations the discrimination that they face in Haiti from the rich and powerful. Only with a foreign education and money could they overcome the discrimination based on color and class background that they face in Haiti.

These Haitian young people saw themselves living in the United States and even obtaining U.S. nationality, but their goals were linked to their expectation that they would always remain Haitian and connected to Haiti. Their achievements would belong to Haiti and would contribute to a brighter future for Haiti and for their families remaining there.

Throughout the country Haitian youth have experienced the Haitian diaspora as a political force within Haiti. As Carmelle explained:

[Those abroad] keep a keen eye on what is going on in Haiti. . . . The Dixième . . . did the same thing that we did in Haiti. We sent news bulletins, and they used to organize demonstrations, voice their opinions, say what they liked and didn't like about what was going on in Haiti. As a result of those actions Aristide was able to return to Haiti.

Several of the program staff went on to say that while the diaspora met their political obligations to Haiti, they were failing to assist Haiti economically. For example, Anna told us:

> We have ample problems in Haiti. There are no roads, there are no indus-
> tries. They could have invested in roads, in opening industries and creating
> jobs, but they don't do that. The country is in poverty. They should have
> put their heads together. This is our country. This is their country too. They
> helped the country politically, but socially the things we need, we don't see
> what they do for us.

Trained in activism, one of the young women, Marjorie, used the occasion of our interview to directly address the diaspora. Speaking into our microphone, she made a passionate appeal: "Those who are listening to my voice, I urge them to concentrate and remember what country they left behind. My brother, see the one on the ground, see the one who has nothing, who is on the ground, help him out."

She spoke of the need to "rebuild Haiti," evoking an image of a past Haiti that was better, stronger, more beautiful than the Haiti that was all around her. Another staff member told us: "You see, what-ever used to be is falling in disrepair is being destroyed. . . . The country is going backward." In their nostalgia for the past these young people who have never left Haiti share the dream of Haiti that made Georges, living in Queens, New York, laugh in delight. That dream, filtered through the nostalgia that other second-generation Haitians living in New York learned from their parents, fuels their commitment to "rebuild Haiti."

In their nationalism and their view of the diaspora the young people at the radio station differed little from the thirty-six other young people we interviewed in Haiti in 1996, who were less po-litically active and by and large had less education and fewer life opportunities. Of those thirty-six, eight were in Aux Cayes and twenty-eight were in Port-au-Prince. In wealth, they varied widely. One, the son of a prominent capitalist, held both a U.S. and a Haitian passport and had houses in Miami and Port-au-Prince, and one was a homeless young man who supported himself by helping persons in an impoverished neighborhood to illegally tap into the electric lines. Twenty-one (60 percent) classified themselves as poor, thirteen (37 percent) as middle-class, and one (3 percent) as a mem-ber of the bourgeoisie. Twenty-eight were students at the time of the interview, although among these some reported having received only a few years of schooling.

Despite the differences in their backgrounds and levels of ed-ucation, the majority of the thirty-six young people (69 percent) expressed some degree of nationalist sentiment, although they were not as fierce in their nationalism as were the radio staff. Most (86 percent), like the members of the radio staff, believed that those who emigrate and change their nationality remain Haitian and therefore remain within the Haitian nation. And most (77 percent) also agreed with the radio station staff in opposing a change in Haitian law to allow dual nationality for those abroad. They opposed this change not because they had a vision of a Haitian polity restricted to those who live in Haiti but because they believed the diaspora could contribute politically (53 percent) and in other ways (42 percent) to the future of Haiti. Most knew the word *diaspora,* and of those who did only 16 percent saw it as a negative word.

Previous generations of Haitian youth had learned patriotic sentiments from nationalist rituals embedded in school curricula and public ceremonies and national holidays. While many of these rituals had been abandoned by the 1980s, the young people in both Aux Cayes and Port-au-Prince grew up in a period of intense political mobilization and also repression. Beginning in the 1990s, the Lavalas slogans calling for rebuilding of the nation were all around them, as graffiti on the walls of houses, churches, and schools, in discussions on the radios that play incessantly in Haiti, and in the Roman Catholic masses of liberation theology priests. They witnessed or participated in street demonstrations with similar slogans. Then, between 1991 and 1995, they experienced the coup that sent Aristide into exile and the transnational resistance to the Haitian military dictatorship that followed.

The sense of awareness of this generation extended far beyond their neighborhood or city. They grew up in a media age dramatically different from what their parents had known. With the advent of cheap transistor radios and inexpensive tape recorders, even people in rural areas of Haiti can now listen to radio programs and exchange audiocassettes.[17] Because of the scarcity of electricity in rural areas, television is less prevalent there, but some poor households in cities such as Aux Cayes have black-and-white sets, and many households living on remittances have color television and video and compact disc players. Television and radio not only introduced images of U.S. and European music, lifestyles, and items of consumption; they also linked Haiti with the diaspora. By the end of the 1980s radio broadcast had become transnational. Interviews with Haitian scholars and political leaders in New York and Miami are now broadcast in Haiti. News about life in Haiti broadcast in New York, Miami, and Boston features telephone conversations with correspondents in Haiti. Some talk shows include audiences calling in from Haiti and the United States at the same time (Glick-Schiller and Fouron 1998). In the 1990s Georges's father-in-law in Aux Cayes regularly followed the radio station that periodically broadcast interviews conducted with Georges in Queens.

However, despite their uniform socialization, not all youth held the same opinions. We found some evidence that young people's opinions were linked to their relationships within transnational social fields. Forty-two percent of those we interviewed lived in transnational households, that is, they had strong ties to family living abroad, defined by either regular remittances to their household or regular communications accompanied by assistance if needed. This group tended to be the fiercest nationalists, and their nationalism was long distance. Because the class status of a household in Haiti is often determined by whether the household receives regular remittances, differences in the degree of nationalist feelings also vary with self-ascribed class status.

Most of the youth, whether from a transnational household or not, displayed some degree of nationalist sentiment. However, except for the radio staff, those who were most strongly nationalist were those who received remittances. At the same time, most of those who displayed no nationalist sentiments had no contact with family living abroad. The radio staff were the exception: even those that had no transnational family ties displayed fierce nationalism. The source of their strong nationalism was their participation in a nationalist organization, the radio station, whose Catholic leaders were part of significant transnational religious and political networks.

The link between Haitian nationalism and transnational ties among the youth is an important one to investigate further. Our exploratory research with small snowball samples can only suggest a direction for further inquiry. However, our interviews reflect patterns we have been observing for many years. They are consistent with our analysis that there is no contradiction between living in a transnational social field and displaying Haitian nationalism. Those young people in Haiti and the United States who live within transnational social fields learn to identify with Haiti, in part because they are positioned within this domain of interaction. At the same time, it is important to note that even young people who have no personal transnational connections often display some degree of long distance nationalism.

THE SECOND GENERATION: A REDEFINITION

In this chapter, we examine the identities of young people of Haitian descent in New York City and young people in Haiti and demonstrate that sectors of young people live within transnational social fields established by networks that cross national borders. Our research on the establishment of transnational terrains that encompass several generations has implications for the concept of the second generation that extend far beyond the specifics of the Haitian case and unsettle the very notion of the "second generation." Far more is at stake here than academic definitions. Categories can illuminate or obscure political processes, and the second generation is just such a category.

We suggest that it is time to redefine the second generation to include the entire generation in both homeland and new land who grow up within transnational social fields linked by familial, economic, religious, social, and political networks. In this approach, young people living in such fields would differ from those who may be exposed to various forms of transnational or global media but do not have direct contacts with persons abroad. However, much empirical research needs to be done to examine the degree to which network density, overlap, and the flow of various resources and personnel within these fields shape the identity and actions of this second generation.

Our research on Haitians indicates that we must look transnationally to understand the dynamics that shape the identity of the children of immigrants living in the United States. This approach provides us with a more complex and dynamic explanation for the identity variability or "fluidity" (Vickerman 1999) encountered by contemporary second-generation researchers. We hypothesize that the children of immigrants living in the United States make their choices and move between different identities not only in relation to their experiences of racialization within the United States but also in relation to the degree to which their lives are encompassed within a transnational terrain. Two postulates emerge from this hypothesis: those young people who grow up within such a terrain develop a sense of self that has been shaped by personal, family, and organizational connections to people "back home"; and at the same time, the production of self in terms of race, ethnicity, and nation is part of a political process that extends transnationally. Participation in transnational social fields can link U.S.-born young people to broader processes that define them as a political constituency that can act on behalf of this "home country."

If we define a second generation on the basis of transnational connections, then we must include children raised in the homeland. Some are children of U.S. immigrants sent "home" to be raised. Other children, while not directly the offspring of immigrants, are supported by relatives who have settled abroad. For example, many young people in Haiti, including eighteen in our sample of forty-two, were supported by transmigrants. They received remittances, regularly or when money was needed, from either one or both parents or a sibling of a parent. In most instances relatives abroad could be considered part of their household.

In the past decade increasing numbers of researchers on immigration have begun to acknowledge and study transnational households (Laguerre 1978, 1998; Lessinger 1995; Pessar 1995; Smith and Wallerstein 1992). Many children, living in emigrant-sending countries, depend for their sustenance, growth, and development on parents and other family members living abroad. These children are nurtured within a terrain of transnational connections, influenced by the economic, social, and cultural capital their parents obtain through emigration. If we can accept households as transnational, what about the generation produced within these households? We suggest that once we define households as transnational, the children living within them become part of a transnational second generation. Yet, once we take the step of including the children dependent on immigrants but still living in the homeland in our definition of a second generation, a further question follows. What of the other young people born within a field of social relations that links the home and host country of their parents through networks of economic activities, religious and social organizations, and transnational media? They too grow up within a transnational terrain that shapes the knowledge, consciousness, and identities of their generation. Young persons growing up in Haiti who are not part of transnational households also experience and are influenced by transnational connections. A transnational second generation can be defined as all persons born into the generation after emigrants have established transnational social fields who live within or are socialized by these fields, regardless of whether they were born or are currently living in the country of emigration or abroad.

It is important to distinguish between transnational connection and transnational identity. The national, racial, and ethnic identities of the transnational second generation must be the subject of research. Our Haitian research provides some preliminary indication, however, that among their multiple identities young people who live within transnational fields are most likely to become long distance nationalists. The young people we interviewed in New York as well as the HACAN activists were members of the transnational second generation. They were embedded in personal or organizational transnational networks. Our analysis of the forty-two interviews of Haitian youth we conducted in Haiti also indicates that those who were most fiercely long distance nationalists had either familial or organizational ties abroad.

To be sure, the Haitian elision of self, family, blood, race, and nation is the product of a two-hundred-year history of nation-state building, so that the propensity of the second generation to embrace long distance nationalism is particularly strong (Glick-Schiller and Fouron 2001). And even in the Haitian case, whether or not personal transnational connections are translated into political actions varies, depending on both the situation in Haiti and the conditions that Haitians face in the United States. However, the attraction for young people born in the United States to return and rebuild a homeland is a force that extends from beyond the particularities of Haitian history and deserves systematic cross-cultural exploration. Just as Georges is a long distance nationalist, so too are several of Nina's relatives who, as supporters of Israel, inculcate loyalty to Israel in their children through fund-raising activities for Israel, including for youth programs there. The U.S. Zionist youth movement flourishes within a well-organized transnational institutional framework that builds long distance nationalism among people whose traceable ancestors never lived in Israel.

Developing this definition of a transnational second generation, which is bounded not by the territorial limits of a state but by the boundaries of social fields that stretch across national borders and link emigrant populations to an ancestral homeland, will greatly enhance migration studies. First, it will allow us to study transnational migration as a phenomenon that extends beyond a single generation. Second, it will allow us to ground and operationalize generational studies within transnational social fields. Moreover, such a definition approaches the entire topic of the second generation with new research questions. We can, for example, begin to explore the ways in which various types and densities of transnational connections shape the identities and political agendas of young people coming of age within transnational social fields, whether or not they themselves have migrated. As we indicate, among Haitian youth, involvement in organizations that have transnational linkages and residence in transnational households are two separate but significant paths to long distance nationalism.

Certainly this transnational definition of the second generation gave us insight into the generation that has come of age in both Haiti and the United States. Those who were born after the beginning of large-scale Haitian migration are affected by it, whether or not they are themselves children of immigrants. One of the outcomes of the establishment of transnational social fields has been the development of a sense of the continuity of Haitian identity after emigration and permanent resettlement. This means that many Haitian youth, regardless of whether they were born in the United States or Haiti and regardless of which country they grew up in, are socialized into a Haitian identity that links persons in Haiti to the Haitian diaspora. Whatever their location, through the transnational media as well as the adult transmigrants among whom they live, they are exposed to and respond to the same identity discourse. However, those who live in transnational fields are more prone to act as well as speak.

Haitian young people living in the different localities of the Haitian diaspora can be influenced by the same adults, as well as by the same political discourse. This is particularly true of those young people who participate in youth activities organized by the Catholic Church, whose clergy are members of transnational networks. For example, in 1998 the clergy from Aux Cayes who initiated the radio program there participated in a retreat for second-generation Haitian youth in New York. Within this transnational second generation, however, there are variations in the ways in which people participate in transnational social fields. A small but significant and vocal section of the transnational second generation moves across borders, well incorporated into the United States yet actively participating in social and political processes in Haiti. A larger group is less likely to move but remains connected across borders in networks that can mobilize them politically in relation to Haiti, according to conditions and events in both Haiti and the United States.

We found evidence of the effect of the dense transnational linkages in the response of Haitian youth to the false labeling of Haitians as carriers of the AIDS virus. Many of the Haitian young people who took to the streets of New York to protest against the stigma of the AIDS label began supporting transnational projects to rebuild Haiti. The second generation in Haiti meanwhile learned to look to the diaspora for the political power to change Haiti.

Although some members of Haiti's second generation living in the United States share with their peers in Haiti an understanding that they live in a transnational space, they have traveled to this place by a different path, and they experience it in different ways. Youngsters living in Haiti in the wake of a massive outmigration were grappling with the disappointments of a bleak and unpromising future and looking to the Haitians of the diaspora for assistance in creating a brighter future. Those in Haiti, faced with the barriers of class, color, gender discrimination, political turmoil, and the lack of economic opportunity, saw migration to the United States and the Haitian diaspora as the hope for both themselves and Haiti.

Meanwhile, some youngsters who are of Haitian descent living in the United States were reclaiming Haiti by reclaiming their ties with their ancestral land and reaffirming their Haitian identity. The members of the second generation in the United States see connection with Haiti as a way to escape racial barriers and the restriction of economic opportunities they increasingly are facing in the United States. Young Haitians in Haiti and in the United States hold different and disjunctive conceptualizations of both of these locations. By arguing that Haitians born and living in the United States and persons born in Haiti after the mass migration that began in the 1960s are part of a transnational second generation, we are not denying the very different experiences these two sets of people have or the very different adults they become. Young people brought up in the United States, whether they were born there or in Haiti, experience multiple assimilative pressures. They are very different culturally from people who never have lived in the United States. Nonetheless, the Haitian second generation, whether living in Haiti or in the United States, is coming of age in a different world from the one that shaped their parents, and the transnational linkages forged by their parents contribute to their shared membership in a single cohort. They are a single cohort because, although they are not pursuing the commitment to a transnational Haiti by following the same path, they believe they are traveling toward the same destination. Located in different daily realities, the members of this second generation share an "imagined community" in the past and in the future (Anderson 1991). They share a claim to a Haitian homeland and nostalgia for a Haiti that never was, binding them across national borders and across generations. Georges's nighttime dreams and the daydreams of the young people he interviewed in New York, Aux Cayes, and Port-au-Prince become a single vision. Underlying their disjunctive images of Haiti and the United States is a common vision of a sweet Haiti of the past and a prosperous peaceful Haiti of the future.

The particularities of location within the transnational terrain matter greatly. The young people we spoke with in Haiti, despite all they share with those growing up in the United States, had a dramatically different set of educational, social, and political experiences. We wish to emphasize that when transnational second generations develop, they can contribute to political projects that join together personal self-identification with broader efforts to reconceptualize nation-states as polities that extend across territorial borders. For a transnational generation to be characterized by long distance nationalism in the sense that we have defined it, young people must not only grow up within a transnational field of social relations but also identify themselves with, and take action on behalf of, an ancestral homeland.

Our discussion of transnational migration, long distance nationalism, and the development of a transnational second generation should not be taken as either a celebration of or a denigration of these forms of interconnection across the borders of nation-states. The merits and problematics of the emergence of a phenomenon such as a transnational second generation can be judged only in terms of the goals and concrete achievements of a specific nationalist project. As we have argued elsewhere, the rhetoric and political practices of a transnational Haiti have so far had the effect of masking the Haitian state's lack of sovereignty (Fouron and Glick-Schiller 1997; Glick-Schiller and Fouron 1998). Debates about the relationship between states such as Haiti and the contemporary processes of globalization have been diverted into the efforts to re-build Haiti by incorporating the Haitian diaspora. Yet the trans-national experiences of the Haitians, including the development of a second generation, also contain possibilities to link struggles in Haiti for justice and equity with similar aspirations of people in other parts of the world. Many of these struggles come together when transmigrants in the United States unite in common cause with op-pressed people, such as in the movement in the 1990s in New York to end police killings and brutality.

We also want to make clear that we do not believe that the con-tinuation of transnational nation-state building across generations is an inevitable outcome of transnational migration. Even if politi-cians in emigrant-sending countries pass laws that extend forms of dual nationality into future generations, as they have done in the Dominican Republic, Mexico, and Colombia, they are not ensuring the long distance nationalism of future generations. On the contrary, the situation we have observed in Haiti since 1996 shows us how nationalist fervor can rapidly turn to cynicism. The paralysis of the political leadership in Haiti, which included members recruited from the diaspora, created cynicism and a loss of nationalist fervor in members of the second generation in both the United States and Haiti. The interaction between transnational social fields and both the growth and diminution of a long distance nationalism that links populations across borders and generations must be systematically explored. Our purpose here is to take the first step by posing a transnational perspective on the second generation.

From "The Generation of Identity: Redefining the Second Generation Within a Transnational Social Field," by Georges E. Fouron and Nina Glick-Schiller, which appears in *Migration, Transnationalization, and Race in a Changing New York,* edited by Hector R. Cordero-Guzman, Robert C. Smith, and Ramon Grosfoguel. Reprinted by permission of Temple University Press. © 2001 by Temple University. All Rights Reserved.

This chapter draws from research supported by grants or institutional support from the National Institute of Mental Health, the National Institute for Child Health and Human Development, the Wenner-Gren Foundation, the University of New Hampshire Graduate Dean's Research Fellowship and the University of New Hampshire Center for the Humanities, the Mellon Foundation's Global Migration Project at Yale University, the Rockefeller Foundation, and CEMI, UNICAMP, Brazil. We would like to acknowledge the encouragement and support of Patricia Pessar, Bela Feldman Bianco, Bert Feintuck, Marilyn Hoskin, Maurice and Solange Fouron, Max Bernard, Maud Fouron, and Stephen Reyna. Special thanks to members of the next generation, including Seendy and Valerie Fouron and Rachel and Naomi Schiller. Portions of this paper appear in Glick-Schiller and Fouron (2001). The names of people interviewed in Haiti and some transmigrants have been changed.

NOTES

1. Within the United States the identities of the second generation are shaped by the particular Haitian settlement within which young people have grown up. Members of the second generation who live in the New York metropolitan area, the largest and oldest Haitian settlement and a center of identity politics, may be more focused on their Haitian identity than those in south Florida, where the Haitian settlement is newer, has had a much smaller core of community activists, and faces a very different configuration of local ethnic politics. See Glick-Schiller and Fouron (1998) for additional thoughts about the differences between the Haitian experience in south Florida and in the New York metropolitan area, and Stepick (1998) for an ethnography based on the Haitian experience in south Florida. In our reference to Haitian immigrants of both the first and second generations we use the word *diaspora,* following a usage of the word that is now widespread both in Haiti and in Haitian settlements abroad. Until the fall of the Duvalier regime in 1986, the word *diaspora* was used by only a handful of Haitian leaders abroad to signal their continuing connection with the Haitian political process. Within a decade the increasingly visible participation of Haitians abroad in daily life in Haiti and in the Haitian political process popularized the word until it entered into the Kreyòl language. Most of the youth we interviewed in Haiti were familiar with the word and took it to mean Haitians living abroad. It is much less fa-

miliar to the second generation living in New York. As we show, they tend to use the word *community* in a way that extends the boundaries of community to include persons of Haitian descent in the many locations of immigrant settlement as well as in Haiti.

2. The term *social field* has also been used by Pierre Bourdieu to refer to "a network, or configuration of objective relations" (Jenkins 1992, 85).

3. We use the term *transnational social field* rather than "transnational community" (Goldring 1996) or "transnational locality" (Smith 1998b) because it is useful to be able to differentiate between various types of transnational connections. The terms *transnational community* and *transnational locality* are best employed for a very specific form of connection to a specific town or location of origin. Past generations of immigrants to the United States (Bodnar 1985; Chun 1990; Soyer 1997; Wyman 1993), as well as contemporary immigrants, have built hometown associations that closely link the locale of origin with members of that town who have settled abroad (Goldring 1996; Levitt 1998; Smith 1998b). Even in such cases the term *community* may be an ideological construction that obscures class differences. We prefer the concept of transnational locality for this set of transnational connections.

4. While many Haitians now use the term *diaspora* to describe those living abroad, we believe that it is important to distinguish between long distance nationalism and a diasporic consciousness such as that described by Paul Gilroy (1993). Diasporic consciousness does not focus on a particular nation-state building project. We also exclude the flexible use of citizenship found in Aihwa Ong's description (1999) of overseas Chinese who may have obtained citizenship in many states but identify with the nation-state of none of them.

5. In approaching long distance nationalism as both words and action so that nationalism constitutes the state and is constituted by it we build on Craig Calhoun's statement (1997, 6), "There is nationalism as discourse: the production of cultural understandings and rhetoric which leads people around the world to think and frame their aspirations in terms of the idea of nation and national identity. . . . There is [also] nationalism as project: social movements and state policies by which people attempt to advance the interests of collectivities they understand as nations."

6. Increasing numbers of the leaders of these countries are transmigrants who were educated in the United States and maintain strong roots there. The president of the Dominican Republic elected in 1998 was a transmigrant with significant ties to Dominicans in New York (Guarnizo 1997).

7. Sunaina Maira's research (2000) among young people whose parents emigrated from India to New York City provides us with evidence of

a second generation of Indians living within transnational social fields that connect them to India through both nostalgia and long distance nationalism.

8. Rob Smith (1998a) has made a similar critique of the research on the second generation.

9. Dandicat's third book, a novel that explores Haitian settlement in the Dominican Republic and the 1937 massacre of Haitians by the Trujillo government, has fanned Haitian nationalist sentiment among Haitian immigrants in the United States, including the second generation. The novel was published in English in 1998, and its Haitian readership is the highly educated sector of the Haitian second generation in the United States, but its message was much more widely disseminated because the book has been discussed extensively on Haitian radio programs that are broadcast every day.

10. The 1990 U.S. census (Bureau of the Census 1993) reports that 41 percent of Haitian immigrants have less than a high school education, 48 percent have at least a high school education, and 11 percent have college degrees or higher. Women are about as likely as men to obtain a high school or college education.

11. Three of these students saw themselves as both Haitian and American at the same time but more Haitian than American. They were generally not comfortable with seeing themselves as "hyphenated Americans," although one of the students explained that a high school teacher had instructed her that "Haitian American" was her proper identity. The one young woman who identified herself as "Haitian American" went on to explain, "I think I'm Haitian before I'm American." The rest were adamant about the fact that they were only Haitian. Although in this chapter we are examining the Haitian long distance nationalism of these U.S.-born students, we are not claiming that this is their sole identity. We attribute some of their adamancy about their Haitian identity to their experiences on a college campus that demands an identity politics and to the fact that Georges, a faculty member on the campus who self-identifies as Haitian, did the interviewing.

12. Even when political repression in Haiti made it difficult for organizations in the United States to actually maintain ties to Haiti or develop ties, we found that Haitian organizations defined their activities in the United States as contributing to life in Haiti and as being part of Haitian life. In 1985 we interviewed the leaders of Haitian clubs at various college campuses, the Caribbean Youth Association, composed of Haitians, and a soccer club. All but one of the persons interviewed saw the actions of their organization in the United States as contributing

to Haiti, arguing that activities that took place in the United States ensured that "people from Haiti lived a better life."

13. All six closely resembled one another in their knowledge of and interest in questions of Haitian identity, their understanding of Haiti as a transnational nation-state, and their desire to migrate to the United States.

14. The use of the word *cultivateur* rather than *paysan* reflects the class aspirations of these young people who have acquired a high school education. The word paysan when it is used in Haiti denotes the bottom of the society. In fact, those in the rural area have been defined as outside political society. Aristide, when he became president, discontinued the practice of issuing special birth certificates with the word paysan for those born in rural areas of Haiti. In contrast, the one professional parent was a land surveyor, a powerful position in the rural area because such persons must certify all land deeds and transactions.

15. Going abroad to study may not necessarily mean to the United States. Many young people are sent to Mexico, the Dominican Republic, or Europe to study fields such as medicine, agronomy, and engineering. With that diploma in hand, at a lesser cost than a U.S. education, young people may then be sponsored or find a way to migrate to the United States, where employment prospects and remuneration for professionals is higher. Even if they cannot enter the United States, their foreign degrees will help them find positions in Haiti or set up their own practices. They reenter Haitian society with the prestige of a foreign diploma as well as with the mystique of having lived abroad.

16. The young people at the radio station averaged 12.3 years of education. One was still attending school. The other five had completed their schooling, but two had only rheto degrees, and one had yet to pass the philo exam, meaning that half of those interviewed could not continue on to a university education in Haiti. In order to enter university in Haiti, a student must attend secondary school for six years and pass a competitive examination at the end of the fifth year (rheto) and the sixth year (philo). However, in the United States, a rheto diploma is considered equivalent to a high school diploma. For young people in Haiti who have not been able to obtain the resources, or have not been able to pass the philo, the only hope for further education lies abroad.

17. The Voice of America broadcast a program in Kreyòl. Radio Tropicale is a radio station that broadcasts simultaneously in Haiti and in the diaspora.

REFERENCES

Anderson, Benedict. 1991. *Imagined Communities: Reflections on the Origins and Spread of Nationalism,* rev. ed. London: Verso.

———. 1993. "The New World Disorder." *New Left Review* 193: 2–13.

———. 1994. "Exodus." *Critical Inquiry* 20(winter): 314–27.

Barnes, J. A. 1954. "Class and Committees in the Norwegian Island Parish." *Human Relations* 7: 39–58.

———. 1969. "Networks and Political Process." In *Social Networks in Urban Situations,* edited by J. Clyde Mitchell. Manchester, Eng.: Manchester University Press.

Basch, Linda, Nina Glick-Schiller, and Cristina Szanton-Blanc. 1994. *Nations Unbound: Transnational Projects, Postcolonial Predicaments, and Deterritorialized Nation-states.* Langhorne, Penn.: Gordon and Breach.

Bodnar, John. 1985. *The Transplanted: A History of Immigrants in Urban America.* Bloomington: Indiana University Press.

Calhoun, Craig. 1997. *Nationalism.* Minneapolis: University of Minnesota Press.

Chun, Sucheng. 1990. "European and Asian Immigration into the United States in Comparative Perspective, 1820s to 1920s." In *Immigration Reconsidered: History, Sociology, and Politics,* edited by Virginia Yans-McLaughlin. New York: Oxford University Press.

Dandicat, Edwidge. 1996. *Krick? Krak!* New York: Vintage.

———. 1998a. *Breath, Eyes, Memory.* New York: Random House.

———. 1998b. *The Farming of the Bones.* New York: Soho.

Fouron, Georges, and Nina Glick-Schiller. 1997. "Haitian Identities at the Juncture Between Diaspora and Homeland." In *Caribbean Circuits,* edited by Patricia Pessar. Staten Island, N.Y.: Center for Migration Studies.

Gilroy, Paul. 1993. *The Black Atlantic: Modernity and Double Consciousness.* Cambridge, Mass.: Harvard University Press.

Gleason, Philip. 1982. "American Identity and Americanization." In *Harvard Encyclopedia of American Ethnic Groups,* edited by Stephan Thernstrom. Cambridge, Mass.: Harvard University Press.

Glick-Schiller, Nina. 1999a. "Transmigrants and Nation-states: Something Old and Something New in U.S. Immigrant Experience." In *The Handbook of International Migration: The American Experience,* edited by Charles Hirschman, Philip Kasinitz, and Josh DeWind. New York: Russell Sage Foundation.

———. 1999b. " 'Who Are These Guys?': A Transnational Reading of the U.S. Immigrant Experience." In *Identities on the Move: Transnational*

Processes in North America and the Caribbean Basin, edited by Liliana Goldin. Austin: University of Texas Press.

———. 1999c. "Citizens in Transnational Nation-states: The Asian Experience." In *Globalisation and the Asia-Pacific,* edited by Kris Olds, Peter Dickern, Philip Kelly, Lily Kong, and Henry Wai-chung Yeung. London: Routledge.

Glick-Schiller, Nina, Linda Basch, and Cristina Szanton-Blanc. 1992. "Transnationalism: A New Analytic Framework for Understanding Migration." In *Towards a Transnational Perspective on Migration: Race, Class, Ethnicity, and Nationalism Reconsidered,* edited by Nina Glick-Schiller, Linda Basch, and Cristina Szanton-Blanc. New York: New York Academy of Sciences.

———. 1995. "From Immigrant to Transmigrant: Theorizing Transnational Migration." *Anthropological Quarterly* 68(1): 48–63.

Glick-Schiller, Nina, and Georges Fouron. 1990. " 'Everywhere We Go We Are in Danger': Ti Manno and the Emergence of a Haitian Transnational Identity." *American Ethnologist* 17(2): 329–47.

———. 1998. "Transnational Lives and National Identities: The Identity Politics of Haitian Immigrants." In *Transnationalism from Below,* edited by Michael Peter Smith and Luis Guarnizo. New Brunswick, N.J.: Transaction Press.

———. 1999. "Terrains of Blood and Nation: Haitian Transnational Social Fields." *Ethnic and Racial Studies* 22(2): 340–66.

———. 2001. *Georges Woke up Laughing: Long Distance Nationalism and the Search for Home.* Durham, N.C.: Duke University Press.

Goldring, Luin. 1996. "Blurring Borders: Constructing Transnational Community in the Process of Mexico-U.S. Migration." *Research in Community Sociology* 6: 69–104.

Gordon, Milton M. 1964. *Assimilation in American Life: The Role of Race, Religion, and National Origins.* New York: Oxford University Press.

Graham, Pamela. 1996. "Nationality and Political Participation in the Transnational Context of Dominican Migration." In *Caribbean Circuits: Transnational Approaches to Migration,* edited by Patricia Pessar. Staten Island, N.Y.: Center for Migration Studies.

Guarnizo, Luis Eduardo. 1997. "Social Transformation and the Mirage of Return Migration Among Dominican Transmigrants." In *Transnational Processes and Situated Identities,* special issue of *Identities: Global Studies in Culture and Power,* edited by Nina Glick-Schiller, 4: 281–322.

———. 1998. "The Rise of Transnational Social Formations: Mexican and Dominican State Responses to Transnational Migration." *Political Power and Social Theory* 12: 45–94.

Haitian American Community Action Network (HACAN). 1996. Conference packet for the Conference on Building a Haitian Community Action Network, New York (October).

Jenkins, Richard. 1992. *Pierre Bourdieu*. London: Routledge.

Kearney, Michael. 1991. "Borders and Boundaries of the State and Self at the End of Empire." *Journal of Historical Sociology* 4(1): 52–74.

Laguerre, Michel. 1978. "Ticouloute and His Kinfolk: The Study of a Haitian Extended Family." In *The Extended Family in Black Societies,* edited by Dmitri Shimkin, Edith Shimkin, and Dennis Frate. The Hague: Mouton.

———. 1998. *Diasporic Citizenship: Haitian Americans in Transnational America*. New York: St. Martin's.

Lessinger, Johanna. 1995. *From the Ganges to the Hudson*. New York: Allyn and Bacon.

Levitt, Peggy. 1998. "Forms of Transnational Community and Their Impact on the Second Generation: Preliminary Findings." Paper presented at the Conference on Transnationalism and the Second Generation, Harvard University, Cambridge, Mass. (April 3–4).

Mahler, Sarah. 1998. "Theoretical and Empirical Contributions Toward a Research Agenda for Transnationalism." In *Transnationalism from Below,* edited by Michael Peter Smith and Luis Eduardo Guarnizo. New Brunswick, N.J.: Transaction Press.

Maira, Sunaina. 2000. "Mixed Desires: Second-Generation Indian Americans and the Politics of Youth Culture." Paper presented at the Conference on Diaspora and Displacement: Researching and Teaching the Asian Diasporas, Brown University, Providence, R.I. (April 15).

Margolis, Maxine. 1998. *An Invisible Minority: Brazilians in New York City*. Boston: Allyn and Bacon.

Mitchell, J. Clyde, ed. 1969. *Social Networks in Urban Situations*. Manchester, Eng.: University of Manchester Press.

Noble, Mary. 1973. "Social Network: Its Use as a Conceptual Framework in Family Analysis." In *Network Analysis in Human Interaction,* edited by Jeremy Boissevain and J. Clyde Mitchell. The Hague: Mouton.

Ong, Aihwa. 1999. *Flexible Citizenship: The Cultural Logics of Transnationality*. Durham, N.C.: Duke University Press.

Pessar, Patricia. 1995. *A Visa for a Dream*. New York: Allyn and Bacon.

Portes, Alejandro. 1995. "Children of Immigrants: Segmented Assimilation and Its Determinants." In *The Economic Sociology of Immigration: Essays on Networks, Ethnicity, and Entrepreneurship,* edited by Alejandro Portes. New York: Russell Sage Foundation.

Portes, Alejandro, Luis Guarnizo, and Patricia Landolt, eds. 1999. *Transnational Communities,* special issue of *Ethnic and Racial Studies* 22(2).

Portes, Alejandro, and Min Zhou. 1993. "The Second Generation: Segmented Assimilation and Its Variants." *Annals of the American Academy of Political and Social Science* 530: 74–96.

Rouse, Roger. 1991. "Mexican Migration and the Social Space of Postmodernism." *Diaspora* 1: 8–23.

———. 1992. "Making Sense of Settlement: Class Transnationalism, Cultural Struggle and Transformation Among Mexican Migrants in the United States." In *Towards a Transnational Perspective on Migration: Race, Class, Ethnicity, and Nationalism Reconsidered,* edited by Nina Glick-Schiller, Linda Basch, and Cristina Blanc-Szanton. New York: Annals of the New York Academy of Sciences, vol. 675.

Rumbaut, Rubén G. 1996. "The Crucible Within: Ethnic Identity, Self-esteem, and Segmented Assimilation Among Children of Immigrants." In *The New Second Generation,* edited by Alejandro Portes. New York: Russell Sage Foundation.

Sanchez, Arturo Ignacio. 1997. "Transnational Political Agency and Identity Formation Among Colombian Immigrants." Paper presented at the Conference on Transnational Communities and the Political Economy of New York, New School for Social Research, New York (February).

Simpson, George, and J. Milton Yinger. 1958. *Racial and Cultural Minorities.* New York: Harper.

Smith, Joan, and Immanuel Wallerstein, eds. 1992. *Creating and Transforming Households: The Constraints of the World Economy.* New York: Cambridge University Press.

Smith, Michael Peter, and Luis Guarnizo, eds. 1998. *Transnationalism from Below.* New Brunswick, N.J.: Transaction Press.

Smith, Robert. 1995. *"Los Ausentes Siempre Presentes:* The Imagining, Making, and Politics of Transnational Community Between Ticuani, Puebla, Mexico, and New York City." Ph.D. diss., Columbia University.

———. 1997. "Transnational Migration, Assimilation, and Political Community." In *The City and the World,* edited by Margaret Crahan and Alberto Vourvoulias Bush. New York: Council on Foreign Relations.

———. 1998a. "Life Course, Cohort, and Gender as Variables Affecting Second Generation Transnational Life." Paper presented at the Conference on Transnationalism and the Second Generation, Harvard University, Cambridge, Mass. (April 3–4).

———. 1998b. "Transnational Localities: Community, Technology, and the Politics of Membership Within the Context of Mexico-U.S. Migration." In *Transnationalism from Below,* edited by Michael Peter Smith and Luis Guarnizo. New Brunswick, N.J.: Transaction Press.

Soyer, Daniel. 1997. *Jewish Immigrant Associations and American Identity in New York, 1880–1939.* Cambridge, Mass.: Harvard University Press.

Stepick, Alex. 1998. *Pride Against Prejudice: Haitians in the United States.* Boston: Allyn and Bacon.

Turner, Victor. 1967. "Aspects of Sora Ritual and Shamanism: An Approach to the Data of Ritual." In *The Craft of Social Anthropology,* edited by A. E. Epstein. London: Tavistock.

U.S. Bureau of the Census. 1993. *1990 Census of Population: Foreign-born Population in the United States.* Washington: U.S. Government Printing Office.

Vickerman, Milton. 1999. *Cross Currents: West Indian Immigrants and Race.* New York: Oxford University Press.

Warner, W. Lloyd, and Leo Srole. 1945. *The Social Systems of American Ethnic Groups.* New Haven, Conn.: Yale University Press.

Waters, Mary C. 1996. "Ethnic and Racial Identities of Second-Generation Black Immigrants in New York City." In *The New Second Generation,* edited by Alejandro Portes. New York: Russell Sage Foundation.

———. 1999. *Black Identities: West Indian Immigrant Dreams and American Realities.* Cambridge, Mass.: Harvard University Press.

Wyman, Mark. 1993. *Round-Trip to America: The Immigrants Return to Europe, 1880–1930.* Ithaca, N.Y.: Cornell University Press.

— Part II —

Questioning Some Underlying Assumptions

—— Chapter 7 ——

On Deconstructing and Reconstructing the Meaning of Immigrant Generations

Susan Eckstein

T HE ESSAYS IN this volume on second-generation post-1965 immigrants focus on two central issues: whether immigrants and their children have different assimilation experiences and different transnational ties, and the adequacy of the long-established assimilationist paradigm to account for the views and involvements of the so-called new immigrants, who have been peopling the United States since the mid-1960s.

Immigrant transnational identity and activity proves to be not unique to post-1965 immigrants. Italians who came earlier in the century, for example, retained close ties with their home country. However, technological innovations have allowed for a speedup in cross-border communication and transportation, and the post-1965 American multicultural milieu is more tolerant of ethnic differences. Both of these factors make new immigrants more likely than earlier émigrés to retain transnational values and involvements.

Of equal if not greater significance is a change in *theorizing* about immigrant experience. In the Kuhnian (1996) sense, there has been a "scientific revolution," a paradigmatic shift. In the pre-1965 period scholars analyzed immigrant experiences almost exclusively from a "straight-line" perspective (and variations thereof), while scholars now, as illustrated in this volume, increasingly draw

211

on a paradigm that highlights homeland ties that coexist with assimilation tendencies.

At the same time the concept of generations has remained virtually intact. The a priori assumption of this book is that generations are biologically based within the context of families, an assumption shared with earlier "assimilationists." The transnational versus assimilationist frame, however, suggests that second generation experiences are likely to differ in accordance with parental experiences. Children's views and involvements should vary if their parents assimilate or retain transnational ties.

How can one group of scholars find assimilation to be the key feature of second-generation experience and another group find transnationalism the key feature? Is the difference analytically explained by the different lenses through which they are viewing immigrant experiences? Or is it empirically explained by contrasting actual immigrant group experiences before and after 1965? Both factors, I believe, are at play. But most of all, the different portrayals tacitly point to a shared problem in the concept of generations embedded in the two schools of thought.

Both schools have tended to use the family as their unit of analysis, and both focus on whether *intra-family* dynamics influence immigrant adaptation. Generational experiences, however, are not only grounded in intra-family dynamics but very much shaped by the historical context in which parents and children live. Karl Mannheim (1952) perceptively argued (though *not* with respect to immigration) that common experiences during youth may create a common worldview or frame of reference that influences subsequent political experiences. Since not all members of an age cohort react the same to the events they experience (for example, reactions vary by social class) and since political experiences may be shaped by age variations, political generations should be understood in terms of key historical experiences and not merely youth-based experiences.

There is reason to believe that political generational experiences are not entirely left behind with emigration. This would be especially likely in the case of refugees. But there is also reason to believe that historically grounded, generationally variable immigrant "baggage" is cultural and economic as well as political, and that it too influences immigrant adaptation.

Meanwhile, people in the homeland may be influenced by family abroad, by new institutions and practices that integrate "diasporas" into their home country, and by the media and the like. Such transnational exposure, in turn, may form part of the historical generational experiences of people who never emigrate or who emigrate at a later point in time. People in the homeland may be absorbed into influential networks and norms that transcend national borders.

Cohorts that differ in their pre-emigration backgrounds can thus be expected to differ, in certain respects, in their post-emigration experiences as well. Yet, also contributing to different adaptation experiences are variations in conditions in the country (and community) of settlement, contingent on the time of arrival. It is thus possible that generational adaptation is shaped more by pre- and post-emigration, historically grounded experiences than by birth order.

It is time to deconstruct the concept of generation and reconceptualize it. If immigrant adaptation is shaped by historical and contextual generational experiences, we would expect first-generation immigrants who resettled in different time periods to adapt differently, and first- and second-generation immigrants at any given point in time to share a range of similar experiences.

Indeed, the very significance of transnationalism among post-1965 immigrants, of *both* the first and second generations, can be traced to specific historical conditions that were nonexistent before the 1960s. Immigrant parents *and* their children who grew up in the immediate post–World War II period and those who grew up in the post-1965 period represent different historical cohorts. In the earlier era economic opportunities for immigrants were greater, the media and the schools emphasized assimilation, and views of the nation and state were territorially grounded. By contrast, since 1965 economic opportunities for immigrants have contracted, both in manufacturing, as the United States has deindustrialized, and in the service sector, where big business increasingly marginalizes possibilities for small start-up firms. Unskilled immigrants under the circumstances are concentrated in jobs that offer few career opportunities and few ties to middle-class Americans and their "habits of the heart."[1] And since the social movements of the 1960s, tolerance toward cultural pluralism and diversity increased, transnational transportation and communications costs decreased, and technological innovations both speeded up cross-border contacts and allowed immigrants to remit money easily to needy family left behind.

At the same time conditions in the immigrant sending countries have changed. In the wake of the debt crises of the 1980s and neo-liberal economic restructuring, Third World economic opportunities have also contracted. With living standards falling, people there increasingly look to the United States for work. Low-paid jobs in the United States are more remunerative than the options for many back home. And the governments themselves have come to look favorably on emigration, which reduces their unemployment rates— and thus political tensions—and generates remittance-based hard currency, desperately needed for both family survival and government import, investment, and foreign debt repayment exigencies. So interested have Third World governments become in encouraging remittance sending that they have established institutional structures to facilitate and encourage monetary transfers and continued homeland ties. The impact of such macro economic and state policies on immigrant adaptation is explicable within a historical generational frame, but not within an intra-family biological frame. Though immigrant experiences are not entirely predetermined by such historical circumstances, they are so circumscribed.

The utility of a sociohistorical generational frame is especially well illustrated by the contribution of Fouron and Glick-Schiller in this volume.[2] In a very interesting analysis, these authors describe, for example, how the political conception of who is Haitian has been redefined with the stepped-up scale of island emigration in recent years. The redefinition takes place at the state level, not merely at the level of individuals and families. The Haitian government has gone so far as to redefine the nation-state to include overseas Haitians as a territorial division. And the scale of immigration has changed the discourse. The word *diaspora,* for instance, has been added to the Kreyòl lexicon and come to have a positive meaning.

Fouron and Glick-Schiller argue that even Haitians remaining on the island should be viewed as second-generation, insofar as they have been influenced, through family networks, the media, and institutional changes, by the Haitian diaspora. The authors' conception of generations is not territorially bounded. They very perceptively conceptualize current generations, not in terms of where people live or where they were born, but rather as grounded in imagined as well as actual experiences shared across borders. They speak of "imagined generations," but historically grounded imagined generations.

The imagined generations do not exist, to borrow Marx's phrase, in "thin air." The second generation, the authors argue, includes all those born after the large-scale transnational immigration gained momentum, whether they live abroad or in the homeland. Today there is great cross-border fluidity among the Haitians—economically, socially, culturally, and politically.

In sum, a historically grounded conception of generations, when sufficiently specified, better explains similarities and differences among immigrants and their children than a biologically grounded conception. We can expect cohort experiences to be shaped more by macro economic conditions and state policies in both the sending and receiving countries and by cross-border networks and norms than by intra-family relations between parents and their progeny.

NOTES

1. On the characteristics of contemporary U.S. culture and their middle-class base, see Bellah et al. (1985).
2. In Eckstein and Barberia (2002), I illustrate how a historically grounded conceptualization of generations accounts for different immigrant experiences and views among first-generation Cuban immigrants who settled in the United States before and after 1980. The two first-generation cohorts differed in their class backgrounds, their reasons for emigration, their frequency of contact with their homeland, and their attitudes toward homeland ties, for example.

REFERENCES

Bellah, Robert et al. 1985. *Habits of the Heart: Individualism and Commitment in American Life.* Berkeley: University of California Press.

Eckstein, Susan, and Lorena Barberia. 2002. "Re-envisioning Generations: Cuban Immigrant Cohorts and Their Transnational Ties." *International Migration Review* 36(3).

Kuhn, Thomas. 1996. *The Structure of Scientific Revolutions.* Chicago: University of Chicago Press.

Mannheim, Karl. 1952. "The Problem of Generations." In *Essays on the Sociology of Knowledge,* edited by Paul Kecksckemeti. New York: Oxford University Press.

— Chapter 8 —

Second-Generation Transnationalism

Joel Perlmann

AMONG HISTORIANS OF the earlier European immigrations, the first question about transnationalism that one often hears is, Just how much is really new in the new transnationalism?, or in this case, How much is really new in the new second-generation transnational behavior? The point most often made about historical precedents for transnationalism is that knowing about the precedents helps dampen excessive claims that particular experiences observed in our own time are novel. Dampening excessive claims, of course, is useful, and yet it should be recalled that even if transnationalism is not entirely novel, it still deserves attention. We do not, after all, argue that just because labor migration existed in the past we should not study contemporary labor migrations. And we do not protest when new and more subtle conceptualizations of labor migration are developed. On the contrary, we may well find ourselves applying these newer and more subtle conceptualizations in historical studies too.

So I want to balance the recognition that transnationalism deserves attention and the urge to dampen excessive claims for transnationalism. I make this point explicitly, because most of my comments derive from the urge to dampen excess. In particular, my comments are organized around the question: What are the implications of the claims for second-generation transnationalism? The implication made for the historical novelty of transnationalism is, I think, in connection with the future of assimilation. Either explicitly or implicitly, transnationalism is related to the notion that the process of assimilation will take a different course now than it has taken in the past. More precisely, the argument that transnationalism is strong, especially in the second generation, makes its broadest claim for attention when it hints, or implies, or boldly asserts that in the face of immigrant and second-generation embeddedness in two societies, assimilation as it occurred in the past cannot be expected in the future. Given this formulation, of course, the need for historical specificity cannot be avoided.

I organize my more specific approach to these issues around three distinctions. The first distinction concerns *immigrant versus second-generation transnationalism,* and specifically, the domains of social embeddedness that are being stressed in connection with each. Many have observed that the concept of transnationalism is too broad; Alejandro Portes, for one, proposes a helpful solution, namely, that immigrant transnationalism is most fruitfully discussed first of all in terms of embeddedness in two economies. However, much discussion of second-generation transnationalism seems to be concerned with the cultural domain. This focus on cultural rather than economic patterns is understandable on numerous grounds— not the least of which is that, as of this writing, the new second generation is young, and evidence for its economic embeddedness would lie in the future. However, I think another reason for the cultural emphasis is the assumption that when the evidence of second-generation economic behavior becomes available, it will show much weaker economic ties to the country of origin than does first-generation behavior—because the comparative advantages of the immigrants may not be available to second-generation members, for example. Language skills are a good example. The question will not be whether, for example, a second-generation Brazilian American knows more Portuguese than the average U.S. citizen, but whether the former's command of Portuguese is at the level of a Brazilian adult's in the world of business.

In any case, what then are the implications of seeking evidence from the domain of cultural practices or adolescent self-identity for understanding how transnationalism might be shaping future American ethnicity? In discussing immigrant and second-generation experiences, the most that can be claimed is that the former provides a context in which the latter can develop—that is, certain kinds of second-generation orientations may be related to certain first-generation arrangements. However, other factors besides first-generation transnationalism may also contribute to the character of second-generation orientations. Here is the relevance of history: if second generations in the past were characterized by much the same range of cultural practices and adolescent identity choices, then how much can the present-day second generation's cultural experience be rooted in a first-generation pattern that is said to be novel, namely, its transnational embeddedness? My point is not to dispute or affirm the novelty of the first-generation transnational embeddedness. Rather, it is to argue the assumption that second-generation cultural patterns are emerging as a result of what is claimed to be new about the first-generation experience. Also, of course, if second generations in the past were characterized by much the same range of cultural experiences as are the present second generations, then the larger implication—that past forms of assimilation will not occur this time around because of those cultural experiences—is also challenged.[1] Finally, I appreciate the claim that we need to be open to a wide spectrum of second-generation cultural responses. However, one might say that we also need to be open to matters of prevalence; claims about cultural orientation cry out for some quantitative grounding.

The second kind of distinction I want to highlight concerns the experience of people in the *sending versus the receiving countries*. Discussions about the impact of immigration on the country of origin may be interesting and important; nevertheless, such discussions cannot directly add to our knowledge about what if anything is special about the experiences of immigrants and ethnics in the United States today. Only the analysis of the people in the receiving country can prove that something distinctive is occurring here.

The third kind of distinction I want to make is among the *various possible receptions in the host country*. Of course, the host country's approach to issues of immigration and pluralism will matter to second-generation identity. But the answer can hardly be that the host society is uniformly hostile. We must deal not only with the impact of anti-immigrant and anti-minority movements but also with encouragement by the state—especially the educational system's stress on multicultural awareness. We need to develop a vocabulary not only for comfortably discussing the hostility of the host society but for discussing the implications of toleration and encouragement of multiculturalism. We must find a vocabulary with which to ask, for example, how much the new school curriculum will contribute to the preservation of cultural distinctiveness. It is true that cultural conservatives and bigoted restrictionists ask such questions. Yet that fact alone should not allow us to ignore the question. Indeed, it has not stopped Gary Gerstle and David Tyack (Gerstle 2001; Tyack 2001)—two historians not usually thought of as anxious conservatives—from trying to find a vocabulary in which to assert the state's rights and responsibilities to educate its citizenry about what is distinctively American even as it offers a multicultural perspective. In other words, these authors seek a vocabulary that would clarify such issues without contributing to immigrant bashing.

And finally, we need a nonpunitive vocabulary with which to ask what affirmative action means for second-generational identity. We are in the third decade of a program through which the state conveys to many immigrants and their offspring (and *their* offspring) a message that is different from the message that the state conveyed in the past. The message is not only that the state reveres the ideal of treating citizens without regard to ethnic origins; it is also that the state recognizes that such origins were far from irrelevant in the past and may well still be relevant today, and so the state will continue to take note of the ethnic origins of immigrants and descendants— for benevolent reasons.[2] We need to find a way to explore whether this difference in the official ideology conveyed to immigrants and their offspring is significant. Of course, we will not want to lose sight of the fact that official ideologies of the past and present may be dripping with hypocrisy, but stating that point does not invalidate the need to explore whether the change in official ideology affects assimilation. This too is part of the question of host-society receptions. If we do not find a humane way to discuss it, others will continue to find inhumane ways to discuss it.

NOTES

1. In searching for distinctive cultural orientations, however, I do not think that the sole (or even the most important) criterion for second-generation transnational embeddedness is the presence of a desire to return permanently to the sending country. Even without such a desire, second-generation youth might still inhabit a novel cultural space.

2. That the original, and central, thrust of affirmative action was to help native-born blacks is not at issue here.

REFERENCES

Gerstle, Gary. 2001. *American Crucible: Race and Nation in the Twentieth Century*. Princeton, N.J.: Princeton University Press.

Tyack, David. 2001. "Schools for Citizens: The Politics of Civic Education from 1790 to 1990." In *E Pluribus Unum? Contemporary and Historical Perspectives on Immigrant Political Incorporation*, edited by Gary Gerstle and John Mollenkopf. New York: Russell Sage Foundation.

—— Chapter 9 ——

The Study of Transnationalism Among the Children of Immigrants: Where We Are and Where We Should Be Headed

Michael Jones-Correa

THIS VOLUME EXAMINES the life trajectories taken by the children of immigrants in the United States, who live in a world where rapid communication and travel make sustained contact with their parents' country of origin more possible today perhaps than ever before. Under these conditions, immigrants' children who have by and large grown up in the United States may orient themselves toward their parents' country of origin, toward the United States, or toward both. How will the second generation's ties and loyalties play out? Will immigrants keep up the transnational ties of their parents or abandon them in favor of new ties in the United States?

The contributions to this volume implicitly pose three questions: Does second generation transnationalism exist? How extensive is it? Finally, what is its significance? This chapter synthesizes the arguments and findings made by the other authors in part II to arrive at some tentative answers to these queries. It proceeds from there to muse on other, still unanswered, questions about second-generation transnationalism before concluding with thoughts on

221

some directions for the further study of transnationalism and assimilation among immigrants and their children in the United States.

DOES SECOND-GENERATION
TRANSNATIONALISM EXIST?

The first question—does transnationalism exist among the children of immigrants?—is the easiest to answer. All of the studies presented in this volume find that transnational behavior—an "interconnectedness across borders that enables individuals to sustain multiple identities and loyalties," as Levitt and Waters put it in their introduction—continues into the second generation. At least some of the children of immigrants, for instance, maintain some knowledge of their parents' native language, travel back and forth to their parents' country of origin, and even send remittances back to extended family.

As Levitt and Waters point out, establishing the fact of transnational behavior in the second generation brings to light patterns of attitudes, behavior, and identification that were overshadowed in the literature of the earlier immigrant wave by the emphasis on assimilation. This does not imply that transnationalism among the second generation today is an entirely new phenomenon; it almost certainly has existed historically. What the contemporary study of second-generation transnationalism does is give us a new understanding of an old process—the multigenerational trajectory of immigrants in their country of settlement (on this point, see Foner 1997, and this volume; Ueda, this volume).

One caveat should be kept in mind. It is worth remembering that while all the studies here focus on the children of immigrants, not all of the members of this younger cohort are truly a native-born "second generation." Some have migrated here at a young age with their parents and so are immigrants themselves. (For instance, more than half of the individuals included in the surveys presented in the chapters by Kasinitz and his colleagues and by Rumbaut are not native-born.) The age at which young immigrants migrate also makes a difference, with those who migrate before adolescence having a greater chance of being socialized in an American context. These distinctions, which might be significant, must be fully explored before we can be confident about making pronouncements about "second-generation" immigrants.

Fouron and Glick-Schiller assert in this volume that "second generation" should in fact apply to the children of immigrants in the United States (or elsewhere) *and* their contemporaries born in their parents' country of origin. In their view, the entire context of life in the United States and in their home country for immigrants and non-immigrants alike has become transnationalized.[1] However, this definition seems at best premature; defined in this way, transnationalism becomes so diffuse as to render it almost meaningless, and what the study of transnationalism requires now is more differentiation in the concept, not less. Despite the fact that the authors here find evidence of extensive transnational behaviors among the second generation, exhibited through language, travel, and remittances, it is less than certain what the real significance of these behaviors is and whether these markers of transnationalism make a personal truly "transnational." Just as there remain uncertainties about the nature of the second generation, there is still a great deal of ambiguity around the term "transnationalism" itself. These require more precise definition and clarification.

One of the dangers in overextending the concept of "transnationalism" or "the second generation" is that we then risk committing a mistake similar to that made by the social science literature when it addressed the previous wave of immigrants in the latter part of the nineteenth century and first half of the twentieth century. This earlier literature ignored the transnational linkages continuing into the second generation and beyond and focused almost exclusively on the integration and assimilation of the second and succeeding generations. The current immigration scholarship at times seems in danger of doing precisely the opposite—overemphasizing the transnational and underplaying incorporation and assimilation. To their credit, the contributors to this volume are quick to point out that assimilation and transnationalism in many ways coexist and overlap.

HOW EXTENSIVE IS SECOND-GENERATION TRANSNATIONALISM?

Determining the extent of second-generation transnationalism is more complicated. The study of transnationalism thus far has largely been conducted through qualitative fieldwork, in which case studies tend to be selected based on their dependent variables. For example, researchers who wish to know something about transnational behavior are likely to base their criteria for case selection around where they are likely to find this behavior. This is a legitimate way of answering the first question—does it exist?—but is less helpful in determining how extensive the phenomenon might be or how it might vary. To begin to answer the second question, one needs more variance along the dependent variable—that is, one needs a wider selection of individuals selecting both transnational and assimilative trajectories and choosing from among a range of transnational and assimilative practices. This requires either qualitative analyses that provide a careful selection of a range of cases or more broad-based quantitative analyses of survey results. This volume provides us with examples of both, in Levitt's multicountry study of second-generation immigrants and in the uses of survey data by Kasinitz and his colleagues and by Rumbaut.

Drawing on larger survey samples, both Rumbaut and Kasinitz and his colleagues find that at least some of the second generation engages in regular transnational behavior. But there are important variations in this behavior. For instance, in their study of eighteen- to thirty-two-year-old children of immigrants in New York City, Kasinitz and his colleagues find that transnational behaviors vary significantly by country of origin: one-third of Dominicans and South Americans have "strong" transnational ties (meaning they travel frequently to, send remittances to, or speak the language of their country of origin), compared with fewer than 10 percent of Russian Jewish and Chinese immigrants. In addition, those children of immigrants who rely on ethnic media or belong to ethnic organizations are also more likely to exhibit transnational behaviors. Rumbaut, drawing on a San Diego–based survey of immigrant children in their twenties (largely of Mexican, Filipino, Vietnamese, and Chinese origin), finds similar patterns of variance. He too finds that transnational behaviors vary across country of origin. Children of Mexican immigrants are much more likely to travel to their parents' home country (particularly those who live just across the border from Mexico in the San Diego area) and to continue to speak their parents' native language, while children of Filipino origin are more likely to send remittances. Levitt's smaller-scale multinational study focusing on immigrants in the Boston metropolitan area also finds variance by nationality, as well as by socioeconomic status and other factors.

Having confirmed the existence of transnational behaviors among the second generation, both of the larger survey studies find that even occasional transnational practices are limited to less than half of their samples, and that those with regular, repeated transnational behaviors account, on the whole, for a small percentage of their second-generation respondents (about 10 percent in both surveys). An overwhelming majority of the second generation is deeply rooted in the United States. In the San Diego survey, for example, by their twenties 88 percent of respondents consider the United States their home, 84 percent are U.S. citizens (even among young adults of Mexican origin this figure is still 81 percent), and 66 percent say they prefer using English. (An additional 32 percent say they are equally comfortable in English and their parents' native language.) Seventy-two percent have never sent remittances, and 75 percent have visited their parents' country less than twice in their lives. In the New York study, Kasinitz and his colleagues have similar findings on language (56 percent prefer English), travel (73 percent have traveled to their parents' home country three times or less), and remittances (71 percent have never remitted money). In New York City 78 percent of the second generation are U.S. citizens (including 58 percent of those not born in the United States). Seventy percent are registered to vote in the United States, and 53 percent voted in 1996. Respondents were more interested in New York City politics than in the politics of their country of origin. For at least some of the groups examined, such as South Americans and West Indians, transnational practices seem to decrease with age, and for Dominicans the more likely immigrants are to have U.S. citizenship, the less likely they are to exhibit transnational behavior.

On the whole, these findings mirror what we can already glean from other sources: immigrants and their children in the United States seem to be here to stay and are increasingly incorporated into the social and political life of this country. Other national survey data indicate, for instance, that:

- Immigrants are no more likely to return to their country of origin today than they were a century ago, and their children, not surprisingly, are even less likely to do so (Immigration and Naturalization Service 1992, table 2).

- Immigrants have increased their rates of citizenship acquisition over the last ten years, and relatively few immigrants (and even fewer of their children) actively acquire dual nationality or take advantage of provisions for voting abroad (Jones-Correa 2001a).
- Immigrant remittances to home countries tend to decrease over time (DeSipio 2000).
- As they settle in as stable residents in neighborhoods across the United States, more and more immigrants are homeowners (Joint Center for Housing Studies 2001). Homeownership implies an increasing stake in American social and political life.
- Immigrants and their children learn English; indeed, their children become English-dominant (Portes and Rumbaut 2001; Rumbaut and Portes 2001).
- The children of immigrants have high rates of outmarriage: at least one-quarter of Asian and Latino immigrants marry outside their broad ethnic-racial categories (as defined by the census) in the first generation; half do so by the second generation (Farley 1998). Keep in mind that these figures are certainly higher for those marrying out of their national origin (rather than racial-ethnic) group, so that in New York City, for instance, one sees increasing numbers of pairings among Latinos of different national origins—Puerto Rican–Mexican, Colombian-Dominican, and so on.

Despite evidence of the continued existence of transnationalism in the second generation, taken overall these data provide evidence for the linear assimilation of immigrants—the further incorporation of immigrants into society over time and with each succeeding generation. The debate about second-generation transnationalism is not, as some conservative policy analysts have pitched it, about whether immigrants and their children "Americanize." Clearly they do. Rather, the question is: What does transnationalism mean within the context of the Americanization of immigrant children?

Levitt and Waters remind us in the introduction (echoed by Smith and by Fouron and Glick-Schiller in their chapters) that even if all this were true, the Americanization of the second generation does not necessarily imply that most children of immigrants will *never* engage in transnational behaviors. Transnationalism may be occasional or sporadic, with the children of immigrants engaging in transnational behaviors in response to life events (like births, marriages, and deaths) or in response to crises in their parents' country of origin or in the immigrant community. This kind of sporadic transnationalism may escape notice, or it may be underplayed in survey results like those reported by Kasinitz and his colleagues and by Rumbaut and may only be adequately captured by qualitative fieldwork. And as Levitt and Waters point out, "selective, periodic transnational practices can add up"—that is, they may be cumulatively significant, though how is yet to be fully determined. Moreover, Levitt argues in her chapter, transnationalism will continue to play an important role in the second generation because its manifestations are likely to vary over an individual's life cycle.

Though the course of transnational activity over an immigrant's life cycle is not explicitly delineated in the contributions here, one can infer from the case studies presented in this volume—as well as from the broader literature on civic and political participation (see Jennings and Niemi 1981; Verba, Schlozman, and Brady 1995)—what this pattern might look like. Second-generation transnationalism may peak in an individual's teens and early twenties (particularly while in college), fall with the introduction of work, marriage, and children, and then increase again after some of these adult responsibilities diminish.[2] For instance, Fouron and Glick-Schiller's interviews were conducted among Haitian Americans in college, where they find there is considerable pressure to display a transnational Haitian identity. Smith's interviews with Mexicans in their mid- to late twenties, however, indicate that the second generation's assumption of adult responsibilities constricts the time and resources they can devote to transnational activities. For many of Smith's interviewees, participation in the Ticuani Youth Group seems to have been a passing phase. They look back wistfully at their activities when they were younger, but none seem to think they will be similarly engaged anytime soon. Finally, Levitt discusses the case of a middle-aged second-generation Irish American who, never having been active transnationally before, finds himself drawn in middle age back into the social networks of his parents' hometown in Ireland and engaged in the town's activities (like the building of a soccer stadium and a discussion of strategies to increase tourism). While these fluctuations over time are captured here only in the snapshots of fieldwork, they might not appear at the moment in survey responses at all.[3]

Both the notions of sporadic engagement with transnationalism and of variance in transnationalism across the life cycle are important contributions to theorizing about second-generation transnationalism. Nonetheless, the general thrust of the findings of Rumbaut and of Kasinitz and his colleagues still hold: only a minority of the second generation seem to be engaged in transnational networks, and most seem to be well on the road to incorporation into American society. How might the regular transnationalism of a few and the irregular transnationalism of others matter?

WHAT IS THE SIGNIFICANCE OF SECOND-GENERATION TRANSNATIONALISM?

None of the authors in this volume deny that transnational behaviors are less obviously present in the second generation than in the first. Indeed, from the studies presented here it appears there is a rather sharp drop in the frequency and intensity of transnational ties from the first generation to the second. So if regular transnational practices appear among 10 percent or so of the children of immigrants, as the surveys in this volume seem to find, what significance do these behaviors, attitudes, and identities have? Will they, as Levitt and Waters ask in their introduction, have any long-term, widespread impact? Among first-generation immigrants, one can readily point to the economic remittances, political participation, and social networks that have unmistakable effects on their home countries, and by implication, on the United States. Given the relatively minuscule proportion of regular transnationalism apparent among the young adults of the second generation, one might be tempted to respond that this second-generation phenomenon is of little or no significance.

However, there are good reasons to reflect before passing judgment. In addition to arguments about "sporadic" transnationalism and changes over individuals' life cycles, there are at least five ways in which second-generation transnationalism could continue to have longer-term effects, for this generation itself, for the United States, and for the parents' countries of origin.

Although transnational actors in the second generation may be quite a small minority among their peers, they may still be quite large in number. This is to say, even if only 10 percent of the 23 million members of the second generation currently living in the United States have regular patterns of transnational behavior, that 10 percent translates into 2.3 million people—not an insignificant number. If these 2.3 million young adults remain active in their transnational networks (or if, as they drop out, others come in to replace them), they could continue to have a considerable impact on both their immigrant communities and their home countries.

The consequences of the second generation's transnational behavior may be exaggerated, for better or worse, by their relative wealth and influence. For instance, the children of immigrants living in the United States can have a disproportionate effect on diaspora politics just by virtue of having more resources to contribute than their compatriots in their countries of origin. Examples might include the relationship between Irish Americans and the Irish Republican Army, or between American Jews and Israel. Benedict Anderson (1994) worries that this disproportionate influence may lead to all kinds of irresponsible meddling by immigrants in their home countries' ethnic, religious, and political feuds. In a less sinister light, second-generation transnationalism can play a significant role in the economy of the country of origin, either as a source of investment and economic development (see Kapur 2001) or as a secondary social safety net in the form of remittances.

Transnationalism is almost certainly unevenly distributed within the United States and among immigrant populations in the United States. The uneven distribution of transnationalism has in part to do with the overwhelming concentration of migrants within a handful of states, the concentration of immigrants within those states, and the clustering of particular country-of-origin groups within these immigrant populations. For example, one of the findings reported by Kasinitz and his colleagues is that second-generation Dominican immigrants are more likely to have regular contact with the Dominican Republic than, say, their Chinese counterparts have with China. Because Dominicans are heavily concentrated in the northeastern United States, and in New York City in particular, the transnational behavior of second-generation Dominicans may continue to have important consequences both for the Dominican Republic and for New York City. In addition, because most transnational behaviors (such as remittances and travel) tend to be directed at very specific localities in the home country,[4] transnationalism is also likely to have uneven effects in immigrants' countries of origin. Even quite limited transnationalism, if it is concentrated in these ways, might have significant local effects.

Latent transnational identities can be triggered by crises in the country of origin—war or other forms of political instability, for instance, or famines or other natural disasters. The mobilization of these networks need not only be focused on the country of origin. Indeed, one of the most persistent debates on immigration and international relations has been on the possible biases introduced by ethnic lobbying on the conduct of U.S. foreign affairs (see, for example, Ahrari 1987; DeConde 1992). It may even be the case that the option of transnationalism—of having alternative networks of social ties available, even if they are never taken up—has a significant impact on people's identities and choices. Knowledge of transnational possibilities, even if they represent the "road not taken," may affect an individual's life choices. These effects, however, are subtle and difficult to measure beyond individual biography.

Transnationalism could continue, or even be rejuvenated and reinforced, among the second generation owing to the continued influx of first-generation immigrants from the home country. Those who speculate on this possibility note that some of these first-generation immigrants will be of the same age as the second generation living in the United States, and so the two groups are more likely to form a single cohort (for more on this point, see Kasinitz et al., this volume). The second generation will be constantly exposed to language, media, and culture from their country of origin in ways that were not true for the second generation at the turn of the last century, when immigration was largely curtailed after 1921. However, this hypothesis relies on at least two assumptions: that immigration will continue indefinitely at its current rate, and that new immigrants in the future will be arriving into the same context as that experienced by current immigrants. There is no guarantee, however, that current patterns will continue indefinitely into the future (as I discuss later).

In sum, the significance of second-generation transnationalism depends very much on the "unevenness" in the distribution of this transnationalism, since this unevenness in time and space may translate into very different consequences for different immigrant populations and for their home-country communities.

TRANSNATIONALISM AND ASSIMILATION

The findings in this volume indicate, on the one hand, that most immigrants are incorporating into American society; the studies presented here also suggest, on the other hand, that second-generation transnationalism will continue (albeit in diminished form) and may well yet have significant consequences. On the face of it, these two conclusions might seem contradictory. Are they? It is worth taking a moment here to delve a bit deeper into the complex relationship between transnationalism and assimilation.

Levitt and Waters argue in their introduction that the two processes of assimilation and transnationalism should not be seen as opposites, and that there are multiple ways in which immigrants and their children can combine transnationalism and assimilative strategies, leading to diverse outcomes, both in the United States and in immigrants' countries of origin. Fouron and Glick-Schiller agree, declaring that "to speak about the transnational connections of persons who have emigrated from their homeland to settle abroad is to describe only one set of relationships that such persons establish." For instance, many Haitian immigrants, they note, "become well incorporated in their new country, developing relationships at work and in their neighborhood," as well as engaging in transnational practices. Other contributors to the volume also note that the second generation is engaged in social networks both within American society and across transnational social fields. Ueda, for instance, remarks that, prior to the Second World War, Japanese American high school students in Hawaii saw no incongruities in affirming their identities as both Japanese and American and indeed saw their multiple identities and loyalties as an advantage. For their part, Kasinitz and his colleagues find that the children of West Indian immigrants who are most engaged in regular transnational practices are also actively participating in New York City politics. Rumbaut discovers that homeownership, which in other contexts signals a commitment to settling permanently in the United States, is also correlated, among second-generation immigrants, with sending back remittances. This complementarity works the other way too: elsewhere I have argued that the option of dual nationality facilitates acquisition of American citizenship, so that transnationalism in this case leads to political incorporation (Jones-Correa 2001a, 2001b). These examples, then, point to assimilation and transnationalism as complementary processes, each having its own social networks, and immigrants can participate in both without contradiction. Neither of these networks contains every immigrant, but because most immigrants are linked to at least some of the individuals in each network, these social networks are able to reach practically the entire immigrant population. Most immigrants are thus at least *potentially* transnational, even as they are also incorporated into American society. Even quite assimilated second-generation Americans might be tempted at times to reengage in the issues and problems of their ancestral countries and hometowns.

What this view underplays is the extent to which there are real disagreements and tensions among immigrants, and even within immigrant families, regarding both assimilation and transnationalism. Immigrants disagree, among many other things, on how to raise a family, whether to learn English or retain their language of origin, whether to return, and where to focus their energies and commitments. Just as there are some immigrants who feel very strongly about being transnational, there are some who want nothing to do with it. These divisions and disagreements can lead to participation in very different social networks that not only may fail to overlap but may actually be in competition with one another.[5] Thus, though assimilation and transnationalism may be going on simultaneously, they are not necessarily complementary. Nor is it the case that these networks are necessarily equally influential. The second generation, in particular, has ties to the broader receiving society through language, education, friendships, work, marriage, and children that their parents may not have. If the children of immigrants are more likely to be engaged in these receiving-society networks than in transnational ones, and the processes of transnationalism and assimilation are competitive rather than complementary, then assimilation will eventually drive transnationalism out.

Nor will the continual flow of new immigration necessarily keep transnational practices alive in the second generation and beyond. The presence of a more established, rapidly assimilating second generation may well result in the more rapid incorporation of new immigrants rather than the transnationalization of immigrants already in the United States. On arrival to a *new* setting, first-generation immigrants set up social networks and organizations, many of which can be described as "transnational." But as this generation ages and the second generation comes into its own, the second generation creates its own networks or takes over those of the first. So new immigrants coming in have two options: they can be covered under the organizational umbrella of the second generation, or they can create their own networks. Nevertheless, given the costs of setting up new organizational networks and the benefits of membership in established networks, new immigrants are more likely to choose involvement with the older immigrant organizations. They would not be arriving to an organizational blank slate, but rather to a previously organized social space that shapes and channels their mobilization and incorporation. For examples of how this might play out we need only look at the situation in Miami after the influx of Cuban refugees—Marielitos and balseros—in the 1980s and 1990s, and at the arrival of Russian Jews in New York City during the same period. In both cases new immigrants were drawn into well-established ethnic communities that played a crucial role in their adaptation and incorporation.

As always, the truth probably lies between these two polar views, with transnationalism and assimilation being both complementary and competitive. Thought of in this way, both processes become more complicated. I argued earlier that there is substantial evidence—both from the data presented in this volume and elsewhere—for the "straight-line" assimilation of immigrants, with increasing incorporation with every generation. However, even if immigrants are overwhelmingly becoming "American," the content of "American" itself may be up for grabs. Immigrants may be assimilating, but not to a mainstream notion of what it means to be an American, but rather to other more hybrid, polyglot, cosmopolitan, or ethnic conceptions of the word. The interaction between transnationalism and assimilation should make it more worthwhile, not less, to pay attention to these processes.

WHAT IS STILL MISSING?

The chapters in this volume offer us a rich stew of findings on transnationalism among the children of immigrants. We have a better idea now of what exists, and of its extent. So now what? What more is needed? What is still missing?

We need to know more about how the second generation will act as independent adults. Rumbaut notes, for instance, that 56 percent of his respondents were still living with their parents. This makes interpretation of indicators of transnationalism such as travel to the parents' country of origin and remittances uncertain at best. Are decisions about the second generation's participation in activities like travel and remittances being made by immigrant parents, by their children, or by both? At what point can we safely say the children of immigrants are making their own decisions about whether to participate in transnational networks?

We need to have a fuller discussion of language loss and its consequences for transnationalism. How important is language for full participation in transnational networks? How successful are groups at transmitting language to succeeding generations, and how does this ability vary across national-origin groups? As noted earlier, on the whole the data seem to indicate that the second generation loses their parents' language over time and acquires English, so that an overwhelming majority of the children of immigrants express a preference for English and most are English-dominant. If one pays close attention to the fieldwork presented in the chapters here (for example, Fouron and Glick-Schiller, Smith, and Levitt), one can see that even the qualitative studies indicate a shift to English, with many of the researchers conducting their interviews with their second-generation respondents in English. The second generation may know some of their parents' language, but they are not as fluent in it as they are in English. The dominance of the English language almost certainly has effects on the ability of the children of immigrants to participate fully in transnational networks and at the very least changes the nature of those networks. Loss of language, or even the degeneration of familiarity with social cues and the ability to navigate social situations, will restrict the scope of transnationalism in the second generation, no matter how much they wish to continue their parents' involvement in transnational social networks.

We need to know more about the second generation's marriage choices and their consequences. What happens as the children of immigrants marry and themselves have children in the United States? Few of the studies here make much of marriage, although marriage choices are likely to be of crucial importance in the continuation of transnational practices. This lacuna may be due to the fact that the second generation is still quite young and so have yet to marry. Rumbaut's findings indicate, for instance, that only 16 percent of the children of immigrants in his San Diego sample are married, and only 21 percent have children. (Kasinitz and his colleagues find a similarly low incidence of marriage among the second generation in New York.) If part of what the surveys are capturing is that the children of immigrants are postponing marriage into their later twenties and thirties, this may already signal a shift in practices from their parents' generation. If when they do marry, marriage patterns among Asian and Latino children of immigrants continue current trends, one-third to one-half will marry outside their "ethnic cluster" (if Asian, for instance, they will marry a non-Asian), and an even higher percentage will marry someone not of their parents' national origin. The evidence suggests that such ethnic outmarriage disrupts transnational practices. Because many transnational ties are intensely local (see Levitt 2001), even marriage to someone of the same national origin but a different *hometown* can disrupt or diminish the transnational focus in the second generation (see Smith, this volume).

We need further explorations of the role of religion in transnationalism. Though nationalism and religion both create strong attachments, immigrants may be attached to religion in ways that they are not, say, to citizenship. Groups that have been successful in transmitting language to succeeding generations, even in the face of societal dominance by another language, have generally done so when language has been linked to religion. The link of language to religion provides a powerful incentive for parents and children alike to maintain linguistic proficiency in that language. Immigrant Jews, Orthodox Christians, and the like may have better success in fostering transnational ties than their counterparts whose religious practices are easily translated into the new vernacular (as would be the case for Catholics and Protestants, for instance). These transnational ties might include marriage arrangements, which could have additional and broader effects on cultural transmission, assimilation, and so on. How do religion, language, and marriage play out among Muslim or Hindu immigrants? On the other hand, immigration may also diminish or change religious affiliations. Because the immigration process is traumatic, it may cause people to rethink their deeply felt attachments. Among some Latin American immigrants to the United States this manifests itself, among other ways, in a shift away from the Catholic Church and toward more personalistic Pentecostal or Evangelical Christian churches. To say that religion is central to many individuals' experience is not to say that it is unshakable or immutable.

It would be useful to have a fuller discussion of power and how it plays out in relations between immigrants and their home countries, between immigrants of different generations, and between male and female immigrants. For instance, Smith notes in his New York City case study that second-generation immigrant youth felt that their organizational efforts were not taken seriously by their (literal) parent organization, which was composed largely of first-generation immigrants. These kinds of intergenerational power conflicts over the control of immigrant networks and resources could derail second-generation transnationalism. Similar power dynamics inhibit the participation of women (Jones-Correa 1998) and lead women to adopt more "assimilationist" political strategies. So even if "diverse and thick" transnational social fields exist in the first generation, contrary to Levitt's hypothesis (Levitt and Waters, this volume; Levitt, this volume), this may not necessarily translate into greater transnational mobilization in the second generation.

Smith also notes that *the second generation's response to racial hierarchies in the United States may push some of them to reconsider their identities as immigrants and attachments to their home country.* Racial discrimination, in this view, leads to greater transnationalism (Waters 2000). Portes and Zhou (1993) note, on the contrary, that in response to encounters with race and discrimination in the United States immigrant children may construct "reactive ethnicities": by assimilating into and identifying with minority cultures in the United States, they presumably become less likely to engage in transnational behavior. What exactly is the effect of race and racial discrimination on immigrant adaptation or ties to the parents' country of origin? Does it matter who is doing the discriminating (whites, blacks, or co-ethnics), or in what context (work, school, police, public space) the discrimination occurs?

We need further study of the impact of local contexts and local institutions. The surveys reported by Kasinitz and his colleagues and by Rumbaut, while largely reinforcing each other's findings, also show some interesting differences. The children of immigrants in San Diego, for instance, seem more likely to favor English (even among Mexican Americans, despite being so close to the Mexican border) than immigrants in New York City. The second genera-tion in New York seems to identify strongly with the city and to participate in the city's politics. These differences raise interesting questions. Is it important, for instance, that immigrants in Califor-nia went through an intense period of anti-immigrant mobilization unmatched in New York City? How would this public discourse have affected immigrants' transnational orientations? Do the chil-dren of Mexican immigrants in California value cosmopolitanism as highly as their counterparts in New York City (see Kasinitz et al., this volume), and if not, is this difference important? If local effects matter for transnational practices, variation in local receiving con-texts might make a significant difference in the outcome of trans-nationalism among the second generation.

In general, we need a better account of how changes in receiv-ing contexts might change immigrants' identity calculus. The usual story, for instance, is that second-generation transnationalism was less apparent among immigrants in the immigration wave a century ago because of the emphasis on assimilation into American life and values, and that any incipient transnationalism was, in any case, curtailed by a number of factors: restrictions on immigration be-ginning in 1917, the Great Depression, and then the Second World War (on Japanese Americans in Hawaii, for instance, see Ueda, this volume). Those who rode the current immigration wave, which began in the 1960s, arrived into a very different context: mobiliza-tion and display of ethnic and racial identities had become part of the accepted repertoire of American politics. However, there is no guarantee that this period of acceptance will continue; indeed, fol-lowing the destruction of New York's World Trade Center in Sep-tember 2001, there have been some indications that this acceptance has diminished, with calls for a renewed emphasis on "American" identity and reduced immigration. How does such a shift in the national context play out in immigrant communities?

Most of the questions raised here could be made into testable hypotheses. Is racism a major factor in the continuity of transnational networks? Then let's treat race as a variable and look at two immigrant groups with very different experiences of prejudice, perhaps Russian Jews and Afro-Caribbeans. Is population concentration a factor? Then we could examine immigrant communities in smaller U.S. cities, towns, and—given the changing demographics—suburbs. Is life cycle important? Let's track a random group of immigrants over the course of their lives. Is time period important? Let's observe an entire group across time, watching how the immigrant community reacts to homeland crises. The studies presented in this volume are good examples of the kind of work that can be done. Apart from all the questions that should be addressed and the kinds of studies remaining to be done, we should always keep in mind the question of falsifiability: When does a group stop being transnational? What does it look like to *not* be transnational? At what point does an immigrant group become an ethnic group?

In answering these questions we need to use methodologies more carefully, and probably in conjunction. If surveys infer transnationalism from individuals' choices to travel or send money, we should keep in mind that these behaviors might have very different meanings for different people. For some, travel to their parents' country of origin might be a chore; for others, a chance to maintain a vibrant connection; and for others, imply a nice place to take a vacation. On the other hand, if surveys indicate that a shift to English has occurred among immigrants in the United States, what *kind* of English are we talking about? Standard American English, slang, a hybrid? What difference does the kind of English make? If we ask about identity in surveys, we need to be aware of the fact that people have multiple identities, and that if we ask them to choose one, we are creating artificial categories. On the other hand, ethnographers should get over their mistrust of survey data and learn to work with it and use it. While social-network research is critical, we need to know we are getting a picture of the full range of network practices out there, not just those that the researcher has targeted. One of the many strengths of this volume is that it presents research that draws on various kinds of methodologies. More of this is needed.

CONCLUSION

Scholarly work on second-generation immigrants in the United States is still a work in progress. As many of this volume's contributors note, this immigrant cohort is still quite young, and it is difficult to predict their future decisions and life trajectories. The excitement generated by these studies lies precisely in the fact that they are charting changes as they occur, changes that will have a significant impact on the shape of American politics and society, and possibly on immigrants' countries of origin as well. Nonetheless, the research presented in this volume allows us to draw some preliminary conclusions about transnationalism and assimilation in the second generation.

While the great majority of second generation immigrants will only rarely or never be "transnational," transnational practices will continue, even in the face of continuing "Americanization"; indeed, these practices will be one of the factors shaping our understanding of what it means to be "American" in the years to come. Still to be determined are the full extent of transnational practices in the second generation and how participation in transnational networks will play out in the future. The full significance of transnationalism in the second generation, both for the United States and for immigrant-sending nations, is as yet unknown. This leaves a lot for us to understand, and much for researchers to do.

NOTES

1. Their actual wording is: "A transnational second generation can be defined as all persons born into the generation after emigrants have established transnational social fields who live within or are socialized by these fields, regardless of whether they were born or are currently living in the country of emigration or abroad" (Fouron and Glick-Schiller, this volume). However, because in practice they see few in the second generation living completely outside transnational social fields, their definition becomes, for all intents and purposes, universal.

2. In passing, note that if we take life-cycle effects seriously, it may be that the survey data presented in the chapters of Kasinitz and his colleagues and Rumbaut overestimate second-generation transnationalism. The reason for this is that the populations for both surveys are largely in their teens and twenties, during or just after college, when peer groups and identity issues can be expected to play a greater role in individuals' lives, and before they have begun to feel the full impact of the responsibilities and roles of adulthood.

3. As the available age range of the second generation increases, surveys may well have more light to shed on this point.

4. This is reflected in some Latin American immigrants' use of the term "patria chica" to describe their hometowns. The term, literally meaning "little country," is untranslatable, but it implies that many immigrants have far stronger loyalties to their hometowns than to their country of origin. The direct ties of immigrants to hometowns (reflected in the profusion of hometown associations among immigrants from every country) have been described elsewhere as "transnationalism from below" (Smith and Guarnizo 1998; Levitt 2001).

5. "Competition" here may be direct, driven by ideological or other disagreements, or it may simply be the result of competition over scarce resources, like time or money. Given the scarcity of resources, the second generation may only be able to commit to one network or another, or may only be able to commit to them both unequally.

REFERENCES

Ahrari, Mohammed E., ed. 1987. *Ethnic Groups and U.S. Foreign Policy.* New York: Greenwood Press.

Anderson, Benedict. 1994. "Exodus." *Critical Inquiry* 20(winter): 314–27.

DeConde, Alexander. 1992. *Ethnicity, Race, and American Foreign Policy: A History.* Boston: Northeastern University Press.

DeSipio, Louis. 2000. "Sending Money Home . . . For Now: Remittances and Immigrant Adaptation in the United States." Working Paper. Inter-American Dialogue/Tomás Rivera Policy Institute, Washington, D.C. (January).

Farley, Reynolds. 1998. "Presentation to the Race Advisory Board, President's Initiative on Race." Accessed July 10, 2002 at: *clinton3.nara.gov/ Initiatives/OneAmerica/farley.html.*

Foner, Nancy. 1997. "What's New About Transnationalism?: New York Immigrants Today and at the Turn of the Century." Paper presented at the

Conference on Transnational Communities and the Political Economy of New York in the 1990s, New School for Social Research, New York (February).

Immigration and Naturalization Service. 1992. *Statistical Yearbook*. Accessed July 10, 2002 at: *www.ins.usdoj.gov/graphics/aboutins/statistics/300.htm*.

Jennings, M. Kent, and Richard Niemi. 1981. *Generations and Politics: A Panel Study of Young Adults and Their Parents*. Princeton, N.J.: Princeton University Press.

Joint Center for Housing Studies. 2001. *The State of the Nation's Housing*. Cambridge, Mass.: Harvard University. Accessed July 10, 2002 at: *www.jchs.harvard.edu/publications/markets/SON2001.pdf*.

Jones-Correa, Michael. 1998. *Between Two Nations: The Political Predicament of Latinos in New York City*. Ithaca, N.Y.: Cornell University Press.

———. 2001a. "Under Two Flags: Dual Nationality in Latin America and Its Consequences for Naturalization in the United States." *International Migration Review* 35(4): 997–1029.

———. 2001b. "Institutional and Contextual Factors in Immigrant Citizenship and Voting." *Citizenship Studies* 5(1): 41–56.

Kapur, Devesh. 2001. "Diasporas and Technology Transfer." Background Paper for Human Development Report, World Bank (January).

Levitt, Peggy. 2001. *The Transnational Villagers*. Berkeley: University of California Press.

Portes, Alejandro, and Rubén Rumbaut. 2001. *Legacies: The Story of the Second Generation*. Berkeley: University of California Press.

Portes, Alejandro, and Min Zhou. 1993. "The Second Generation: Segmented Assimilation and Its Variants." *Annals of the American Academy of Political and Social Science* 530: 74–96.

Rumbaut, Rubén, and Alejandro Portes. 2001. *Ethnicities: Children of Immigrants in America*. Berkeley: University of California Press.

Smith, Michael Peter, and Luis Guarnizo. 1998. *Transnationalism from Below*. New Brunswick, N.J.: Transaction Publishers.

Verba, Sidney, Kay Lehmann Schlozman, and Henry Brady. 1995. *Voice and Equality in American Politics*. Cambridge, Mass.: Harvard University Press.

Waters, Mary. 2000. *Black Identities: West Indian Immigrant Dreams and American Realities*. Cambridge, Mass.: Harvard University Press.

Chapter 10

Second-Generation Transnationalism, Then and Now

Nancy Foner

MUCH HAS BEEN written about transnational practices among immigrants who come to the United States—about the origins of these practices, the forms they take, how extensive they are within and among different groups, and their consequences. A critical question is whether transnationalism is in fact a first-generation phenomenon, or whether it will persist among the children of immigrants who are born and raised in this country.

In thinking about this question it is useful to make some comparisons with the past as a way to better understand the social, economic, and political conditions that may promote and sustain transnational relations and attachments among today's second generation. The paths that the children of contemporary immigrants are taking, and will take in the future, are made clearer if we place the analysis in the context of the experiences of the descendants of earlier immigrants. In discussing second-generation transnationalism then and now, I draw on my comparative study of the two great waves of immigration to New York, America's quintessential immigrant city. In speaking of the earlier wave, I refer to the influx of eastern European Jews and Italians between 1880 and 1920; the current wave, in the main from Asia, Latin America, and the Caribbean, began in the late 1960s and still going strong (see Foner 2000). In discussing transnational practices, I have in mind the way migrants sustain multistranded social relations along family, economic, and political lines that link their societies of origin and settlement (Basch 2001).

Among earlier European immigrants, transnationalism had a fairly short life, in that ongoing, day-to-day involvement in and connections to the communal life of sending societies fell off sharply after the first generation. To be sure, some members of the second generation continued to play a role in sending-society politics or international political movements, such as Zionism and the struggle for Irish independence, but they tended to do so as ethnic Americans whose ethnic identities and sense of connection to their parents' homeland were shaped and created in the U.S. context (Kasinitz et al., this volume). Many second- and third-generation Jews have identified with and given financial support to Israel, but most do not have close relatives in Israel or regular contact with people there.

Connections with their parents' homelands became extremely attenuated among the children of Jewish and Italian immigrants. Consider the Jewish landsmanshaftn, or hometown associations, which sent massive aid to their war-ravaged home communities both during and immediately after World War I. In addition to sending millions of dollars in aid, many delegates from New York traveled back to eastern Europe after the war to deliver the money. A writer in one Yiddish daily observed that "the 'delegate' has become, so to speak, an institution in the Jewish community. There is not a single *landsmanshaft* here in America which has not sent, is not sending, or will not send a delegate with money and letters to the *landslayt* on the other side of the ocean" (Soyer 1997, 177). The Jewish landsmanshaftn of New York, however, were a one-generation phenomenon that had

> little attraction for most of their members' American children, who had developed their own sense of Jewish-American identity and to whom their parents' parochial loyalties seemed irrelevant at best. The fact that the aging societies continued to utilize Yiddish and Yiddish-accented English as their official languages made them seem all the more old-worldly. (Soyer 1997, 204)

Jews, of course, were exceptional in their low rates of return migration—and in having most of their number wiped out in eastern Europe by the Holocaust. But transnational ties appear to have largely atrophied among second-generation Italians too. A recent study that discusses the transnational links maintained by Philadelphia's Italian Americans speaks of the "American born second generation of individuals with loose ties to the land of their parents" (Luconi 2001, 149).[1] Among Irvin Child's second-generation Italian informants in New Haven in the late 1930s, only one mentioned even wanting to return to Italy. "I don't care for the country and I don't care what they do there," said one informant. "My father may care, but I don't. I was born in this country, and I'm only interested in it" (Child 1943, 88–89). How widespread such attitudes were is unclear, but as Robert Smith (1998, 202) comments: "Given the series of questions Child asks about the informants' opinions about Italy and things Italian, and a chapter devoted entirely to 'in group' Italian Americans, it seems likely that if return to Italy was an important part of the second generation's experience it would have been mentioned" (see also Smith, this volume). In East Harlem in the 1920s and 1930s, according to Robert Orsi (1990, 141), Italian immigrant parents created an idealized version of southern Italy "into which they demanded their children gaze while making it clear that their children could never enter it. . . . They were 'Americani.' "

What happened to undercut transnationalism among second-generation Italians and Jews in the past? For one thing, there were the processes of assimilation that went on in schools and other institutions as those born and bred in the United States learned English and American ways and became engaged with life in this country. Indeed, in the early twentieth century schools, settlement houses, and Progressive reformers put pressure on immigrants and their children to abandon their old-fashioned customs and languages and attachments to the Old World. Although in the 1920s and 1930s educators began to "Americanize" the second generation at a less frenetic pace, the schools continued to be, as the historian Paula Fass (1989, 75) puts it, "the great institution of assimilation" (see also Tyack 2001, 352).[2] Many members of the earlier second generation also managed to climb the socioeconomic ladder, if only in small steps. Another critical factor was that Italian and Jewish communities received hardly any fresh recruits after the 1920s in the wake of legislated immigration restrictions and the back-to-back cataclysms of the Great Depression and World War II. Without replenishment, the number of Italians and Jews with fresh memories of and connections to the homeland became steadily smaller. The economies of Italy and eastern Europe, moreover, had little to offer the children of immigrant parents. And political events— World War II and the Holocaust—cut off connections there and heightened their patriotic embrace of the United States.

What about today? Some of the same factors still operate to un- dermine second-generation transnationalism. Most of the current second generation do not function in transnational social fields in the sense of engaging in regular practices and sustaining continu- ous relations that link them with their parents' home societies. As members of the second generation enter the labor force, a good number will do well and carve out successful careers in the United States. The forces of assimilation are still strong. English, as Rubén Rumbaut has observed, is triumphing with "breathtaking rapidity" (quoted in Dugger 1998). In his chapter, Rumbaut reports that by the time the children of immigrants in an ongoing longitudinal San Diego survey were in their midtwenties, the vast majority preferred English over their parents' native language, fewer than one-third said they could speak a foreign language very well, and fewer than one-quarter could read it very well. English may have become the global language of money, but the loss of the parental language surely has implications for the second generation's ability to maintain ongoing ties with their parents' homelands.[3]

But if members of the present second generation, like their pre- decessors, are becoming more and more American, there are also differences from the past. Different circumstances today and in the years ahead are likely to support ongoing transnational connections for at least some of the current second generation so that trans- nationalism will have a longer life than it did in the past. Indeed, in their study of over 2,000 young adult New Yorkers born to immigrant parents, Kasinitz and his colleagues (this volume) find that trans- national ties continue to play a regular, sustained, and integral role in the lives of a minority in every group (Anglophone West Indi- ans, Dominicans, South Americans, Chinese, and Russian Jews), with especially significant minorities of Dominicans, West Indians, and South Americans "highly embedded in transnational social structures" into the second generation.

Let's hope there's no World War III—because if there is, no one will be left in any generation. One hopes too that no Holocaust will wipe out all the relatives of any one immigrant group. Even if there is some move toward restrictionism, it is likely that the United States will remain an immigration country, allowing substantial numbers of new immigrants to enter for a good time to come. Continued inflows will bring new recruits who will enrich and replenish ethnic communities—and include substantial numbers of people, of all ages, with close ties to their homelands.

Moreover, in today's multicultural America, where there is an official commitment to cultural pluralism and cultural diversity, transnational ties are more visible and acceptable—and sometimes even celebrated in public settings. Today members of the second generation often feel pride—not shame—in their connections to their parents' homelands. In cities like New York, exhibits in museums and libraries highlight the cultural background of different immigrant groups; special school events feature the foods, music, and dress of various homelands; and school curricula include material on different ethnic groups. Practically every ethnic group in New York has its own festival or parade, the largest one being the West Indian American Day parade on Brooklyn's Eastern Parkway, which draws crowds of more than one million people every Labor Day. Moreover, in the quest for votes, established New York politicians of all stripes recognize the value of visits to immigrant homelands. Of course, racial and ethnic inequalities have not disappeared in the United States, and the realities of discrimination may be a factor motivating some second-generation individuals to seek out involvements with their parents' home communities (Fouron and Glick-Schiller, this volume; Smith, this volume).

Where dual citizenship provisions extend to the second generation—as is now the case for Dominicans—this may foster continued political involvement in the home country among the second generation. The Dominican Republic not only recognizes the right to dual citizenship but also, as Levitt notes in her chapter, counts children of Dominican parents born in the United States as Dominican citizens. When recent electoral reforms in the Dominican Republic go into effect, adult children of Dominican parents born in the United States will have the right to vote from abroad in Dominican elections. Some are bound to exercise this privilege.

Then there is the fact that some members of the second generation will have spent significant periods of their childhood and teenage years in their parents' homeland, thereby creating and reinforcing ties to relatives and friends there. Some immigrants send their children home to grandparents because they need child care. Others ship teenagers home for high school to protect them from the drugs, gangs, and sexual precociousness in inner-city neighborhoods and to expose them to cultural values and institutions in the home society. In the late 1990s Dominican educators and government officials estimated that as many as ten thousand students from schools in the United States, mainly from the New York area, were enrolled in schools in the Dominican Republic (Rohter 1998). Kasinitz and his colleagues (this volume) note that, in their study, a surprising number of West Indians and Latinos were sent back home to live with relatives at some point in their teen years by parents terrified of the dangers of the New York City streets. Even if extended homeland visits are less frequent—or end—in the adult years, they may form the basis for ties that persist into adulthood, especially if there is at least some visiting back and forth.

At the other end of the life course, parental retirement patterns may also strengthen transnational ties. Some of the first generation will end up retiring to their birthplace, ensuring that their children will make trips to see them and keeping children and grandchildren connected, however tenuously, to the sending country. Indeed, some second-generation Mexican New Yorkers send their third-generation youngsters to Mexico during winter and summer vacations from school to live with grandmothers who, after many years in the United States, have retired in the home community (Smith, this volume). Language may also play a role, particularly among Latinos who, studies show, are most likely to be bilingual in the second generation (Portes and Hao 1997; Portes and Rumbaut 2001; Rumbaut, this volume). In the context of a huge Spanish-speaking community in New York and other U.S. cities, including Spanish-language newspapers, radio, and television programs, many children of Latino immigrants will speak and understand Spanish, thereby facilitating the maintenance of ties to the homeland. And Rumbaut's analysis (this volume) suggests another intriguing possibility: that some children will assume the responsibility of maintaining ties to relatives in the country of origin, including remittance assistance, at the death of their parents.

If, as some predict, economic restructuring of the American economy and the declining demand for less-educated labor threaten the ability of many members of the second generation to advance, then some may try their hand at ventures (including illegal ones) that involve transnational connections. In today's global economy this is a tack the more successful may take up as well. Robust and growing economies in some countries of origin may attract a number of educated and well-trained descendants of the current immigrants, who will find it profitable to invest in their parents' homeland, return there for a time to work, or end up commuting back and forth. These paths may be especially attractive to those who experience professional barriers to mobility in the United States (see Levitt, this volume).

Cheap air travel and widespread global tourism in the modern era will also increase the firsthand contact that members of the second generation have with their homelands, the evidence already showing that those in some groups are more frequent visitors than others. In the surveys reported in this volume, Dominicans in New York and Mexicans in San Diego stood out, with around one-fifth having visited their parents' home country more than ten times. Overall, however, the vast majority had visited much less often—only once or twice, maybe three times, if at all (Kasinitz et al., this volume; Rumbaut, this volume). In any case, caution is needed in evaluating whether short vacations or special tours to the homeland are evidence of, or lead to, significant transnationalism. Indeed, trips "back home" may end up reinforcing notions of how American the second generation are—and bring out the fact that it is the United States that is indisputably home (Kasinitz et al., this volume).

The verdict is not yet in how important transnational ties really are—or will be—in the lives of today's second generation, particularly as they grow up, move into the workforce, and establish their own families. We are only starting to get studies of the second generation, and those we have are of schoolchildren, teenagers, and college students, or young people only beginning to enter the workforce. In addition, many of the people in the studies are not really second-generation at all but were born abroad and in some cases spent their early childhood there.

It is possible, of course, that some members of the second generation who had little involvement in their parents' homelands in their youth and young adulthood will develop stronger ties when they get older and become more interested in their roots; growing older may also bring the time, money, and resources to cultivate transnational ties (see Levitt, this volume, on Boston Irish Americans). Another possibility is that unforeseen political events in the home country—war, revolution, or ethnic persecution, for example—could revitalize or intensify intermittent and weak transnational involvements among second-generation adults, particularly when a small minority have continued to sustain strong transnational political connections to political organizations in the homeland (see Kasinitz et al., this volume; Levitt, this volume).

On the whole, however, it is when they are young and still living with their parents that children of immigrants are more likely to be influenced by their parents' transnational connections—and sometimes they are even sent back to the homeland to stay with relatives. Whether these youths will maintain the same kind of transnational links when they marry and form their own families and have children of their own is, at the moment, an open question.

To the extent that members of the second generation do maintain transnational ties, we need to know just what the consequences are for their opportunities, relationships, and engagements in the United States, from their occupational prospects to their family relations and political behavior. Second-generation transnationalism is likely to be a mixed blessing. On the positive side, transnational ties can provide access to resources, skills, and connections in two societies. In this way, they may operate as a safety net for those who have trouble making it in the U.S. economy or, for the more successful, as an avenue for economic and social mobility through business, investment, and other occupational opportunities. Peggy Levitt (this volume) notes that some of her highly educated respondents saw their transnational connections as a "Plan B" that could be put into action to circumvent blocked mobility or as a way to diversify risk and produce additional income. As in the case of the Mexican New Yorkers whom Robert Smith (this volume) studied, ties to the home community can bolster a sense of ethnic pride among adolescents and counter the negative influences they experience in New York schools and neighborhoods. For some West Indians and Latinos, going to school "back home" has even given them a leg up in getting into U.S. colleges and jobs, as compared to their cousins who remained in New York City public schools (Kasinitz et al., this volume).

Yet transnationalism may have negative consequences for immigrants' children. Those who move back and forth between the United States and their parents' country of origin may feel that they do not completely belong to either place, and such movement can add to children's educational difficulties and be a drain on family resources (see Levitt, this volume). Moreover, when children spend long periods apart from their parents, family relations can be strained. As among the first generation, involvement in the political and organizational affairs of the home country may draw energies and interests away from engagements in this country, although this is certainly not inevitable. One of the great insights of the recent transnational literature is that individuals can keep up ties to their own (or their parents') home countries at the very same time as they are committed to, and influenced by, involvements in activities, institutions, and relationships in this country. Assimilation and transnationalism, in other words, are not mutually exclusive but can go hand in hand.

From a comparative perspective, it seems clear that connections to their parents' homelands will be more important for the present second generation than they were for immigrants' children of an earlier era, and such ties are thus a topic that requires careful study. Yet a note of caution is in order. Although researchers need to be sensitive to the role of transnational ties among the second generation, there is a risk of seeing transnationalism everywhere and overemphasizing its centrality. Some members of the second generation will maintain ongoing and close connections to their parents' country of origin, but they are likely to be a minority. The vast majority, having been born and raised in the United States, will be primarily oriented to people, institutions, and places in this country—and it is the implications of growing up in the United States, not ties to their parents' homelands, that should be our primary object of study.

NOTES

1. The transnational links documented by Luconi for Philadelphia's Italian Americans in the post–World War II era included: the mobilization of aid to Italy during World War II through the heavily Italian local of the Amalgamated Clothing Workers of America; anti-Communist letter-writing campaigns to friends and relatives in Italy in the late 1940s sup-

ported by Italian newspapers and religious leaders; and fund-raising efforts, spearheaded by ethnic associations, to help earthquake victims in Friuli in the 1970s (Luconi 2001, 110–11, 120, 147). Luconi does not specify whether these efforts involved only the first generation, but his observation that the American-born second generation had only loose ties to their parents' homeland suggests that transnational connections were mainly a first-generation phenomenon.

2. David Tyack (2001, 354) notes that education policies of the World War II period stressed that it was all right to be a hyphenated American if one put the emphasis on the American side of the hyphen. Tyack suggests that the children of immigrants often learned American ways most powerfully not from teachers but from peers who were intolerant of cultural differences and made fun of their accents, clothes, food, and ignorance of American children's ways and games (357). See Paula Fass (1989) for an account of the complicated process of assimilation in New York City public high schools in the 1930s and 1940s.

3. In the past, the Jewish second generation was, by and large, an English-only group; members of the Italian second generation often spoke Italian dialects at home and on the streets. (On the Italian second generation and language, see Alba and Nee, forthcoming; Child 1943.)

REFERENCES

Alba, Richard, and Victor Nee. Forthcoming. *Remaking the American Mainstream.* Cambridge, Mass.: Harvard University Press.

Basch, Linda. 2001. "Transnational Social Relations and the Politics of National Identity: An Eastern Caribbean Case Study." In *Islands in the City: West Indian Migration to New York,* edited by Nancy Foner. Berkeley: University of California Press.

Child, Irvin. 1943. *Italian or American?: The Second Generation in Conflict.* New Haven, Conn.: Yale University Press.

Dugger, Celia. 1998. "Among Young of Immigrants, Outlook Rises." *New York Times,* March 21.

Fass, Paula. 1989. *Outside In: Minorities and the Transformation of American Education.* New York: Oxford University Press.

Foner, Nancy. 2000. *From Ellis Island to JFK: New York's Two Great Waves of Immigration.* New Haven, Conn., and New York: Yale University Press and Russell Sage Foundation.

Luconi, Stefano. 2001. *From Paesani to White Ethnics: The Italian Experience in Philadelphia.* Philadelphia: Temple University Press.

Orsi, Robert. 1990. "The Fault of Memory: 'Southern Italy' in the Imagination of Immigrants and the Lives of Their Children in Italian Harlem, 1920–1945." *Journal of Family History* 15: 133–47.

Portes, Alejandro, and Lingxin Hao. 1997. "English First or English Only?: Bilingualism and Parental Language Loss in the Second Generation." Paper presented at Conference on the Second Generation, Annandale-on-Hudson, N.Y.: Jerome Levy Economics Institute, Bard College.

Portes, Alejandro, and Rubén Rumbaut. 2001. *Legacies: The Story of the Immigrant Second Generation*. Berkeley: University of California Press.

Rohter, Larry. 1998. "Island Life Not Idyllic for Youths from U.S." *New York Times,* February 20.

Smith, Robert. 1998. "Reflections on Migration, the State, and the Construction, Durability, and Newness of Transnational Life." *Socziale Welt* 12: 197–217.

Soyer, Daniel. 1997. *Jewish Immigrant Associations and American Identity in New York, 1880–1939*. Cambridge, Mass.: Harvard University Press.

Tyack, David. 2001. "School for Citizens: The Politics of Civic Education from 1790 to 1990." In *E Pluribus Unum?: Contemporary and Historical Perspectives on Immigrant Political Incorporation,* edited by Gary Gerstle and John Mollenkopf. New York: Russell Sage Foundation.

Part III

Using a Transnational Lens to Understand the Children of Immigrants

—— Chapter 11 ——

There's No Place Like "Home": Emotional Transnationalism and the Struggles of Second-Generation Filipinos

Diane L. Wolf

S OCIOLOGISTS OF IMMIGRATION have recently turned their attention to the next generation—the children of immigrants, or "the second generation," asserting that the future success and well-being of particular immigrant groups can be partially discerned from their children's ability to assimilate, adopt English, and succeed in school (Rumbaut and Cornelius 1995; Portes 1995). Children of immigrants, or "second-generation" youth, are defined as children born here to immigrant parents and children born abroad who emigrated at a very early age (Portes 1996, ix).[1] In comparative studies of English language rates, test scores, and GPAs, Filipino second-generation youth look relatively successful and assimilated (Rumbaut 1996). These statistics cohere with what we know about their parents: in general, post-1965 Filipino immigrants have been predominantly middle-class, college-educated, English-speaking professionals who integrated easily into the labor force and quickly blended into the American landscape (Wolf and Hoffman 1996). Despite these optimistic demographics, however, there is more lurking beneath these confidence intervals.

255

Based on fieldwork in two California sites, this chapter examines, in more depth, some of the issues and problems confronting second-generation Filipino youth. "The family" seems to offer an extremely magnetic and positive basis of Filipino identity for many children of immigrants, yet it is also a deep source of stress and alienation that, for some, has led to internal struggles and extreme despair. Indeed, McCoy (1993) suggests that Filipino social and political processes cannot be fully understood without incorporating an analysis of the family. More specifically, this chapter suggests that many Filipino second-generation youth are beset by transnational struggles, some of which are deeply connected to their relationships to their families. It is certainly neither new nor surprising that children of immigrants experience some familial conflict as their parents attempt to impose their values in new social contexts. What is surprising in this case, however, is the high level of Filipino assimilation and economic success in the United States, particularly when compared with other immigrant groups, and juxtaposed with the despair, alienation, and unhappiness experienced by a significant proportion of Filipino youth.

Many studies of immigrant groups focus on socioeconomic issues, such as wages, labor force participation, and economic enclaves, in part because such data are easier to acquire than more personal information about problems that might air the family's "dirty laundry." This chapter complements such approaches by focusing on the more personal and familial levels, particularly the gap between family ideology, on the one hand, and family processes and practices, on the other. Furthermore, although Filipinos are the largest Asian American group in the United States, they are strikingly absent from contemporary literatures on immigration and on Asian Americans.[2] This chapter begins to close that gap by focusing on some serious contradictions within this important but somewhat invisible group.

ANALYTICAL FRAMING

In a recent paper, Luis Guarnizo (1998) points out that the sociological literature on immigration and assimilation still tends to view the process of assimilation in fairly narrow, usually dichotomous terms—either groups assimilate to mainstream U.S. culture or they do not. In an effort to add another dimension to our thinking about assimilation, Alejandro Portes (1995) has put forth the notion of segmented assimilation, suggesting that there are three general possibilities: assimilation into the majority culture coupled with economic mobility; preservation of the immigrant culture coupled with economic mobility; and assimilation into the underclass linked with poverty.

Using Portes's framework, Filipinos would be categorized in the first group—as assimilated, acculturated, and economically upwardly mobile owing to impressive numbers that paint a "model minority" picture. These statistics, however, reflect only a point in time rather than the dynamics and interactions that typify the daily lives, quandaries, and struggles of immigrants and their children. Indeed, the feelings revealed by some second-generation Filipino youth suggest that assimilation involves a process far more complex than English language proficiency rates and good grades can portray.

Scholars working in the new field of transnational studies (Basch, Glick-Schiller, and Szanton-Blanc 1994; Guarnizo 1998; Ong 1996) have pointed to more complex patterns that challenge the use and utility of certain accepted sociological categorizations for understanding migration and change. Using a transnational framework for understanding these dilemmas goes beyond the dichotomous notion that a process of acculturation occurs when the migrant and his or her children travel from point A (native culture) to point B (new receiving culture). A transnational approach acknowledges a plurality of cultural codes and symbols that go beyond the nation-state and also the multiple locations of "home" that may exist not only geographically but ideologically and emotionally as well. The concept of transnationalism avoids the assumption of linearity in immigrants' thinking, decisionmaking, and changes in practices and focuses instead on migration as a complex set of processes that involve multiple, interacting, and perhaps conflicting layers.

My use of the term "transnational struggles" is meant to underscore the notion of differing codes, cultures, ideologies, and goals that circulate in the lives and minds of children of Filipino immigrants. Although their parents are more active in maintaining relationships that directly link the Philippines and the United States (Espiritu 1994, 257; Basch, Glick-Schiller, and Szanton-Blanc 1994, 3), the children of immigrants maintain these ties, at the very least, at the level of emotions, ideologies, and cultural codes. Indeed, I suggest that second-generation Filipino youth experience an *emotional transnationalism* that situates them between different generational and locational points of reference, both the real and the imagined—their parents', sometimes also their grandparents' and other relatives', and their own.[3]

By using the term "emotional transnationalism," I wish to inject a dynamic sense of the interaction between places and ideologies for children of post-1965 immigrants as they construct their identities, since these struggles do not exist in a vacuum. With global connections unparalleled to what migrants experienced in previous waves, these families are keeping up their ties to relatives "at Home," a phrase that always refers to the Philippines, usually with reverence, by making inexpensive phone calls, visiting, and sending money and other goods, often through specialized companies such as Balikbayan. For today's children of Filipino immigrants, the Philippines is often right in their home, locally in California, both literally and figuratively.

Thus, using a different terminology is meant to illustrate the fluid movement back and forth that persists as young people establish their identities, moral practices, educational goals, and careers within families that are deeply connected to the Philippines both symbolically and physically. This terminology also underscores that ethnic identity is formed not simply in one place, the United States, but that this process includes interactions with the Philippines on multiple levels. The point is not that Filipino children of post-1965 immigrants are suddenly experiencing something new and different from other similar groups of children of immigrants. Rather, I wish to suggest that because of this particular historical moment, using a transnational framework infuses the negotiations that lead to identities and life decisions with a kind of dynamic and fluid interconnectedness between Home and home that did not exist for previous generations of immigrants.

Finally, much but not all (Hondagneu-Sotelo 1994) of the immigration and assimilation literature is cast in a gender-neutral light, and I wish to take a more gendered view of these processes. Male and female children of Filipino immigrants are treated differently, given different messages about what it means to be Filipino, and are reacting differently to their environment. In particular, Filipinas seem to be subject to greater parental control over their movements, bodies, and sexuality than their brothers, and more of them are exhibiting signs of distress.

BACKGROUND AND METHODS

Filipino immigrants in the post-1965 period paint a "model minority" picture: they have relatively high educational attainment (Kao 1995; Woo 1985), a high level of labor force participation (particularly among women), a high percentage work as professionals (Cabezas, Shinagawa, and Kawaguchi 1986), and they have the lowest rate of poverty in the United States and in California (Rumbaut 1995; Oliver et al. 1995). For example, Filipinas are well represented in professional occupations (Wong and Hirschman 1983), and foreign-born Filipinas constitute a higher percentage of professionals compared with other Asian females (both native and foreign-born) and Anglo women (Wong and Hirschman 1983; Cabezas et al. 1986). In 1980 foreign-born Filipinas had the highest mean income compared with Chinese, Japanese, and Anglo women (Woo 1985, 312).

These statistics partially account for the lack of attention to Filipinos in immigration studies. Filipinos appear to be assimilated and successful; to some extent, and for various historical and cultural reasons—many of which are connected to colonialist history—Filipinos tend to blend into American society and become relatively invisible to the eye of the average American or U.S. academic. This invisibility is historically and politically significant and needs to be further problematized (Takaki 1989; Kaplan 1990; Campomanes 1995b; Wolf and Hoffman 1996).

I was drawn to study second-generation Filipino immigrant youth when wrapping up—or so I thought—a study of Filipino immigrants in Vallejo, California. Interviews with teachers, counselors, and principals in two high schools suggested some disturbing and unexpected patterns among second-generation Filipino youth. Additionally, a random survey of San Diego public high school students conducted under the auspices of the Federal Centers for Disease Control and Prevention (CDC) as part of a larger study of teen risk behavior in U.S. cities found that an extremely high number of

Filipino female students surveyed (45.6 percent) said they had seriously considered attempting suicide in the year preceding the survey.[4] Perhaps more important, half of those who *considered* suicide (23.3 percent) had actually *attempted* suicide at least once in the preceding year. As the *San Diego Union-Tribune* noted on February 11, 1995, compared with other ethnic groups, "a far greater ratio of Filipino girls made plans to kill themselves, attempted to do so one or more times or sustained injuries while trying to commit suicide."

Both the general and Filipino presses in San Diego emphasized the high rates of Filipinas in these statistics. For example, *Filipinas* magazine reprinted the *San Diego Union-Tribune* article, entitling it "For Filipino Girls Who Have Considered Suicide" (Lau 1995b, 38). However, Filipino males also ranked fairly high in these categories.[5] Although suicidal thoughts have not always been matched with actions, the high preponderance of desperate and despairing Filipina and Filipino youth suggests that serious problems and patterns exist.[6] Since only 30 percent of Filipinos in the United States today are native-born (as opposed to foreign-born; Espiritu 1994, 251), it is reasonable to assume that the majority of the Filipino students surveyed in San Diego are children of immigrants.

Finally, Rubén Rumbaut's (1996) study of ethnic identity and self-esteem among second-generation immigrant youth also reveals some unexpected patterns among Filipino students. Competence in English and educational achievement, two areas in which the subsample of 818 Filipino students surveyed scored highly, are "typically significantly and positively related to self-esteem and psychological well-being" (Rumbaut 1996, 162). Yet he found that the Filipino students had statistically significant lower levels of self-esteem and higher depression scores. Although lower socioeconomic status, poor parental English skills, and a higher degree of stress in the immigration process may help explain these same patterns among the Vietnamese students (Portes and Rumbaut 1990, 157), there are no such obvious explanations for these scores among the Filipinos. Furthermore, Filipinas have consistently higher depression scores than their male counterparts for all variables measured (Rumbaut 1996).[7] Rumbaut's data suggest that "in comparison with other groups certain psychosocial vulnerabilities or dynamics among Vietnamese and Filipino children of immigrants not captured by our data may be linked to a diminished sense of self-worth" (Rumbaut 1996, 163).

To explore further my findings from the high school interviews,[8] I conducted four focus groups[9] among Filipino second-
generation youth who were students at the University of California
at Davis (hereafter UC Davis) during the 1995–96 academic year.[10]
Twenty-one undergraduates and one graduate student participated
in the focus groups; all of them were either born in the United
States or born in the Philippines and brought to the United States at
an early age, before most of their childhood socialization or schooling had occurred. The majority of their parents had arrived in the
United States in the mid-1970s. The gender breakdown was four
males and eighteen females. Most of the students had at least one
parent who was a professional, and often two.

Although my previous research had focused on adult Filipino immigrants, the generation of parents, this project exclusively focused
on youth. The kinds of concerns expressed by the parents echoed
those typically found among other immigrant groups—children
becoming Americanized and losing respect for their elders, or exposure to violence, sex, gangs, and drugs. However, none of the
parents interviewed alluded to any real problems among their children. Clearly, the responses of the children of immigrants reported
in this chapter are situated within an intergenerational dynamic that
is not fully represented without the voices of their parents. That
context needs to be kept in mind as their narratives unfold so as
not to reify the views and responses of youth relative to those of
their parents or to cast their parents in a shadowy light.

THE FAMILY AS CENTER

When asked what it means to them to be Filipino, students referred
to Filipino languages and culture, with several references to pride
and respect. However, the most common response (from almost
half the sample) was a strong, spontaneous, and emotional statement about family as the center of what it means to be Filipino.
These responses may not be particularly striking coming from a
group of Filipino immigrants or their children (Tompar-Tiu and
Sustento-Seneriches 1995, 111; Rumbaut 1997); they became significant, however, in light of subsequent revelations about family relations. The following narratives are taken from some of the

family-oriented responses to the question, "What does it mean to you to be Filipino American, or Filipino?"

> I guess the get-togethers are the big thing, because family is just so important. The structure of the family is important with being Filipino because I know families who don't really talk outside the first cousins, but my family has always kept in touch with eighth and ninth cousins. We all know each other, and we speak to them all the time because we call them and stuff even though it's not a holiday.

> The family is really close-knit. For holidays it's all my mom's four brothers and their families, all get together, and my family and friends, so whenever we get together we have to have this huge house. Last Christmas was the first year we rented a hall for our Christmas party. It was so big.

> For me being a Filipino is tradition and loyalty, because I know my parents always tell me to be proud of who you are, and just because you live here in America, don't be influenced by everything you see, because you are Filipino and you should know who you are and where you come from. Loyalty—my family is very loyal to each other; my cousins and I were really close, it's like my cousins are like my brother and sisters. We look out for each other, and if any one of us have problems we just try to solve them no matter what it is. It is just a close-knit family relationship.

> For me, being Filipino, I guess it is basically the family. I mean, this is my second year here, and my mom still calls me every night. . . . Being Filipino, I really miss my family.

> I don't know . . . things like . . . I can't explain it. It's just certain things that your parents hold dear, like no premarital sex. Things like that are what I call "Filipino" values, just because those are the values my parents hold, and those are the types of values that they tried to give to us. And that's what I consider "Filipino." Whereas in America it's more liberal.

> To me being Filipino means having strong family ties, having values instilled from the time you are born. And warmth, hospitality, just really caring for the people around you. . . . All those values, the strong family ties . . . seem to dominate my whole life, and just about the same with all my friends. We always talk about family, and there is always a big influence with what our parents have to say, and we always care about our peers. And we are very family-oriented. For a lot of us, the reason why we joined MK [Mga Kapatid] was to find another family after leaving home, so it is always that family thing in us. That kin network, the hospitality.

> I think that being Filipino means having family values. Whenever we can we like just sitting at the table and just having dinner together and doing a lot of family stuff.

Yen Le Espiritu (1994) found that when asked what was "Filipino" about their household, most Filipino immigrants she interviewed in San Diego mentioned food and family closeness, and both converged with family reunions and get-togethers (see also Strobel 1997). However, second-generation Filipinos, she argues, tend to have a "largely symbolic" sense of ethnicity, since they experience Filipino culture through family get-togethers and trips to the Philippines, events that are intermittent, brief, and disconnected from most other areas of their lives (Espiritu 1994, 257). Although some interviewees could speak their parents' language of origin, a number of the students in the focus group referred to Filipino language and culture in a manner that suggested a "nostalgic but unacquainted allegiance to an imagined past" (253).

The students I interviewed identified themselves as "Filipino" or "Filipino American." In either case, the "Filipino" part of that identity came first and was more clearly definable than the "American" part. This notion of being Filipino often meant being clear about and proud of who they were. "What Filipino means to me . . . first of all . . . it means pride," explained one student. Another stated it this way: "To me being a Filipino is tradition and loyalty, because I know my parents always tell me to be proud of who you are."

At the same time notions of home—"at home" or "back home"—almost always referred to the Philippines. Some references to the Philippines were positive, such as: "I'm a straight Pilani. And that's the bottom line of it. And I consider home Sicijor. That's me. It's an emotional thing, but I love it." Home was also referred to in more neutral terms; for instance, one student observed that "back home children don't talk back to their parents." This statement reflects the kinds of reprimands with which parents rebuked their Americanizing children. Finally, the Philippines had some negative associations for some students: "When we do something bad, they threaten to send us back home." But all in all, despite place of birth, and whether or not they had lived in or visited the Philippines, the students, in their references to "home," always meant the greater Home across the ocean. In this sense, their association with the Philippines echoed their parents' transnational connections, suggesting more of a sojourner's sense of roots in a diasporic setting. Indeed, some of their parents did plan to retire in the Philippines, although it remains to be seen whether they will move that far away from their children when the time comes.

Although they chose to emigrate to the United States for economic and educational reasons, Filipino immigrants often "look back to the old country as where they really belong psychologically, socially, and culturally" (Santos 1983, 145). Regardless of the students' actual connections with the Philippines, their notion of the Philippines as Home made it an implicit if not explicit point of reference for their behavior and their relations with their parents. Such constant referencing of Home juxtaposed with the daily realities of home in California creates a kind of transnationalism, even if it is based on an "imagined community." In that sense, I would suggest, these children of immigrants experience "emotional transnationalism" with multiple notions of home.

At the same time the students' responses about family as the center of their Filipino identity did not seem to draw on nostalgia or (re)created, (re)imagined events. Instead, those responses stand out as strong, experientially based statements, some quite emotional, about the central role and importance of family in their formulation and understanding of what it means to be Filipino.[11] However, these strong and positive aspects of family and family values began to wither when the students talked about other aspects of their lives.

EDUCATION AND THE PRESSURE TO SUCCEED

In response to our question as to whether Vallejo teachers and high school counselors had noticed anything that set their Filipino students apart from their non-Filipino students, particularly the children of immigrants, most referred without hesitation to the intense academic pressure that Filipino immigrant parents put on their children, especially their daughters. These respondents attributed this pressure to the parents' immigrant status, their desire to succeed in the United States, and their hope that their children would achieve at least their same middle- to upper-middle-class status. Many teachers reported to us that they were aware that "anything less than an A was unacceptable." Teachers' awareness of this pressure came from direct interaction with students and, in certain classes, from reading papers and journals in which students sometimes confided their concerns and problems. Counselors, on the other hand, dealt with students or their parents who were concerned about grades. One head counselor noted that, among Filipinos, "there is less margin for grade acceptance than in any other group."

In both Vallejo schools, Filipino students excelled in academic achievement, receiving the highest average GPAs compared with all other racial-ethnic groups (Vallejo Senior High School 1995). Filipinas especially were also the school leaders, school valedictorians, and salutatorians; they predominated in the honors classes and in the California Scholarship Federation and were extremely active in extracurricular activities. Most teachers thought that Filipinas did better and were more focused than male Filipino students because they were pushed to succeed and make their families proud or to bring honor to their families. Many teachers felt that Filipino families were more indulgent with their sons, giving them more latitude and not controlling or reining them in as much, and that as a result male Filipino students were less motivated and achieved less than their female counterparts.

The children of Filipino immigrants we interviewed at UC Davis, particularly the females, corroborated that grade pressure in their families was intense, and they offered numerous examples of how they experienced this pressure from their parents. The following examples, all of which are from daughters, suggest that some parents were more concerned with grades and achievement than their child's well-being.

> I remember once when I was younger I had four Bs and two As, and I had more Bs than As, which pissed my mom off, and so she just said, "What is this?" and she started yelling at me, and I just started crying. It's like, I am trying and she didn't care, she just wanted the grades and always told us, "I was the valedictorian when I was your age," and I am like, "So what?"

> There is a lot of pressure on me now where they don't care for me. The first thing they ask me is, "So how are you doing in school?" Nothing is easy so far. I have had a rough time and am not doing as well as I would like to. But I have to just say that "things are great," and so they expect me to be out of college in four years and not to take six. There is a lot of pressure when you are their child and they expect you to do well.

> At times I felt bad telling my mom that I got bad grades, I mean during high school, because my mom was valedictorian of her school. She would always tell us, "And when I went to high school, I only got As and Bs." If I even got a C, my parents would hit the fan. Actually, not my dad, he would be like, "Better luck next time," but if it was my mom, I would be scared to even show her my test grades because she would always say, "You have to

get the best grades." It was kind of confusing, because I always went to my dad, and my mom would get mad at my dad for like, "Why are you doing this to her? You are not rooting her on, you are not helping her any," and then she would get mad at me, and say, "Why didn't you show the card to me? I would have understood." It made me more confused, because I really didn't want to get in trouble. And she says, "No, but you can come to me." She changes, it's kind of hard.

"I just totally don't want them to know," explained one female student on academic probation, "and it's just really hard because I know that for a fact that it was my fault that I failed, but to feel their disappointment would hurt more." What is striking in this response is that her parents' disappointment over her academic failings seems to bother this student more than doing poorly academically.

At UC Davis most of the undergraduates we interviewed were involved in majors that would lead to a job or to a graduate degree in a field chosen by their parents. Parental expectations were central, and there did not appear to be any rebellion against or rejection of parental desires for fear of confronting and disappointing them, and for fear of sanctions. The males were majoring in the sciences, computing, or engineering, and the females in the biological sciences, computer science, or sociology–human development; one was majoring in American studies. Those in the sociology–human development fields expressed an interest in social services, public health, nursing, teaching, or law.[12]

Accepting parental decisions about education—what to major in and what career path to follow—is double-edged. On the one hand, students who accept parental choices have a clear sense of direction and security about the future and avoid the uncertainty and insecurity that many students experience; as one female UC Davis student put it, "I had my whole future mapped out." On the other hand, parents may be choosing safety, economic returns, and a known entity (for example, their own profession) rather than an area well suited to their child's interests and talents. For example, the daughter of a doctor spoke of the intense, almost unbearable pressure on her to follow in her father's footsteps, particularly after her two sisters got pregnant out-of-wedlock. "My parents are very, like, you know, 'You've got to get straight.' As, you gotta go here, you gotta do this, you gotta help your cousins back home, you've gotta go to school, you gotta get that degree so you can pay for your brother's college education." Two other Filipina students spoke of similar pressures:

It's true that they say, What do you want to be? and if you come out with you want to be a doctor, they will be really happy, or any of the other two categories [lawyers or engineers], but if you were to come back after your first year and say, I want to be a musician or an artist, they would have a cow. They say, We encourage you to do what you want, but they don't want you to do anything that is risky. They want the steady, secure job.

My parents and my grandparents have always instilled in me that I can do whatever I want as long as I was happy. But now and then they always push, "Well, you can be a doctor," or, "Do you like medicine?" Little hints now and then. "We want you to be this, but if you want to be like that then that is fine."

It is surprising, but perhaps not coincidental, that the dropout rate for Filipino students at UC Davis from 1980 to 1989 was on the high side—about 33 percent (University of California 1995, 3).[13] This could very well be related to a bad fit between students and their majors, which often result in a lack of interest and/or poor grades and an inability to cope with such pressures.

EDUCATIONAL AMBIVALENCE

The pattern of excessively pushing their children to do well in school or to follow a major that will lead to a "safe" profession is not particularly unusual among Asian immigrant parents (see Kao 1995; Okamura and Agbayani 1997). However, we were alerted to a contradictory practice that may contribute to the transnational struggles that many children of Filipino immigrants experience, and daughters perhaps more than sons. The teachers and counselors we interviewed spoke of the relentless pressure from parents on their children, particularly their daughters, to succeed academically. They were concerned about a pattern they observed among their high-achieving Filipino students, particularly the Filipinas, during the senior year: parents would put "roadblocks" in their children's paths, discouraging them from excelling or from going to an excellent university nearby (Vallejo is a twenty-five-minute drive from UC Berkeley and forty-five minutes from UC Davis). Teachers of both regular classes and more challenging classes (such as honors, physics, French, and accounting) were disturbed by this final push for underachievement, particularly among their very bright Filipina students, who often ended up going to a local community college—if they continued their schooling at all—instead of a University of California campus.[14] None of their Filipino students applied to out-of-state universities. Teachers and counselors found this excessive pushing and then sudden braking to be puzzling and disconcerting.[15]

When asked whether this pattern of keeping children, particularly daughters, from going to the University of California, or to college at all, was familiar, the UC Davis students in the focus group would nod their heads, often giggling. They recounted many examples of this dynamic, drawn from their own experience or that of siblings or friends. Some were the only one in their group of friends to go to the University of California, and some said that their parents had tried to get them to go to a campus near home so that they could live at home. When we asked whether this pattern was related to finances (not being able to afford UC tuition), their responses suggested that it was related more to parental control, particularly over daughters' whereabouts and their sexuality, than to money, since many parents bribed their child to stay home with the offer of a new car. This pull homeward directly contradicts the push to excel academically but makes it very clear that parents want to control their daughters' bodies and sexuality.

Young women talked about how strict their parents were with them compared with the leniency granted to their brothers; male students spoke of experiencing the reverse situation. The first of the following narratives is from a male student, and the next three from female students:

> Well, they want you to go to college, but they don't want to let you go. . . . My sister, for example, she wants to go to San Diego State, which is ten, eleven hours away. But they bribed her—my parents bribed her with a car so she could commute to San Francisco State instead. I think they want you to achieve that high goal, but then, they don't want to let you go because they don't trust you . . . 'cause they are used to, you know, "as long as you're under my roof" sort of thing, "you're under my control and you have to follow my rules." So as soon as you move out of their home, then you're on your own, and they don't want you to do that, as much as possible.

> They put a lot of pressure on us girls growing up. The two boys got the most freedom from all of us, because it's like they are invincible, nothing can happen to them. But the girls are so fragile and something might happen to them, so they have to make sure that they can do something and that they are protected all the time.

> I went to community college for two years before I transferred here to Davis. I had the grades and I could have gone to UC, but my parents de-

cided it would be easier for me so that I would just transfer to UC. And I think the same happened to all my friends, most of them stayed there . . . and they got involved in relationships and they ended up wasting their lives because they got pregnant and they got married and they had a lot more potential.

My parents and grandparents . . . say, "Americans, they just let their kids out at the age of eighteen, and they say you are independent. Well, we are not like that. We will support you and be together until you are done in college and educated, and then once you are ready to get married, then you can move out of the house, or you and your husband can stay in the room here that we have available for you." Again, that goes back to family. Because of strong family ties, they tend to be strict sometimes, not knowing the boundaries, when to let go and when not to let go, and that's probably the reason, especially with Filipinas, they are so afraid that if they let them go and give them their freedom, that something like that might happen. Unfortunately, whether they stay home or not, they can still get pregnant and they can still get into drugs.

Although some Filipino immigrant parents also attempt to keep their sons at home as long as possible, the pattern is clearly stronger in relation to daughters, who thus have a very different experience, one based on their parents' gendered notions of propriety. Parental controls over daughters often surpassed their concerns about academic achievement, but daughters were nevertheless still expected to have a career. Many of them have a professional mother to emulate and know that the family depends on her income. Indeed, the labor force participation rates for Filipinas is one of the highest for females among all racial-ethnic groups. Daughters are expected to combine their work lives with marriage and children, and until their marriage, they are expected to remain virgins.[16]

In their study of Filipino educational enrollments in California, Okamura and Agbayani (1997) also found evidence of a substantial decrease in educational enrollments after high school among Filipinos. Reflecting the second-generation Filipino youth's inability to replicate their parents' high levels of education were lower college and university enrollment rates and high dropout rates (Okamura and Agbayani 1997, 187). The authors attribute these lower educational levels to structural factors, such as not being actively recruited by colleges, not being strongly encouraged to pursue further study by teachers and counselors, and not having many

Filipino American faculty who could become role models (188). Although it may be true that many students have not been sufficiently encouraged or recruited, the data from the high school counselors and teachers I interviewed suggests otherwise, and the data from Filipino students also suggests otherwise.

To summarize these data, Filipino immigrant parents appear to resemble other Asian immigrant parents in their emphasis on education. Their tendency to pressure their children to achieve good grades and to choose "safe" professions seems to be in keeping with what we know from other research on Asian American families (Kao 1995; Kao and Tienda 1995). However, these data underscore three additional dynamics. First, qualitative responses from the perspective of students and children offer us a process-oriented and dynamic view of this interaction, providing a sense of how difficult and harsh these pressures are for those struggling to do their best and to please their parents. These responses illuminate the sense of alienation from their parents that many children develop as a result of these pressures, in that they often feel that their parents have no concern or understanding for them and their situation but care only about what they produce.

Second, some Filipino immigrant parents pursue contradictory tactics with their children's (particularly their daughters') education. They push their children relentlessly to achieve and succeed at first, and then pull the emergency brake just as they are coming to an important junction, slowing or even stopping them in their tracks, and then sending them in a different direction, often on the local rather than the express train. Instead of continuing to push children to achieve by going to an excellent four-year university, such as the University of California campuses that are within close proximity, many parents prefer that their children stay at home, even if that means going to a lesser college, if at all. It was our strong impression from the interviews that this was usually not an economically based decision. This process obstructs and derails the drive for excellence that parents previously pursued and replaces it with the more gendered priorities of control and safety. This pattern may very well impede possibilities for more substantial economic mobility among the second generation, as parents limit the educational and career opportunities of their children, especially their daughters.[17]

FAMILY CONTRADICTIONS:
PARENT-CHILD COMMUNICATIONS

Parent-child communication varied among the students we interviewed, with examples of both closed and open lines, as well as estrangement. The paradox many young people faced, however, was that while parents wanted or expected their children to come to them with their problems—reflecting Filipino family ideology—parents were often at the root of some of these problems. Furthermore, the prospect of sanctions, punishment, or feelings of guilt led some of the students to withdraw and withhold their problems. This notion of family as the locus of contradictions best summarizes these poignant experiences.

Although a few of the female students stated that they had a good and open relationship with their mother, we also heard narratives of alienation from parents; these were particularly striking in light of the earlier responses about the centrality and importance of family in daily life and identity formation, and in the ideology of what it means to be Filipino. The students described their alienation as a result of not being able to communicate with their parents and not being seen for who they were. They expressed a sense of being pushed to be someone they were not and said that their parents often compared them to a cousin or a friend's child, or even the parent when she or he was young. When they ventured to tell a parent about their thoughts, their lives, or their problems, these young people immediately regretted sharing that information because they once again experienced the pain of not being seen or heard. Instead of the empathy, understanding, support, and love that they had hoped for, they received a lecture, anger, disappointment, or emotional punishment.[18] Again, while these dynamics may not differ significantly from intergenerational relations in other immigrant (and non-immigrant) families, the emotional outcomes do seem to be significantly different. This may provide insight into the feelings of aloneness and despair that can translate into desperate and suicidal thoughts. Three responses from female students are followed by four from male students:

> I have never been close to my mom, I don't know why. I have always felt that she didn't love me because she's not the type to show feelings. All she

says to us is to get good grades. . . . My dad . . . tries to be more open with us. He always tells me that if I have a problem I am here not just as father but as a friend but I still don't want to talk to my dad.

There are strong repercussions for going to your parents. You know that they are there for the support, but then you get punished and you don't want that. You'd rather wait till the very end and take the real huge punishment rather than face it up at the very beginning and deal with it everyday. . . . It is common when there is something wrong with the family, they'll send that member or threaten to send that member back home.

I think that a lot of my Filipino friends don't like sharing problems with their own parents because a lot of our parents are really old-fashioned and they don't understand. . . . As for my mom, I kept a lot of things from her problem-wise . . . [in speaking about family pressures for her success] because my family is prestigious and want you to succeed, they want you to be on top. . . . They don't want you to mess up, they want you to be perfect. . . . It's scary because they expect a lot, and when you can't they keep pushing you, and you have a problem with it, you can't even go to them because they might find out what your problem is.

I know for a fact that my mom really wishes that I would talk to her and my dad really wishes that I would communicate more, and that they complain that I am like a boarder. I just come in to eat and sleep, I play with my brothers, I play with the kids my mom baby-sits, and then I go back to college and that's it. They wish that I would talk to them about what is happening in college. . . . They go about it all wrong. I tell them something, and then I instantly regret it the minute later, and you just like don't want to bother with it, so just like keep it to yourself and say, "School is fine, Mom," and just let them keep their illusion of what the perfect family is. And try to keep from messing up. [*This young man cried while he spoke.*]

[When I talk to my parents] they are thinking that whatever I say doesn't matter because they are the grown-ups and I am just a little kid; I am just their baby boy. . . . I know what I want for myself, and it's hard for them to understand that. . . . I tried talking to my mom one time, and she just said, "Okay, whatever," and she ignored everything I said . . . and said, "No, my way is right because I am the grown-up, I am older than you, and I know better than you." I am like "Okay," and so I just pretty much stick to myself with the problems.

My cousin Ronnie goes here and is a medical student, and my mother made a big thing of me following Ronnie, and she just couldn't get it through her head [*he begins to cry and has to stop momentarily*] that there is something I can't do as well as Ronnie or some things that he can't do as well as me, but Ronnie just always excelled at school in general, and she would always force me to be . . . her answer for everything was, "Well, Ronnie did it." And I would be going, "I am not Ronnie," and I know that totally shot me from ever deciding to ever try to talk to my parents because that was the worst thing for me growing up.

[My brother and I] don't tell them anything because somehow if there is something wrong with our lives, somehow it is like our fault, and we don't want to tell them because they'll listen to us and then they'll start to give us grief about our problems and say, "Why did you do that or this?" And then that's kind of why we don't go to counseling. If we can't go to our parents, we figure why should we go to a stranger? Right now [*speaking of the focus group*] my dad would say, "Why are you here right now, why are you telling them, these strangers, your problems?" [*laughter*]

Filipino family ideology has taught these students that all problems should be kept within the family. Revealing a problem to an "outsider," whether a friend, a teacher, or, in the worst case, a counselor would create gossip and bring shame (hiya) and embarrassment to the family because of the insinuation that the family has a problem. In other words, owing to a sense of self that is highly identified with the family (Tompar-Tiu and Sustento-Seneriches 1995, 115), the family as a collectivity loses face when an individual member's problems are revealed, suggesting that the parents did not do their job. Since many young people cannot turn to their parents, in part because their parents are causing some of the problems, and in part because of a lack of sympathy and receptivity, they feel caught in an extremely lonely bind, with no one to turn to for help. A few of the students in the focus groups felt able to turn to friends, siblings, or cousins in the knowledge that confidentiality would be observed, but others either did not have these outlets or could not trust their friends or relatives to not betray them. Such individuals feared that someone would tell his or her parents, leading to a wide chain of gossip about the young person that would shame the family. A young man shared the following feeling:

They expect so much of you, and that's why there are so many problems sometimes with Filipino youth, because they can't turn to anyone. They might want to go to a counselor, but then they have always been taught that this is a stranger and that you shouldn't go outside the family, you should just go inside the family. And then it just doesn't work because then they just never say anything and they keep it bottled up inside until one day they explode and it's too late.

One young woman who wanted to see a counselor was told by her mother:

"You know, Filipino families, it's just whenever there's a problem, we don't tell anyone else, because it would bring shame to our family; it would say that we don't know how to take care of our own. And if there's a problem we, the unit, the immediate family, can deal with it, or will have to deal with it." Well, once in a while, you know, Mom and Dad just can't take care of it, and so now you're getting like mixed signals. You know you're supposed to come to Mom and Dad, but you know Mom and Dad can't help you, so can I go to a counselor? Oh no, I can't. Why? Because I'd bring shame down on them. . . . You're just not supposed to tell anyone about "our" family problems, about anything that happens with you, or with your brothers and sisters or your family, because that would just bring shame on to the family. . . . You can't go to a counselor. There are a lot of secrets in my family. If something bad happens, you don't tell anyone. No matter what, you don't tell anyone. You don't want to bring shame upon your family. Keep your mouth shut. And we say, "Okay."

Family business should stay in the family and should be private. It doesn't have to include strangers because strangers don't know what is going on with you. They are saying, "Okay, if you have a problem, come to us," but then when you tell them, it is like they are so disappointed in you, and you don't want to feel the disappointment from them, because that hurts more than when you failed yourself.

I think part of the reason that parents don't want their children to go to counselors is because they see it as a reflection on them personally, because if their kids have to go to a counselor, that means they're not doing their jobs as parents—they're not taking care of their children that well.

Our interviews in high schools suggested the same patterns. Filipino students in need of help are averse to seeking counseling for fear that their friends and parents will find out; high school counselors told us of students begging them not to tell their parents of their meetings. The head counselor at one Vallejo high school for over fifteen years stated, "I am concerned about the mental health of Filipino students as a group," because they are more reluctant to seek help for their problems than others.[19] The director of counseling services at UC Davis, a Filipina psychologist, also finds that Filipino students are hesitant to seek counseling, and the few she has seen discuss their friends but never their families. This avoidance of mental health services is not unusual among Asian American populations (Kuo 1984; Sue and Morishima 1988).

FAMILY SECRETS

The family ideology of keeping problems within the circle of immediate kin seems to be working, to some extent, in that most children are very reticent with others about their problems. They keep quiet about their problems and rarely disclose them. However, where this ideology fails is in the practice of children turning to their parents for help.[20] Attempting to cope with the pressures and problems they feel, the children of Filipino immigrants described a situation of "no exit"—they could not turn to their parents for help, but they also could not turn to others for fear of further sanctions. This bind often created intense feelings of loneliness, deep unhappiness, and at times despair. A few mentioned a religious belief that "suffering in silence" was a way to accept their pain: if Jesus could withstand carrying and being nailed to the cross, they should be able to handle their own suffering. However, not all succeeded in keeping their pain and their problems in check. Indeed, six of the twenty-two university students we interviewed (27 percent), all female (one-third of the female students), acknowledged having had suicidal thoughts, and a few others gave examples of suicide attempts by their siblings or other family tragedies. This more gendered pattern is in keeping with the CDC's finding of rates of suicidal thoughts (Kann et al. 1995) and with Rubén Rumbaut's findings of higher depression scores among young Filipina women (1996).

Suicidal thoughts not only encompass deep despair and alienation but also speak of anger and a desire for power. Because of the highly emotional content of these responses, I did not feel able to probe further when students discussed their suicidal thoughts, but some did allude to a fantasy of how that act would affect their parents: perhaps suicide would make them see the child for who she was and also make them regret their behavior toward her. One young woman spoke of how difficult it was for her in high school to have parents who were so strict that they would not allow her to have a boyfriend and grandparents who threatened not to help her financially with college if she had one:

> I would just sit in my room and cry, and [my father] wouldn't care, and I would just want to kill myself. I felt that was the only solution for me, and I felt that so many times and just wanted to do something. I don't think I could

ever go through with it because it is just scary, but I always wanted to do it in a way to scare them so they would wake up and realize that they can't treat me like that and maybe they'll change. Some way to make them realize to stop doing what they were doing because that was the only thing that I could think of to reach them because any other way, they won't listen.

Another young woman responded in the following way:

> I don't know about you guys, but now I can say it, because I'm far from it now. I always felt that I really must have been a bad child, because when I was little I always used to think I did a lot of things wrong. I don't know why I thought that. Maybe it's that Filipino American thing that I was dealing with. . . . And I always had a lot of suicidal thoughts. . . . I was looking back at my old journals, what I was writing at ten years old. A ten-year-old should not be writing this! . . . I remember thinking that I was a bad child, that I didn't deserve to live. I have no clue why I thought that. But it's a pressure that you feel, and it's coming from your own family, and you don't ever want to tell anybody that it's your own family because that would bring shame not just onto your family but onto you.

One student spoke of her desperation and the unempathic and threatening response she received from her parents:

> I have had suicidal thoughts before. I am anemic, and I was so stressed this past year trying to transfer that there were times when I felt like I didn't have a friend in the world. My parents were yelling at me, my sister didn't even support me or anything, and my grandparents weren't there. I have a very close tie with my grandparents. . . . I felt that it would be better for me if I wasn't around anymore and that it would be better for everyone else if I wasn't around anymore, and I went to the extreme where I almost cut my wrists. It was like almost there and then my parents saw me and they are like, "What are you doing?" and they said, "God is going to punish you if you do that." . . . My parents also said, "Look at the effect you are having on your sister. Your younger sister looks up to you." I am like, "You don't need to tell me that, it is like adding more pressure."

Another young woman related her desperation to immigration and the experience of being uprooted:

> I wanted to kill myself because of what has come down to this. My parents brought me here to America to get my best life, but at that time [early in college] I was experiencing the worst that I wanted to kill myself, and it boils down to going to my parents and saying that I hate them for bringing me here. It's not the best, they think it's the best, but it's not. It's not all money, education, and stuff. . . . I don't understand why they could say the best thing is in America but yet when we do something bad they threaten to send

us back there. It is very ironic. And so when I was thinking those thoughts like, "I just want to go," and then I think about how I am the only child and how they have all these expectations of me, how I am going to hurt them and how God will punish me, and I said, "No."

In one focus group of four women, all of whom were the eldest in their families, one said, "I wouldn't be surprised if any of us here eldest members of the family did *not* have suicidal thoughts; I think the pressure that we have and the stress that is placed on us is just enough to push you." This pressure is related to the remnants of a traditional family practice in the Philippines, namely, that a first-born daughter (manong) was expected to endure substantial sacrifices to take care of her natal family and often did not marry.[21] Although none of the male students directly mentioned being suicidal, two broke down and cried when they spoke of their alienation from their parents, their relationship with whom was clearly one of respect, fear, and hatred.

Family problems and secrets tumbled out at this point in the focus groups—in a family with a great deal of pressure on the daughters to follow the father's professional footsteps in medicine, one student's two sisters had both attempted suicide. One student described her eating disorder. Another spoke of her younger brother who got involved with a gang and was killed. Another told the group that her younger brother had been jailed for gang-related criminal activities.[22]

In these cases, parents not only created some of the pressures that caused distress and anxiety in their children but were unavailable to help them and forbade all other possible outlets for help. Speaking with friends or other relatives about a problem could cause gossip, embarrassment, and shame, as could breaking the taboo of keeping things within the family and speaking with a stranger, such as a counselor. Indeed, the students saw these thoughts or acts of despair as acts of family sabotage for which they might be sanctioned. Rather than receiving the empathy they so clearly needed, those who had been suicidal (including suicidal siblings) instead had been scolded, shamed, and further alienated. None of the six women who had been suicidal sought or were sent to counseling. Given the strength of Catholicism among Filipinos, it was somewhat surprising that none of those interviewed even mentioned the possibility of talking with a priest. This is less surprising, however, in light of the fact that suicide is sanctioned by the church.

TRANSNATIONAL STRUGGLES
AND FILIPINO IMMIGRANT YOUTH

Given their hybrid identity, some of which draws on an image of Filipino culture and language, a close connection with parents, and Filipino notions of the family (see McCoy 1993), the children of Filipino immigrants are experiencing multiple and contradictory tugs, messages, and pushes and pulls. Privileging the notion of family with which they were brought up, these young people have accepted patriarchal family dynamics and the predominance of parental wishes over their own voices, resulting in internal struggles and an inability to approach their parents openly for fear of sanctions. Part of the struggle seems to stem from living and coping with multiple pressures and with the profound gap between family ideology and family practices.[23] This gap may be more apparent or disturbing in the United States than in the Philippines because some American societal pressures and practices constitute direct challenges to particular Filipino American family practices.

I was unsuccessful in finding current studies on depression, low self-esteem, or suicidal ideation in the Philippines that would bear upon my findings. Filipino academic psychologists and social psychologists have been trained either in the United States or by U.S.-trained Filipino academics. They tend to apply positivist research techniques from U.S. psychology that are neither adapted to Filipino culture nor sensitive to nuanced emotions in general. Although it is difficult in general to study family dynamics anywhere, the kinds of academic research done on Filipino mental health and family life do not begin to seek out the kinds of behaviors and practices found here, and the methodology utilized would not detect it either.

It is actually in the somewhat older research on the Philippines done by anthropologists, many of whom were American, that some of these dynamics and values are delineated, such as the primacy of the family, the authority of parents, the role expected of the eldest daughter, and the strength of shame and embarrassment as deterrents to certain behaviors that would affect the family's name, such as sharing one's problems with an outsider (Bulatao 1964; Guthrie 1971; Lynch and de Guzman 1981; Yengoyan and Makil 1984). We have seen how the primacy of family has led to particular ideologies among children of Filipino immigrants. We have also seen how these young people are, for the most part, following their parents' wishes by going to certain colleges and declaring certain majors that will lead to certain careers, often nursing and accounting. However, these choices may reflect a transnational lag in that parents, as noted earlier, may be choosing and judging careers from the perspective of their pre-emigration experiences in the Philippines.

Shame or embarrassment (hiya) is one important principle with which children are socialized and coerced in the Philippines. It is a powerful tool that keeps children of Filipino immigrants from seeking out therapy for fear that they will shame their parents for admitting a problem, sharing it with a stranger, and possibly incurring gossip about the family. For example:

> Just as an individual's fortunes are closely bound to those of his family, so are his mistakes. It is clearly in the best interests of each family member for all others to keep out of trouble. . . . Quarrels within the family are concealed so that a solid front can be presented and because family conflicts are deemed a disgrace. (Guthrie 1971, 75)

This description and others I have read in texts published on average twenty-five years ago most aptly reflect the kinds of values that Filipino young people expressed in the focus groups. These studies strongly suggest that the values, emotions, and ideologies underlying contemporary dynamics within Filipino immigrant families are rooted in the Philippines. Thus, the case I am making here is for a cultural transnationalism that plays itself out in the realm of the emotions. That the young people I interviewed were able to speak about these problems so freely in the focus groups, most for the very first time, suggests that many of them are ready and willing to break the silence and abandon part of a cultural tradition, but not in a manner that would endanger the family name.

Although we can establish that these practices stem from Filipino gendered values and ideologies, that does not explain what causes these disturbing dynamics. Compared with other Asian immigrant groups, and owing to their particular colonialist history, Filipino immigrant parents are uniquely situated in that they tend to speak excellent English and have a greater familiarity with American institutions. As postcolonial subjects, their parents' Americanization did not start at the Los Angeles International Airport but years before, in the Philippines:

> Most are products of a public school system established by Americans and patterned after the American educational system, with English as the language of instruction and, until recently, a curriculum that was heavily American oriented. For years, every Filipino child in the Philippines was raised and educated as a "developing American." (Santos 1983, 132)

Filipino parents' knowledge of U.S. life, along with their middle-to upper-middle-class status, may intensify the controls they exert over their children, particularly when compared with other Asian immigrant parents, who lose control because their children gain English proficiency faster (Kibria 1993).[24] And as I have argued elsewhere (Wolf 1992), better-off parents can and do exert greater controls over their children than poorer parents. They are more likely to be able to orchestrate a parental or household strategy because they have more resources and therefore can call upon more significant sanctions with which to keep their children in line.

However, while parents and the ideology of family may be creating some of these problems, I do not wish to argue for a mono-causal explanation, nor do I wish to demonize Filipino parents, who, after all, are also going through their own transnational struggles. Indeed, as others have pointed out, living in the United States is a quick and acute "apprenticeship in disillusionment under the impact of discrimination and rejection," in the words of Joel San Juan, a sociologist working within the Filipino community in San Diego (quoted in Campomanes 1995b, 147). Clearly, there are other social forces and structures in the broader society that can also be detrimentally affecting these young people. As Espiritu (1994, 253) points out, the children of Filipino immigrants simultaneously face the pressure of assimilation and "the racism that signals to them that they will never be accepted." Among the almost two-thirds of Rumbaut's (1996) Filipino sample who had experienced discrimination, depression scores were higher than the scores of those who had not experienced it; among the females, the difference in scores was still substantially higher compared with the males. Furthermore, Filipinos faced with discrimination may be caught in a very particular racial-ethnic bind in that they are from Southeast Asia (although very few Filipino American students identify as "Asian" or "Southeast Asian") but have Hispanic surnames and can easily be mistaken for Latino.

San Juan suggests that these higher rates of depression and suicidal thoughts among Filipino youth are connected to a history of colonialism in the Philippines and racism in the United States, both of which have created feelings of inferiority (Rimonte 1997). In Filipino colonialist history, shame, martyrdom, and suffering played important roles (Ileto 1979), and these notions may still be reverberating among Filipino immigrant parents and their children. Indeed, Filipino colonialist history, marked by socialization into North American life, values, and practices while still in the homeland, resembles the Puerto Rican case more closely than any other Asian group, suggesting an interesting comparative study.

San Juan also feels that the divisive and amorphous nature of the Filipino community in the United States offers young Filipinos little to identify with compared with other Asian ethnic groups. A young woman's recounting of her earlier struggles with her Filipino identity in Leny Mendoza Strobel's (1997) participatory research on Filipino decolonization corroborates San Juan's contention. As one of Strobel's research participants examined her Filipino identity at a younger age, "she went through a period of depression that led to suicidal thoughts, because, she said, 'Nothing that I could claim as my identity was defining who I was. So I had to begin reconstructing this identity and discovering and rediscovering who I wanted to be and who I was before' " (Strobel 1997, 73). San Juan suggests that the gender differentials in the patterns discussed earlier are related to a double standard in that males are given more leverage to externalize their feelings and to exhibit more aggressive behavior (Joel San Juan, personal communication, October 23, 1996). His insights point to several research questions deserving attention.

These internal conflicts among the children of Filipino immigrants are not simply constituted by a dichotomous push and pull between two homogeneous sides, between two sides of the ocean (the United States and the Philippines), or between dual systems (the American system and the Filipino system), but by multiple and heterogeneous understandings and meanings of what it is to be Filipino, American, and Filipino American. In other words, a binary model of immigrant assimilation, of pushes and pulls between two systems, the old and the new, does not adequately represent the complex and contradictory processes occurring among the children of Filipino immigrants.

Despite high and rapid naturalization rates, Filipino immigrant parents in the United States preserve "strong transnational ties" with the Philippines; they live in "worlds that very much include the Philippines both ideologically and literally" (Szanton-Blanc 1996, 187, 191). Children of Filipino immigrants are dealing with their parents'—and often their grandparents'—experiences and images of the United States. Some of those images have been shaped by the older generation's time here (such as notions of American inhospitability, sexual immorality, and lack of respect for elders), some by the Philippine educational system—created by American colonialists—during colonial and postcolonial times (depending on their generation), and some by the changing political-legal structure of U.S. immigration (for example, export-oriented careers). This image of the United States is held in conjunction with their images of life in the Philippines, some of which are reconstituted through selective memories. Thus, at home with their parents—and very possibly with their grandparents as well[25]—children of Filipino immigrants confront multiple and sometimes conflicting transnational and transhistorical images, cultural codes, discourses, and notions of what it means to be both Filipino and American, in addition to nostalgia for Home. And as Espiritu (2001) has pointed out, the ways in which the "margins" (Filipinos) construct the "mainstream" (Americans) end up affecting constructions of what proper young Filipino—and especially Filipina—young people should do and be.

Thus, the Philippines and the United States as "imagining" and imagined communities exert particular pressures on U.S. Filipino formations and Filipino-ness (Campomanes 1995b, 151). The father who yells at his children, "We are in America, but you are still Filipinos, and I'll raise you however I want to. I'll raise you as Filipinos because you are Filipino, and I don't care if you are in America," has a very different image of being Filipino and being American than do his children. Furthermore, his image of what is appropriately Filipino or American is highly gendered (Espiritu 2001). His notions are partially reflected in his children, who have multiple and hierarchical notions of home and Home.

CONCLUSIONS

I do not wish to suggest that all Filipino children of immigrants are suffering from alienation from their parents and are potentially suicidal. Clearly, that is not the case. However, this study and others with larger statistical bases do suggest some unexpected patterns that are significant in light of the relatively successful integration of post-1965 Filipino immigrants into the American economy and society.

First, the broad socioeconomic statistics that paint a "model minority" picture of Filipino immigrants suggest that they have successfully assimilated, but this study finds that those demographics do not capture or portray the painful and problematic contradictions in the lives of many children of those immigrants. In other words, while a demographic and comparative analysis of Filipino immigrants' position is important and useful, it portrays only a limited part of the story. Such comparative measures need to be broadened and deepened.

Second, the findings from this study suggest that the term "assimilation" in and of itself can be misleading and needs to be reconceptualized by sociologists of immigration—or at the very least, used more critically. Although Filipino immigrant youth appear to be assimilated in form, many are not reflecting the adaptation and acceptance that this concept implies. The problem may be in the terminology and its implications more than in the population under discussion, since assimilation connotes a kind of functionalist, nonconflictual adaptation. The bipolar choice between assimilated and non-assimilated is not particularly helpful in explaining this case (Espiritu 1994, 268). In this chapter, I use the concept of emotional transnationalism to evoke a sense of the multiple discourses circulating and competing in the emotional lives and minds of Filipino children of immigrants and to go beyond binary and segmented notions of assimilation.

Third, this study highlights that immigration and transnationalism are gendered processes in which control over women's bodies, mobility, sexuality, and education play an important role that affects the future success of Filipina children of immigrants. Furthermore, the higher rates of depression and despair among young

Filipinas suggest that assimilation is also a highly gendered process. The gender-neutral theoretical approaches in much of the immigration literature need to be revised and sensitized, taking these differential cultural codes into account.

Fourth, these data leave us asking, Why are some Filipino youth, particularly females, suffering from so much distress, and what appears to be more distress than that experienced by other groups? There does not appear to be one clear answer to that question. I have suggested some possibilities that need to be further explored in individual interviews and contextualized within the historical, political, and racialized relations between the Philippines and the United States and between Filipinos within the United States. All of this must be factored in with the strong role that Catholicism plays among Filipinos and others in restricting and constraining women's mobility and choices.

Given the paucity of in-depth data on the psychological, political, and social interactions and processes among the children of immigrants in general, we must ask whether these levels of alienation and despair are occurring among other groups as well and how they manifest themselves. Although it is very likely that children of immigrants from other groups, particularly from East Asia, are experiencing these tensions and some alienation from their parents who are pushing them educationally, they do not seem to be reacting in the same way as many Filipino children of immigrants. However, such reactions may be difficult to discern, since the role of culture in the "manifestation, perception [and] recognition . . . of psychiatric symptoms within ethnic minority groups is almost completely overlooked in contemporary psychiatric epidemiology" (Vega and Rumbaut 1991, 356; Kuo 1984). In-depth qualitative research on the emotional life of children of immigrants is needed to complement the important quantitative work that has been done and to contextualize these dynamics over time and transnational spaces. Additionally, appropriate policy measures and community services need to be designed for Filipino youth to create forms of help that are culturally appropriate and sensitive to the needs, fears, and concerns of those wanting assistance.

Families are a "theater" of multiple relationships between genders and generations (Morris 1990, 2). Although families create the ties that bind and bond, they can also be sites of intense conflict and contradiction, especially among immigrants (Rumbaut 1997, 8). The family ties of Asian immigrants are praised and admired by those who argue for "strong families" and "family values," but we must look more closely at family practices and the price they exact from the children upon whom they are imposed.

I have introduced the concept of emotional transnationalism here to suggest a more complex way to think about immigrants' children, who for the most part can only imagine the Home that constitutes their parents' and grandparents' primary point of reference. This Home is morally superior to the home they now inhabit and constitutes the foundation for judging behaviors as proper, appropriate, or shameful. Thus, although many children of immigrants may not pursue the kinds of transnational economic and emotional ties with relatives or friends in the Philippines that their parents pursue, they nevertheless live a kind of transnational life at the level of emotions, even if it is based in one geographical place. As they manage and inhabit multiple cultural and ideological zones, the resulting emotional transnationalism constantly juxtaposes what they do at home against what is done at Home. While this may offer the security of a source of identity, it also creates tensions, confusion, and contradictory messages that, as has been demonstrated, can lead to intense alienation and despair among some. The son who is told, "Just because you live here in America, don't be influenced by everything you see, because you are Filipino and should know who you are and where you come from," is being told to differentiate between home and Home. In doing so, at the level of emotions and behaviors, he becomes a transnational subject.

We might ask, Is this so-called transnational emotional jockeying between two sites of home any different from what all ethnic groups experience in diasporic settings? Wouldn't Indian children of immigrants in Great Britain, especially the girls, experience similar references to Home and similar admonitions to act and be Indian rather than British? My response would be, Yes, these experiences are very similar. But are they also similar to the ways in which children of immigrants from earlier waves experienced Home and negotiated their identities? Although certain attempts to constrain children with notions of traditional culture may be similar, the context of children's connections with Home and the presence of Home at home are vastly different factors, owing to new and intensified global connections. And still, many of these Filipino children of immigrants find that there is no place like Home, which is a welcoming and warmly imagined place.

This is a revised version of "Family Secrets: Transnational Struggles Among Children of Filipino Immigrants," 1997, *Sociological Perspectives* 40(3): 457–82. I wish to thank Rubén Rumbaut, Chuck Holms, Peggy Levitt, Mary Waters, and the anonymous reviewers who made comments on this paper.

NOTES

1. Those who emigrated at a very young age—by age three or four—may still be considered to belong to this category, since most of their childhood socialization and schooling took place in the United States.
2. In a study of Filipino source materials at the University of California at Los Angeles, Ciria-Cruz (1994) found that an average of 2.7 pieces a year were published on Filipino Americans between 1920 and 1990. Lisa Hoffman's search of Sociofile for the past twenty years, covering 1,600 journals and dissertation abstracts, revealed that Filipinos were the focus of only 8 of the 254 pieces (3 percent) produced on Asian Americans. In the psychology abstracts, 25 of the 675 studies (again 3 percent) done on Asian Americans were on Filipinos.
3. I do not intend to dichotomize "the real" and "the imagined" in order to privilege one over the other. Both are extremely important in the creation and maintenance of particular identities.
4. This compares strikingly with 33.4 percent among Hispanic females, 26.2 percent among whites, and 25.3 percent among black females.
5. Twenty-nine percent of Filipino males had suicidal thoughts as well, compared with 21.4 percent among Hispanic males, 19.1 percent among white males, and 23.7 percent among black males. Filipino males ranked third (11.9 percent) among those who had attempted suicide, after Filipina and Hispanic females. The rate of suicide attempts among Filipino males is close to double that of all other males.
6. Because of the high proportion of Filipinos in San Diego, a special category was created for them in that city only. These rates are much higher than the national average of all groups and both genders who had suicidal thoughts in the previous twelve months—24 percent

(Dr. Laura Kann, personal communication, August 7, 1996; see Kann et al., 1995, 32).

7. This and other references to statistical breakdowns of the Filipino sample in Rumbaut's (1996) study are based on further analyses of his data, for which I am extremely grateful (Rubén Rumbaut, personal communication, October 12, 1996).

8. We interviewed ten teachers, five counselors, and two principals in two Vallejo senior high schools with similar racial and socioeconomic mixes of students, where Filipinos constituted 25 to 30 percent of the student population. Filipinos constituted approximately 20 percent of Vallejo's population in the 1990 census; the slightly higher proportion in the public schools may reflect that more white children go to private schools.

9. In determining how many focus groups to run, I followed the general advice of the literature on focus groups—when the outcomes and responses become predictable, one has done a sufficient number. Such predictability developed during the second focus group, but I continued in order to increase the sample size. The focus groups were run in the same manner each time, lasting 90 to 120 minutes maximum. The advantage of using the focus group format for this research was that it allowed us to ask about certain findings from the high school interviews in a manner that facilitated open discussion among the students. Indeed, in each group, it seemed as though a door had been suddenly opened on to their personal lives that had not been previously opened in front of others. Hearing others' stories seemed to encourage students to share their own. The disadvantage of the group setting was that more in-depth probing of individuals was not possible (see Merton, Fiske, and Kendall 1990).

10. I contacted the president of the main and largest Filipino student organization on campus—Mga Kapatid ("Our Brothers and Sisters," or "The Siblings"), known as "MK." With approximately 250 student members, it is the largest of six Filipino organizations on campus and one of the largest ethnic associations on campus. Calculating from the 1995 UC Davis student ethnic census, approximately 40 percent of Filipino students at UC Davis are members of MK. By sending out e-mails to its members through the president and by attending several MK meetings to explain my purpose and ask for volunteers, I was able to get many student volunteers, twenty-two of whom were able to fit a focus group into their schedules. After the first focus group met, my announcements in MK were followed by spontaneous and enthusiastic endorsements from students who had participated in a previous focus group, who would state that, in their view, the focus group was a worthwhile and

interesting experience. Students who had participated in them were also helpful in soliciting volunteers through their own networks.

11. The strength of family ties among these students is not surprising in light of the anthropological literature on the importance of sa pamilya (at least ideologically) in the Philippines (Yengoyan and Makil 1984; Lynch and de Guzman 1981; McCoy 1993; see also Hirtz 1995).

12. The "lawyer, doctor, engineer" career choice triad is reflected in some of the Filipino campus organizations for preprofessionals: the Filipino American Society of Engineers (FAE), the Filipino Americans in Health Sciences (FAHS), and Filipino Americans in Liberal Arts and the Humanities (FILA).

13. The director of student affairs reports that approximately 25 percent of all those who drop out do end up graduating; however, no study has been done to follow the dropouts in order to see whether they re-enroll elsewhere, return to UC Davis, or simply choose another option. What is surprising is that the majority of Filipino students have college-educated and professional parents, and that is less likely to be the case for the groups whose dropout percentages are similar—for example, Latinos (32 percent) and Chicanos (39 percent).

14. Kao's (1995) analysis of the 1988 National Education Longitudinal Study, which surveyed eighth-graders and their parents, found that 45 percent of the Filipino parents expected their children to graduate from college, and 43 percent of the Filipino children expected to graduate from college. These percentages were among the highest among Asian groups. This finding may not necessarily contradict what we heard at the Vallejo high schools, since community college can be part of that trajectory. State eligibility rates on Filipino high school students who could attend the University of California are not very clear, since the sample size is too small for a reliable estimate. A 1986 study done by the California postsecondary educational commission found that somewhere between 15 and 23 percent of eligible Filipino high school students in California apply to the University of California. Owing to the small sample size, there is a confidence interval of +/−4.1 percent (Jean Suhr Ludwig, personal communication, July 30, 1996). This does not tell us how many applied to the California State University system but does suggest that many Filipinos who are otherwise eligible do not attend an excellent state-run university. In 1995, 63 percent of Filipino applicants accepted to the University of California actually enrolled in the fall. This percentage is similar for other Asians (University of California 1995).

15. Of the 459 Filipino students who graduated from Vallejo Senior High School between 1985 and 1992, an average of 6.7 percent per year went on to the University of California, 8.75 went to a California State

University campus, and 28.3 went to a California community college (Vallejo Senior High School 1995). Although I do not have test scores by race-ethnicity, the grade distribution alone for the same school does suggest that it is highly likely that there were far more Filipino students who were eligible for the UC system or the California State University system than who actually went.

16. High school teachers and counselors recounted to us examples of Filipino parents not allowing their high-achieving daughters to go on certain field trips, especially if they included an overnight. Parental controls were often a source of deep frustration for female students who wished to date, have boyfriends, or attend the prom. Parents either forbade those activities or set strict conditions, such as a sibling-chaperone or early curfew, making it difficult for many young people. The strictness of parents was noted in the San Diego newspaper article as one of the possible reasons for the high Filipina rate of suicidal thought (Lau 1995a, 1).

17. This obstruction must be understood, however, within the fairly limited range of career options seen by many Filipino immigrant parents. For example, if it is decided that a daughter will become a nurse, going to a community college rather than the University of California is not likely to affect her career possibilities. These choices may reflect a transnational lag in that parents may be choosing and judging careers from the perspective of their pre-emigration experiences in the Philippines, where nursing, other medical degrees, and accounting were seen as "export" degrees.

18. In Tompar-Tiu and Sustento-Seneriches's (1995, 35) study of depression among Filipino Americans, they note that "some Filipino child-rearing practices . . . do not allow the expression of negative feelings to parents or authority figures."

19. High school counselors spoke of Filipino parents seeming to be unaware of their children's problems and then often denying these problems when confronted with them. For example, some parents attempted to change a child's teacher or class rather than look at the child's problems. Some counselors and teachers at one high school provided anecdotal evidence of more suicidal thought and perhaps more suicide among Filipino students in their school: three of the past five suicides were Filipino students, and there were many more attempts among these students.

20. The results of a peer survey conducted among 254 Filipino youths between the ages of fifteen and seventeen in Vallejo, under the auspices of the Fighting Back grant to the Filipino Task Force, shocked many Filipino parents by what they showed about their children's involve-

ment in gang membership, sexual behavior, and drug and alcohol use. One finding of interest here concerned young people's perceptions of where they would receive help and support. Although mothers were viewed as slightly more supportive than fathers in response to questions about how a parent would react to an alcohol or drug problem or an unwanted pregnancy, most of those interviewed (65 to 85 percent) felt that their parents would *not* be supportive if confronted with their child's problem. Furthermore, *76 percent knew of no place in the Filipino community where they would feel safe seeking help with personal problems.* Clearly, these young people in the midst of adolescence felt that there were few options, if any, if they had problems.

21. I am grateful to David Szanton for pointing this out to me.

22. These tragic family stories were disconcerting to hear. If they had been taking my course, I would have judged these students, from their appearance as cheerful and socially involved, to be among the better-adjusted and higher-achieving students. I also worried about opening up painful wounds but not having the skills to deal with them appropriately. After the first focus group, I asked the head of the counseling services, a Filipina psychologist, whether she would be willing to speak to MK about family issues or run a support group (which did not get off the ground). In subsequent focus groups I spoke directly to these problems, telling the students that they should feel free to call me and that they might want to consider talking with the psychologist. After one group I sent e-mails to particular participants, thanking them and inviting them to contact me should they wish to talk further.

23. It is important to note that in his study of children of immigrants, Rumbaut found that depression scores were directly related to the level of parent-child conflict, as reported or experienced by the child. Filipino respondents scored slightly higher than average in terms of the degree of parent-child conflict they experienced, but their score was certainly not as high as that of the Indochinese groups. In a further analysis of the Filipino sample, the direct relationship between parent-child conflict and depression scores holds, and the females' depression scores are consistently higher than those of the males. Of the four hundred Filipinas interviewed, one of the highest depression scores is among the one-quarter of them who reported a high level of parent-child conflict (Rumbaut 1996).

24. I am grateful to Yen Le Espiritu for pointing this out to me.

25. The Filipino youth in Rumbaut's (1997) comparative study of fourteen different groups of children of immigrants had the highest proportion of grandparents living in their homes—about one-quarter.

REFERENCES

Basch, Linda, Nina Glick-Schiller, and Cristina Szanton-Blanc. 1994. *Nations Unbound: Transnational Projects, Postcolonial Predicaments, and Deterritorialized Nation-states*. Langhorne, Penn.: Gordon and Breach.

Bulatao, Jaime. 1964. "Hiya." *Philippine Studies* 12: 424–38.

Cabezas Amado, Larry, Hajime Shinagawa, and Gary Kawaguchi. 1986. "New Inquiries into the Socioeconomic Status of Filipino Americans in California." *Amerasia* 13: 1–21.

Campomanes, Oscar V. 1995a. "Filipinos in the United States and Their Literature of Exile." In *Discrepant Histories: Translocal Essays on Filipino Cultures,* edited by Vincent Rafael. Philadelphia: Temple University Press.

———. 1995b. "The New Empire's Forgetful and Forgotten Citizens: Unrepresentability and Unassimilability in Filipino-American Postcolonialities." *Critical Mass* 2(2): 145–200.

Ciria-Cruz, Rene P. 1994. "How Far Have We Come?" *Filipinas* 3(October): 40–44.

Espiritu, Yen Le. 1994. "The Intersection of Race, Ethnicity, and Class: The Multiple Identities of Second-Generation Filipinos." *Identities* 1: 249–73.

———. 2001. " 'We Don't Sleep Around Like White Girls Do': Family, Culture, and Gender in Filipina American Lives." *Signs* 29(21): 415–40.

Guarnizo, Luis Eduardo. 1998. "Transnationalism from Below: Social Transformation and the Mirage of Return Migration Among Dominican Transmigrants." Unpublished paper, University of California at Davis.

Guthrie, George M. 1971. "The Philippine Temperament." In *Six Perspectives on the Philippines,* edited by George M. Guthrie. Manila: Bookmark.

Hirtz, Frank. 1995. *Managing Insecurity: State Social Policy and Family Networks in the Rural Philippines*. Saarbrucken: Verlag fur Entwicklungspolitik Breitenbach.

Hondagneu-Sotelo, Pierrette. 1994. *Gendered Transitions: Mexican Experiences of Immigration*. Berkeley: University of California Press.

Ileto, Reynaldo C. 1979. *Pasyon and Revolution: Popular Movements in the Philippines, 1840–1910*. Quezon City: Ateneo de Manila University Press.

Kann, Laura, et al. 1995. "Youth Risk Behavior Surveillance—United States, 1993." *Morbidity and Mortality Weekly Report* 44: 1–56.

Kao, Grace. 1995. "Asian Americans as Model Minorities?: A Look at The Academic Performance of Immigrant Youth." *Social Science Quarterly* 76: 45–64.

Kao, Grace, and Marta Tienda. 1995. "Optimism and Achievement: The Educational Performance of Immigrant Youth." *Social Science Quarterly* 76: 1–19.

Kaplan, Amy. 1990. "Romancing the Empire." *American Literary History* 3: 659–90.

Kibria, Nazli. 1993. *Family Tightrope: The Changing Lives of Vietnamese Americans*. Princeton, N.J.: Princeton University Press.

Kuo, Wen. 1984. "Prevalence of Depression Among Asian-Americans." *Journal of Nervous and Mental Disease* 172: 449–57.

Lau, Angela. 1995a. "Filipino Girls Think Suicide at Number One Rate." *San Diego Union-Tribune,* February 11.

———. 1995b. "For Filipino Girls Who Have Considered Suicide." *Filipinas* 4: 38–40.

Lynch, Frank, and Alfonso de Guzman II, eds. 1981. *Four Readings on Philippine Values*. Quezon City: Institute of Philippine Culture.

McCoy, Alfred W. 1993. " 'An Anarchy of Families': The Historiography of State and Family in the Philippines." In *An Anarchy of Families: State and Family in the Philippines,* edited by Alfred W. McCoy. Madison: University of Wisconsin Press.

Merton, Robert K., Marjorie Fiske, and Patricia Kendall. 1990. *The Focused Interview*. New York: Free Press.

Morris, Lydia. 1990. *The Workings of the Household*. Cambridge: Polity Press.

Okamura, Jonathan Y., and Amefil R. Agbayani. 1997. "Pamantasan: Filipino American Higher Education." In *Filipino Americans: Transformation and Identity,* edited by Maria Root. Thousand Oaks, Calif.: Sage Publications.

Oliver, J. Eric, Fredrick Gey, Jon Stiles, and Henry Brady. 1995. *Pacific Rim States: Asian Demographic Data Book*. Oakland: Office of the President, University of California.

Ong, Aihwa. 1996. "Citizenship as Subject-Making: Immigrants Negotiate Racial and Cultural Boundaries in the United States." *Cultural Anthropology* 37(5): 717–62.

Portes, Alejandro. 1995. "Segmented Assimilation Among New Immigrant Youth: A Conceptual Framework." In *California's Immigrant Children,* edited by Rubén G. Rumbaut and Wayne A. Cornelius. La Jolla: Center for U.S.-Mexican Studies, University of California at San Diego.

———. 1996. "Introduction: Immigration and Its Aftermath." In *The New Second Generation,* edited by Alejandro Portes. New York: Russell Sage Foundation.

Portes, Alejandro, and Rubén G. Rumbaut. 1990. *Immigrant America: A Portrait*. Berkeley: University of California Press.

Rimonte, Nilda. 1997. "Colonialism's Legacy: The Inferiorizing of the Filipino." In *Filipino Americans: Transformation and Identity.* edited by Maria Root. Thousand Oaks, Calif.: Sage Publications.

Rumbaut, Rubén G. 1995. "The New Californians: Comparative Research Findings on the Educational Progress of Immigrant Children." In *California's Immigrant Children,* edited by Rubén G. Rumbaut and Wayne A. Cornelius. La Jolla: Center for U.S.-Mexican Studies, University of California at San Diego.

———. 1996. "The Crucible Within: Ethnic Identity, Self-esteem, and Segmented Assimilation Among Children of Immigrants." In *The New Second Generation,* edited by Alejandro Portes. New York: Russell Sage Foundation.

———. 1997. "Ties That Bind: Immigration and Immigrant Families in the United States." In *Immigration and the Family: Research and Policy on U.S. Immigrants,* edited by Alan Booth, Ann C. Crouter, and Nancy Landale. Mahwah, N.J.: Erlbaum.

Rumbaut, Rubén G., and Wayne A. Cornelius, eds. 1995. *California's Immigrant Children: Theory, Research, and Implications for Educational Policy.* La Jolla: Center for U.S.-Mexican Studies, University of California at San Diego.

Santos, Rolando A. 1983. "The Social and Emotional Development of Filipino-American Children." In *The Psycho-social Development of Minority Group Children,* edited by Gloria Johnson Powell, Joe Yamamoto, Annelisa Romero, and Armando Morales. New York: Brunner/Mazel Publishers.

Strobel, Leny Mendoza. 1997. "Coming Full Circle: Narratives of Decolonization Among Post-1965 Filipino Americans." In *Filipino Americans: Transformation and Identity,* edited by Maria Root. Thousand Oaks, Calif.: Sage Publications.

Sue, Stanley, and James Morishima. 1988. *The Mental Health of Asian Americans.* San Francisco: Jossey-Bass.

Szanton-Blanc, Cristina. 1996. "Balikbayan: A Filipino Extension of the National Imaginary and of State Boundaries." *Philippine Sociological Review* (special issue on "Filipinos as Transnational Migrants") 44(1–4): 178–93.

Takaki, Ronald. 1989. *Strangers from a Different Shore: A History of Asian Americans.* Boston: Little, Brown.

Tompar-Tiu, Aurora, and Juliana Sustento-Seneriches. 1995. *Depression and Other Mental Health Issues: The Filipino American Experience.* San Francisco: Jossey-Bass.

University of California. 1995. "Final Report for New Students." Oakland: Office of the President, University of California.

Vallejo Senior High School. 1995. *General Summaries of Educational Data.* Main Office, Vallejo Senior High School, Vallejo, Calif.

Vega, William, and Rubén G. Rumbaut. 1991. "Ethnic Minorities and Mental Health." *Annual Review of Sociology* 17: 351–83.

Wolf, Diane Lauren. 1992. *Factory Daughters: Gender, Household Dynamics, and Rural Industrialization in Java.* Berkeley: University of California Press.

Wolf, Diane, and Lisa Hoffman. 1996. "Filipino Invisibility in the American Landscape." Paper presented at the meeting of the Pacific Sociological Association, Seattle (March 28).

Wong, Morrison G., and Charles Hirschman. 1983. "Labor Force Participation and Socioeconomic Attainment of Asian American Women." *Sociological Perspectives* 26: 423–46.

Woo, Deborah. 1985. "The Socioeconomic Status of Asian American Women in the Labor Force: An Alternative View." *Sociological Perspectives* 28: 307–38.

Yengoyan, Aram, and Perla Makil, eds. 1984. *Philippine Society and the Individual.* Ann Arbor: Center for South and Southeast Asian Studies, University of Michigan.

Chapter 12

Of Blood, Belonging, and Homeland Trips: Transnationalism and Identity Among Second-Generation Chinese and Korean Americans

Nazli Kibria

I
N AMY TAN'S 1989 best-selling novel *The Joy Luck Club,* Jing-Mei Woo, an immigrant mother, tells her incredulous and Americanized second-generation daughter that "once you are born Chinese, you cannot help but feel and think Chinese. . . . Someday you will see, . . . it is in your blood, waiting to be let go." The mother's words ring true for the daughter on her first trip to China: "The minute our train leaves the Hong Kong border and enters Shenzhen, China, I feel different. I can feel the skin on my forehead tingling, my blood rushing through a new course, my bones aching with a familiar old pain. And I think, My mother was right. I am becoming Chinese" (306).

This chapter looks at recollections of and reflections on homeland trips—visits to the society of immigrant parental origin—among second-generation Chinese and Korean Americans and the dynamics of identity associated with them. An analysis of homeland trip experiences can offer important insights into the conditions that

295

surround the development of transnational engagements among second-generation immigrants.

My findings suggest the complex, often contradictory ways in which homeland trips shape the relationship of second-generation Chinese and Korean Americans to the homeland of their immigrant parents. For the most part, the second-generation Chinese and Korean Americans did not identify transnational engagements—ongoing involvement in activities and networks spanning U.S. and Chinese or Korean borders—as a part of their lives. Homeland trips had affirmed the value and appeal of such engagements but also the difficulties of creating them. Building on primordialist conceptions of what it means to be Chinese or Korean ("a matter of blood") that had been conveyed to them by their immigrant parents, homeland trips affirmed to these second-generation Chinese and Korean Americans the potency and significance of Chinese or Korean membership. Among other things, Chinese or Korean membership came to be understood as strategically valuable, a way to reap rewards from the globalizing world economy. At the same time homeland trips also worked to highlight to the second generation their marginality, or the ways in which they were not accepted and did not belong in Chinese or Korean societies.

ASSIMILATION, TRANSNATIONALISM, AND HOMELAND TRIPS

Transnationalism is among the ideas that have come to challenge assimilationist understandings of the immigrant experience in the United States. Transnationalism implies the embeddedness and regular and sustained engagement of persons in activities and networks that span societies of origin and settlement (Portes, Guarnizo, and Landolt 1999). Glick-Schiller, Basch, and Szanton-Blanc (1992, 1–2) have noted the potential importance of transnationalism for understanding the development of identities, which "transmigrants" form, they suggest, within social networks and structures that span national borders. In contrast to the image evoked by transnationalism—of a seamless web running across societies—the assimilation paradigm is marked by a conception of American society and the immigrant group's society of origin as distinctly bounded and culturally dichotomous entities ("modernity" versus "tradition"). From this perspective, immigrant groups are successfully incorporated into the United States when their identification and ties with the society of origin are progressively weakened. For immigrants and their descendants, then, the dynamics of identity are increasingly marked by the conditions and challenges of incorporation into the United States and an absence of ties to the society of origin.

Although transnationalism offers a fresh lens through which we can view the immigrant and ethnic experience, it remains in many ways a speculative one. We know especially little about transnationalism among the second-generation ethnics of today—the forms that it takes and the forces that surround its development. In analyzing the experience of homeland trips among second-generation Chinese and Korean Americans, I am not looking for evidence per se of transnationalism. Rather, my analysis focuses on the ways in which accounts of homeland trips provide insight into some of the conditions that surround and shape the development of transnational engagements. For second-generation Chinese and Korean Americans, the experience of homeland trips provided an important forum, a thematic focal point for reflection and discussion of their relationship to Chinese or Korean societies and, more generally, the meaning of membership and belonging in the Chinese or Korean collective.

The movement of immigrants back and forth between societies of origin and settlement is certainly not new, but it has assumed particular prominence in the contemporary era, reflecting advances in communication and travel technology. We should distinguish, however, between these movements, which differ in character in important ways. In this chapter, I use the term "homeland trips" to refer to voluntary visits to societies of ancestral origin that are limited and fairly short in duration and generally focus on such goals as tourism, leisure, seeing family and friends, and learning, discovering, or rediscovering the cultural aspects and other elements of the ancestral society. Although I recognize the complexity of the motivations and circumstances that surround such visits, I distinguish them from those that are more clearly associated with transnational activity, such as extended forays to the homeland of uncertain duration, as well as those taken for distinctly work-related purposes.

Many second-generation Chinese and Korean Americans take private homeland trips, often accompanied by immigrant family members. But homeland trips have also become institutionalized for them in the form of study tour programs that offer local travel and classes in Chinese or Korean language, culture, and history and are usually geared quite specifically toward the descendants of expatriates. The very fact of this institutionalization highlights the apparent absence of strong ties with the homeland for many second-generation Chinese and Korean Americans. Reflecting their interest in cultivating ties with their overseas populations, the Korean and Chinese governments have supported or sponsored many of these study tour programs. Although there are many different programs, two are particularly popular and well known among second-generation Chinese and Korean Americans. For Korean Americans, Yonsei University in Seoul is a favored destination. For Chinese Americans, there is the Overseas Chinese Youth Language and Study Abroad Tour to Taiwan, more popularly known as "The Love Boat" owing to its reputation as an opportunity for fun, parties, and romantic encounters.

STUDY METHODS

The materials presented here are drawn from sixty-four in-depth interviews with Chinese Americans and Korean Americans in the Los Angeles and Boston areas, conducted from 1992 to 1997. The study was limited to second-generation Chinese and Korean Americans between the ages of twenty-one and forty. I define "second-generation" to include those who are the children of immigrants and were born or raised in the United States since the age of twelve or earlier. Interviewees were asked to talk about the role and meaning of their racial and ethnic affiliations in such spheres as work, family, and neighborhood over the life course. The interviews, which lasted from one and a half to four hours, were tape-recorded and later transcribed. Informants were initially located through the membership lists and referrals of a variety of churches, professional and social clubs, and college and university alumni associations. The sample was expanded through "snowballing": informants were asked for referrals to others who fit the criteria for inclusion in the study.

In terms of family of origin, the social background of the sample was varied. Some, for example, had grown up in working-class or small-business families, while others were from professional, upper-middle-class homes. However, the majority of the sample were college-educated. Fifty-five of the sixty-four informants had a bachelor's degree from a four-year college or university, and some had earned a graduate or professional degree as well. Fifty-one of the sixty-four informants indicated that they had taken one or more trips to the ancestral homeland during their late adolescence or early adulthood years. The numbers were a little higher for Korean Americans (twenty-eight) in comparison to Chinese Americans (twenty-three), a reflection perhaps of the history of travel restrictions to mainland China as well as the greater national and institutional solidarity of Korean Americans (Min 1991). Of the fifty-one informants who had made a homeland trip, twenty-seven indicated that they had been on a study tour program to South Korea, Taiwan, or mainland China. In terms of duration, the programs ranged from a couple of weeks to a year, with the most common time frame being one to two months during the summer.

The second generation's[1] accounts of the homeland trips were marked by particular conceptions of what it means to be Chinese or Korean, formed around ideas to which they had been introduced by their parents and other immigrants. These conceptions provided a framework and set of expectations, albeit highly contested, for interpreting and gauging homeland trip experiences. I begin, then, with a discussion of these conceptions, followed by an exploration of homeland trip experiences.

"A MATTER OF BLOOD": THE MEANING OF CHINESE AND KOREAN MEMBERSHIP

During interviews, many of my informants spoke without conscious thought of belonging to the "Chinese race" or the "Korean race." Their use of these terms reflected particular notions of national identity that are prevalent among Chinese and Koreans. This is a conception of Chinese or Korean membership as primordial, based on the ties of blood or shared descent from a common ancestor

(Dikotter 1992; Kim 1991). In writing of Chinese beliefs about membership, Lyn Pan (1994, 267) asserts that it is "not so much language, or religion, or any other markers of ethnicity, but some primordial core or essence of Chineseness which one has by virtue of one's Chinese genes." Those writing of Korean nationalism emphasize the significance of a shared history of national oppression and struggle. An understanding of the Korean collectivity as inexorable and primordial is affirmed against the backdrop of this history and the continued force and potency of Korean nationalism within it. Koreans' frequent use of the word "chong" to describe the nature of Korean relations with each other also suggests that these ties have an essential quality. "Chong" refers to a complex mixture of relational qualities that work together and have a primordial cast to them: love, affinity, empathy, obligation, entanglement, bondage, and blood (Abelman and Lie 1995, 39).

For the second-generation Chinese and Korean Americans, these primordialist identity notions provided an important counterpoint to the uncertainties they felt about their membership and belonging as Chinese or Korean. That is, in ways that could be enhanced by limited knowledge of such important cultural markers as language, the second generation's claims to "Chinese-ness" or "Korean-ness" were suspect, both from their own perspective and that of others. Unlike their immigrant parents, they could not make claims to these identities based on birth or a personal history of residence in the homeland. Primordialist notions, however, offered an alternative means to affirm them.

The immigrant community was an important channel of exposure to primordialist notions of Chinese and Korean identity. Besides informal interactions with Chinese or Korean immigrants and nationals, the second generation was also exposed to these ideas in Chinese or Korean language schools and church programs. But most important in the recollections of my informants were interactions with family members, in particular their immigrant parents. The topic of intermarriage or marriage partner choice, for example, was one that immigrant parents often framed with reference to a notion of Chinese or Korean ties as rooted in blood and thus not to be violated. Sandra, a Korean American in her late twenties, described her father's objections to Korean outmarriage:

Koreans are very very proud and stubborn people, and my father is even more so than most Koreans. A lot of his friends, the old-timers, their children can't speak Korean, have married non-Koreans, and in general are not really Korean-identified. It really bothers him; he says, I don't even want to talk about it. Koreans are very nationalistic, they want to keep the Korean blood pure. He's told me that it was unacceptable for me to marry a non-Korean. When he came here, you know, he really felt the prejudice; it was the sixties, and there weren't too many Koreans around. He remembers that, and he tells me, "You think you're American and you think that you're widely accepted, but remember that people still see your physical features. If you spend time with them, they realize that you were raised here and you speak English fluently. But you don't have the time to sit with every person, to educate every person on the bus or the subway."

Faced with such admonitions to protect "blood purity," some informants explicitly rejected primordial conceptions of Korean or Chinese ties, describing them as "racist" and "xenophobic." More generally, however, the second generation held these immigrant notions, but in a state of uneasy and unresolved tension with more individualistic ones. That is, the notion of Chinese or Korean affiliation as given or immutable was present along with the idea that one's identity or group membership is voluntary, a matter of choice or whatever one wants to make of it. To some extent, the contradiction between primordialist and individualistic identity notions was muted for the second generation by their recognition of the significance of race in the United States. We see this in the excerpt from Sandra's interview: she implied that for her immigrant father the need to maintain Korean boundaries was not simply a matter of lineage purity but also a defense against racism. It was in the face of racism that group solidarity and the primordialist notions of identity intertwined with it assumed significance.

In fact, experiences of racial exclusion were closely intertwined for my informants with the message of primordialist Chinese or Korean membership. In their work on the children of contemporary immigrants, Fernandez-Kelly and Schauffler (1994) note that ethnic identities constitute important resources for those who are labeled in stigmatizing ways. For the second-generation Chinese and Korean Americans, the message of primordialist Chinese or Korean membership provided them with some important means of resisting and coping with racial experiences. For one thing, the idea that

Chinese or Korean ties are a matter of blood asserts the significance of a Chinese or Korean identity over an Asian one. Given that persons of Chinese and Korean descent are automatically labeled as "Asian" in the United States, my informants' experiences of racial exclusion and discrimination were vitally linked to their ascribed identity as Asian. Thus, affirming one's identity as Chinese or Korean could be a way to distance oneself from the racial environment of the United States. More generally, by providing one with a sense of deep-seated belonging in a collectivity other than the United States, the message of Chinese or Korean primordialist membership also provided a focus and means of asserting self-esteem and pride in the face of racial assaults.

Many of my informants recalled incidents of racial taunting and teasing during their childhood. In helping their children to cope with these situations, immigrant parents emphasized Korean or Chinese identity and pride. Sonia, a Korean American in her early twenties, recalled a vivid early memory in which a group of neighborhood children followed her as she went home from school. They poked fun at her by pulling their eyelids up and chanting slurs like "slanty" and "chink." Sonia recalled crying as she got home. After hearing about it, her mother and father counseled her in the following ways:

> They told me to not pay any attention, that the kids were just ignorant and mean. They also told me that I was Korean, I would always be Korean no matter what, and I should always remember that and be proud of it. Being proud of your Korean heritage was something that they always stressed to us.

Although a primordial conception of Chinese and Korean identity as I have described it was a common aspect of the second generation's childhood experiences, it was not, interestingly enough, accompanied by uniform or consistent parental attitudes and behaviors with regard to the transmission of Chinese or Korean culture to the next generation. As reflected, for example, in the differing degrees of knowledge of the Korean or Chinese language among them, my informants were a diverse lot in the extent of their learning and exposure to Korean or Chinese cultural practices during childhood. This diversity highlights the fact that the transmission of a strong sense of ethnic identity may not necessarily be accompanied by an emphasis on the transmission of explicit ethnic markers or behaviors.

My informants' accounts suggested that primordialist notions were flexible and could bolster a variety of orientations. On the one hand, these ideas could provide support for asserting the importance of practicing and knowing about one's ethnic heritage, since it was an identity that was a given and not something that one could discard. We see this in the recollections of Jane, a Chinese American in her midthirties, about her parents' reaction to her declaration when she was a child that she no longer wanted to go to language school:

> We were forced to go to Chinese school for a few years. It was after school, three or four days a week. I hated it because it was so strict and boring. My parents weren't too happy when I told them I wanted to quit. They said I would always be Chinese on some level, no matter how Americanized I was. They said it was really important to know something about the Chinese culture because it was a deep part of me.

At the same time, the message of one's inherent "Chinese-ness" or "Korean-ness" could also support the idea that cultivating one's Chinese or Korean heritage was not an urgent matter and could be postponed. Since complete escape was not possible, given the essential nature of these ties, a lack of active cultivation did not fundamentally threaten them. Renee, a Chinese American in her midthirties, described a childhood in which she had little explicit exposure to Chinese community and culture. She had recently embarked on a quest to get in touch with her Chinese roots. She saw this quest as one that drew on previously untapped forces of blood:

> I feel that even if you've grown up like me, without much connection to Chinese culture, there's still something deep inside you that's Chinese. It's in your blood. It's like a potential that you can choose to ignore. But when you're ready to get back in touch with it, it's there.

Embedded in the message of primordialist Chinese or Korean membership is a certain promise of true belonging or community in the Chinese or Korean collectivity. That is, unlike membership in the United States, which is circumstantial and artificial—an accident of migration—one's Chinese or Korean membership is organic and genuine. It was with these notions, along with the many doubts and uncertainties surrounding them, that the second-generation Chinese and Korean Americans approached homeland trips.

HOMELAND TRIPS:
OF BLOOD AND BELONGING

The second-generation Chinese and Korean Americans often described particular instances or moments during homeland trips, especially at the time of entry into the homeland, in deeply emotional
terms. Jeff, a Korean American, spoke of going to Korea on a study
program after his senior year in high school. He recalled a feeling
of deep connection to the homeland as he flew into Seoul:

> I remember actually flying into Seoul, and it was late at night, but I could see
> these little houses, farms in the country. That brought back some memories,
> of being with my grandfather. Something about it felt good. I remember
> thinking, This is where I was born, this is an important part of me.

But for Jeff as for others, such dramatic and emotional moments of
feeling connected to the homeland were invariably followed by
other, far less positive recollections. As I have described, embedded
in the primordialist conception of Chinese or Korean membership
is an implicit promise or expectation of belonging and acceptance.
Although this promise was certainly affirmed in some ways, the
overall effect of the homeland trips was to highlight the complexity
of membership and belonging in the Chinese or Korean collective.

For some informants, especially those who had grown up outside Chinese or Korean enclaves in the United States, a notable part
of the homeland trips was being surrounded, perhaps for the first
time in their lives, by others who "looked like them." They found
themselves, in other words, in a setting in which they did not stand
out from most others owing to their physical characteristics. They
experienced a certain comfort or ease in this situation. In ways that
affirmed the elemental conception of membership embedded in
primordialist notions, some said that, at least in a physical sense,
they had felt like they belonged. This was the case for Tammy, a
Korean American who had taken a family trip to Korea in her teens:

> Going back to Korea for the first time was a real eye-opener. It was frankly a
> shock to go to a place where everybody was Korean, and where everybody
> looked just like you. Here you kind of stand out no matter what you do. You
> can never exactly just blend in. (*How did you feel about that? Did you like it?*)
> Oh, yeah. It felt comfortable, because I didn't stand out. I felt like I belonged.

Some also observed that the trip had brought them closer to their immigrant parents. It had made them more appreciative and understanding of the cultural traditions and practices with which they had been raised, ones that they may have rebelled against in the past. The trip had worked to normalize these cultural traditions and practices, which, if they seemed aberrant or peculiar in the United States, in the Chinese or Korean context were normal and expected. This fostered not only a greater empathy for their immigrant relatives but also a certain sense of belonging in China or Korea. Cynthia, a Chinese American, described this sense of affinity as springing from the realization that her childhood upbringing had been similar in many ways to that of Chinese natives. She had something significant in common with them, perhaps more so than with "Americans." Cynthia had attended a study and travel program in southern China during her college years:

> I learned a lot on the trip. You know, I learned where my parents came from, how they grew up and how different it was from here, and why they act the way they do. When we were younger, we could never understand why they did certain things that were not like other Americans—like white people, I guess. Like why they were so undemonstrative in terms of kissing and hugging, showing affection. Going to China made me realize that the way I grew up was not so bizarre. In that way, I kind of belonged there; we had grown up with the same things.

Even as the homeland trips fostered a sense of affinity, however, they also challenged notions of blood and belonging in profound ways. As described earlier, Jeff, a Korean American, had felt an intensely emotional sense of intimacy with Korea when he flew into Seoul. But his recollections of the time he spent there on the ground were far less rosy:

> The natives looked down on us because a lot of us couldn't speak Korean. Although I could understand what they were saying, they were basically saying, "You're so stupid. You're Korean, but you can't speak Korean." There were some isolated incidents when we were . . . yelled at, harassed. I guess I felt a little weird with my relatives because I couldn't really communicate that well, and sometimes I felt they were talking about me behind my back: "Oh, he's American, that's why he's like that."

Recollections of homeland trips were in fact prominently marked by experiences of being seen and treated as "different" by the local population. As suggested by Jeff, language was an especially prominent issue in the experience of this difference. Even if the second-generation Chinese and Korean Americans were able to blend in with the local environment owing to their physical characteristics, it was also the case, as one interviewee put it, that they "stuck out like a sore thumb." Although there were many reasons for this, the inability to speak the language or to speak it in expected ways was clearly a central concern. Here it is important to mention that in the United States too it is not uncommon for Chinese and Korean Americans to experience condemnation from Chinese or Korean immigrants for not speaking Chinese or Korean. But during the homeland trips this censure was particularly virulent, especially in the experiences of Korean Americans. They encountered not only surprise and disapproval but, at times, overt anger. They explained that their limited Korean language knowledge marked them to some natives as traitors, or persons who had renounced loyalty to the ties of their blood. Kyung Sook, a Korean American, had spent part of a summer during her college years in a study program in Seoul. Rather than fostering a sense of affinity, the trip had given her a sense of bitterness about her Korean heritage:

> When I went to Korea, I was traumatized by the language thing. Ever since that trip, I never think of myself as Korean; I'm of Korean descent, but not Korean. Koreans are really shocked by people like me, Americanized Koreans who don't speak Korean. They look down on us. I'm not one of those people who's rah-rah Korean.

Besides language, the second generation found themselves distinguished by cultural mannerisms—dress, demeanor, and so forth. One person, for example, described an unpleasant incident on a bus in Seoul, when he and his companions were scolded for laughing and talking loudly in public. Women spoke of experiencing disapproval, either implicit or explicit, for not conforming to norms of appropriate behavior for women. That is, they were seen as too loud, aggressive, and not appropriately deferential to men.

Thus, in a variety of ways, the second generation found that the homeland trips made them more aware of their differences with the Chinese or Korean collectivity than their commonalities. The sense of belonging implied by the ties of blood seemed to be overwhelmed by differences of culture as well as of nationality. Many of the second-generation Chinese and Korean Americans described gaining a heightened sense of their identity as American on the trip. If in the United States their racial identity as Asian dominated others' perception of them, in China or Korea it was their identity as American that was significant. Depending on the specific context, as Americans they could be seen as wealthy, privileged, spoiled, naive, and aggressive, and implicated in U.S. imperialist agendas. A March 1995 article by Nina Chen in *AsianWeek* ("Love Boat: Scamfest or Cultural Exchange") describing the Overseas Chinese Youth Language Training and Study Abroad Tours to Taiwan suggests some of the ways in which these perceptions could be aggravated by the structure and approach of the study tour programs:

> The students are treated like "little diplomats." Motorcades lead the buses carrying the students wherever they go. Radios broadcast their whereabouts in advance, hoping traffic will be less congested—and traffic literally stops to allow the students to pass first. Unsurprisingly, the American students are viewed as extremely spoiled.

A sense of difference and distance from Chinese or Korean nationals could also be enhanced for the second generation by limited contact with the local Chinese or Korean populace during the trip. Many of those traveling on organized programs spoke of spending their time primarily if not exclusively with other program participants. For some, in fact, especially those who had grown up in relative isolation from local Chinese or Korean communities in the United States, one of the most memorable aspects of the homeland trips was the opportunity to interact, perhaps for the first time in their lives, with other second-generation Chinese and Korean Americans like themselves. For James, a Chinese American, these interactions were a significant opportunity for discussion and reflection on what it meant to be Chinese:

> I became friends with some of the other folks on the trip. Good friends, close friends; we still keep in touch. It was the first time I got to know other Chinese kids like me, who were basically American but had Chinese faces. We talked about what that was like—it was a very big part of the trip for me.

If there were ways in which the homeland trips highlighted for the second generation the uncertainty of belonging in Chinese or

Korean society, they also ironically suggested the potency and significance of Chinese or Korean membership. The very depth of the censure encountered for not displaying the appropriate cultural markers or behavior affirmed the symbolic potency of blood—its ability to evoke powerful expectations and responses. But Chinese or Korean membership also acquired significance in another, quite different respect. Many of my informants spoke of coming away from the trips with an appreciation of the strategic value of Chinese or Korean membership. Being of Chinese or Korean ancestry gave them a particular ability to take advantage of economic globalization processes. During the 1980s and much of the 1990s the Chinese and Korean economies were widely seen as dynamic and increasingly powerful players in the global arena. In ways that built on these perceptions, informants spoke of coming away from the trips with a sharpened sense of the economic dynamism of Chinese and Korean societies and, relatedly, of pride in their achievements. Jane, a Chinese American who had toured Hong Kong and mainland China with a study group, noted that the trip had lifted a certain sense of inferiority that she had associated with being Chinese while growing up. The trip had made her regret her own lack of Chinese language and other cultural knowledge, but it also strengthened her resolve to look for ways to forge connections to China in the future:

> It changed my feelings or my understandings of China. I got a sense of the economic potential of the country, and how people thrived and worked under all kinds of conditions. I guess I realized I was proud to be Chinese. It's such a rich culture. Now I've started to think about business connections, if there's some way to get into that. I'm at a disadvantage since I don't speak much Chinese. When I have children, I definitely want them to learn Chinese, to be able to take advantage of all this.

For Jane as for many others, the homeland trip had resulted in a greater appreciation of the strategic value of membership in the Chinese or Korean collective. Although less explicit, running through these accounts was also a sense of the potency of this membership when coupled with an American one. The popular language of globalism, infused with an aura of glamour, provided a way of talking about these perceived advantages. Thus, the second generation referred to the world as "getting smaller" and to the value of having access to resources and relationships in several societies.

For some informants, their understanding of Chinese or Korean membership as strategically valuable had affected their career choices. That is, they spoke of deriving advantages of some form in the workplace from their Chinese or Korean heritage. For a few informants, this membership had become deeply intertwined with their employment history, as, for example, when they took positions with multinational companies that called for a connection with Chinese or Korean societies. But for the most part, the second-generation Chinese and Korean Americans expressed much uncertainty about the actual ways in which the advantages could be realized and about the effects on their lives. These advantages, then, were seen as potential, as possibly realizable in the future. Thus, like Jane, our other second-generation informants often spoke of the importance of making sure that their children—the third generation—remained somehow connected to China or Korea. They often contrasted the deficiency of their own knowledge with what they hoped would be the case for their own children. But this deficiency, coupled with the value they put on individual preference and choice, often made them vague and unsure about the actual ways in which they might ensure this proficiency in their children. For example, Curt, a Korean American married to a white woman and the father of two, was adamant about the value of exposing his children to Korea as they grow up. At the same time, like many others, he expressed a strong preference for letting children make their own choices and an aversion to forcing children to be interested in their heritage:

> When they're a little older, I want to take my kids to Korea and spend a year or two there. It's good for them. You have to take advantage of whatever you have. And if you're part Korean, then I say, Go for it, use it! I really believe that in the next century the people who are going to be the most successful are the ones who can move freely in different environments. . . . Be American, be Korean, speak as many languages as possible. (*How are you going to teach them Korean?*) I don't know, it really depends on them. I don't think it's fair to force kids. They have to choose to be interested in their Korean heritage.

To summarize, in their recollections the second generation said that the homeland trips had given them an understanding of the complexities and contradictions of Chinese or Korean membership.

The expectations of belonging based on blood were affirmed in some ways, but also profoundly challenged. The trips highlighted for the second generation the strategic value of Chinese or Korean membership. For the most part, however, this strategic value remained unrealized in practice and was cast as a possibility for the future.

CONCLUSIONS

Transnational engagements were not visible or common aspects of the lives of the second-generation Chinese and Korean Americans interviewed in this study. However, many were attracted to the possibilities of such engagements and expressed a desire to explore and cultivate them.

Sometimes the second-generation Chinese and Korean Americans saw transnational involvements as a way of coping with the dilemmas of racial marginality in the United States, that is, with the ways in which their minority racial status complicated and bounded processes of incorporation for them. The attractions of transnationalism also related to the perceived strategic and instrumental advantages of Chinese or Korean membership, especially when coupled with American membership. They perceived these memberships as giving them a special ability to tap into the dynamism of the East Asian economies. The Asian economic recession of the late 1990s brings our attention to the fluid and situational character of these perceptions and also raises the possibility, yet to be investigated, that these attitudes have shifted. More generally, however, beyond the fluctuations indicated by shifting economic currents, my informants' accounts suggest the importance of popular understandings of globalism, infused with an aura of glamour and vigor, in encouraging people to view transnationalism in positive ways.

My findings highlight the complexity of primordialist notions of homeland membership as an ideological context for the development of transnationalism among second-generation persons. The idea of membership as rooted in blood offers a means for the descendants of migrants to see themselves, and for others to see them, as having ties to the homeland of enduring significance. At the same time, as shown in especially vivid ways in the experiences of my Korean American informants, such notions can also be corrosive to ties when they are coupled with strongly nationalistic and culturally homogenous homeland settings. When homeland environments offer ways of being part of the homeland that are not wedded to particular national boundaries and cultural behaviors, they are likely to be more conducive to transnationalism among the second generation.

NOTE

1. For ease of presentation, I refer to my informants as "the second generation" throughout the chapter.

REFERENCES

Abelman, Nancy, and John Lie. 1995. *Blue Dreams: Korean Americans and the Los Angeles Riots*. Cambridge, Mass.: Harvard University Press.

Chen, Nina. 1995. "Love Boat: Scamfest or Cultural Exchange?" *AsianWeek* (March).

Dikotter, Frank. 1992. *The Discourse of Race in Modern China*. Palo Alto, Calif.: Stanford University Press.

Fernandez-Kelly, Patricia, and Richard Schauffler. 1994. "Divided Fates: Immigrant Children in a Restructured U.S. Economy." *International Migration Review* 28(4): 662–89.

Glick-Schiller, Nina, Linda Basch, and Cristina Szanton-Blanc. 1992. "Towards a Definition of Transnationalism." *Annals of the New York Academy of Sciences* 46: 1–24.

Kim, Jae-On. 1991. *The Koreans: Their Mind and Behavior,* translated by Kim Kyong-Dong. Seoul: Kyobo Book Central, Korea Research Foundation.

Min, Pyong Gap. 1991. "Cultural and Economic Boundaries of Korean Ethnicity: A Comparative Analysis." *Ethnic and Racial Studies* 14(3): 225–41.

Pan, Lyn. 1994. *Sons of the Yellow Emperor: A History of the Chinese Diaspora*. New York: Kodansha International.

Portes, Alejandro, Luis Guarnizo, and Patricia Landolt. 1999. "Introduction: Pitfalls and Promise of an Emergent Field." *Ethnic and Racial Studies* 22(2): 217–37.

Tan, Amy. 1989. *The Joy Luck Club*. New York: Putnam.

— Chapter 13 —

Creating Histories for the Present: Second-Generation (Re)definitions of Chinese American Culture

Andrea Louie

I think that for me I'm looking at it more as a Chinese American now, not necessarily as an ABC [American-born Chinese], or as a Chinese, but as a Chinese American. I'm very comfortable sort of knowing my personal family history, knowing [about] exclusion laws, knowing factual things, teaching, and researching on that. . . . And that's my community, that's the stuff that I do, and definitely [the roots program] is important, Asian American studies, my friends, family. All those things are definitely Chinese American. And I'm still trying to figure out exactly what does that mean. I don't want to make it that, well, we pull some Chinese stuff, we pull some American stuff. It's a lot more complex, and I don't even know how to approach it, it's a much bigger thing, and I think that's why . . . even though it's hard to describe what it is, I'm growing comfortable in saying I know what Chinese American culture is, but don't ask me to define it.

—"In Search of Roots" participant in roundtable discussion, 1996

T HIS CHAPTER BRINGS together multiple themes to provide a new perspective on how second- (and later-)generation children of immigrants create transnational relationships with their country

312

of ancestral origin. For my analysis, I draw from my research on American-born Chinese Americans who participate in family history and genealogical projects that culminate in their return to their ancestral villages. Within the context of studies of transnationalism and the second generation, the key question is, Why and how is China important for American-born Chinese Americans? How do they learn about China and Chinese culture and make this information relevant to their identities as American-born Chinese? I argue that relations between Chinese Americans and China are shaped by: mainland Chinese politics toward Chinese populations abroad; U.S. racial and cultural politics; transnational mass media flows originating from but circulating far more broadly than their ancestral homelands; and historical and cultural continuities emanating from the experiences in the United States of Chinese American families and communities.

By focusing on a cultural heritage program, "In Search of Roots," I examine the politics of culture and identity that define relations between American-born Chinese Americans and China within the context of transnational and global flows. Specifically, I examine how Chinese Americans use the experience of visiting China to create narratives of family history and personal identity exploration, and then use these narratives to contextualize their lives within the broader picture of Chinese–Asian American experiences (at the same time that they help form this very picture through their narratives).[1] I argue that through this process Chinese Americans create their own knowledge about and redefine their attitudes toward China and Chinese culture. Furthermore, while some transnational generations build ties abroad as a means of establishing themselves despite forms of racial, economic, and political exclusion in the United States (Basch, Glick-Schiller, and Szanton-Blanc 1994), these Chinese Americans make connections to China primarily to build ties to the United States. In other words, they create relationships to China and Chinese culture to legitimize their identities in the United States rather than to attain political or economic goals in China.

By creating family history narratives out of their visits to China, Chinese Americans legitimize their identities within a U.S. racial and cultural politics that forces them to be associated with essentialized views of China and Chinese culture. These histories provide a basis from which to construct identities that go beyond the narrow focus of U.S. racial and multicultural politics on quantifiable cultural elements (which produce narrow conceptions of Chinese-ness). By producing their own knowledge about Chinese culture, Chinese Americans can bridge the divide between "China" and "Chinese American" that is inherent in U.S. multicultural politics and legitimize U.S.-based identities that are not dependent on direct connections to China. Examining the relationships that American-born Chinese Americans craft with China allows for the academic exploration of these less concrete and more symbolic aspects of transnationalism. These processes of identity construction distinguish American-born Chinese Americans from other immigrant generations for whom relations with the homeland are often based in more concrete economic or political concerns. The less tangible elements that constitute the cultural politics of Chinese-ness in the United States and China are inextricable from other transnational political and economic flows. But as I argue later in the chapter, they affect particular populations, including later generations, to a greater extent.

CHINESE FIELD SITES

Multi-sited research on Chinese identities serves as the ethnographic focus of this chapter. From 1992 to 1995 I conducted research on Chinese American attitudes toward Chinese culture and toward China as a place of origin, using as my focal group a cultural heritage program based in San Francisco's Chinatown called "In Search of Roots." Participants in this program are drawn from around the San Francisco Bay Area and must be between seventeen and twenty-five years of age and of Cantonese descent. The majority are high school or college students. The geographical focus, composition, and organization of the program are derived from a number of historical factors.

First, the majority of emigrants to the United States from the mid-1800s until the 1960s originated from the Pearl River Delta area of Guangdong province in the People's Republic of China (PRC). This region, marked roughly by a triangle between the former British colony Hong Kong, Guangzhou (Canton), and Macao, is dotted with qiao xiang, or hometowns of Chinese who have gone abroad. Most U.S. Chinatowns have historically been dominated by groups from these areas of the Pearl River Delta: Sze yup (si yi), Sam yup (san yi), and Junggsan (zhongshan).

The second factor is demographic change in the Chinese American community as it has made the transition from being a community shaped by the limitations of legal exclusion[2] to one composed of families with second-generation children as well as third-generation children and beyond. At the same time, new immigration after 1965 has greatly diversified the Chinese population in the United States in terms of class background and region of origin (Hing 1993; Liu and Cheng 1994), bringing in immigrants from different parts of the mainland, Taiwan, Hong Kong, and other parts of the diaspora. As the second and third generations of Chinese Americans in San Francisco, of primarily Cantonese origin, gained middle-class economic stability, they moved out of Chinatown and into other parts of the city or the suburbs. The "In Search of Roots" program was formed as part of an effort by Chinatown cultural organizations to reconnect to the suburban Chinese community.

Finally, this program arose in response to programmatic initiatives on the part of the PRC government to sponsor Chinese youth from "abroad" on cultural heritage tours of the mainland. China's coastal cities and regions, such as the Pearl River Delta, have historically been frontiers for contact between China and the outside world (Wakeman 1998 [1966]).[3] Following the initiation of the PRC's open policy in 1978, the Office of Overseas Chinese Affairs resumed its focus on Chinese in foreign nations. This office viewed the Chinese heritage of Chinese abroad as a basis for their continued connection to China and glorified overseas Chinese investors as "patriotic" sons of the yellow emperor who had returned to build the Chinese "motherland" (jian shi zu guo) (see also Ong 1999; Woon 1989, 1990). These ethnic Chinese investors fit nicely into China's plans to develop "socialism with Chinese characteristics." At the same time policymakers recognized that the political, cultural, and economic distance between Chinese in other parts of the world and China had grown large during the Communist era, when China was essentially cut off from the outside world. The formation of Summer Youth Festival programs sponsored by the Guangdong Provincial Office of Overseas Chinese Affairs, China Travel Service, and local municipal officials marked the PRC's acknowledgment of these differences.[4]

The Summer Camp programs[5] invoke a "politics of native roots" (Siu 1992). According to this long-standing idea, a Chinese person, no matter how many generations removed from China, retains a connection and a loyalty to China. Loyalty and patriotism, which are assumed to exist even for generations born abroad, translate into investments and donations by Chinese abroad to the home regions. These connections are best represented by the Chinese person's sentiments toward his native place and the people there. A municipal-level overseas Chinese official whom I interviewed remarked, "A little stream flows long." He recognized that Chinese youth from the United States and other parts of the world may lack sufficient funds to make generous contributions to their "motherland." However, he also believed that something may come in the future from instilling a nostalgia for China in them. It is somewhat ironic, then, that attitudes toward Chinese culture and tradition are rapidly changing for Guangdong Chinese, both officials and non-officials. At the same time, their assumptions about how Chinese abroad feel toward China increasingly differ from the ways in which the political and cultural identities of American-born Chinese Americans have been constructed (see Louie 2000).

THE "IN SEARCH OF ROOTS" PROGRAM

The "In Search of Roots" program focuses on the researching and writing of family histories and narratives of identity exploration that trace family roots back to emigrant villages in China. This is done with the aid of detailed history lessons provided by a noted Chinese American historian as part of the program's bimonthly meetings. The history taught begins in the emigrant regions of the Pearl River Delta, from which the ancestors of "Roots" participants originated. It continues by tracing the history of Chinese immigration to the United States and the experiences of Chinese in this country up until the present. The course chosen for this historical narrative is significant, because it emphasizes a continuity between China and Chinese Americans that until recently has been neglected in discussions of Chinese and Chinese American history.[6] Though the program focuses on family history and genealogy, it also relates to the present experience in its emphasis on identity exploration. In doing so, it allows participants to understand the history of past transnational connections to China within a contemporary, transnational Chinese American context.

Instructors teach participants techniques of oral history interviewing and bring them to the National Archives in San Bruno, California, to search for the immigration files of their relatives who passed through Angel Island Immigration Station during the exclusion era.[7] Understanding the history of exclusion is essential to providing the larger sociopolitical context that shaped a family's story of emigration. For example, awareness of this context helps explain why immigrant ancestors assumed paper names—the citizenship papers or birth certificates that Chinese immigrants purchased from others during the exclusion era (1882 to 1943).[8] This illegal act was necessary to skirt unfair immigration laws designed to restrict the entry of Chinese laborers. Knowledge of this historical background allows participants to understand what seem to be idiosyncrasies and details specific to their family's story as part of broader historical, political, and social patterns. Through this process, participants can recontextualize "illegal" acts, such as entering the country under a false name, as reasonable and creative responses to an unjust system. Such actions can be redefined as collective acts of resistance that connect one's own family history to a shared Chinese or Asian American history (see Wong and Chan 1998). "Roots" participants are taught that, although much of the information found in the Immigration and Naturalization Service (INS) files may be fictional information from the coaching books—the handwritten "crib sheets" that would-be immigrants studied and then threw overboard before going through interrogation by U.S. immigration officials[9]—these stories and processes were integral to shaping their family's history. These preparations form a central and necessary background for the group's experience when they collectively visit their ancestral villages in China under the guidance of a Chinese American leader. Indeed, without an organizational structure through which to experience the village, Chinese Americans would be ill prepared for a visit to China. Most would not be able to find their ancestral village on their own, as few speak the language fluently or know how to get around in contemporary China.

A PREMATURE CELEBRATION?

Where, then, do these Chinese Americans, generations removed from China, fit into transnational flows? To what extent has increased access to China opened up new possibilities for their formation of identities within the context of a racist U.S. society that constructs Chinese-ness in restrictive ways? To what extent do Chinese Americans control this information and to what extent are they controlled by it? Diasporic or historically transnational (Hsu 2000; Glick-Schiller 1999a, 1999b) relationships between immigrant populations and their homelands are being redefined under globalization. Processes of globalization are reshaping the borders of historical diasporas, multiplying the channels through which identities can be negotiated. As Clifford (1997, 247) has observed, parts of diasporas that have spread out over time are being relinked through processes associated with transnationalism as "dispersed people, once separated from homelands by vast oceans and political barriers, increasingly find themselves in border relations with the old country, thanks to a to and fro made possible by modern technologies of transport, communications, and labor migration." The abundant and highly flexible symbolic resources made available under globalization have been viewed by some scholars as opening up endless possibilities for the formation of new hybrid, mobile identities. Featherstone (1996, 55) notes that "there has been an extension of the cultural repertoires and an enhancement of the resourcefulness of various groups to create new symbolic modes of affiliation and belonging, to rework and reshape the meanings of existing signs, and to undermine existing symbolic hierarchies."

Others, however, acknowledge the significance of these links but observe that this discussion of the concepts of globalization, transnationalism, and diaspora takes on a tone that is far too celebratory. These critics note that this "abstract celebration of travel, hybridity, and multiculturalism" (Mitchell 1996, 220) avoids looking at the ways in which identities and identity politics are appropriated or used as mechanisms of control in local contexts. Mitchell, in her study of Hong Kong transnationals in Vancouver, British Columbia, shows how the liberal, "emancipatory" rhetoric of multiculturalism and racial harmony in Canada is appropriated by the

Canadian government to smooth the way for wealthy Hong Kong investors. The Hong Kong transnationals to whom Mitchell refers use their flexibility in language and citizenship—as well as speed of movement through space and across time zones—to their advantage in doing business and in negotiating identities. For them, multicultural rhetoric is not so much a strategy for getting along with their new neighbors as a base for establishing solid business relations in Vancouver.

Anthropologist Aihwa Ong's work on flexible citizenship (1993, 1999) among Hong Kong managers and professionals has been highly influential in describing how the mobility of capital, resources, and bodies yields new form of identities. She is careful, however, to define the particular conditions and populations to which the term applies. Flexible citizenship is a strategy used by investors and professionals "who seek to both circumvent and benefit from different nation state regimes by selecting different sites for investments, work, and family relocation" (Ong 1993, 136). These individuals have the social, cultural, and economic capital and the strategic foresight that is a necessary part of running a family firm or doing business and that places them in a position to be strategically mobile. Ong also emphasizes, however, the importance of understanding the constraints under which even these "astronauts" work—those of capitalist markets and nation-states (136).[10] She also makes an important distinction between the peasant Chinese laborers who swelled the first waves of Chinese immigration to the United States and the savvy, cosmopolitan Chinese businessmen who arrive in the West today (149). In addition, she is careful to point out that not all of today's immigrants—who include refugees, victims of political persecution, and migrant workers—possess the flexibility of those she studied (156).

A case in point is the Chinese American population with whom I worked. They are for the most part U.S.-born (second, third, fourth, or fifth generation), comfortably middle-class, and college-educated. However, they find themselves at the margins of global flows. For the most part they lack the social, cultural, or economic capital to participate skillfully in cross-border flows. At the same time they are more strongly influenced by the essentialist discourses of Chinese-ness that pervade both folk and academic writings about Chinese populations outside of China. As Ong and Nonini

(1997) have discussed, the majority of the scholarship on overseas Chinese, much of it written by diaspora Chinese, is pervaded by binary oppositions between East and West and a belief in a timeless and static set of characteristics that define Chinese-ness.

THE QUESTION OF THE SECOND GENERATION

In focusing on the second generation,[11] I take an opportunity to move away from these essentialized portrayals of diasporic and transnational subjects to examine a type of transnational relationship that over time will become even more central to transmigrant experiences. My goal is not to predict how transnational these generations will be based on the patterns of previous generations. I avoid using evidence of actions, behaviors, or sentiments among the second generations that do not fit existing models as a basis for altogether dismissing these generations as transnational. Asking whether their activities are really transnational creates a difficult analytical problem. If these generations do not fit any of the accepted definitions of transnationalism, is this because they are not transnational or because we need to modify our definitions of transnationalism? It is important to consider the second generation as part of the transnational literature in order to establish the boundaries of the term (Portes, Guarnizo, and Landolt 1999). Rather than predicting or assuming continuity, this is an opportunity to explore the various forms that relations with the homeland take over time.

As it has developed, the field of transnationalism has come to be defined more broadly as something more than the movement of bodies and the establishment of social networks. It has grown to encompass popular culture, capital, and information flows that affect even those who do not move (Appadurai 1991). Examination of transnationalism in these broader terms allows for the exploration of the complex transnational dynamics between the country of origin and the country of residence that often affect first-generation transmigrants and their descendants in different ways. We can push the field to examine the questions that these generations raise: How do transnational flows of culture, capital, and information affect migrants and descendants of migrants differently? How might the local politics of the nation-state come to influence these later generations?

Increasingly, scholars have begun to examine not only migration flows—the movement of bodies and creation of social ties across national borders—but also flows of ideas, information, and popular culture. Studies of transnationalism have begun to examine different types of transnational practices and flows that are distinguished by various types of mobility. Scholars of transnational communities have identified historical precedents to current forms of transnationalism (Glick-Schiller 1999a, 1999b; Hsu 2000; Chen 2000). (Some fifth-generation Chinese Americans, for instance, are descended from families that moved back and forth across the Pacific for two or three generations before settling in the United States.) Contemporary forms of transnationalism under late capitalism are qualitatively different from these precedents. However, these earlier forms of cross-border movement in combination with contemporary flows centrally define the relationship of certain generations to their places of origin. As contributors to Smith and Guarnizo's (1998) volume observe, it is important to acknowledge that transnational practices may vary among people of different classes or generations ("astronauts" versus fourth-generation Chinese Americans, for example), who may have different degrees of mobility. They question whether actual migration is necessary for participation in transnational processes, or whether other types of transborder practices may exist (Mahler 1998; Smart and Smart 1998). In particular, Sarah Mahler (1998, 77) discusses the importance of examining cultural flows of "things, not bodies." Indeed, Grewal, Gupta, and Ong (1999) observe the impact that the mass media have had in reconnecting diasporic populations to their places of origin.

At the same time transnational flows and processes do not take place in a vacuum. Numerous scholars have discussed the continued impact of nation-states in regulating the mobility and access to capital and other resources of both citizens and noncitizens (Schein 1998; Smith and Guarnizo 1998). Far from liberating people from attachments to nation-states and territories, people are reterritorialized in complex ways in relation to past histories, contemporary politics, and popular culture flows (Louie 2000). Glick-Schiller (1999a, 1999b) has discussed the simultaneous processes of racialization and transnationalization that affect immigrants to the United States. In other words, transnational connections that link immigrants back to their places of origin do not provide a total escape from the racializing practices of the nation-states in which they reside.

The mediating influence of nation-states is key to understanding Louisa Schein's (1998) concept of forged transnationality, a term that she coined to describe the creation of relationships based on a shared heritage (often imagined) across national borders by Hmong American refugees and ethnic Miao minorities in China. These relations are defined by multiple layers of representation of the other as well as language and culture barriers. In combination with those discussed earlier, Schein's concept is particularly useful in understanding the connections between the American-born Chinese Americans whom I studied and their ancestral homeland. Relations between the second (and later) generations and their places of ancestral origin involve a mixture of the transnational processes discussed earlier: forged transnationality (of which the "Roots" program is a form), forms of reterritorialization that draw on imagined connections to place and history, and the increasing influence of the mass media.

CHINESE AMERICANS AND CHINA: REDEFINING THE RELATIONSHIP

While American-born Chinese Americans may identify with China to differing degrees as an exotic tourist site, a geopolitical entity, a historical region, or a place of origin, most have had little firsthand contact with China or mainland Chinese people. Most American-born Chinese have not been to China and do not speak Chinese fluently, if at all. Prior to their involvement in the "Roots" program, many of the people I interviewed had little knowledge about China or their family history. During the exclusion era, many Chinese families avoided talking about family history for fear that their "paper son" status would be discovered. In addition, during the Communist period most members of the Chinese American community seldom acknowledged connections with mainland China. For these Chinese Americans, their family history and experiences, on the one hand, frame their images of Chinese culture and of China as an ancestral home. On the other hand, it becomes difficult to distinguish between what is particular to one's own family and friends and what is true of the larger context of Chinese and Chinese American culture and society. Because they live in a society where there are multiple and conflicting images about Chinese and Chinese culture, it can become difficult for Chinese Americans to contextualize their own family culture within a broader picture of Chinese and Chinese American culture. Family experiences and home culture must be resolved with what is learned about China and other Chinese outside the home from the media, school textbooks, and popular culture.

Images of Chinese culture and authentic Chinese-ness often derive from the media rather than from sources inside the home. One twenty-two-year-old second-generation Chinese American said that he grew up thinking he should know how to do kung fu because he was Chinese. Growing up in the Midwest, the only images he saw of Chinese were on TV, and in many ways he thought these media images taught him how to be Chinese. For some Chinese Americans, these conceptions of their (lack of) Chinese-ness shape their images and attitudes toward China as a reservoir of an essentialized Chinese culture and source of family secrets that can be tapped to fill in the holes of their own incomplete and perhaps quirky understandings of their Chinese-ness.

Increasing contact between the United States and China through trade, immigration, and popular culture constantly reminds Chinese Americans of their motherland. The prominent presence of the Pacific Rim in the media makes representations of Chinese culture available on a daily basis. These representations are attached to discussions of economics, international relations, illegal immigration, and campaign finance scandals. Through these transnational flows—of commodities, popular culture, and media—Chinese Americans are sometimes unwillingly reattached to their homeland. Media hype over transnational overseas Chinese business and social networks portrays a Chinese diaspora, driven by Confucian values and a culturally engrained business drive, as a united world force to be reckoned with.[12] As one participant in the "Roots" program remarked, images of China, though changing, still strongly affect his ideas of what it means to be Chinese in America:

> I think the idea of China always having an effect on your perception of Chinese-ness, I would tend to agree with that, because no matter what I think, I think the media plays a role in what I absorb and what I don't. Whether I agree with it or not, it affects the way I think. Whatever is going on in China,

or about what Congress says about China, or what movies are out about China, it always has this effect. . . . Basically it seems to me like it's opening up a little more, and China is becoming more like any normal country. Whereas twenty years ago I thought it was this dark, Evil Empire II kind of thing.

This distance from China combined with the pressure to know and identify with China results in a complex and confusing relationship between Chinese Americans and their country of origin, a relationship that is mediated by the discourses of multiculturalism and race in the United States. While Mitchell's (1996) Hong Kong transnationals use multiculturalism to their advantage, Chinese Americans are in many ways controlled by American multiculturalism without realizing the extent of its impact. The global flows of capital and culture created by and used to the advantage of Hong Kong transnationals reattach Chinese Americans to their places of origin, sometimes unwillingly. This opens up new alternatives for them but also raises new complications for rooting (and routing) identities. Though meant to be empowering, the identity politics of U.S. multiculturalism provide a distorted lens through which Chinese Americans view their Chinese-ness, their American-ness, and their relationship to China and the United States.

CHINESE AMERICANS
AND THE ASIA-PACIFIC REGION

The relationship between Chinese Americans and China emerges from historical processes that go far beyond the particulars of the individual stories of their ancestors who emigrated. As Arif Dirlik (1998) observes, Eurocentric thinking and capitalist processes created the Asia-Pacific region, which is not an objective geographical entity but a sociohistorical construction. Through processes integral to its formation, the creation of the Asia-Pacific region has determined the relationships between Chinese Americans and China, and between Chinese Americans and the United States. Dirlik argues that Asian American history and identities have been shaped by the historical prominence of ideas of cultural difference in U.S. definitions of relations between East and West. From the beginning of U.S. history, he points out, the relationship between Asians and the United States has taken form around issues of labor and capital (Dirlik 1998, 296).

However, the debates have always been framed in terms of cultural difference rather than political or economic tensions. The legal exclusion of Chinese immigrants, then, was justified not in terms of the threatening labor competition posed by Chinese workers but in terms of irreconcilable differences between Eastern and Western cultures (297). Though Chinese were integral to building the U.S. economy, they remained exotic and dangerous outsiders who needed to be controlled.

Thus, the problem faced by Asian Americans is the difficulty of comfortably claiming either Asian or American roots. Dirlik (1998, 294) observes that "to the extent that trans-Pacific ties of Asian Americans have been recognized within the dominant culture, . . . this recognition has served primarily to deny their 'Americanness'—and their history." The recent attention paid to the Asia-Pacific region has newly emphasized the potential in those connections (284). However, for the Chinese Americans I interviewed, this focus puts them in a double bind. Lacking strong connections to Asia, they are nevertheless viewed through the prism of cultural difference that has historically defined relations between Asian immigrants and the United States. As Ebron and Tsing (1995) observe, while black Americans are seen as lacking a cultural heritage, Chinese Americans are viewed as having too much culture. The "Asian" and "American" parts of "Asian American" become two irreconcilable parts of a single identity. Dirlik (1998) and others have referred to this problem as a dual or split personality, neither side of which can be recognized as whole. The idea that the "Asian" and "American" parts of "Asian American" cannot be integrated into a cohesive, singular identity makes it very difficult to conceive of processes of cultural change that blend Asian and American elements. Rather, assimilation becomes the dominant model, in which one culture is exchanged for the other. Some people are judged or judge themselves as more or less Chinese than others. As one "Roots" participant observed:

> In some ways I think I have this internal jealousy of people who have closer connections—who can speak the language or know more traditions . . . but I think there's also another part of it, which is going around Chinatown and being, "Oh, don't speak to me in Chinese." I mean, I can understand parts of what they're saying, but I don't respond. And . . . people of other ethnicities . . . [are] always surpris[ed] that I don't speak Chinese. I'm third-generation, what do you want?

U.S. MULTICULTURAL POLITICS

Thus, Chinese American culture is defined within U.S. multicultural politics as a form of inherent and immutable difference from the U.S. mainstream culture (whatever that might be). As mentioned previously, from the beginning of Chinese emigration, the class and labor tensions that the Chinese presence in the United States represented have been framed by opponents in terms of cultural difference. Chinese have been portrayed as unassimilable and unable to live democratic, civilized lifestyles (Choy, Dong, and Hom 1995). They have thus been marginalized and excluded from mainstream American culture, not only in political and economic realms but also in cultural ones. By emphasizing the inherent difference of Chinese people within U.S. cultural politics, these opponents feel justified in criticizing Chinese Americans as less American, and at the same time this focus forces Chinese Americans to reference China and Chinese culture (about which they know little) as a basis for their identities. Even as Chinese Americans are forced to define their differences as cultural, the hybrid blend that Chinese American culture has become is not recognized by mainstream U.S. society, or by Chinese Americans themselves, as legitimately "Chinese." Therefore, Chinese Americans are forced to form a relationship with mainland China or attempt to claim a wholly American identity (an effort that is difficult, if not impossible, in racialized U.S. society).

Conceptions of cultural change and adaptation to U.S. culture must be understood within the larger context of the social science, folk, and official models that have been used to describe minority experiences in the United States. Each of these models falls back on basic assumptions about culture and identity. U.S. multicultural politics is based on implicit assumptions that one's true identity is "out there" somewhere, waiting to be found through self-reflection, or by "finding" oneself. Within the consciousness-raising identity politics (Bondi 1993) of U.S. multiculturalism, assumptions about culture change, preservation, and authenticity constrain avenues for identity exploration and expression.

The assimilationist models originally used to understand minority experiences in the United States have inadequately dealt with processes of cultural change and issues of race. At the same time they have provided a framework for folk understandings of cultural change. As Omi and Winant (1994) have observed, models of race relations for U.S. minorities have been shaped by the legacy of Robert Park's race relations cycle, which described a continual drive toward assimilation. Though it has become evident that racial minorities do not melt into a uniform blend, this model of assimilation remains influential despite the discourses of multiculturalism that have arisen in its place. This influence is due in large part to the inadequacies of these models in dealing effectively with the question of race. Within academic models, race has been relegated to the realm of biology, subsumed under class, or hidden by the idea of ethnicity (Omi and Winant 1994; Visweswaran 1998).

Asian American scholar and cultural critic Lisa Lowe (1996) describes the ways in which both folk and academic discourses on Asian American adaptation to U.S. culture have been subsumed under the model of assimilation to American culture. Within this model, the differential abilities of immigrant versus U.S.-born generations to adapt to American ways is the main source of intergenerational conflict. Lowe argues that this vertical, generational model of understanding both conflict and diversity within the Asian American community and family should be replaced by a horizontal model. In acknowledging the heterogeneity of the Asian American community, a horizontal model would serve as a first step toward strategic political action.

A particular difficulty with generational models, Lowe observes, is the relationship that they construct between authenticity and assimilation, and therefore with China as a place of origin. The farther one is removed from China, the more assimilated to U.S. culture one will be, and therefore the less authentically Chinese. As an illustrative example, Lowe uses a fictional story about two Chinese American girls, each of whom assumes that the other is more "authentically" attached to China and more culturally Chinese. They come to find out that they are both U.S.-born and that neither knows much about China.

This idea that one can be more or less authentically Chinese places Chinese Americans in an ambivalent relationship with people whom they view as "more Chinese" (those who speak the language or have immigrated more recently). While, on the one hand, Chinese Americans, under assimilationist models, should identify strongly with their U.S. roots, the realities of racial politics cause them to remain perpetual foreigners. Chinese Americans have always been told that "home" is in the United States but that their "roots," and therefore a missing piece of their identity, is somewhere in China.

Segal and Handler (1995, 392) observe that U.S. multiculturalism conceives of some societies, such as the United States, as being composed of multiple cultures, and others as constituting a single culture. They point out that

> culture, in this view, is not itself "multi"; rather, multiplicity and diversity arise from the aggregation of cultures. Cultures, in short, are figured as elemental. From this perspective, it is not that diversity is intrinsic to social formations, nor simply that the U.S. is diverse, but more specifically, that the U.S. consists of some unspecified number of cultural elements.

Similarly, Richard Handler (1988) observes that there is a tendency in Western thinking to objectify and commodify culture within movements for cultural preservation.

In the Chinese American context, culture is objectified and then broken down into discrete practices, customs, and traditions (using chopsticks, eating certain foods, celebrating certain holidays). These elements carry symbolic weight as features and traits that can be measured to indicate the authenticity of a culture. Within this context, Chinese-ness becomes a measurable and commodified form of cultural capital (Bourdieu 1984). Some people have more Chinese culture, while others, having lost it, have less. This sets up a situation in which some lack culture and others have too much. For Chinese Americans, this dilemma is a double-edged sword: they are thought of as having, in contrast to African Americans (Ebron and Tsing 1995), too much culture, but at the same time they often worry about lacking culture (Lowe 1996). Chinese American culture, compared to authentic Chinese culture, becomes something that is impure, diluted, and devolved. Meanwhile, Chinese tradition and culture are rendered static, something either "left over" or in need of "preserving."

Thus, within folk Chinese American culture, Chinese Americans critically describe one another as "not being very Chinese" or "being too Chinesey." Some are accused of being "jook sing" (hollow bamboo). Others are viewed as "bananas" (yellow on the outside, white on the inside). The term "ABC" (American-born Chinese) carries a negative connotation, implying assimilation to the dominant American culture and loss of Chinese culture.

The question of the past is especially problematic for Chinese Americans. However, at the same time it is their past, in terms of their connections to their ancestral homeland of China, that defines them as Chinese people in the United States. Popular ideas about Chinese culture are often essentialized and static representations of "Chinese tradition" that have been shot through an Orientalized filter. These notions of tradition, customs, food, language, and history are viewed by the broader American public as deeply rooted historically in a mainland Chinese past. At the same time this is a past about which many American-born Chinese Americans feel they know little. Under U.S. multiculturalism, specific racial backgrounds become associated with sets of essentialized cultural traits. As Chinese people, Chinese Americans are expected by the broader society to possess knowledge of Chinese language and cultural practices. The specifics of family history are disassociated from these more visible identity markers, so that Chinese Americans are expected to know something about China and Chinese culture despite the fact that many Chinese American families have been in the United States for generations.[13] Thus, many view Chinese culture with ambivalence, and as mysterious, foreign, and irrelevant to their everyday lives. In comparison to popularly accepted views of China and Chinese culture, they see their own Chinese American family practices as diluted or inauthentic versions of "real" traditional Chinese culture.

The emphasis in mainstream American constructions of Chineseness on knowledge of such visible identity markers as language and customs makes many Chinese Americans feel inadequately and inauthentically Chinese when judged according to these criteria. Yet at the same time they feel inescapably Chinese because racialization in the United States marks them as inherently and immutably Chinese. Anthropologist Jean Jackson (1995) observes that folk models of culture conceive of it as something natural, possessed, and innate. These attitudes form the basis of popular attitudes toward culture change. Popular conception holds that pure cultures can be neither created nor invented. People "possess" culture "just like animals have fur." Culture is acquired slowly through one's lifetime of personal development, and cultural change occurs gradually. Rapid cultural change is viewed as resulting in acculturation—in other words, the loss of culture (Jackson 1995, 18). For Chinese Americans, these naturalized conceptions of culture and culture change imply that consciously learned culture is a less authentic or inauthentic type of culture. One fourth-generation Chinese American woman shared the following event in a discussion session with fellow American-born Chinese:

> I was having a conversation with a friend of mine who was born in Hong Kong. He was saying that . . . I think this was a fairly harsh term . . . but he was kind of disgusted how ABC I was. I think he used the wrong word. He was kind of joking to me . . . and was saying that I have no culture. And I was saying that I can't help the way I was born, I'm fourth- or fifth-generation, and whatever culture that I have is going to be learned culture, and then he said, and I think that this is controversial, he said that you can't learn culture, it's something that you're born with.

The idea expressed by the Hong Kong friend that culture cannot be learned but rather is "something that you're born with" is consistent with the earlier discussion of folk ideas about culture change. This type of thinking leaves no room for processes of re-ethnicization. Many Chinese Americans consciously research and adopt practices, material culture, and beliefs that signify "Chinese-ness" or "Chinese American-ness" to them. Or they may mark as ethnic certain values, traits, and customs that they view as being part of their family's core. Reethnicization often involves learning more about Chinese history and culture or Chinese–Asian American history. It may involve becoming active in Asian American or Chinese American community issues, or going to China to learn to speak Chinese. Or it may consist of consciously associating with other Chinese or Asian Americans, or watching Chinese or Hong Kong movies. But in claiming Chinese culture, Chinese Americans must negotiate a politically charged atmosphere in which both the sources of this culture and the content of the parts to be "preserved" are contested by other Chinese people and by the broader U.S. society.

This framework for understanding identity is inadequate for a discussion of the new set of differences that come to the fore in border experiences under globalization. These represent a different set of discourses that attempt to internationalize Chinese Americans, bringing them into contact with China, Chinese people, and discourses on China about which they know little.

WRITING HISTORIES

For Chinese Americans born and raised in the United States, the geographical and temporal distance from China puts them in a double bind (Dirlik 1998; Ang 1994). Their American-ness makes them not Chinese enough according to the essentialized standards defining Chinese culture in both China and the United States. At the same time they are excluded from full participation in American culture because their Chinese-ness makes them somehow not American enough. How, then, are they affected by the transnational currents that are reattaching diasporic peoples to their homelands on a worldwide scale? What does visiting China represent for Chinese Americans who often know little about China or Chinese culture? How is the contradiction between their forced association with China and their often ambivalent feelings about China and Chinese culture resolved? In the end "Roots" participants find their experience productive. The question is, How do they create meaning out of their experience that goes beyond these limitations?

Bruner (1996), in his account of African Americans "returning" to slave castles in Ghana, and Gable, Handler, and Lawson (1992), in their analysis of how the history of slaves is presented in Colonial Williamsburg, emphasize the role of contemporary identity politics and the political and constructed nature of history and memory. In visiting China, Chinese Americans participate in what appears to be a mythical return of a diasporic people to their homeland. But it is a return that is highly mediated through transnational processes and contemporary identity politics. Chinese Americans make meaning out of their visits to ancestral villages by reconstructing family memory through multilayered filters: contemporary U.S.-China relations, Chinese American history, identity politics as defined by U.S. multiculturalism, and transnational discourses about China and Chinese people produced from a variety of sources.

In discussing here how Chinese Americans recollect their experiences upon return to the United States, my description of village visits will be brief (for more detailed discussion, see Louie 2001).

These visits are well choreographed, highly emotional affairs during which Chinese government officials, tour guides, local village leaders, and the Chinese American tour group come together for a series of meetings, village tours, and banquets. The "In Search of Roots" group visits each participant's village in turn. The purpose of the visit differs depending on the perspective of those involved. For the government officials, it symbolizes the patriotic return of overseas Chinese to their ancestral villages. For the Chinese American leader and most of the "Roots" participants, it represents an opportunity to connect present and past and to fill in holes in the genealogical and family history record. At the same time it is an opportunity to meet relatives and friends of the family who may still be living in the area and to see any physical marks that their ancestors may have made on the village (the ancestral home, the schoolhouse, and so on). On yet another level, Chinese American visitors glimpse contemporary Chinese life as they tour the countryside, shop at night markets, and interact (to a limited degree) with Chinese people.

For Chinese Americans, the first physical encounter with the village in China is almost never the first metaphorical or imaginative encounter with it. Village visits are in many ways prefigured by the workings of the diasporic imagination particular to the generations removed from the place of origin. The disjuncture between immigrant generations and the homeland creates a complex interplay of history, memory, and politics that mediates the ways in which Chinese Americans perceive and experience the village.[14] Participants expect that the village visit will help them fill in missing pieces of the family story, which has of yet been only partially written, and in this way complete an important part of personal identity. One participant described how sincerely moved she was when a villager, upon their arrival in her ancestral county of Hoiping, welcomed her "home." She felt that the experience helped her "finally complete the missing piece of the puzzle of my existence as a Chinese American."

Chinese American narratives are characterized by a dual focus— that of their experiences in contemporary China, and that of details and interpretations relating to family history. Within these narratives, the point of immigration (the imagined moment in time itself, and the events preceding and following it) takes on magnified importance. The village itself and the surrounding region, though representing a relatively small part of China, are a focal point. Specific physical structures take on increased importance within the physical and cultural geography of the village—the ancestral home, the school built with the family's donations from overseas, the grave site. Newer structures and the homes converted into small factories or occupied by migrant workers from northern rural areas fade into the periphery. The contemporary setting of southern China, though peripheral to the "Roots" mission, becomes a locus of fun and entertainment. In fact, many popular culture icons found in China are familiar elements of Asian American youth culture (see Louie 2001).

As Dirlik (1998) has observed, the politics of multiculturalism not only separates the "Asian" and "American" parts of "Asian American" but also misrepresents them. The "Asian" portion glosses over the diversity that exists in the region known as "Asia," which is ultimately a creation of the West. The "American" portion refers only to the United States, leaving out Canada and Latin America. Through the linking of the Chinese and Chinese American aspects of their histories, these Chinese Americans are trying to redefine these restrictive meanings of "Asian" and "American." They do this by linking localized forms of identity—their ancestral villages and the homes that their families have created in the United States—within the context of broader historical processes.

Though while in China they are—as participants in the Youth Summer Camps— subject to the Chinese government's imposed interpretations of their identity as Chinese overseas, they incorporate these claims on their identities into their narratives of return (for more on Youth Summer Camps, see Louie 2000). In this way, they view their welcome "home" more within the context of historical linkages and family connections than through the prism of contemporary PRC politics and national loyalty. Rather than subscribing to China-centered notions of identity based on static views of culture (a danger raised earlier by Ong and Nonini 1997), Chinese American visitors to ancestral villages begin to rework these "traditional" notions of Chinese-ness through the mediated lens of a heritage tour. Although Chinese American visitors usually rely on their Chinese American leader to interpret for them the traditional Chinese customs and practices found in the villages, these practices take on new significance for them. In fact, the very experience of visiting the village becomes a new aspect of their family tradition, reconnecting parts of the family history. In addition, local customs, specialty foods, and traditional products become a part of Chinese culture that Chinese Americans claim proudly as part of their family's heritage. Together, these newly learned aspects provide a basis for an "authentic" connection to China and China culture that they have felt they were lacking.

Both women and men visit ancestral villages, often both the maternal and paternal side, write genealogies, including both women and men, and create histories that link the Chinese past to a Chinese American present. Participants reframe their interpretations of history within the context of contemporary ethnic and gender politics. One female "Roots" participant shared the following opinion during an informal group discussion of Chinese traditions that touched on the practice of assigning formal names in a generational cycle to male children in a Chinese lineage: "To me the [generational] name doesn't mean as much, but it could also be because I'm a woman. . . . But I also think the most important thing is that we remember our history, so I think that if we just remember that and remember how the [paper] name got changed, then I think that's sufficient for me."

The village visits encouraged the development of a Cantonese, place-focused, historically grounded, nonpolitical identification with China. This connection ultimately referred to a U.S.-based identity. To a large extent, this Cantonese American identity was based on contrasts between an elite Mandarin "high" culture and a Cantonese family-based culture. This more personal version of Chinese culture was represented by an identification with local customs, food, dialect, and other points of pride that the "Roots" participants learned about on their visit to China. Noted one participant, who has since become involved in the preservation of Angel Island and is pursuing graduate work in Asian American studies:

When we went to Beijing after we did the "Roots" part, I think, for me, it was cool climbing on the Great Wall, but I think it was a lot more significant seeing the village my grandfather was from and things like that. . . . I'm glad I went to Beijing afterwards, but . . . I definitely want to go back to my village again, but there's no strong pull to go to Beijing for a second time. . . . It was very much just a touristy thing, what we learned and what we had. And I think the first part of the trip there was definitely a lot more connection because of the family, the history, though I don't understand Cantonese, just the tonality of it—you know it feels more comfortable.

The specifics of the village visit—experiences with relatives and representations of continuity between people or things in the village and their own family histories (pictures of relatives from the United States, sometimes themselves, on the walls, newspaper clippings from the United States, and so on)—were the basis for this "culture." In addition, for many, involvement in Asian American politics and academic pursuits in combination with having visited China provided a sense of legitimacy to being Chinese American without necessarily knowing the language.

Chinese Americans may not be key players in creating or controlling capital resources, images, or social relations, but they still negotiate information and images as they craft identity narratives out of their family's past and contemporary resources about China and Chinese–Chinese American culture. These narratives create a connection to China that is not dependent on knowledge of Chinese culture or language. They come to view their own family's experiences as a legitimate part of a broader Chinese American culture, based on both a shared past and, more important, a shared present. Although the connections of second (and later) generations of Chinese Americans to China can be said to be largely symbolic, involving information about China and Chinese culture that is filtered through multiple layers (both national and transnational), they are nevertheless still powerful. Through producing and appropriating meanings of Chinese-ness for themselves, they use transnational flows and border-crossing experiences to create and legitimize identities that blend Chinese and American influences and go beyond the constraints of U.S. multiculturalism.

NOTES

1. By narratives, I refer to both the formal papers written by participants in the "In Search of Roots" program and the frameworks that they develop for understanding and talking about their family histories and identities more informally.
2. From 1882 to 1943 Chinese immigration was severely restricted by the U.S. government in an effort to reduce labor competition. Only select

classes, such as merchants and students, and the children of citizens were allowed to enter the United States during this time period. Because of exclusion, families could not be brought to the United States.

3. From the beginning of Chinese emigration, the empire, and later the government, has mediated relations between itself and Chinese abroad. Prior to this practice, the Qing empire viewed all Chinese who left their motherland as traitors who had committed a crime punishable by death. These relations were marked by a major shift in 1954 from extra-territorial rule to acknowledgment of Chinese abroad as subjects of foreign nations. For periods prior to and at times during the Communist period, overseas Chinese were viewed as a valuable source of foreign capital. However, associations with overseas relatives were often dangerous in pre-Communist years because one's relative prosperity made one the target of bandits, and during the Communist era because one was suspected of association with capitalist roaders.

4. For more information on the PRC's construction of these programs and the limitations of their effectiveness, see Louie 2000.

5. The Taiwanese government was the first to institute such cultural heritage programs. Theirs is now called "the Love Boat" by Chinese Americans, many of whom participate less for the sake of learning about Chinese culture than of socializing with other Chinese Americans while in Taiwan.

6. More recently, research by historians such as Madeline Hsu (2000) and Yong Chen (2000) has redefined early Chinese immigration as a form of transnational practice.

7. Not all participants were able to find family records in the archives. Some families had emigrated to Hong Kong, to places in Southeast Asia or Latin America before entering the United States. Therefore, many families entered after the repeal of the Exclusion Acts in 1943.

8. Immigrants would have to memorize the information pertinent to these identities to make it past the interrogation of immigration officials, under a system that was designed to make entry very difficult.

9. Because many immigrants assumed paper names and the family histories that went along with them, it was important that they record this information for later arrivals so that their stories would match, thus convincing immigration officials that they were legitimate relatives and not "paper sons."

10. Aihwa Ong (1999, 127) uses the word "astronaut" to refer to the Hong Kong businessman who is continually in the air while his wife and children are located in Australia, Canada, or the United States, earning rights of residence.

11. Owing to the nature of transnationalism itself (the continuous back-and-forth movement that marks it), clearly defining generations in a

way that is analytically meaningful is difficult. A second-generation Chinese American born in the 1930s may have little in common with the second-generation children of post-1965 immigrants.

12. China is discussed in the news media and is found on product labels, in popular culture, and in many other dimensions of American life. Andrew Lam (1997), a Pacific News Service commentator originally from Vietnam, satirizes the ease and extent to which Asian Americans are tied to Asia in the American imagination. He marvels at the power and influence that he and his Asian American friends must now have to influence politics. All they have to do, he quips, is to make "a few well-placed campaign contributions" to ruin the careers of politicians. After all, his "transpacific web of connections is extensive"—he has an uncle in Saigon, cousins in refugee camps in Hong Kong, and the ability to make a "wicked Thai soup."

13. A cartoon strip, "Angry Little Asian Girl," makes fun of these assumptions. In this strip the girl walks into a classroom, and the teacher says, "Oh, my, you speak English so well, where did you learn to speak so well?" The ALAG says, "I was born here, you stupid dipshit, don't you know anything about immigration? Read some history, you stupid ignoramus."

14. For a more detailed account of how Chinese American visitors use their mobility and contemporary transnational references to experience and interpret their visits to their ancestral villages, see Louie (2001).

REFERENCES

Ang, Ien. 1994. "On Not Speaking Chinese." *New Formations* 24(winter): 1–18.

Appadurai, Arjun. 1991. "Global Ethnoscapes: Notes and Queries for a Transnational Anthropology." In *Recapturing Anthropology,* edited by Richard Fox. Santa Fe, N.M.: School of American Research Press.

Basch, Linda, Nina Glick-Schiller, and Cristina Szanton-Blanc. 1994. *Nations Unbound: Transnational Projects, Postcolonial Predicaments, and Deterritorialized Nation-states.* Langhorne, Penn.: Gordon and Breach.

Bondi, Liz. 1993. "Locating Identity Politics." In *Place and the Politics of Identity,* edited by Michael Keith and Steve Pile. New York: Routledge.

Bourdieu, Pierre. 1984. *Distinction: A Social Critique of the Judgment of Taste,* translated by Richard Nice. Cambridge, Mass.: Harvard University Press.

Bruner, Edward. 1996. "Tourism in Ghana: The Representation of Slavery and the Return of the Black Diaspora." *American Anthropologist* 98(2): 290–304.

Chen, Yong. 2000. *Chinese San Francisco, 1850–1943: A Transpacific Community*. Stanford, Calif.: Stanford University Press.

Choy, Philip, Lorraine Dong, and Marlon Hom. 1995. *The Coming Man: Nineteenth-Century American Perceptions of the Chinese*. Seattle: University of Washington Press.

Clifford, James. 1997. "Diasporas." In *Routes: Travel and Translation in the Late Twentieth Century*. Cambridge, Mass.: Harvard University Press.

Dirlik, Arif. 1998. "The Asia-Pacific in Asian-American Perspective." In *What Is in a Rim?: Critical Perspectives on the Pacific Region Idea,* edited by Arif Dirlik. Boulder, Colo.: Rowman and Littlefield.

Ebron, Paulla, and Anna Tsing. 1995. "From Allegories of Identity to Sites of Dialogue." *Diaspora* 4(2).

Featherstone, Mike. 1996. "Localism, Globalism, and Cultural Identity." In *Global/Local: Cultural Production and the Transnational Imaginary,* edited by Rob Wilson and Wilmal Dissanayake. Durham, N.C.: Duke University Press.

Fitzgerald, Stephen. 1972. *China and the Overseas Chinese: A Study of Peking's Changing Policy, 1949–1970*. Cambridge: Cambridge University Press.

Gable, Eric, Richard Handler, and Anna Lawson. 1992. "On the Uses of Relativism: Fact, Conjecture, and Black and White Histories at Colonial Williamsburg." *American Ethnologist* 19(4): 791–805.

Glick-Schiller, Nina. 1999a. "Transmigrants and Nation-states: Something Old and Something New in U.S. Immigrant Experience." In *Handbook of International Migration: The American Experience,* edited by Charles Hirschman, Philip Kasinitz, and Josh DeWind. New York: Russell Sage Foundation.

———. 1999b. "Who Are These Guys?: A Transnational Perspective on National Identities." In *Identities on the Move: Transnational Processes in North America and the Caribbean Basin,* edited by Liliana Goldin. Austin: University of Texas Press.

Grewal, Inderpal, Akhil Gupta, and Aihwa Ong, eds. 1999. "Introduction: Asian Transnationalities." *Positions: East Asia Cultural Critique* 7(3): 653–66.

Handler, Richard. 1988. *Nationalism and the Politics of Culture in Quebec*. Madison: University of Wisconsin Press.

Hing, Bill Ong. 1993. *Making and Remaking Asian America through Immigration Policy 1850–1990*. Stanford, Calif.: Stanford University Press.

Hsu, Madeline. 2000. *Dreaming of Gold, Dreaming of Home*. Stanford, Calif.: Stanford University Press.

Jackson, Jean. 1995. "Culture, Genuine and Spurious: The Politics of Indianness in the Vaupes, Colombia." *American Ethnologist* 22(1): 3–27.

Lam, Andrew. 1997. "An Asian American Argues It's Better to Be Feared Than to Be Invisible." Pacific News Service.

Liu, John, and Lucie Cheng. 1994. "Pacific Rim Development and the Duality of Post-1965 Immigration to the U.S." In *The New Immigration in Los Angeles and Global Restructuring,* edited by Paul Ong, Edna Bonacich, and Lucie Cheng. Philadelphia: Temple University Press.

Louie, Andrea. 2000. "Reterritorializing Transnationalism: Chinese Americans and the Chinese Motherland." *American Ethnologist* 27(3): 645–69.

———. 2001. "Crafting Places Through Mobility: Chinese American 'Roots-Searching' in China." *Identities* 8(3): 343–79.

Lowe, Lisa. 1996. *Immigrant Acts: On Asian American Cultural Politics.* Durham, N.C.: Duke University Press.

Mahler, Sarah. 1998. "Theoretical and Empirical Contributions Toward a Research Agenda for Transnationalism." In *Transnationalism from Below,* edited by Michael Peter Smith and Luis Eduardo Guarnizo. New Brunswick, N.J.: Transaction Press.

Mitchell, Katherine. 1996. "In Whose Interest?: Transnational Capital and the Production of Multiculturalism in Canada." In *Global/Local: Cultural Production and the Transnational Imaginary,* edited by Rob Wilson and Wilmal Dissanayake. Durham, N.C.: Duke University Press.

Omi, Michael, and Howard Winant. 1994. *Racial Formation in the United States.* New York: Routledge.

Ong, Aihwa. 1993. "On the Edge of Empires: Flexible Citizenship Among Chinese in Diaspora." *Positions* 1(3): 745–78.

———. 1999. *Flexible Citizenship: The Cultural Logics of Transnationality.* Durham, N.C.: Duke University Press.

Ong, Aihwa, and Donald Nonini. 1997. *Ungrounded Empires: The Cultural Politics of Modern Chinese Transnationalism.* New York: Routledge.

Portes, Alejandro, Luis E. Guarnizo, and Patricia Landolt. 1999. "The Study of Transnationalism: Pitfalls and Promise of an Emergent Research Field." In *Ethnic and Racial Studies* 22(2): 218–22.

Schein, Louisa. 1998. "Forged Transnationality and Oppositional Cosmopolitanism." In *Transnationalism from Below,* edited by Michael Peter Smith and Luis Eduardo Guarnizo. New Brunswick, N.J.: Transaction Press.

Segal, David A., and Richard Handler. 1995. "U.S. Multiculturalism and the Concept of Culture." *Identities* 1(4): 391–407.

Siu, Helen. 1992. "Cultural Identity and the Politics of Difference in South China." In *China in Transformation,* edited by Tu Wei-Ming. Cambridge, Mass.: Harvard University Press.

Smart, Josephine, and Alan Smart. 1998. "Transnational Social Networks and Negotiated Identities in Interactions Between Hong Kong and

China." In *Transnationalism from Below,* edited by Michael Peter Smith and Luis Eduardo Guarnizo. New Brunswick, N.J.: Transaction Press.

Smith, Michael Peter, and Luis Eduardo Guarnizo, eds. 1998. *Transnationalism from Below.* New Brunswick, N.J.: Transaction Press.

Visweswaran, Kamala. 1998. "Race and the Culture of Anthropology." *American Anthropologist* 100(1): 70–83.

Wakeman, Frederic, Jr. 1998 [1966]. *Strangers at the Gate: Social Disorder in South China 1839–1861.* Berkeley: University of California Press.

Wong, K. Scott, and Sucheng Chan. 1998. *Claiming America: Constructing Chinese American Identities During the Exclusion Era.* Philadelphia: Temple University Press.

Woon, Yuen-Fong. 1989. "Social Change and Continuity in South China: Overseas Chinese and the Guan Lineage of Kaiping County, 1949–1987." *China Quarterly* 118: 324–44.

———. 1990. "International Links and the Socioeconomic Development of Rural China: An Emigrant Community in Guangdong." *Modern China* 16(2): 139–72.

Chapter 14

Second-Generation West Indian Transnationalism

Milton Vickerman

IN RECOGNITION OF the growing importance of globalization, recent research on immigration has focused increasingly on transnationalism (see, for example, Cordero-Guzman, Smith, and
Grosfoguel 2001). This focus underscores how the global interconnectedness of national cultures, political systems, and economies—
to cite only a few of the more important arenas of action—shapes
the flow and adaptation of migrants in different regions of the world.
In this way, transnationalism avoids representations of migration as
a simple movement of people from sending to receiving countries
and emphasizes that it is a process in which cross-border contacts between such societies are consciously cultivated. As Portes, Guarnizo,
and Landolt (1999, 219) note, transnationalism refers to "occupations and activities that require regular and sustained social contacts over time across national borders for their implementation."
Underlying these flourishing contacts is the reality of social spaces
that bisect national boundaries and are characterized by the inter-
mingling of multifarious cultures. Although the resiliency of national
borders should temper notions of a rapid crumbling of political
barriers between countries, there is little doubt that in many areas
these borders are becoming increasingly permeable and social life is
taking on a more global flavor.[1] Patterson (1994, 106–7), for instance,
has argued for the existence of at least four distinct transnational
"cosmoses" in the United States, all of which are characterized by

342   The Changing Face of Home

a "system of flows between a metropolitan center and a set of independent satellite countries." These are the "West Atlantic regional cosmos," encompassing the Eastern Seaboard and the circum-Caribbean societies; the "Tex-Mex" regional cosmos of the Southwest, which embraces the Euro-Indian culture of that part of the United States and northern Mexico; the southern California cosmos, which is characterized by a mixture of Asian, Latin, and African American cultures; and the Pacific Rim cosmos of the Northwest, which embraces traditional Euro-America and industrialized Asia.

Transnational social spaces facilitate transnational contact between sending and receiving countries, but we need to distinguish between these spaces and the possibility of such contact. More generally, it is important to "unpack" the notion of transnationalism, recognizing that it contains several distinct subprocesses. Vertovec (1999), for instance, notes that in the literature the term is used to refer not just to social spaces but to consciousness and to the globalization of capital; transnationalism also denotes a mode of cultural reproduction, a site of political engagement, and a way to reconstruct a sense of "place" or locality. Often the assumption is that since modern immigrants operate in a transnational social space, at minimum they must also possess a transnational consciousness. Brazilian immigrants, for example, have been said to have their "heads . . . in two places," inasmuch as they utilize American society's better opportunities for upward mobility but continue to feel deep attachment to their homeland (Margolis 1998). Similarly, Dominicans are held to view New York City (home to the bulk of Dominicans) as a "waiting room." The greater present-day tolerance in the United States for multiculturalism allows these immigrants to " 'imagine' and negotiate worlds where national boundaries, national cultures, and national identities are far less constraining and socially binding than was the case for earlier immigrant groups" (Pessar 1995, 69–70). Thus, Dominicans, like Brazilians, routinely shuttle between the United States and the Dominican Republic. They operate businesses in both countries simultaneously, repatriate funds, and even remain active in island politics to the point of returning there to vote in national elections (Bray 1987; Pessar 1990, 1995).

While it is likely that the various forms of transnationalism frequently accompany each other, the possibility that they do not must be held open. An immigrant can benefit from living in a transnational social space but not be consciously (for example, ideologically or emotionally) transnational (see, for example, Wolf 1997; Vickerman 1999). This might be even more true of the "new" second generation. Less research has been done on this group compared to post-1965 immigrants, so less is known about them. However, this situation has been rapidly changing as researchers have increasingly focused on the question of how this second generation will incorporate into American society (see, for example, Fernandez-Kelly and Schauffler 1994; Zhou and Bankston 1994; Portes, 1996; Oropesa and Lansdale 1997; Perlmann and Waldinger 1998). Another issue that has drawn attention is the question of whether second-generation immigrants are transnational (see, for example, Wolf 1997; Glick-Schiller and Fouron 1999). Because of immigrant settlement patterns in the United States, many second-generation individuals live in areas that would be considered integral parts of transnational social spaces. However, because they are oriented toward the United States (through birth or arrival at an early age), theoretically their consciousness should be less transnational than that of their immigrant parents. Moreover, questions of ethnic-racial identity should be more problematic for the former than for the latter.

This chapter addresses the issue of second-generation transnationalism by focusing on second-generation, English-speaking West Indians. I argue that it is important to distinguish between transnational social spaces, on the one hand, and transnational behavior and consciousness on the other. Second-generation West Indians in the New York City area live in and benefit from a transnational social space, the vibrancy of which is becoming ever more evident. Ironically, however, the existence of this space may undermine incentives to participate in transnationalism on an individual level and, more generally, transnational consciousness. Although many second-generation West Indians maintain some contact with their parents' homelands, they may well downplay the importance of such contact because the existence of a West Indian transnational social space facilitates wide dissemination and easy availability of information about the West Indies in the United States. More important, the growth of the American West Indian population has spurred the re-creation of West Indian culture in the New York area's West Indian enclaves. Although "secondary," in a sense, this culture is probably primary and sufficient for many of the second generation, who may feel no need for the "genuine" West Indian culture that might be available to them from cultivating contact with the region. Overall, second-generation West Indians are less transnational than their parents in their personal behavior and consciousness. However, notable variation exists within this general orientation: some of the second generation maintain close ties with the West Indies, and others have virtually none. Most second-generation West Indians probably lie somewhere between these two extremes, drawing their ethnic identity primarily from their immigrant families and the West Indian culture they find in the enclaves of the New York City area.

WEST INDIAN TRANSNATIONALISM

It would probably be fair to say that most of the literature on West Indian migration does not explicitly adopt a transnational framework. (For a discussion of transnationalism in the Caribbean, see Robotham 1998.) Nevertheless, some of the migratory experiences of West Indians could be construed as lending support to the theory. A number of writers (for example, Rouse 1995; Foner 1997; Mintz 1998) have shown that transnationalism is not a new phenomenon, and it is probably also a mistake to view all previous eras of migration as being necessarily transnational. However, if the essence of transnationalism is the idea that migratory populations cultivate multifarious and necessary links between their homelands and new foreign homes, thereby making borders increasingly permeable, then important phases of West Indian migration since the middle of the nineteenth century would qualify. Undoubtedly, some phases would not qualify. In the case of post–World War II immigration to the United Kingdom, for instance, the movement was decidedly one-way. However, mid-nineteenth-century to early-twentieth-century West Indian migration to Central America and the United States was transnational. Specifically, in terms of Portes, Guarnizo, and Landolt's (1999, 222) useful typology of transnationalism, West Indian migration during this period reflected high- and low-level economic transnationalism and low-level political transnationalism. As these writers note, transnationalism may be conceived of in terms of degree of institutionalization, with some such activity (high-level) involving the state or other large organizations, and other transnational activity (low-level) being more spontaneous. They also see transnationalism as occurring in three primary spheres—economic, political, and sociocultural. Consequently, at least six different types of transnationalism are possible: high-level economic, political, and sociocultural transnationalism, and low-level economic, political, and sociocultural transnationalism.

West Indian migration in the latter half of the nineteenth century was transnational because it was persistently circular, involving the creation and nurturing of strong links between the West Indies and West Indian communities in many countries, especially in Central America (see, for example, Eisner 1961; Koch 1977; Thomas-Hope 1986; Fraser 1990; Richardson 1983, 1984; Conniff 1985). Richardson, especially, in his *Caribbean Migrants,* shows the extent to which migration became a deeply rooted part of the cultures of many West Indian societies. Males were expected to migrate repeatedly, to live in the West Indian towns that had been created abroad by previous waves of migrants, and to return home to their families in the West Indies. This cycle, perpetuated over many decades, created vibrant and self-sustaining links between Anglophone Caribbean territories and places such as Santo Domingo, Panama City, and Havana. The motives for these migrations were decidedly economic: poverty and overpopulation were endemic to many of the countries from which the immigrants came. Some of this migration operated at a low level of institutionalization, representing a spontaneous flight from dire economic conditions. However, much of it also operated at a high level, since some economic projects—notably the construction of the Panama Canal—demanded large numbers of laborers. The level of organization required to set such large-scale labor migration into motion entailed the cooperation of colonial governments in the various West Indian territories. Thus, for instance, they helped organize the migration to Latin America and assumed limited responsibility for their foreign-resident citizens (Eisner 1961; Conniff 1985).[2]

After about 1900 West Indians increasingly migrated to the United States and established themselves in places such as Boston and, especially, New York City's Harlem. During this period some West Indian immigrants were motivated by a confluence of factors to work toward a type of low-level political transnationalism.

Despite British racism in their homelands, many West Indian immigrants found that racism in the United States was relatively harsher, and they found it difficult to adjust to their role as "blacks." One result was an ironic tendency to emphasize their "British-ness" (see, for example, Reid 1939; Osofsky 1966). A potentially more important response to racial alienation was the attempt by some immigrant West Indians—especially intellectuals such as Cyril Briggs, Marcus Garvey, and Claude McKay—to ground black identity in a transnational project. This attempt dovetailed with and drew on the fervor for nationalism that accompanied the end of World War I. As other peoples clamored for a sense of identity in separate nationhood, so these West Indians argued that blacks throughout the diaspora could end their subordination only by developing an overarching sense of "blackness" that transcended national boundaries. These individuals foresaw a future in which people of African ancestry would be blacks, first, and West Indians, Africans, and African Americans second (Stephens 1998). In short, some early-twentieth-century West Indian immigrants attempted to develop political transnationalism in response to their racial subordination. (For a discussion of political transnationalism, see Vertovec 1999.)

Explicit analysis of West Indian immigrants within a transnational framework is most focused, of course, on the current wave of "new" immigrants (see, for example, Sutton 1992; Sutton and Chaney 1987; Glick-Schiller, Basch, and Szanton-Blanc 1994, 1995; Foner 1998; Basch 2001). Most of this analysis has focused on West Indian immigrants; relatively little research has been conducted on the second generation, and even less on the question of whether they are transnational. This gap most likely stems from the newness of the field. As noted previously, theoretically these American-born West Indians should be more assimilated than their parents and therefore less likely to maintain ties with the latter's homelands. However, there are hints that some of the second generation are enmeshed in transnational networks and may have transnational sensibilities. For instance, Soto (1987) and Ho (1993) point to child-minding—the practice whereby American-resident West Indians temporarily relegate parental rights and duties to extended kin and friends in the West Indies—as one mechanism whereby second-generation West Indians maintain contact with the West Indies. Other immigrant West Indian parents send their children back to their homelands to obtain a "quality" education (see, for example, Gmelch 1992; Basch 2001). Waters's (1994) work among second-generation West Indians, though not focusing on transnationalism, implies that some of these individuals may have transnational sensibilities. She argues that the second generation falls into three groups: the American-identified, the ethnic-identified, and the immigrant-identified. The first group tends to be poor, to experience and internalize racial rejection, and consequently to develop pessimistic attitudes about achieving success in American society. The second group tends to be middle-class and better educated and to emphasize an ethnic identity as West Indian in an attempt to counter racism by attaining upward mobility. The third group, the immigrant-identified, is of most importance here since Waters maintains that they are so oriented toward the West Indies that the question of whether they should identify as black does not even occur to them.

METHODOLOGY

Although they raise good points, these arguments relate only tangentially to possible second-generation transnationalism. Immigrant-identified West Indian youth may be oriented toward the West Indies, but their identity, Waters notes, is unstable, and over time they may become either "American"-identified or "ethnic"-identified. This implies that they will orient themselves less to the West Indies and more toward the United States. Also, child fostering, though it enmeshes some second-generation West Indians in transnational networks, originates with the parents of the second generation, not the children. Such enmeshment does not necessarily tell us about the attitudes and behavior of the second generation with respect to transnationalism. The present research does this by focusing on a sample of thirty-five second-generation individuals who most closely resemble what Waters refers to as the ethnic-identified.[3] Moreover, "snowball" sampling was employed. Thus, the findings should be viewed as illustrating broad trends among a particular group of second-generation West Indians. "American"-identified and immigrant-identified second-generation West Indians may view transnationalism differently (although, as noted earlier, the latter may tend toward transnationalism).

TABLE 14.1 **Demographic Characteristics of the Sample of Second-Generation West Indians**

Demographic Characteristics	Percentage	Mean
Gender		
Female	62.0	
Male	38.0	
Age		25
Marital status		
Single	85.0	
Married	12.0	
Divorced	3.0	
Level of education		
Postgraduate	9.0	
First degree	70.0	
Some college	15.0	
High school	6.0	
Percentage in college	42.0	
GPA		2.9
Ethnic identity		
American	10.0	
Hyphenated identity	63.0	
National origin identity	10.0	
Racial identity	10.0	
Other	7.0	
Household income		
$25,000 to $39,999	24.0	
$40,000 to $54,999	16.0	
$55,000 to $70,000	36.0	
Over $70,000	24.0	

Source: Author's compilation.

Twenty-five of the respondents were born in the United States, and on average the others were five years of age when they migrated to this country. The respondents traced their ancestry to several Caribbean nations, including Jamaica, Guyana, Barbados, St. Martin, Grenada, Trinidad and Tobago, and Panama.[4] Averaging twenty-five years of age, 62 percent of the respondents were female, 85 percent were single, and 79 percent were college-educated. Sixty-three percent identified themselves as "West Indian–American," and 60 percent came from families in which the annual household income was $55,000 or over (see table 14.1). The telephone interviews (only one interview was face to face) were tape-recorded (with permission) and lasted an average of forty minutes, although some went on much longer. Thirty-one of the respondents were originally from the New York City area, three lived in the Washington, D.C., area, and one lived in the Virginia Beach, Virginia, area. The parents of these second-generation respondents had lived in the United States for decades: mothers averaged twenty-eight years of residence and fathers thirty-one years.

FINDINGS

The interviews probed for ways in which the second generation maintain contact with their parents' country of origin and for their ethnic identity. The modes of contact included e-mail communication, child-minding, property ownership, letter writing, remittances, telephone contact, and travel to the West Indies. These modes of contact are ranked based on the frequency of the responses given by the second-generation sample. Of least importance were contact through e-mail and child-minding. Only one person reported keeping contact with the West Indies through e-mail. When interviewees were asked this question, they typically responded that relatives and friends in the West Indies do not have computers. Also, only two individuals reported having contact through child-minding: both had been sent, while quite young, to live with relatives in the West Indies. One woman had spent two years in Jamaica, and the other had spent approximately ten years in Panama.[5] Only one person owned property in the West Indies. However, this individual stressed that he had no intention of returning to occupy this inherited property.

Another respondent had a stake in property owned by his parents and expressed serious interest in building a vacation home on that property. A third respondent reported that she had been visiting various countries in the West Indies with an eye to buying property for a summer home.

Letter writing proved to be a more popular method of maintaining contact with friends and relatives in the West Indies than child-minding, e-mail, and property ownership, but only six respondents reported writing on a regular basis. Nine respondents reported sending money or gifts to the West Indies. However, they usually stressed that they did not typically follow their parents' habit of sending barrels of material to the West Indies.[6] Although some reported helping in the preparation of these barrels for transport, the general sentiment was that sending barrels is more typical of the immigrant generation. The process of preparing and transporting these heavy drums was viewed as being too troublesome, whereas, as one child of Jamaican parents put it, the second generation likes to "travel light." Thirteen respondents reported that they telephoned the West Indies on a regular basis; these individuals averaged sixteen calls per year. Twenty-eight of the thirty-five respondents reported traveling to the West Indies at some point in their lives. However, this figure masks wide variation, since ten of the twenty-eight (with a mean age of twenty-five) had traveled to the region four times or fewer in their entire lives. On the other hand, four second-generation respondents reported traveling to the West Indies at least once a year. The other fourteen respondents fell between these two extremes.

DISCUSSION

Although these data support the thesis that second-generation West Indians maintain contact with their parents' country of birth, the main trend among the respondents was a perception that the second generation is less interested in the West Indies than their parents are. As Stewart,[7] a thirty-year-old truck driver, put it:

> My mother's generation is the one that will send barrels and give money because you see that's their home. That's not my home, you know. My mother talks to Jamaica; she talks about home. . . . I don't have that passion for it

because I wasn't born and raised out there. You know, I have been there plenty of times. I like to go there. Don't get me wrong. When I go there, it's like a little vacation, but I don't think of it as home. . . . People that are in my position, that was born here, they don't worry about Jamaica.

Stewart's sentiments were typical of how the respondents viewed the West Indies vis-à-vis their parents. Although he stated that he had visited Jamaica many times, he later admitted that he had been there only four times in his entire life. Nevertheless, most respondents regarded themselves as being, in some sense, "West Indian." For instance, though Stewart felt somewhat detached from his West Indian heritage, his mother was deeply enmeshed in it, and being close to her, he admitted that he was constantly influenced by West Indian culture. From the perspective of ethnic identity, the main difference between the respondents was the degree to which they stressed their West Indian-ness. The three respondents who expressed this identity most enthusiastically (that is, a national origin identity) were also the ones who expressed the greatest desire to maintain contact with the West Indies.[8] However, sustained personal contact does not appear to be necessary for the development and maintenance of an ethnic identity. Second-generation respondents who maintained fairly loose connections to the West Indies also viewed themselves as being, at least partially, West Indian. The difference is that the latter primarily drew their ethnic identity from their immigrant parents and from the critical mass of West Indian culture that has been created in New York City by dynamic flows of information and culture linking the West Indies and the United States.

West Indian immigrant parents are a crucial component in these dynamics, since they are a central—perhaps *the* central—means whereby West Indian culture is transmitted to the second generation. In many cases—though not always[9]—these immigrants are transnational in the truest sense of the word: they help to construct the West Indian–North American social space and possess a transnational consciousness. The respondents in the present study indicated that by immersing the second generation in West Indian culture within the home, parents and other immigrant West Indian family members effectively transmitted certain values and norms to their American-born and -reared children. These mostly traditional values and norms included having respect for elders in word and deed, the importance of hard work and education, and the need to achieve. As indicated later in the chapter, in some cases this cultural immersion also succeeded in transmitting a transnational consciousness to the second generation. Ironically, however, in other cases West Indian culture in the home seems to have acted as a substitute for direct sustained contact with the West Indies. In this way, it was possible for some second-generation respondents to feel "ethnic" without personally maintaining sustained contact or feeling strong emotional or ideological ties to the region. Without making much effort, these individuals could gain a great deal of information about their parents' homelands.

Stewart is an example of how this could work. During the interview (and as indicated in the quote), he admitted to possessing a low level of transnational consciousness. His infrequent visits to Jamaica are the most tangible manifestation of this fact. Despite this, because of his mother's close ties to the island and the Jamaican community in New York City, he found it impossible not to view himself as being, in some sense, Jamaican, but he derived his ethnic identity primarily from the New York context. To take a second example: a number of the respondents reported that they did not actually initiate phone calls to the West Indies. These calls were initiated by their parents or other elders within the household, and once the telephone contact had been made, the second-generation individuals could participate in the conversations freely. Alternatively, they could wait to glean important bits of information from other members of the family who had participated in the phone conversation. That is, these second-generation individuals treated the process of telephoning their West Indian relatives as being of secondary importance. The information gleaned from these conversations might be interesting, but it was of less significance to them than it was to their parents, who had a more recent and direct connection to events back home. Still, even secondhand information about the West Indies could help reinforce the second generation's ethnic identity by adding to the overall West Indian atmosphere in immigrant families. Because of dynamics such as these, in some ways many of the second-generation individuals I interviewed could be viewed as "free riders" in the sense that they cherished an ethnic identity that ultimately was nourished by living in a thriving transnational social space. But the respondents themselves were not necessarily undertaking transnational activities that nourished this identity. The mere fact of living in ethnic enclaves was sufficient to sustain their ethnic identity. Apart from family, the respondents mentioned a number of other factors that were crucial in this regard: attending schools with large numbers of West Indian students, participating in ethnic churches, participating in ethnic festivals, and obtaining information from friends who had traveled to the West Indies.

In discussing the notion that for many second-generation individuals ethnicity may be rooted in American ethnic enclaves more than in the West Indies, we also need to note the importance of hybridity in ethnicity. For approximately 60 percent of the respondents in the present study, being West Indian was intermingled with a sense that they were also American. That is, they held a hybrid identity such as "West Indian American" or, say, "Barbadian American." This fact is noteworthy because those with a hyphenated identity are oriented to the United States in important ways. A number of respondents related experiences that underscore the significance of American birth as far as identity is concerned. For instance, Janet, a young professional of mixed Barbadian-Guyanese ancestry, reported that her immigrant parents maintained close contact with their homelands and wanted their American-born children to view themselves as West Indian. However, jarring encounters with Barbadian students when she was in college caused her to reevaluate her self-identity. Though friendly, these students resisted her claims to a Barbadian identity, arguing that being American-born, affluent, and without a trace of an accent, Janet could not really understand their financial and cultural adjustment struggles. Instead, the Barbadian students insisted that Janet claim the more accurate identifier "Barbadian American."

Similarly, John, a twenty-three-year-old construction site supervisor, recounted the painful struggles within his family over questions of ethnic authenticity. Three of his siblings had been born in Jamaica, while he and a younger sister had been born in this country. This made for problems in his family whenever John attempted to assert his Jamaican-ness by manipulating symbols of Jamaican culture (such as speaking patois). His Jamaican-born siblings resisted his right to manipulate such symbols, claiming that John was a "Yankee" rather than a "true Jamaican."

Although experiences such as these did not end Janet's and John's desire for a West Indian identity, they underscored that American birth (and also probably socialization in the United States from an early age) added a distinctive new element to the second generation's identity options. Both Janet and John reported that their painful experiences had caused them to view themselves as more American than they had originally thought. At the time of the interview Janet was planning to marry her African American boyfriend, and John reported that though he still participated in Jamaican cultural events, he—unlike the rest of his family—had visited Jamaica only once in eighteen years.

VARIATION IN TRANSNATIONAL BEHAVIOR AND CONSCIOUSNESS

The previous discussion points to the importance of variation where transnationalism is concerned. Although this research found a low level of transnational consciousness overall among the second-generation West Indians who were studied, other research has pointed to high levels of such consciousness (see, for example, Glick-Schiller and Fouron 1999). In all likelihood, transnational contact and consciousness vary over time (recall the previous conclusion that some periods of West Indian immigration have been transnational but not others) and between groups. The between-group variation arises from the simple fact that the context of immigration varies from group to group and hence responses also vary by group. For instance, because of Haiti's history and relationship with the United States, Haitian immigrants tend to be intensely involved with Haiti. However, such intensity of involvement does not necessarily characterize other West Indian immigrants. Compared with Haitian immigrants, for example, Jamaican immigrants may be less concerned with day-to-day politics in their homeland because Jamaican politics is generally more predictable.

This argument, however, would probably have been less valid in the 1970s, when Jamaican society was more convulsed than it is today by a combination of political turbulence, economic woes, and crime. A similar point could be made for Grenada in the 1980s during and after the Maurice Bishop regime. Both countries experienced stresses during those time periods that called their very existence into question. Under such circumstances, immigrants from those two nations understandably evinced more than run-of-the-mill interest in the events taking place back home. In the 1970s, for instance, Jamaican immigrants had good cause to worry about the physical safety of their relatives in Jamaica because the crime rate reached extraordinarily high levels (see, for example, Stone 1989). Thus, it is likely that Jamaican immigrants in the 1970s and Grenadian immigrants in the 1980s had more intense contact with their respective societies than is the case today.

Despite reporting lower levels of transnational contact and consciousness overall than their immigrant parents, the second-generation individuals in this study also displayed noticeable variation in both of these variables, as well as in intensity of ethnic identification. The reasons they cited for this variation may be grouped into five categories: the influence of the migration cycle; parental influence; the influence of the life cycle; cost; and fortuitous events.

The Migration Cycle

It has been argued that immigration should be conceived of as a cycle instead of as a linear process in which an individual leaves one country and enters another. The latter movement constitutes migration, but it also implies that once the individual reaches his or her destination the process is ended. In contrast, viewing immigration as cyclical underlines the point that immigration often involves whole families and that typically, as in the case of West Indians, the family migrates in piecemeal fashion. A mother or father will migrate first, establish herself or himself, then send for the remaining family members. This process may take years, but until all family members—"family" being defined here in subjective terms—have arrived in the new country, migration cannot be said to have been completed. The migration cycle comes to a close when all members of the family have arrived in the host society (Palmer 1990).

This view of migration helps to explain one of the dynamics that emerged from this research on second-generation West Indians. As it turns out, the number of family members remaining in the West Indies is a key factor in explaining the extent to which second-generation West Indians maintain contact with the region. The respondents defined "family" differently. For some, family includes uncles, aunts, cousins, and grandmothers; for others, it includes only closer kin, such as brothers and sisters. Typically, a large number of remaining family members leads to closer contact with the West Indies, while a small number of remaining family members leads to less contact. For instance, Sharon, a twenty-one-year-old college student, emphasized during our interview that she maintains close contact with Jamaica. She phones at least six times a year and travels to the island at least three times a year. Notice the following exchange:

> Q: Why do you maintain such close contact with Jamaica?
>
> A: Most of my family is still there, and . . . it's only my generation and my parents' generation—like their brothers and sisters—that are really in the U.S. For the most part, everybody else is in Jamaica still. . . . I have uncles and aunts that have actually never left.
>
> Q: So then that means that you are close to your aunts and uncles?
>
> A: And my cousins.

Compare this response with that of Carla, another twenty-one-year-old college student. She maintains virtually no contact with Jamaica and last visited the island at age nine for a funeral. During our interview she hastened to explain why my questions on transnational contact did not apply to her:

> A: Let me explain further. My dad's family doesn't live in Jamaica anymore.
>
> Q: They all live here?
>
> A: Well, his immediate family does, because they all came over. My mom, she only came to the States because she met my dad. . . . The rest of her siblings went to Canada, and then the one went to Trinidad. . . . The only people who are left back in Jamaica are my . . . grandfather. My grandmother died. None of his children are left in Jamaica; and, oh, one, his son, his only son is in Jamaica. . . . His kids, all three of them left, too. They went to Canada, and I think ——— is in New York. So, like, no one is left in Jamaica.

Parental Influence

It emerged from the interviews that West Indian immigrant parents exercise significant influence over the degree of transnational contact maintained by their American-born (or -reared) children and over their ethnic identity. There were several cases in which parents had soured on maintaining ties with their countries of birth and actively discouraged their children from cultivating a West Indian identity. As might be expected, these second-generation West Indians maintained little contact with the West Indies, though several expressed regret that this was the case. Of course, the dynamics also work in the opposite direction. Parents who maintained close contact with the West Indies encouraged their children to do the same. They were most successful in accomplishing this goal when children were young and had little choice over decisions to maintain contact (see the later discussion on the life cycle).

A good example of a situation in which parents discouraged the development of ethnic identity and transnational contact in their children comes from my interview with Yvonne, a twenty-three-year-old administrative assistant. I asked her how she identifies herself. She replied:

> I would have to say . . . American, because my mother and my father both, I think, they wanted us really Americanized. Totally. So, ah, they were really strict about that. Like, for example, my mother doesn't want us to talk with an accent. She didn't want us to really pick it up; so she was really like: "You're in America, you're not in Guyana. Talk the way you're supposed to talk." She was really strict about that part. . . . She just feels it sounds nasty for someone who was born in America to have an accent even when they were not even from that country.

A closer examination of this attitude revealed that Yvonne's mother really disliked Guyana. One measure of this was that, since migrating to the United States in 1967, she had returned to Guyana only once, and that visit, Yvonne stated, was disastrous: her mother literally tried to leave the day after arriving. Yvonne, then twelve, accompanied her mother in what turned out to be her only visit to Guyana. During the interview Yvonne expressed a desire to revisit Guyana, but her mother had consistently discouraged this. Yvonne had continued to maintain tenuous contact with the one remaining relative in that country (a grandfather), telephoning approximately three times a year. However, this rate of contact placed Yvonne well below average, since overall the second-generation sample telephoned an average of sixteen times a year.

Two other examples of parental discouragement came from my interview with two sisters, Beverley and Laura. During the interviews both expressed regret that they had been discouraged from developing a Jamaican identity and pursuing contact with that country. They expressed a sense of loss that, at ages twenty-three and twenty-eight, respectively, neither felt authentically Jamaican. Both traced this to parental discouragement in their upbringing; Beverley stated that whenever the children asked about Jamaica the parents avoided the subject. Instead, their parents actively tried to Americanize them. (Although, significantly, both sisters agreed that their parents had also passed on many of the values—for instance, the centrality of education and discipline—that other second-generation respondents reported.) In probing Beverley's self-identity, I posed the following question:

> Q: So they pretty much left it up to you therefore to choose your own identity?
>
> A: Yes . . . I think that they didn't want us to identify with Jamaica like that. I mean, they . . . were from Jamaica. They could identify. They were born there, but they figured that because we were born here, we were Americans. . . . We would . . . ask questions about Jamaica, and they like, you know, either avoided the subject or didn't really tell us much; or it was pretty much short answers. So you kind of got it that they didn't want us to ask them any questions.

From our conversation it became apparent that Beverley regarded herself as more African American than West Indian. It also seemed apparent, however, that she regretted not having developed a Jamaican self-identity and not having kept in touch with Jamaica. I inquired whether this was the case:

> Well, yeah, because, you know, they [her Jamaican relatives] are, they are family; . . . but like I said, my mother never really spoke about, you know, her relatives very much and so, it's like, we feel like we don't know them . . . even though they are family. . . . Even though we are blood-related, we [do] not, you know, know one another that well. . . . It's not too late, but sometimes it feels like it is. Like, when will I ever get the time or the money to visit?

Beverley's situation contrasts sharply with that of someone like Murphy, a nineteen-year-old college student. He maintained very close contact with Jamaica and in fact indicated that over the past five years his contact with the island had intensified. Also, though he migrated to this country at age one, he strongly affirmed that he was Jamaican. For instance, he held almost a primordial view of his ethnicity, arguing that his sense of Jamaican-ness was something in him "that needs to come out." He also stated that at the age of seven he started fantasizing about becoming prime minister of Jamaica. In our conversation Murphy attributed this strong sense of ethnicity to his parents' influence:

> I know a lot [about] . . . Jamaican culture. Like Christmas, you know, we eat curried goat and everything . . . curried chicken. . . . I know about all the foods, all the national holidays . . . national heroes, you know. . . . My parents taught me a lot about Jamaica. . . I know a lot about America, too, but they made sure that I knew about Jamaica; and from there . . . it just got into me. And I think the clincher was I just . . . knew where I was born, and it is from there that I moved on.

Rose, a second-generation woman of Grenadian-Barbadian parentage, along with Murphy, was one of the three individuals who strongly identified as West Indian. Notice the similarity of her response to Murphy's:

> Sometimes I wish I was born there, you know, so I could have that experience of going to school over there. . . . I guess over there schooling is so much different, also because of the respect that is given in the school. It's not like over here, where sometimes you can't even learn sometimes because the classes are so disruptive.

The Life Cycle and Cost

An individual's stage in his or her life cycle emerged from the interviews as one of the important factors determining degree of transnational contact. It was found that, for some second-generation respondents, the present level of contact is not a reliable guide to previous intensity of contact. A pattern emerged for some of the second generation: as children, they had frequently accompanied their parents on visits to the West Indies, but as they grew older they visited less often and then almost not at all after they entered college, with its demanding schedule. After college, however, the frequency of contact picked up again, although not necessarily to the same level as when they were young.

Carol, a thirty-four-year-old professional, is a good example of this pattern. She migrated to the United States at the age of two, and as a child, she made frequent visits to the island with her Jamaican-oriented mother. However, she stopped traveling to Jamaica, she stated, "the moment my mother stopped paying the ticket." That happened when she became a teenager. As Carol grew older and attained professional success, however, she started to feel an urge to rediscover her "roots." Her young children proved to be an important catalyst for these sentiments, since they were very close to their grandmother. They started to express a desire to know where their grandmother and mother had come from. Carol's desire to reestablish contact with Jamaica intensified sharply in 1995 when she entered a relationship with a Jamaican man.

Reflecting a desire to distance herself from her ethnicity, she stated that for years she had specifically avoided dating co-ethnics. However, this relationship had proved to be a turning point in her life. Her new friend was deeply steeped in Jamaican culture (for example, he visited the island at least once a year) and was transmitting that attitude to her: in the previous four years she had visited at least three times and was planning a visit the year I interviewed her. She attributed this increased frequency of contact to her new friend's insistence that she know her culture. During the interview Carol expressed delight at being shown places in Jamaica that she never knew existed.

One sign of the reinvigoration of Carol's Jamaican identity was that, at the request of her new friend, she had started to learn how to cook Jamaican food. Also, her self-perception had begun to change. Despite the strong Jamaican presence in her mother's home, over the years she had put more and more emphasis on the American side of her identity. A recent dispute at her job had caused her to see that the Jamaican side of her self-identity had begun to reassert itself. She related that a debate had broken out among her coworkers over the proper term to use when describing people of African ancestry. She responded: "You can call me 'black,' I don't care. But at this point in my life I have to put 'Jamaican' in there somewhere. And since I have lived all my life in America . . . I guess I would just say, you know, 'Jamaican American' or 'American Jamaican,' or something like that."

Carol's story shows that cost overlaps with stage of life to influence the likelihood of maintaining contact with the West Indies. Although airfares to the Caribbean are relatively cheap, they can still look daunting—as they did to Carol (and Beverley in the previous example)—to a young adult who is not economically secure and whose parents do not want to underwrite the costs of travel. Costs can be especially pressing for college students, and signifi-

cantly, the students who reported close contact with the West Indies also reported having part-time jobs or supportive parents. As
Nell, a college student who visits Jamaica often, stated, she visited
the island frequently because her father "always pays." However,
once the second generation becomes economically secure—as
Carol had done—cost considerations become less of a factor where
travel, phoning, and remittances are concerned.

Fortuitous Circumstances

Carol's story also illustrates that fortuitous (random) circumstances
can influence both the likelihood of maintaining contact with the
West Indies and ethnic identity. In Carol's case, these circumstances
took the form of a relationship with a co-ethnic who was more committed to his ethnic identity than she was: he felt more Jamaican
than she did and maintained closer contact with the island. After
their relationship began, he essentially pulled Carol in his direction.

My interview with Mira also illustrates the impact of fortuitous
(and mundane) circumstances on the extent to which some second-
generation individuals maintain contact with the West Indies. In
Mira's case, the natural environment and the relative underdevelopment of the West Indies were the circumstances that pushed her
away from close contact with the region. Mira was seventeen, on the
verge of graduating from high school, and had last visited Jamaica
when she was only two years old. Yet she reported having vivid
memories of that visit—memories that prevented her from wanting
to make a return visit. During our conversation she expressed a
strong sense of self as Jamaican, even though she had not visited the
island in fifteen years. Probing into this, I elicited her response that
she did not need to visit Jamaica to maintain her identity as Jamaican,
since the culture was strong in her family and among her friends. She
also explained why she has been reluctant to return to Jamaica, and
specifically to the rural district from which her parents had come:

> [It is] not that I don't like Jamaica, but it's dark at night. There's a lot of bugs
> and things [that the] American part of me [dislikes]: I can't stand bugs—
> especially the foreign ones. I don't like them, and when I come from here
> and I go there and I get mosquito bites . . . it's annoying! . . . It was torturous,
> so I didn't want to go back. I said if I was in a resort, fine! I'll be fine. But
> it was dark. I had to walk in the dark, and it was so rocky.

CONCLUSION

As immigration research has increasingly focused on transnationalism, second-generation transnationalism has become an issue. This logical extension of research interests is part of the larger issue of what is to become of the "new" second generation, and it has revealed how little we know about this group. As a contribution to this new field, this chapter has discussed attitudes toward transnationalism among one subgroup of second-generation West Indians. These individuals live in a transnational social space that has become more vibrant over the years as immigration into the United States has continued at high levels. Many of the individuals I studied were aware that they have benefited from living in West Indian enclaves,[10] even if they took them for granted. Ironically, these enclaves may also inhibit transnational behavior and consciousness among the second generation. This does not necessarily mean that second-generation West Indians completely distance themselves from their parents' homelands. That was rarely the case among the individuals I interviewed. Rather, ethnic enclaves undermine their incentive to maintain contact by facilitating the spread of West Indian culture, as well as news about the region, in the United States. In essence, West Indian ethnic enclaves represent reservoirs of West Indian culture that, to some extent, can substitute for actual contact with the West Indies. This substitutability, combined with the fact that American birth (or socialization from a young age) already predisposes the second generation to view itself as American, competes against tendencies toward transnationalism that arise from living in a transnational social space. Most of the respondents in this study regarded their immigrant parents as relatively more interested in the West Indies, and they seemed content with this assessment. They saw themselves as American but also as West Indian, and they drew their ethnic identity primarily from their families and the ethnic enclaves in which they had been reared. Still, the respondents exhibited variation within the limits of their lessened interest in the West Indies. Although a few maintained close contact with their parents' homelands and a few had very little contact, most respondents fell somewhere in between these poles: they maintained contact but attached less significance to such contact than did their parents. In this research, the variation was explained by the influence of the immigration cycle, parents, the stage of life, cost, and fortuitous events. However, these variables were probably but a few of many possibilities, and more research needs to be conducted to investigate other factors that may influence second-generation West Indian transnationalism.

NOTES

1. The trend toward dual citizenship in the United States is a good example of this. See, for instance, Cortese (2001) and Zachary (1995).
2. For instance, Eisner (1961, 149–50) reports that the failure of the first Panama Canal project in 1888 caused mass suffering among immigrant Jamaican workers, and this led to efforts on the part of the Jamaican colonial government to repatriate some of these workers.
3. Thirty-nine respondents in all were interviewed, but four were dropped from the final sample either because they did not self-identify as Anglo–West Indian or because they migrated to the United States as adolescents.
4. I include Panama as West Indian because of its connections to the islands and because a Panamanian individual I interviewed viewed herself as Anglo–West Indian.
5. This woman considered herself West Indian because her ancestors were of West Indian descent and she primarily associated with West Indians from the islands.
6. Many West Indians routinely export to their relatives in the West Indies large barrels stocked with a variety of merchandise, ranging from foodstuffs to electronic appliances. A whole industry catering to the exporting of these barrels has grown up in West Indian enclaves throughout New York City.
7. All names are pseudonyms.
8. Two respondents expressed ambivalence about their identity, and another four identified as black, though their responses did not differ substantially from those respondents who expressed a hybrid identity.
9. In previous research conducted among West Indian immigrants, I also encountered a few individuals who evinced little interest in the West Indies. They attributed this lack of interest to the presence of vibrant West Indian enclaves in New York City that reproduced many aspects of West Indian culture. They argued that because of these enclaves they did not need to go back to the West Indies often (see Vickerman 1999).

10. Here I am using this term simply to mean an area with a high concentration of a particular ethnic group, and not in the sense in which Alejandro Portes uses it—that is, to refer to an ethnic group's demographic, economic, and political dominance of a distinct geographical area (see, for example, Portes 1996).

REFERENCES

Basch, Linda. 2001. "Transnational Social Relations and the Politics of National Identity: An Eastern Caribbean Case Study." In *Islands in the City,* edited by Nancy Foner. Berkeley: University of California Press.

Bray, David B. 1987. "The Dominican Exodus: Origins, Problems, Solutions." In *The Caribbean Exodus,* edited by Barry B. Levine. New York: Praeger.

Conniff, Michael L. 1985. *Black Labor on a White Canal: Panama, 1904–1981.* Pittsburgh: University of Pittsburgh Press, 1985.

Cordero-Guzman, Hector R., Robert C. Smith, and Ramon Grosfoguel. 2001. *Migration, Transnationalization, and Race in a Changing New York.* Philadelphia: Temple University Press.

Cortese, Amy. 2001. "As Rules Ease, More Citizens Choose to Fly Two Flags." *New York Times,* July 15.

Eisner, Gisela. 1961. *Jamaica: 1830–1930.* Manchester: Manchester University Press.

Fernandez-Kelly, Patricia, and Richard Schauffler. 1994. "Divided Fates: Immigrant Children in a Restructured U.S. Economy." *International Migration Review* 28(4): 662–89.

Foner, Nancy. 1997. "What's New About Transnationalism?: New York Immigrants Today and at the Turn of the Century." Paper presented at the conference "Transnational Communities and the Political Economy of New York in the 1990s," New School for Social Research, New York (February 21–22).

———. 1998. "The Transnationals." *Natural History* (March 3): 34–35.

Fraser, Peter D. 1990. "Nineteenth-Century West Indian Migration to Britain." In *In Search of a Better Life: Perspectives on Migration from the Caribbean,* edited by Ransford W. Palmer. New York: Praeger.

Glick-Schiller, Nina, Linda Basch, and Cristina Szanton-Blanc. 1994. *Nations Unbound: Transnational Projects, Postcolonial Predicaments, and Deterritorialized Nation-states.* Langhorne, Penn.: Gordon and Breach.

———. 1995. "From Immigrant to Transmigrant: Theorizing Transnational Migration." *Anthropological Quarterly* 68(January): 48–63.

Glick-Schiller, Nina, and Georges E. Fouron. 1999. "Terrains of Blood and Nation: Haitian Transnational Social Fields." *Ethnic and Racial Studies* 22(2): 340–65.

Gmelch, George. 1992. *Double Passage: The Lives of Caribbean Migrants Abroad and Back Home.* Ann Arbor: University of Michigan Press.

Ho, Christine. 1993. "The Internationalization of Kinship and the Feminization of Caribbean Migration: The Case of Afro-Trinidadian Immigrants in Los Angeles." *Human Organization* A52(1): 32–40.

Koch, Charles W. 1977. "Jamaican Blacks and Their Descendants in Costa Rica." *Social and Economic Studies* 36(3): 339–61.

Margolis, Maxine L. 1998. *An Invisible Minority.* Boston: Allyn and Bacon.

Mintz, Sidney W. 1998. "The Localization of Anthropological Practice." *Critique of Anthropology* 18(2): 117–33.

Oropesa, R. S., and Nancy S. Lansdale. 1997. "In Search of the New Second Generation: Alternative Strategies for Identifying Second-Generation Children and Understanding Their Acquisition of English." *Sociological Perspectives* 40(3): 492–55.

Osofsky, Gilbert. 1966. *Harlem: The Making of a Ghetto.* New York: Harper and Row.

Palmer, Ransford. 1990. "Caribbean Development and the Migration Imperative." In *In Search of a Better Life: Perspectives on Migration from the Caribbean,* edited by Ransford Palmer. New York: Praeger.

Patterson, Orlando. 1994. "Ecumenical America: Global Culture and the American Cosmos." *World Policy Journal* 11: 103–17.

Perlmann, Joel, and Roger Waldinger. 1998. "Are the Children of Today's Immigrants Making It?" *The Public Interest* 132: 73–96.

Pessar, Patricia R. 1990. "Dominican International Migration: The Role of Households and Social Networks." In *In Search of a Better Life: Perspectives on Migration from the Caribbean,* edited by Ransford Palmer. New York: Praeger.

———. 1995. *A Visa for a Dream.* Boston: Allyn and Bacon.

Portes, Alejandro. 1996. *The New Second Generation.* New York: Russell Sage Foundation.

Portes, Alejandro, Luis E. Guarnizo, and Patricia Landolt. 1999. "Introduction: Pitfalls and Promise of an Emergent Research Field." *Ethnic and Racial Studies* 22(2): 217–37.

Portes, Alejandro, and Rubén Rumbaut. 1996. *Immigrant America.* Berkeley: University of California Press.

Reid, Ira D. A. 1939. *The Negro Immigrant.* New York: Columbia University Press.

Richardson, Bonham. 1983. *Caribbean Migrants.* Knoxville: University of Tennessee Press.

————. 1984. "Slavery to Freedom in the British Caribbean: Ecological Considerations." *Caribbean Geography* 1 (3): 164–75.

Robotham, Don. 1998. "Transnationalism in the Caribbean: Formal and Informal." *American Ethnologist* 25(2): 307–21.

Rouse, Roger. 1995. "Thinking Through Transnationalism: Notes on the Cultural Politics of Class Relations in the Contemporary United States." *Public Culture* 7: 353–402.

Soto, Isa Maria. 1987. "West Indian Child Fostering: Its Role in Migrant Exchanges." In *Caribbean Life in New York*, edited by Constance R. Sutton and Elsa M. Chaney. New York: Center for Migration Studies.

Stephens, Michelle. 1998. "Black Transnationalism and the Politics of National Identity: West Indian Intellectuals in Harlem in the Age of War and Revolution." *American Quarterly* 50(3): 592–608.

Stone, Carl. 1989. *Politics Versus Economics.* Kingston: Heinemann.

Sutton, Constance. 1987. "The Caribbeanization of New York City and the Emergence of a Transnational Sociocultural System." In *Caribbean Life in New York City: Sociocultural Dimensions,* edited by Constance Sutton and Elsa M. Chaney. New York: Center for Migration Studies.

————. 1992. "Transnational Identities and Cultures: Caribbean Immigrants in the United States." In *Immigration and Ethnicity,* edited by Michael D'Innocenzo and Josef P. Sirefman. Westport, Conn.: Greenwood Press.

Sutton, Constance, and Elsa M. Chaney, eds. 1987. *Caribbean Life in New York City: Sociocultural Dimensions.* New York: Center for Migration Studies.

Thomas-Hope, Elizabeth. 1986. "Caribbean Diaspora—The Inheritance of Slavery: Migration from the Commonwealth Caribbean." In *The Caribbean in Europe,* edited by Colin Brock. London: Frank Cass and Co.

Vertovec, Steven. 1999. "Conceiving and Researching Transnationalism." *Ethnic and Racial Studies* 22(2): 447–62.

Vickerman, Milton. 1999. *Crosscurrents: West Indian Immigrants and Race.* New York: Oxford University Press.

Waters, Mary. 1994. "Ethnic and Racial Identities of Second-Generation Black Immigrants in New York City." *International Migration Review* 28(4): 795–820.

Wolf, Diane L. 1997. "Family Secrets: Transnational Struggles Among Children of Filipino Immigrants." *Sociological Perspectives* 40(3): 457–73.

Zachary, Pascal. 1995. "Dual Citizenship Is a Double-edged Sword." *Wall Street Journal,* March 25.

Zhou, Min, and Carl L. Bankston. 1994. "Social Capital and the Adaptation of the Second Generation: The Case of Vietnamese Youth in New Orleans." *International Migration Review* 28(4): 821–45.

— Chapter 15 —

"Việt Nam, Nước Tôi" (Vietnam, My Country): Vietnamese Americans and Transnationalism

Yen Le Espiritu and Thom Tran

If you are disconnected from your homeland, it's difficult to know where you come from or where you are going.

—Andrew Lam (cited in Nguyen 2000, 59)

T HE GLOBALIZATION OF labor, capital, and culture, the restructuring of world politics, and the expansion of new technologies of communication and transportation—all have driven people and products across the globe at a dizzying pace. In the last decade, reflecting the current saliency of transnational processes, scholars have shifted their analytical paradigms from the dualism inherent in the classic models of migration—the assumption that migrants move through bipolar spaces in a progressive time frame—to nonbinary theoretical perspectives that are not predicated on modernist assumptions about space and time (Kearney 1995, 227–28). Recent writings on the "transnational socio-cultural system," the "transnational community," "transmigrants," the "deterritorialized nation-state," and "transnational grassroots politics" have challenged our notions of *place*, reminding us to think about places not only as specific geographic and physical sites, but also as circuits and networks (Lipsitz 1999). They also have contradicted localized and bounded social science concepts such as community and culture, calling attention instead to the transnational relations and linkages between overseas communities and between them and their homeland (Clifford 1994; Okamura 1998; Basch, Glick-Schiller, and Szanton-Blanc 1994).

Transnational migration studies form a highly fragmented field; there continues to be much disagreement as to the scope of the field and the outcome of the transnational processes under observation (Portes, Guarzino, and Landolt 1999; Glick-Schiller 1997). Our interest in the concept of transnationalism is less empirical and more epistemological. That is, we are interested in transnationalism not (only) because it captures a novel and emergent phenomenon, but because it is a valuable conceptual tool, one that disrupts the narrow emphasis on "modes of incorporation" characteristic of much of the published work in the field of U.S. immigration studies. Although no longer bound by a simplistic assimilationist paradigm, the field has remained "America-centric," with an overwhelming emphasis on the process of "becoming American" (Goldberg 1992; Archdeacon 1983; Handlin 1973). The concept of transnationalism, as a heuristic device, highlights instead the range and depth of migrants' lived experience in multinational social fields (Goldberg 1992).

It is important to note that transnational activities are not new. As early as 1916, Randolph Bourne, in his classic essay "Trans-National America," argued that the nation might have to accept "dual citizenship" and "free and mobile passage of the immigrant between America and his native land." Given the notoriety of Bourne's essay, why did the concept of transnationalism never really enter the lexicon of political and scholarly debates on immigration? Instead, "pluralism," "the melting pot," and "assimilation"—terms that presumed unidirectional migration flows—dominated our discussion. Barry Goldberg (1992, 212–13) suggests that the idea of transnationalism, regardless of the observable dimensions of the transnational social fields, was sidelined because it posed too much of a challenge to the "mythistory" of the United States as the beacon of hope and the land of opportunity. Veblen calls this willful nonrecognition "trained incapacity": the inability to see what is there because of how we have been trained to look (cited in Smith 1998, 197).

This chapter examines identity formation and behavior among Vietnamese American young adults in San Diego, including their transnational practices. We begin with the premise that Vietnamese immigrants and their children do not merely insert or incorporate themselves into existing spaces in the United States but also transform these spaces and create new spaces for themselves, such as the transnational space. Commenting on the transnational lives of Tongan migrants, Cathy Small (1998, 193) urges us to pay attention to the dynamics that occur in the "space between"—the transnational space within which new forms of economy, family, tradition, and identity are forged. Our conceptualization of transnationalism includes both actual transnational activities (in the form of home visits, kinship ties, and remittances) and imagined returns to the homeland (through selective memory, cultural rediscovery, and sentimental longings). That is, we argue that transnationalism takes place not only at the literal but at the symbolic level—at the level of imagination, shared memory, and "inventions of traditions" (Hobsbawm and Ranger 1983). Along the same line, we conceive of homeland not only as a physical place that immigrants and their children return to for visits but also as a concept and a desire—a place to return to through the imagination. Ketu Katrak (1996, 201) has described this return through the imagination as the "simultaneity of geography . . . the possibility of living here in body and elsewhere in mind and imagination."

We contend that the practice of symbolic transnationalism is most evident—and most poignant—in the lives of the second generation: How do young Vietnamese who have never been "home" imagine the "homeland"? And how do they recall that which is somewhere else, and that which was perhaps never known? The specificities of the Vietnamese experience also encourage the development of symbolic transnationalism. From 1975 to 1994 exiled Vietnamese in the United States could not legally travel to, invest in, or send large sums of remittances to Vietnam. Declared an "enemy nation" by the U.S. government under the Trading with the Enemy Act, Vietnam remained out of reach for most Vietnamese Americans, particularly the second generation, who had very little, if any, direct experience with their parents' homeland. Additionally, prior to the đổi mới period instituted in 1986, Vietnam's policy was to not welcome "Việt Kiều" (overseas Vietnamese, in the term used by national Vietnamese) to return. In other words, until 1994 symbolic transnationalism was more available to the Vietnamese American community. To say that certain transnational practices are symbolic is not to say that they are unimportant; indeed, we argue that symbolic transnationalism influences the ways in which young Vietnamese Americans imagine themselves, their social membership, and their future plans. We are particularly interested in the ways in which young Vietnamese Americans imagine Vietnam, their perceived responsibilities toward the country, and the critical role that the representation of Vietnam plays in the construction of their ethnic identity in the United States.

HISTORICAL CONTEXT FOR VIETNAMESE RESETTLEMENT IN THE UNITED STATES AND IN SAN DIEGO

Why the United States?

Calling attention to global structures of inequality, recent social theorists have linked migration processes with the global penetration of Western economic systems, technological infrastructures, and popular cultures into non-Western countries (Burawoy 1976; Petras 1978; Portes 1978; Zolberg 1986). Although their details vary, these works posit that the internationalization of the capitalistic economic system to Third World countries has produced imbalances in their internal social and economic structures and subsequently has spurred migration (Portes 1987). A transnational approach that stresses the global structures of inequality is critical for understanding Vietnamese migration to the United States; that is, Vietnamese are in the United States because of U.S. military action and economic expansion in Vietnam and in Asia more generally.

Throughout the period from 1945 to 1975, North and South Vietnam dueled in a bloody civil war. With each side receiving significant foreign assistance, what started out as a civil war became a war of foreign intervention (Viviani 1984, 11). As the Communist Viet Minh (supported by China and the Soviet Union) consolidated their power in the North, the United States pledged military and political support to the anti-Communist regime in South Vietnam. With the Communist victory in China in 1949 and the outbreak of war in Korea in 1950, Vietnam had become vital to the U.S. mission of containing the spread of communism. In 1965 the United States and its allies committed large numbers of combat troops to Vietnam; the North Vietnamese retaliated by sending troops to the South to assist the Viet Cong. By the end of 1967 there were half a million U.S. troops in Vietnam and the United States was pouring $2 billion of aid per month into the war (Chan 1991, 154). Between 1971 and 1973 South Vietnam was almost completely dependent on U.S. financial and material assistance for the military, for administration, and for the economy (Viviani 1984, 13).

With the collapse of the U.S.-backed government in South Vietnam in 1975, about 200,000 Vietnamese fled war-torn Vietnam in search of asylum in other countries. Influenced by the pervasive U.S. presence in Vietnam in the decade before 1975, some 130,000 Vietnamese refugees fled to the United States that year; the majority of them were leaders of the last regime who had the most to lose under the new government—military personnel, government officials, the well-to-do, and the educated.[1] Vietnamese remain one of the largest refugee groups resettled in the United States since the mid-1970s. The 2000 census counted 1,122,528 Vietnamese in the United States, almost doubling the 1990 census count (see table 15.1). This population increase is due not only to fertility rates but to continuing immigration.[2]

Why San Diego?

The Interagency Task Force (IATF) set up to resettle the first wave of refugees adopted a policy of dispersal in an attempt to reduce the economic impact on any single community and to speed up the process of assimilation (Liu 1979; Rumbaut 1995; Do 1988). Although all fifty states resettled Vietnamese refugees, California received the largest share—21 percent of the first 130,000 refugees. Texas was second with 7 percent. Thus, in spite of IATF's dispersal policy, secondary migration led to the congregation of Vietnamese in only a few states: 52 percent of the 2000 population and 60 percent of the 1990 population was concentrated in California and Texas (see table 15.1). Vietnamese favored these two states for their

TABLE 15.1 Ten States in Which Vietnamese Americans Congregate: 1990 and 2000 Censuses

| State | 2000 | | 1990 | |
	Population	Percentage of Vietnamese Americans in the United States	Population	Percentage of Vietnamese Americans in the United States
California	447,032	39.8	280,223	45.6
Texas	134,961	12.0	69,634	11.3
Washington	46,149	4.1	18,696	3.0
Virginia	37,309	3.3	20,693	3.4
Massachusetts	33,962	3.0	15,449	2.5
Florida	33,190	3.0	16,346	2.7
Pennsylvania	30,037	2.7	15,887	2.6
Louisiana	24,358	2.2	17,598	2.9
New York	23,818	2.1	15,555	2.5
Illinois	19,101	1.7	10,309	1.7
Total in the ten states	829,917	73.9	480,390	78.2
Total in the United States	1,122,528	100.0	614,547	100.0

Source: U.S. Bureau of the Census, Census of Population and Housing (1990, 2000).

temperate climate and socioeconomic opportunities. Texas provided opportunities in the fishing industry, and California in the aerospace and microelectronic industries (Desbarats 1985).

According to the 2000 census, about 40 percent of the U.S. Vietnamese population resided in California, with most clustering in southern California (see table 15.2). San Diego ranked as the sixth most popular metropolitan destination for Vietnamese resettlement in the United States, and the fourth most popular in California. In 2000 there were 33,504 Vietnamese in San Diego, up from 21,111 in 1990. Although the Vietnamese make up only a small proportion of the total population of San Diego, they are the second-largest Asian American population there after the Filipinos.

STUDYING VIETNAMESE IN SAN DIEGO

This study consists of both quantitative and qualitative data. In the summer and fall of 1998 we surveyed 114 Vietnamese American youth who attended the University of California at San Diego (UCSD), Miramar Community College, or Mesa Community College. All three college campuses have a significant Asian American population. In the fall of 1998, 38 percent of UCSD's total population were Asian American students. As the fourth-largest Asian American group on campus (behind Chinese, Filipinos, and Korean), Vietnamese American students made up 4 percent of the campus population. The Asian American population constituted 20 percent of the total population at Mesa and about 30 percent at Miramar. Detailed ethnic breakdowns were unavailable for the fall of 1998, but based on statistics gathered prior to this time, half of the Asian American students at Miramar were Filipino and the rest were Vietnamese. Reflecting the large number of Vietnamese who lived in Linda Vista and East San Diego, the majority of the Asian American students at Mesa Community College were Vietnamese Americans.

We selected a public research institution (UCSD) and two community colleges (Miramar and Mesa) in an attempt to diversify the socioeconomic backgrounds, generation, and immigration cohort of our sample. Our sample consisted of students who were active in ethnic organizations such as the Vietnamese Student Association

TABLE 15.2 Ten California Counties with the Highest Number of Vietnamese Americans: 1990 and 2000 Censuses

County	2000		1990	
	Population	Percentage of Vietnamese Americans in California	Population	Percentage of Vietnamese Americans in California
Orange	135,548	30.3	71,822	25.6
Santa Clara	99,986	22.4	54,212	19.3
Los Angeles	78,102	17.5	62,594	22.3
San Diego	33,504	7.5	21,111	7.5
Alameda	23,817	5.3	13,374	4.8
Sacramento	16,372	3.7	9,497	—
San Francisco	10,722	2.4	9,712	3.5
San Bernardino	10,003	2.2	6,697	2.4
Riverside	6,612	1.5	4,618	1.6
San Joaquin	6,032	1.3	6,958	2.5
Total in the ten counties	420,698	94.1	251,098	89.6
Total in California	447,032	100.0	280,223	100.0

Source: U.S. Bureau of the Census, Census of Population and Housing (1990, 2000).

(VSA) and the Asian Pacific Islander Association (APSA) as well as students who were not. To reach the latter, we visited general education courses such as sociology, psychology, political science, biology, and English as well as Vietnamese language courses. We also asked respondents, professors, and counselors to refer us to other Vietnamese American students. The survey asked a series of questions about the respondents' family history and socioeconomic status, their ethnic identities and practices, their experiences with racism, and their ties to Vietnam.

To supplement the quantitative data, we conducted in-depth interviews with fifty students drawn from the larger survey pool. We began each interview by referring to the survey that the respondent had completed and then asking him or her to clarify or elaborate on certain answers. We were particularly interested in family ties to Vietnam, perception of Vietnam, experiences growing up in San Diego as racialized and gendered subjects, and relationships with parents. As discussed later in the chapter, the interview data were crucial in our analysis of the survey data: they provided not only missing information but also some *unexpected* or even *conflicting* interpretations of survey answers.

We believe that our own personal and social characteristics influenced the process of data collection, the quality of the materials we gathered, and our analysis of them. Both of us were born in Vietnam and came to the United States in 1975. We both identify ourselves as members of the 1.5 generation: Espiritu arrived in the United States at the age of twelve, and Tran at the age of seven. The fact that we grew up primarily in the United States made a difference to our respondents. Because they perceived us as being more like them than their parents and other first-generation Vietnamese adults, they were quite eager to speak to us and to share many intimate and even painful experiences with us. Our near-fluency in Vietnamese also facilitated the process, making it easier for some respondents to express certain words and phrases or to describe specific memories about Vietnam in the Vietnamese language. Although the majority of the respondents chose to speak primarily in English, we believe that the ability to switch to Vietnamese, when relevant, allowed these young Vietnamese Americans to relate a wider range of their experiences and to express themselves more fully.

DESCRIPTION OF SAMPLE

We believe that our study is among the first to examine Vietnamese American young adults. Previous studies of children of Vietnamese immigrants have focused primarily on adolescents under the age of eighteen (Portes and Rumbaut 2001; Kibria 1993; Zhou and Bankston 1998). In contrast, our respondents ranged between eighteen and twenty-five years old, with the average age being twenty-one. About two-thirds of the 114 students surveyed came from the second generation (62.5 percent) and about one-third came from the 1.5 generation (37.5 percent).[3] More females (56 percent) were represented in the sample than males (44 percent). The sample distributed almost evenly between UCSD (54 percent) and the two community colleges (46 percent). It is interesting to note that the community college sample contained more U.S.-born second generation than the UCSD sample. Given the specific context of exit and entrance of the different waves of refugees to the United States, the year in which these respondents and their parents arrived was a useful indicator of the historical context under which the respondents adapted. For those who were U.S.-born, we used the year in which their parents immigrated to categorize the wave in which they arrived in the United States. Thus, in this sample, 26 percent of the respondents were children of the first wave, 40 percent were children of the second wave, and 33 percent were children of the third wave. These figures roughly correspond to the proportion of refugees admitted under the three waves of migrants. Based on the numbers of Vietnamese resettled in the United States between 1975 and 1992, provided from the Office of Refugee Resettlement and the U.S. Department of Health and Human Service, we calculated that about 20 percent came in the first wave, 51 percent came in the second wave, and 29 percent came in the third wave. Accordingly, this sample can offer useful insight into the experiences of children arriving from different immigration waves.

Sociodemographic Profile of the Vietnamese in the United States and in San Diego

A 1990 analysis of the socioeconomic profile of Vietnamese in the United States reveals that Vietnamese refugees have made much progress since their resettlement in this country (Zhou and Bankston

1998). Nationwide, English proficiency rose from 27 percent in 1980 to 39 percent in 1990, and the proportion of college graduates over the age of twenty-five rose from 13 percent in 1980 to 17 percent in 1990. The labor force participation rate for males over sixteen also increased, from 66 to 72 percent. By 1990 the median household income of the Vietnamese nationwide was $33,500, above the average of $30,000 for all American households.[4] Public assistance also declined to 8 percent in 1990 (from 8.8 percent in 1980). Yet despite these measures of progress, the poverty rate among Vietnamese in 1990 still stood at 25 percent, significantly higher than the national average of 15 percent. The 1990 census data for San Diego reveal that the local Vietnamese population appeared to be less well-off than the general Vietnamese population: a higher proportion registered lower educational attainments and relied on public assistance. The overall San Diego population was also marked by a poverty rate higher than the national rate—27.2 percent, up from 22.1 percent in 1980. These bleaker economic indicators may be due to the influx of less-skilled refugees in the early 1980s and to the exodus of the more affluent Vietnamese to other California counties, such as Santa Ana and San Jose (Zhou and Bankston 1998, 9).

These objective socioeconomic indicators notwithstanding, we still found it difficult to measure the social class backgrounds of our respondents. Although it has been common to depict Vietnamese refugees as entering the bottom of the U.S. economic ladder and relying on public assistance, owing to a lack of English proficiency, formal education, and transferable skills, this broad picture glosses over the complex economic circumstances of these refugees. For example, how would one classify parents who received college degrees and worked as teachers in Vietnam but who now toil as a landscaper and a manicurist in the United States? Likewise, how would one classify parents who have only a third-grade education, now work as microelectronics assemblers, and own a home in a middle-class suburb through the pooling of family incomes and resources, overtime work, and multiple jobs? Nevertheless, in taking into consideration parental educational level, current occupation, and whether they own or rent their homes, we assessed that 65 percent of our sample came from a working-class background, while 22 percent were classified as middle-class and 13 percent as poor. The community college sample and the UCSD sample did not differ much in proportion of working-class students (62 percent and

66 percent, respectively). However, we found that the community college sample had more respondents in the poor category (21 percent) when compared to the UCSD sample (7 percent). Those whom we categorized as poor classified their families as poor themselves and also had parents who had little formal education, were not working, and rented their home.

GROWING UP AS VIETNAMESE AMERICANS

As indicated earlier, most adult Vietnamese are heavily concentrated in low-status, minimum-wage jobs. The parents' social and economic marginality has a profound impact on the lives of their children. The Vietnamese Americans in our qualitative sample grew up with parents who were always "so busy running around" trying to provide economically for the family. In contrast to the close-knit Vietnamese families depicted in popular discourse, our respondents seldom saw their parents and relied on peers almost exclusively for emotional support. Most reported growing up in mixed neighborhoods and attending primarily nonwhite schools. As a result, their reference group was not always white but included other groups of color. For example, a twenty-year-old female recalled that "in junior high, everyone wanted to be Filipino. It was 'cool.' To be a Filipino means to be in the popular crowd. To be really sociable." Although all reported that their parents discouraged them from socializing with African Americans, some related that their best friends during their adolescent years were African American. A twenty-two-year-old who grew up in a predominantly African American neighborhood described his speech as "black English": "People ask me if I am in a gang because I talk ghetto style. I think I get a lot of discrimination, even from fellow Asians, they just look down upon me. They just don't understand why I talk this way. I'm like, 'I can't speak white.' I can imitate it, but I am not comfortable doing it." When asked why she felt more comfortable with African Americans than white Americans, a twenty-three-year-old referred to their shared history: "I think it's understanding oppressions and sufferings, and understanding what it means to have your history just pulled out from under you."

The majority—about two thirds—in our quantitative sample related that they had experienced racial discrimination. When asked to elaborate on these experiences, all those interviewed complained that "Americans" often assumed that they did not speak English, made fun of their Vietnamese names, or teased them when they spoke Vietnamese among themselves. A twenty-two-year-old woman related that she learned at an early age how difficult it was to present herself as an American, because "American" was reserved for "whites":

> I was always called a Twinkie or a banana: yellow on the outside, white on the inside. I laughed about it. But really, if you think about it, I can't help but being white-washed, you know. I was born here! This is all I know. How can I not be American if I was born and raised here? If I am immersed in this culture growing up, going through the school system, watching the television programs, I'm going to be a part of this generation, knowing what they know.

Even though she considered herself to "be a part of this generation," she was often reminded that she was not. She recalled an incident when she was in Washington, D.C.: "I was waiting for the Metro when this old gentleman, like probably in his sixties, he comes up to me and he asks, 'Well, were your parents born in Vietnam?' and I said, 'Yeah.' And he tells me, 'Our boys died in your jungle.' And my whole life I tried to prepare for something like that to happen to me, but I was still in shock when it happened."

It's important to note that experiences with racial discrimination are gendered. Almost all of the young men in our sample reported being harassed by the police. A nineteen-year-old male recalled being randomly stopped by the police "about fifteen times": "They do it 'cause they see that there is a bunch of Asians and think that they're up to no good. Like, they see five Asians, and they think they're probably going to steal a car. If it was a car full of five, you know, American white guys, I believe that they wouldn't have stopped them." Another nineteen-year-old agreed, relating that he had been pulled over "tons of times" for no apparent reason: "They always ask the same questions: 'Do you belong in a gang? Do you have weapons? Is this a stolen car?' One time my older brother got pulled over. He had a high school tassel hanging on his rearview mirror, and the officer asked, 'What's that? Is that some sort of gang symbol?' " A twenty-two-year-old had a slight twist on his experiences with the police. He reported that when he fought with white kids, he got into trouble with the authorities; in contrast, when he fought with black or Vietnamese kids, there were "no worries about the authorities getting involved."

In comparison, racism targeted girls' self-esteem, particularly their image of what constitutes "beautiful." Several young women reported wanting to "be white, with blond hair and blue eyes." Another young woman reported that in high school she "did everything in the book" to fit in, including "trying to talk a lot, being really outgoing, joining the different clubs and plays, . . . stuffing my bra, . . . trying to . . . get into the in group." But she reported that since she was bussed into the school from a nearby neighborhood, she never could fit in. "The group aspect didn't happen. Because they just did different things. They went surfing and hung around the neighborhood after school. And, you know, went out to play on the streets. But I got bussed home so I couldn't really do that so."

These young Vietnamese Americans reacted to racism in different ways. Most felt angry but decided to ignore these incidents since "there is not much that we can do to change them." Some Vietnamese Americans attempted to protect themselves from racial harassment by shunning other Vietnamese Americans, especially the recent arrivals. As a twenty-two-year-old female related:

> In high school, most of my friends were not Asians. I look back and I'm mad at myself because I would be with my friends and we would make fun of the Vietnamese kids who just came over. We'd call them FOBs. We had this one hallway that we called the FOB Hall. They all hung out there, and they all talked. And it really bothered me because these guys especially would always cuss. I just felt bad because I know that a lot of people were going to base their understanding of Vietnamese just on those people.

Some young men responded to racism by joining gangs. One nineteen-year-old related that he joined a Vietnamese gang of about thirty members because he liked the "relationship that was part of a gang." He recalled being expelled from school, fighting with Filipinos, stealing cars, doing drugs, and being detained in juvenile hall. He also repeatedly ran away from home because "my parents and I have fights about my grades, school, going out late, getting kicked out of school, and the way I was dressing." Still others dealt with racism by getting involved in the Vietnamese American community. For example, a twenty-two-year-old became very active in a local Buddhist youth group in which she learned how to read and write Vietnamese and perform traditional Vietnamese dances. She explained that going to temple on Sundays helped her to cope with going to a predominantly white school:

> I kind of have two lives. Like, I go to school, and then I have temple. So I don't feel lonely. I go to school, I play sports, and then I go home. And on Sundays I go to temple. And those are the people that I talk to and hang around with, practice "tập múa, tập hát" [dancing and singing]. School was just a place to study. And the place to relax and have fun was the temple. I don't have much of a social life, other than temple. I go to a white school, and I don't hear Vietnamese. The only time I hear it is when I go home, like when my parents talk with me. But then sometimes I have to study, and I go to my room and just study and I read English, the whole day, just plain English. . . . Sunday [is] the only day I am exposed to Vietnamese and people speaking Vietnamese.

She related that it was what she learned from temple that allowed her to challenge racism: "In temple, I am surrounded by Vietnamese people, and Vietnamese parents and the elders, and the love. I learn about the Vietnamese customs and culture and this and that. I am proud of myself! I'm Vietnamese. Who gives you the right to put me down?"

ETHNIC SELF-IDENTIFICATION AND ETHNIC BEHAVIORS

Ethnic self-identification has often been used as an indicator of the degree to which individuals have acculturated. As indicated in figure 15.1, over half of the respondents in our sample (53 percent) identified with the national-origin category of Vietnamese; 32 percent identified as Vietnamese American; and an insignificant proportion identified as Asian American (3 percent) or American (1 percent).

However, we caution against the common interpretation that a national-origin ethnic self-identification signals ethnic resilience. When probed during the in-depth interviews, most respondents explained that they chose the "Vietnamese" designation because they were racially Vietnamese. Sample answers included "Because my parents are Vietnamese" and "Look at me, I have black hair and my skin is not white." Along the same line, they disidentified

FIGURE 15.1 **Ethnic Self-Identification**

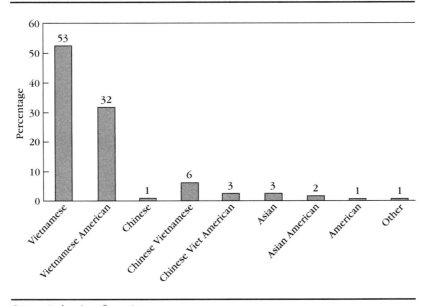

Source: Authors' configuration.

with the term "American" because they conflate "American" with "white." For others, "Vietnamese" is simply a shorthand for "Vietnamese American." When one nineteen-year-old, second-generation, male Chinese Vietnamese was asked why he identified himself as "Vietnamese" instead of "Vietnamese American" or "Chinese Vietnamese," he responded: "If someone asks me what I am, that's my first answer. I'm Vietnamese. If they wanted to get in more depth, I would say, Vietnamese Chinese. That's as far as it goes." When asked why he did not include "American" in his self-identification, he replied: "It isn't important to put 'Vietnamese American.' That's almost like . . . you can see it. I'm basically Americanized. So if someone asks, I'm Vietnamese. . . . If I ask someone, they don't need to say 'Chinese American.' They should just say 'Chinese.' "

On the other hand, those who identify as Vietnamese American tend *not* to view their ethnic identity only in terms of racial characteristics and stress instead their cultural knowledge in both cultures. According to a twenty-two-year-old, U.S.-born female: "I checked 'Vietnamese American' because I feel that I definitely am Vietnamese but a part of me is American because I've grown up here all my life and that's all I know. I can just compare with others. . . . I have combined both aspects of the cultures."

To supplement the ethnic self-identification questions, we included four quantitative measures of ethnic practices in our survey: speaking Vietnamese, reading Vietnamese-language newspapers or magazines, watching Vietnamese-language videos, and listening to Vietnamese-language music. The data that we collected on Vietnamese language use and proficiency revealed mixed linguistic practices. On the one hand, the majority of the respondents reported that they and their parents communicated in Vietnamese. Ninety-one percent indicated that their parents spoke with them in Vietnamese "all" or "most of the time," and over three-quarters (77 percent) noted that they spoke Vietnamese "all" or "most of the time" with their parents. Not surprisingly, a generational difference emerged: more of the 1.5 generation (91 percent) used Vietnamese with their parents than the second generation (69 percent). On the other hand, when asked about their proficiency in Vietnamese, over 40 percent of the second generation reported that they did not speak Vietnamese well, suggesting that English monolinguals may not be far off for the third generation (see figure 15.2). In the following excerpt, a U.S.-born twenty-two-year-old female described the struggle and conflict surrounding the maintenance of Vietnamese language within her family:

The way [my stepfather] was with me is not how he raises his own son now. He used to get mad at my mom for speaking to me in English. He would refuse to speak to me in English. If I spoke to him in English, he would, like, not listen to me; he'd ignore me, like I didn't exist. I had to speak Vietnamese to him. And I could never talk back to him. And I know they were always fighting because he would tell her she had to speak Vietnamese to me. Now, my brother, oh . . . he speaks exclusively in English. His Vietnamese is really bad. He sounds like a white person.

Her cousins also had limited proficiency in Vietnamese: "My one cousin, he speaks Vietnamese so bad. Like he says, 'Cái áo nó sé' [The shirt is doing the ripping]. . . . We all understand more than we speak. . . . It's kind of ironic, because his mom purposely chose to name him Minh because she wanted him to have a Vietnamese name. But he can't even speak Vietnamese."

FIGURE 15.2 **Vietnamese Language Proficiency**

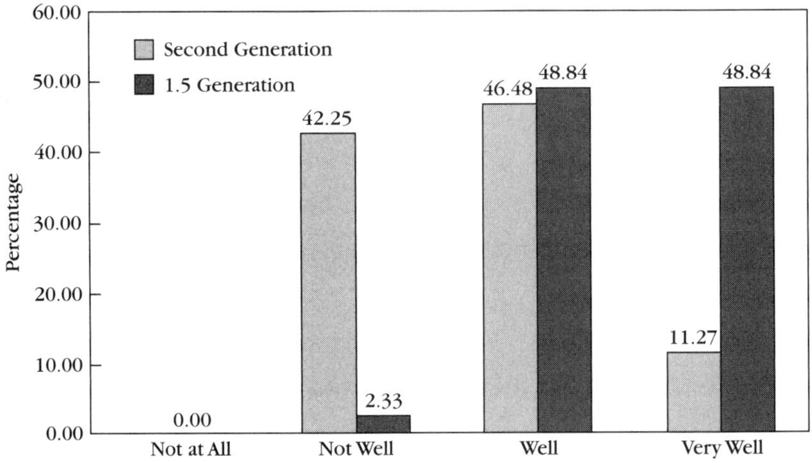

Source: Authors' configuration.

The children's inability to speak Vietnamese well is linked in part to the parents' lack of time. Some parents simply are unable to cram language lessons into their hectic work schedules. One nineteen-year-old female reported: "My mom speaks to me in Vietnamese, but they're working so much. When she comes home, it's like, 'Hi Mai, làm bài chưa?' [Have you done your homework yet?] Then I say, 'I'm going to sleep.' I don't talk to them that much." Other structural factors also affect the younger generation's proficiency in Vietnamese. Children of the first-wave refugees tended to go to either predominantly white or ethnically mixed schools with few other Asians, let alone other Vietnamese children. Quite a few of these respondents recall feeling marginalized, isolated, and wanting "to be white, like all the other kids." Even though they may have entered school with limited English, this phase lasted only a short time, since most of their friends were native English speakers. The Vietnamese who immigrated to the United States during the early and mid-1980s were derogatorily regarded as "FOBs," or "Fresh Off the Boats." Massey's (1995, 642) prediction that perpetual immigration would provide the "grist mill for ethnicity" was not borne out by the response of the U.S.-born children of the first and second waves: they derided these recent arrivals so as to distance themselves from the foreignness displayed and embodied by the newcomer Vietnamese. In the process they were also trying to protect themselves from the ever-present racism that regards all Asian Americans, regardless of ethnicity and nativity, as foreign. One male U.S.-born respondent recalled: "The ones who came here recently, they tend to talk really loud and just be really rude to each other . . . at the lunch court, they're screaming at each other and stuff. It's almost embarrassing." Looking back, he regrets his mistreatment of the recently arrived Vietnamese. "I feel badly. I wish I could've reached out a little more and do something and help them understand a little more of what's going on, because they were so isolated in high school."

Many of our respondents deeply regretted their inability to speak Vietnamese well. According to a twenty-two-year-old, his limited proficiency in Vietnamese and his father's limited facility in English restricted their communication and affected their relationship:

> There are times when me and my dad would drive in a car and there's nothing to talk about because there is that language barrier. I can't find the right words in Vietnamese, and he can't find the right words in English. . . . It's hard because there are parts of my life that he'll never get to know because they are just outside of his access and because of the situation in which we grow up in. I could never communicate it to him. . . . It's like my public side has to be separate.

This respondent recounted the obstacles he faced in trying to improve his Vietnamese-language skills: "I tried to enroll in a class in January at Mesa College, but it was full. I tried to enroll in UCSD last September, but they cut the program for undergraduates. So it's not like I haven't tried, there's all these budget cuts." Others felt reluctant to practice their Vietnamese in the fear that their more fluent co-ethnics would chastise them for not knowing the language in the first place. Instead of encouraging the children to practice the language, many Vietnamese elders chide the second generation for being "too Americanized," or "mất gốc" [having lost one's roots], and laugh at their "broken" Vietnamese. A nineteen-year-old Vietnamese female reported that she and her friend stopped going to their Vietnamese-language class because they "were sitting there basically saying the same thing over and over again" owing to a lack of vocabulary. When directed to Vietnamese-language courses at her college, she quickly rejected this option because she did not "want to be made fun of" by other Vietnamese. Many of the second-generation children may similarly refuse to speak Vietnamese altogether in order to avoid derision.

As with ethnic language proficiency, ethnic practices also varied by generation. With "frequent" defined as twice or more per month, 74 percent of the 1.5 generation but 51 percent of the second generation reported that they listened to Vietnamese-language music frequently; 63 percent of the 1.5 generation but 38 percent of the second generation watched ethnic videos frequently; and 40 percent of the 1.5 generation but only 21 percent of the second generation read Vietnamese-language newspapers frequently. While generational variation is expected, a more interesting statistic can be gleaned from the percentage of the second generation who reported that they did not engage in any of these ethnic activities: 58 percent did not read ethnic newspapers, 38 percent did not watch ethnic language videos, and 26 percent did not listen to Vietnamese-language music *at all*. This is quite interesting considering that 57 percent of the second generation reported speaking Vietnamese "well" or "very well."

In sum, while ethnic practices among the second generation may be on the decline, they have not disappeared. At least half of our sample reported that they could still speak Vietnamese "well or very well," and that they listened to Vietnamese-language music, watched ethnic videos, and read Vietnamese-language newspapers occasionally (at least once a month).

TRANSNATIONAL TIES AND PRACTICES

In this section, we continue our discussion of the lived experiences of Vietnamese American young adults by focusing on their transnational ties and activities. Unlike other scholars of transnationalism, we do not privilege these transnational practices but instead view them as one among several frames of reference within which Vietnamese Americans construct their identities. That is, Vietnamese Americans are "self-making" and "being made" within local, national, and transnational contexts (Ong 1996).

We surveyed our respondents about their participation in the following activities: communicating with relatives and friends in Vietnam through letters and phone calls, sending remittances, visiting Vietnam, or participating in charitable causes and investing in Vietnam. An overwhelming majority (90 percent) of our respondents still had familial ties to Vietnam: still living in Vietnam were parents (2 percent), siblings (15 percent), grandparents (49 percent), and uncles, aunts, and cousins (87 percent). But how well did they know these relatives, and did they write, phone, or return to Vietnam for visits? If they did, what impact, if any, did these familial ties have on their self-conception and behaviors?

Ninety-five percent of our respondents reported that their parents telephoned or wrote to relatives in Vietnam. Among the young adults, two-thirds (68 percent) of the 1.5 generation continued to keep in touch with their relatives in Vietnam, but only one-fifth (22 percent) of the second generation did. The second generation reported that they lacked the language and cultural skills to communicate with these relatives, some of whom they had never met or barely remembered. This finding calls attention to the possible relationship between class and transnationalism. As discussed earlier, many of the second generation received little cultural and language tutelage from their parents, who worked long hours to make ends meet. This lack of exposure, in turn, made it more difficult for these young Vietnamese to maintain ties with their relatives in Vietnam, even when they so desired. In other words, transnationalism is in part an outcome of class resources, more of which are available to affluent refugees than to poor refugees and migrants.

Since the United States lifted its economic embargo against Vietnam in 1994 and reestablished diplomatic relations in 1996, Vietnamese Americans have been able to travel to and from Vietnam. In our sample, 26 percent of the 1.5 generation and 18 percent of the second generation had returned or traveled at least once to Vietnam. While this proportion is not substantial, the impact of the journey on the second generation provides a glimpse into the potential of future transnational activities among this generation. Of those interviewed who had returned to Vietnam for visits, many reported that they had a difficult time adjusting to Vietnam's "unbearably" hot and humid climate and lack of amenities. On the other hand, the majority of those interviewed reported that they were happy to have met their relatives in Vietnam and were able to maintain these newly forged relationships by writing, telephoning, and sending remittances after they returned to the United States. One respondent related that she sent money so that her friend in Vietnam could buy a motor scooter to replace a stolen bicycle.

Because our sample consisted of young adults between the ages of eighteen and twenty-five, they may have lacked the money and perhaps the time required to participate in certain transnational activities, such as traveling and sending remittances to Vietnam. Thus, we included two measures on their transnational intentions: whether they had a desire to return to Vietnam to live permanently, and what country they considered their home. Whereas 34 percent of the respondents reported that their parents had expressed a desire to return to Vietnam and live permanently, both the 1.5 and second generations overwhelmingly rejected this option (86 percent and 93 percent, respectively). The question on "home" provided yet another indicator of the second generation's intention to stay permanently in the United States: 87 percent asserted that the United States was their home (see figure 15.3). Only 1 percent considered Vietnam home, and 8 percent claimed both the United States and Vietnam as home. The 1.5 generation expressed more attachment to Vietnam, with 19 percent considering Vietnam home and another 23 percent considering both the United States and Vietnam their home.

LOOKING FORWARD AND BACKWARD: THE CONSTRUCTIONS OF VIETNAM

The data above indicate that the children of Vietnamese refugees maintain minimal ties with their families in Vietnam. The fact that few could write or speak Vietnamese well enough to communicate with their relatives in Vietnam—and the fact that many did not even know or remember these relatives—suggest that the second generation, and even the 1.5 generation, will have few if any transnational *familial* ties in the future. Some of our respondents voiced this possibility, wondering what would happen to their tenuous connections to their overseas families once their parents, especially their mothers, were no longer alive to maintain these ties. More-

FIGURE 15.3 **Where Is "Home"?**

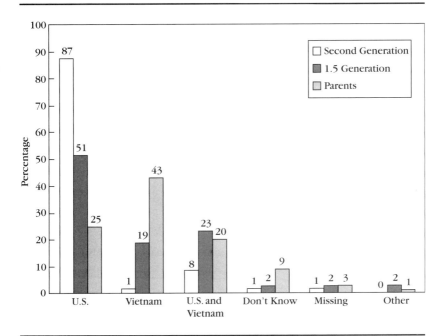

Source: Authors' configuration.

over, the data also indicate that the overwhelming majority did not consider Vietnam their home and did not want to live in Vietnam permanently. Taken together, these data strongly support the thesis that the children of Vietnamese refugees view themselves as permanent residents of the United States. Even as we acknowledge this fact, we want to call attention to two other facts: the *symbolic* hold that Vietnam continues to have on young Vietnamese Americans, and relatedly, the desire that most young Vietnamese Americans have to help Vietnam in the future.

Even though our respondents were disconnected from Vietnam, the country continued to loom large in their imagination through the stories told to them by their parents. Largely unacquainted with the home country, young Vietnamese Americans depend on their parents for information on Vietnam in order to craft and affirm their ethnic self. As such, they are particularly susceptible to their parents' memories of and stories about Vietnam. When asked to recite the stories that their parents told them about Vietnam, most respondents indicated that their parents often compared the hardships that they endured in Vietnam to the opportunities they perceived to be available to their children in the United States. The following comment by a U.S.-born, twenty-two-year-old female is typical: "[My parents] would tell me all the time how easy it is that I have, how I could eat whatever I want or I am never hungry. . . . They always stressed poverty. If I don't finish something on my plate, my family is like, 'In Vietnam you'd be lucky to even have that plate.'" From the perspective of the respondents, their parents told these stories to control, socialize, or motivate them to work hard, to do well in school, and to get a good job. A nineteen-year-old who did not perform well in school said that his parents used these stories to "make me feel guilty for not doing well. They make it look like they had it really hard, which they probably did. And I have it really easy, which I do." A twenty-two-year-old female concurred: "My mom always says, 'We give you this opportunity. Study hard, because in Vietnam you don't have this opportunity. Your father and I came over here to give you this opportunity. Focus on studying.'" And these stories worked. Many of our respondents explained that they worked hard in school to repay their parents for the opportunities that they had given them. As a twenty-two-year-old female stated: "I have this really heavy thing on me to succeed. I have to repay what they sacrificed. I feel it. I want to be something up there just to show them that their efforts are not wasted on me." Even those who did not do well in school expressed deep regrets and guilt for failing to live up to their parents' expectations.

Parents also used stories about Vietnam to regulate the misbehavior of their children, especially their daughters, by linking such behavior to cultural betrayal. As some of the young women recounted, their parents often compared their behavior to that of Vietnamese girls in Vietnam. One young woman related the criticisms that she received from her mother: "My mom tells me that no matter what I do, I am totally disrespectful compared to Vietnamese girls in Vietnam. That in Vietnam the kids grow up to take care of their parents and they appreciate their parents. That they never met another kid who is so rude like me, stuff like that." Another self-described "Americanized" young woman remembered that, "growing up, I was really bad. I would always talk back, and she would always get mad and blame it on being in America, like kids here aren't raised to respect the elderly like in Vietnam. Like I was copy-ing the bad stuff." Many of these women complained that their par-ents' criticisms were unfair. As one woman exclaimed: "I am not a bad kid. It's just that I want to go out and experience the world. . . . They think I am the worst kid in the world, but I don't do anything bad." These women particularly resented what they saw as gender inequity in their families: far more restrictions were placed on them than on their brothers. A young woman explained this inequity: "[My mom] was afraid of me doing bad things, hanging out with the wrong crowd, sleeping with guys. That's her big one, 'Girls can get pregnant. Guys can't.' That was always her rationale for my brother going out, he could get a girl pregnant, but it's not really on him unless he wants it to be. But she tells me, 'If you get pregnant, your life is over.' " On the other hand, parents also used stories about unequal gender relations in Vietnam—the fact that women have fewer opportunities compared to men—to urge their daughters to aim for success. As a twenty-two-year-old woman recounted:

> My mom says, "Mấy người ở Việt Nam không có điều kiện dễ" [Women in Vietnam don't have the chance], to be successful, to be who they want to be. That's why they have to depend on their husbands. And my mom says, "Bây giờ ở Mỹ rồi, con không có cần đó, con có phương tiện để làm bác sĩ, kỹ sư, con không có cần" [Now, you are in America, you don't need that, you can be a doctor, engineer, you don't need to], depend on the guys. You have the opportunity to be what you want. That's what my mom stressed to me.

It is true that what we have just described is not new; earlier gen-erations of immigrant parents have similarly required their children to conform to prescribed "ethnic" norms and values (Gabaccia 1994; Orsi 1985; Yung 1995; Ruiz 1992). However, our decision to call these practices "transnational" rather than "ethnic" is a matter of em-phasis: "transnational" emphasizes the power and appeal of both "here" *and* "there" in the constructions of immigrant lives. In this case, Vietnamese immigrant parents use (selective) memory of the homeland to mold their children into ideal "ethnic" subjects. The source of their parental power lies precisely in their ability to claim to be guardians of "authentic" cultural memory—that is, to claim to have had direct ties to Vietnam. These direct ties bequeath them the authority to determine whether their children are "authentic" members of the Vietnamese community. Because they have few direct ties to Vietnam, these young adults depend on their parents' assessment of their ethnic selves and thus are particularly vulnerable to charges of cultural betrayal. Since Vietnamese Americans are also excluded from full American membership through racism, the parental accusation "You are not Vietnamese enough" essentially strips the young Vietnamese American of all meaningful identity.

These stories—told to them by their parents but also by other Vietnamese—also inadvertently constructed Vietnam as a poor, dirty, and even dangerous Third World country. The respondents who had not visited Vietnam described it in the following ways: "It is a poor country"; "From what I've heard, how dirty it is, I probably wouldn't last"; "They don't have toilets there, you know"; "Some houses are infested with like rats and stuff like that"; "I'm kind of scared of getting ripped off over there"; "Vietnam doesn't have all these things, all the luxuries"; and, "Not much to do over there." A twenty-two-year-old related that her experience with remittance-sending as a young child impressed in her mind that Vietnam was an impoverished country:

> When I was young, I remember always going to Chinatown in L.A. with my grandma and buying so many things to send home. Everything you can think of, like razor blades, a lot of candies, lemon drops, a lot of gums. It was always fun. I remember going to those fabric stores and always picking out fabrics, yards and yards of different fabrics. They sent electronics too. I remember they sent portable radios. Sometimes I would ask [my grandma], "Why do you need to send this stuff?" and she would say, "They don't have this stuff there." I was like, oh, my God, they don't have pens, you know?

For those who had visited Vietnam, these images were confirmed in their minds. For example, an eighteen-year-old who visited Vietnam twice, at the ages of nine and eleven, gave his impression of Vietnam: "It didn't look that pretty. And the economy. . . . I look at the people over there, and they are thirty and still smaller than me because they don't get enough food to eat, so I know I am pretty well off over here."

Partly because of these stories—the construction of Vietnam as an impoverished and needy country—some of our respondents expressed a desire to go back and help the country. The proposed assistance ranged from giving money to "everyone there" and "tak[ing] the whole block out to eat or something" to being involved in the economic and political affairs of Vietnam. When asked why they wanted to help Vietnam, these respondents replied that Vietnam is "a part of who I am." One young woman explained that she wanted to help Vietnam because "it is your homeland. You kind of have that bond. I don't know how to describe it. If you didn't get out of there, you'd be one of them. And you would want someone to help you. That's how I feel. If I was capable financially and physically, I would help out. I would send money." Another woman who left Vietnam at the age of two indicated that she wanted to go back there because she wanted "to see how far I have come from and to see if I can help to improve the lives of people who still live there. I mean I don't want to go there thinking that I am like the Westerner on the white horse who's going to help everyone out, but I do want to do what I can. I want to go there because it's a part of who I am." According to a young Vietnamese American woman who left Vietnam at the age of five, her desire to help Vietnam did not contradict the fact that she did not consider Vietnam her home:

> Vietnam is not my country because I don't live there. But the people are my people. The people here, the Americans, they are not my people. They can't relate to who I am; they don't know who I am. But the people in Vietnam cũng là người Việt [are also Vietnamese]. Người Việt với nhau [You are Vietnamese with each other], and there is a connection, you know? I want to help the people. They need help.

In sum, for the majority of the respondents in our sample, their visit to Vietnam or the stories that were told to them about Vietnam constructed the country as a humid, dirty, poverty-stricken, Third World nation. This bleak account had motivated some young Vietnamese Americans to vow to contribute to the well-being of their families and friends in Vietnam and to the rebuilding and developing of the country. We do not claim that these interview data on intentions to return mean that U.S.-born and -raised Vietnamese Americans *will* forge dense transnational ties with Vietnam in the future. Their future plans are subject to verification and likely to change over time and context. What the data do suggest, however, is that if young Vietnamese Americans do forge such ties, they are more likely to do so with Vietnamese hometown associations, service organizations, local churches, and the media, and not necessarily or only with their families.

CONCLUSION

Our research on Vietnamese American lives in San Diego reveals that these young adults felt strong symbolic loyalty to Vietnam but knew very little about it and had little contact with their parents and other adults who might have educated them about it. A high proportion of these young adults had linguistic expertise in Vietnamese but seldom spoke it, read it, or encountered Vietnamese-language entertainment. They felt pressured to become like "Americans," but their experiences as racialized individuals living in minority neighborhoods, and as the children of low-wage workers, had left them with an uneasy relationship with both Vietnamese and U.S. culture. These complex experiences thus demonstrate the impossibility of both complete assimilation within U.S. society and return to Vietnam for these youths. They also underscore the multiplicity of Vietnamese American lives and work against definitions that would fix Vietnamese Americans in one identity or one place.

First and foremost, we are indebted to the young Vietnamese Americans we interviewed. We are also grateful for research grants from the UC Pacific Rim Research Program and the UCSD Academic Senate, and for the important input and support of Diane Wolf and David Lopez.

NOTES

1. Today the Vietnamese diaspora consists of more than two and a half million refugees and immigrants who have resettled in over one hundred nations throughout the world (Nguyen and Le 1998).
2. The "first wave" commonly refers to the initial 130,000 refugees admitted in 1975. This first wave did contain an elite group from urban South Vietnam who on average were well educated and wealthy and had some knowledge of English. However, studies mentioning the first

wave rarely acknowledge that half of this group of immigrants did not fall into the so-called high-risk category and instead were labeled the "catchall" group. The catchall group consisted of students, street vendors, small shopkeepers, local policemen, fishermen, and farmers. The catchall group also included thousands who had simply followed the crowd to escape combat zones and were picked up in the evacuation chain by chance, including fifteen thousand who persevered on the long trek from the highland cities of Kontum, Pleiku, and Phu Bon to Vung Tau (Liu 1979; Lewins and Ly 1985, 13). Commonly referred to as the "boat people" because they stealthily escaped Vietnam on small boats, this second wave arrived in the United States between 1979 and 1984. Fleeing from political repression and the economic dislocations caused by trade sanctions from the West, natural disasters, failed economic plans, and drained resources diverted to Vietnam's warfare with Cambodia and China (Beresford 1989; Tran 1994), those who came in the second wave were more heterogeneous in class, religion, and ethnic background. Unlike the first wave, which was predominantly ethnic Vietnamese, middle-class, Catholic, and urban, those who arrived in the second wave included a significant proportion of ethnic Chinese, Buddhists, fishermen, and farmers from rural provinces. These refugees either crossed dangerous zones through Cambodia to reach Thailand or set sail on the South China Sea, only to endure long stays in demoralizing refugee camps in Hong Kong, Thailand, Indonesia, Malaysia, and the Philippines. About four hundred thousand of these refugees entered the United States in the early 1980s (Caplan et al. 1985). The third wave of Vietnamese refugees began in the late 1980s and continues to this day. Many third-wave immigrants either are pursuing family reunification through the Orderly Departure Program (ODP) or have been designated as refugees through the Humanitarian Operation Program (HOP) and the 1988 Amerasian Homecoming Act (Rutledge 1992, 64–67). The ODP allowed family members of U.S. legal residents to sponsor their immediate family for reunification, while the HOP and Amerasian act allowed former military officers released from reeducation camps and any Amerasians to immigrate to the United States with their families. This third wave has now trickled down to mainly immigrants who are seeking family reunification and who resemble immigrants of the voluntary type. It is important to remember that each refugee wave faced complex contexts of exits and resettlement that affected family dynamics and adaptation processes. For example, there are refugees in all three waves who face reunification issues with separated family members if they migrated at different times or if family members were imprisoned for attempting to escape or ordered to reeducation camps after the war. These reunification issues must be negotiated not only between spouses, who may fear the infidelities made possible by years of separation, but also between parents and children and between siblings, who may see each other as strangers.

3. In this study, we defined the second generation as respondents who were born in the United States or who came to the United States prior to the age of five and who had at least one foreign-born parent. The 1.5 generation was defined as respondents who immigrated to the United States between the ages of six and thirteen.

4. This figure may be misleading and should not be viewed too optimistically, because there are often more income earners per household in the Vietnamese family as well as more household members sharing the income.

REFERENCES

Archdeacon, Thomas. 1983. *Becoming American: An Ethnic History*. New York: Free Press.

Basch, Linda, Nina Glick-Schiller, and Cristina Szanton-Blanc. 1994. *Nations Unbound: Transnational Projects, Postcolonial Predicaments, and Deterritorialized Nation-states*. Langhorne, Penn.: Gordon and Breach.

Beresford, Melanie. 1989. *National Unification and Economic Development in Vietnam*. London: Macmillan Press.

Bourne, Randolph. 1916. "Trans-National America." *Atlantic Monthly* 118: 778–86.

Burawoy, Michael. 1976. "The Functions and Reproduction of Migrant Labor: Comparative Material from Southern Africa and the United States." *American Journal of Sociology* 81: 1050–87.

Caplan, Nathan, John Whitmore, and Quang L. Bui. 1985. "Southeast Asian Refugee Self-Sufficiency Study." Report prepared for Office of Refugee Resettlement by the Institute for Social Research, University of Michigan.

Chan, Sucheng. 1991. *Asian Americans: An Interpretive History*. Boston: Twayne.

Clifford, James. 1994. "Diasporas." *Cultural Anthropology* 9(3): 302–38.

Desbarats, Jacqueline. 1985. "Indochinese Resettlement in the United States." *Annals of the Association of American Geographers* 75(4): 522–38.

Do, Hien Duc. 1988. "The Formation of a New Refugee Community: The Vietnamese Community in Orange County, California." Master's thesis, University of California at Santa Barbara.

Gabaccia, Donna. 1994. *From the Other Side: Women, Gender, and Immigrant Life in the United States, 1820–1990*. Bloomington: Indiana University Press.

Glick-Schiller, Nina. 1997. "The Situation of Transnational Studies." *Identities* 4(2): 155–66.

Goldberg, Barry. 1992. "Historical Reflections on Transnationalism, Race, and the American Immigrant Saga." In *Towards a Transnational Perspective on Migration: Race, Class, Ethnicity, and Nationalism Reconsidered,* edited by Nina Glick-Schiller, Linda Basch, and Cristina Szanton-Blanc. New York: New York Academy of Sciences.

Handlin, Oscar. 1973. *The Uprooted.* 2nd and enlarged ed. Boston: Little, Brown.

Hobsbawm, Eric, and Terence Ranger. 1983. *The Invention of Tradition.* New York: Cambridge University Press.

Katrak, Ketu. 1996. "South Asian American Writers: Geography and Memory." *Amerasia Journal* 22(3): 121–38.

Kearney, Michael. 1995. "The Effects of Transnational Culture, Economy, and Migration on Mixtec Identity in Oxacalifornia." In *The Bubbling Cauldron: Race, Ethnicity, and the Urban Crisis,* edited by Michael Peter Smith and Joe Feagin. Minneapolis: University of Minnesota Press.

Kibria, Nazli. 1993. *Family Tightrope.* Princeton, N.J.: Princeton University Press.

Lewins, Frank, and Judith Ly. 1985. *The First Wave: The Settlement of Australian's First Vietnamese Refugees.* Sydney: George and Unwin.

Lipsitz, George. 1999. "No Shining City on a Hill: American Studies and the Problem of Place." *American Studies* 40(2): 53–69.

Liu, William. 1979. *Transition to Nowhere: Vietnamese Refugees in America.* Nashville, Tenn.: Charter House.

Massey, Douglas S. 1975. "The New Immigration and Ethnicity in the United States." *Population and Development Review* 21(3): 631–52.

Nguyen, Phuong Madison. 2000. "Beyond the Fountain Pen." In *25 Vietnamese Americans in 25 Years: 1975–2000.* San Jose, Calif.: New Horizon/Chân Trời Mới.

Nguyen, Quang Vinh, and Le Thanh Sang. 1998. "Preliminary Study on Remittances from Overseas Vietnamese and Their Socioeconomic Impact on the Recipient Households in Ho Chi Minh City." Ho Chi Minh City: Institute of Social Sciences, Center for Sociology and Development. Unpublished paper.

Okamura, Jonathan Y. 1998. *Imagining the Filipino American Diaspora: Transnational Relations, Identities, and Communities.* New York: Garland.

Ong, Aihwa. 1996. "Cultural Citizenship as Subject-Making." *Current Anthropology* 37(5): 737–62.

Orsi, Robert Anthony. 1985. *The Madonna of 115th Street: Faith and Community in Italian Harlem, 1880–1950.* New Haven: Yale University Press.

Petras, James. 1978. *Critical Perspectives on Imperialism and Social Class in the Third World.* New York: Monthly Review Press.

Portes, Alejandro. 1978. "Migration and Underdevelopment." *Politics and Society* 8: 1–48.

———. 1987. "The Social Origins of the Cuban Enclave Economy in Miami." *Sociological Perspectives* 30(October): 340–72.

Portes, Alejandro, Luis E. Guarnizo, and Patricia Landolt. 1999. "The Study of Transnationalism: Pitfalls and Promise of an Emergent Research Field." *Ethnic and Racial Studies* 22(2): 217–37.

Portes, Alejandro, and Rubén Rumbaut. 2001. *Legacies: The Story of the Immigrant Second Generation.* Berkeley: University of California Press.

Ruiz, Vicki. 1992. "The Flapper and the Chaperone: Historical Memory Among Mexican American Women." In *Seeking Common Ground: Multidisciplinary Studies,* edited by Donna Gabaccia. Westport, Conn.: Greenwood Press.

Rumbaut, Rubén. 1995. "Vietnamese, Laotian, and Cambodian Americans." In *Asian Americans: Contemporary Trends and Issues,* edited by Pyong Gap Min. Thousand Oaks, Calif.: Sage Publications.

Rutledge, Paul. 1992. *The Vietnamese Experience in America.* Bloomington: Indiana University Press.

Small, Cathy. 1998. *Voyages: From Tongan Village to American Suburbs.* Ithaca, N.Y.: Cornell University Press.

Smith, Robert C. 1998. "Transnational Localities: Community, Technology, and the Politics of Membership Within the Context of Mexico and U.S. Migration." In *Transnationalism from Below,* edited by Michael Peter Smith and Luis Eduardo Guarnizo. New Brunswick, N.J.: Transaction Press.

Tran, Dang. 1994. *Vietnam: Socialist Economic Development 1955–1992.* San Francisco: Institute for Contemporary Studies.

Viviani, Nancy. 1984. *The Long Journey: Vietnamese Migration and Settlement in Australia.* Carlton, Victoria: Melbourne University Press.

Yung, Judy. 1995. *Unbound Feet: A Social History of Chinese Women in San Francisco.* Berkeley: University of California Press.

Zhou, Min, and Carl Bankston III. 1998. *Growing up American: The Adaptation of Vietnamese Adolescents in the United States.* New York: Russell Sage Foundation.

Zolberg, Aristide. 1986. "International Factors in the Formation of Refugee Movements." *International Migration Review* 20(summer): 151–69.

Index

Numbers in **boldface** refer to tables or figures.